DATE DUE

ALGERNON BLACKWOOD

ALGERNON BLACKWOOD

An Extraordinary Life

MIKE ASHLEY

CARROLL & GRAF PUBLISHERS
New York

Carroll & Graf Publishers
An imprint of Avalon Publishing Group, Inc.
161 William Street, 16th Floor
New York
NY 10038-2607
www.carrollandgraf.com

First published in the UK by Constable
an imprint of Constable & Robinson Ltd 2001

First Carroll & Graf edition 2001

ISBN 0-7867-0928-6

Printed and bound in the EU

Contents

Contents

Illustrations

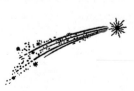

Harriet Sydney Blackwood, *by kind permission of Lord and Lady Kintore*
Sir Arthur Blackwood, *by kind permission of Lord and Lady Kintore*
Wood Lodge at Shooter's Hill, *by kind permission of Lord and Lady Kintore*
Blackwood's sisters Ada, Beatrice and Cecilia and his brother Arthur, *by kind permission of Lord and Lady Kintore*
Algeron aged 4 or 5, *by kind permission of Mrs Reeves on behalf of the Blackwood estate*
Blackwood in his late teens, *by kind permission of Mrs Reeves on behalf of the Blackwood estate*
Algernon at Wellington College, *by kind permission of Wellington College*
Offices of the New York Times, 1893, *reproduced from King's Handbook of New York City, 1893 by Moses King; copyright expired*
Alfred H. Louis around 1908, *reproduced from My Own Past by Maude ffoulkes, copyright expired*
Edwyn R. Bevan
Maude ffoulkes, *reproduced from My Own Past by Maude ffoulkes, copyright expired*
Cover of the first edition of John Silence
Blackwood and Fred Dufferin, in the Alps, 1925, *by kind permission of Mrs Reeves on behalf of the Blackwood estate*
Blackwood, August 1905, *by kind permission of the Syndics of Cambridge University Library*
Church and pension at Bôle, *by kind permission of Bibliothèque universitaire de Neuchâtel*
Blackwood with Sir Edward Elgar, *by kind permission of Mrs Reeves on behalf of the Blackwood estate*
Blackwood reading to Lena Ashwell and children
Maya Philipson in 1923, *by kind permission of Mrs Barbara Lindsay*
Encombe at Sandgate, 1923, *by kind permission of Mrs Barbara Lindsay*
Blackwood with Sinclair Lewis and others in 1921, *by kind permission of Mrs Reeves on behalf of the Blackwood estate*

Acknowledgments

In the twenty-three years since I started research for this biography I have been helped by hundreds of people. It is impossible to acknowledge them all, but I must thank all of those without whom it would have been difficult, if not impossible, to finalize this book.

First and foremost I must thank Patricia Spanoghe, who is eternally Patsy Ainley to me. She not only brought Blackwood alive in my mind but she opened up her network of contacts, which made my research so much easier. Together with Barbara Lindsay, the great-niece of Maya Philipson, they helped recreate Blackwood's world from the 1920s onwards.

I could not have started on my research without the help and permission of Sheila Reeves, who now represents the Blackwood estate, and of Michael Horniman and Linda Shaughnessy of A.P. Watt Ltd, agent for the Blackwood estate. They allowed me access to many primary documents without which it would have been almost impossible to begin my research. I am also grateful to Sheila Reeves for her comments and advice on the final typescript and for her authorization to write the biography.

Derek Hudson was another early port of call in my research and I thank him for the benefit of his own research and his suggestions of people to contact. Similarly Professor Jean-Louis Grillou who, like me, has spent over twenty years researching Blackwood's life for his doctoral thesis. He has been a valuable source of help and support.

Very early in my work Richard Dalby was an ever reliable source acquiring books and hitherto lesser known items by Blackwood and unearthing snippets of information. I have lost track of just how much data originated with Richard but I know that early on, whenever I was stuck for something, Richard usually had the answer.

I owe tremendous thanks to Michael Pointon. Ever since he contacted me in 1986 he has been a constant source of help, support and inspiration. Michael kept the Blackwood flag flying during my 'wilderness years', when pressure of work on other projects kept me away from the Blackwood research. It's thanks to Michael that I never lost sight of my goal and he, more than anyone, shepherded me back onto the right track. Michael has been a constant lifeline, as has his friend Elsbeth Schmidt, and I owe both of them a huge debt of thanks.

Likewise Alan Bundy, whom I have never met, yet who since 1985 has been regularly supplying me with the products of his painstaking and thorough research through the New York newspapers and other archives. Without Alan's help much of Blackwood's American years would still remain a mystery and though much still remains to be resolved, Alan's work has prised open a hundred doorways into the past.

It was a wonderful moment when I met Ella Maillart with whom I had corresponded for some years. She gave me many memories of Blackwood and shared with me her many letters from him. I also have very fond memories of my meeting with Dr John Nesfield and his wife and sister. Their house had scarcely changed since the days when Blackwood regularly visited and with their detailed and lively memories of him, I almost felt he was there with me.

Early in my work I contacted the indefatigable Canadian researcher John Robert Colombo, who was the first to publish an individual Blackwood bibliography, *Blackwood's Books*. John has since been an unflagging help, not only fielding my many queries on Blackwood's Canadian days but in offering his own thoughts and views on Blackwood's life and character.

I am most grateful for the help provided by Lord and Lady Kintore, especially allowing me unrestricted access to their archives and the amazing photograph albums from Blackwood's early days, and for providing copies of many of these photographs.

In addition to all of the above I had three lifelines at the other end of my e-mail helping me with *ad hoc* queries as I was writing the biography. These were librarians Victor Berch and Dennis Lien and writer and researcher S. T. Joshi. Their illuminating responses to obscure queries, often in only a matter of minutes, was a tremendous boost during those darker moments when the weight of research and writing becomes suffocating. They were always there to pull me back towards the light.

I must also thank Ted G. Davy for his expertise over the years on the Theosophical Society; James Moore and Walter Driscoll for their help on Gurdjieff and Ouspensky; R.A. Gilbert and Ellic Howe for their help on the Golden Dawn; Christopher Andrew for his advice on the Secret Service in the First World War; Derek Bartlett for his guidance with Louis N. Parker; Ethel Hardie for the loan of her unpublished biography of Henry Ainley; Lavender Jones and Rosemary Linnell for their help on Violet Pearn; Cecil Madden, Stephen McCormack and Robert Barr for their wonderful memories of working with Blackwood at the BBC; Neil Somerville of the BBC Written Archives for his immense help in detailing Blackwood's work for the BBC; Anthony Gilkison for his memories of filming Blackwood; Donald A. Prater for his guidance on Rainer Rilke; Dr Ken Simmons for the benefit of his research into Elgar and *The Starlight Express*; and Bengt Dahlquist, Ola Svensson, Sue O'Brien, James Carter and many others on the Blackwood e-mail discussion group for their views, advice and help on a variety of matters.

I hope the following will excuse me mentioning them by name only, as all of them were generous and helpful in either their own personal memories of Blackwood or allowing access to family papers or correspondence. Lord Ashbourne, Basil Ashmore, Michael Asquith, David Astor, Elaine Baly, Jill Balcon, Cecil Barclay, Sir Colville Barclay, Robert Barclay, Alan Baxendale, Sir Basil Blackwell, E.F. Bleiler, Charles Bocking, Major E.A. Boylan, Captain S. Bullock-Webster, Susan Carnagham, Thelma Cazalet-Keir, Katharine Cockin, Gerry de la Ree, June de Schanschieff, Gilly Flower, F. Gerald Gough, Felicity Hardcastle, Megan Hatch, Josephine Heyworth, Louis Jebb, Mary Jennings, Richard Joseph, Raymond Keen, Matilda Kessler, Rev. Marcus Knight, Preston Lockwood, Allen McElfresh, Cynthia Mackay, Bice McKean, Pauline Matarasso, Lady Mills, Gunilla and Malcolm Munthe, Robin Murray-Philipson, Paul Myers, Andrew Napier, Charles Palmer, O.J. Philipson, J.B. Priestley, Raymond Raikes, John Reed, Alan Richardson, Peter Rowe, Murray Sanderson, Mrs L.H. Shave, David Simeon, Agnes Stapledon, Hilda Strickland, Robert Temple, Alex Todd, Peter Underwood, Lady Vansittart, Edward Wagenknecht, Richard Waller, J. Sterling Williams, A.N. Wilson, and Olive Wilson.

I must also acknowledge the various sources, archives and libraries who have provided copies of Blackwood material and given permission for selective quotations:

Sheila Reeves and A.P. Watt for permission to quote from Blackwood's works and correspondence.

BBC Written Archives, Caversham for copies of their correspondence with Blackwood.

Boston College for Blackwood's correspondence with Hilaire and Elodie Belloc.

Boston University Libraries for Blackwood's correspondence with Mary Borden.

University of Birmingham Library for Blackwood's correspondence with St John Ervine.

University of Bristol Library for Blackwood's correspondence with Penguin Books.

The British Library for access to Blackwood's correspondence with Macmillan & Co., and Vera Wainwright.

British Red Cross Society (Miss M. N. Slade) for details of Blackwood's Red Cross service.

The Churchill College Archives Centre, University of Cambridge, for Blackwood's correspondence with Cecil Roberts and Sir Edward Spears.

Cardiff University College for Blackwood's correspondence with Brian J. Morse.

The Garrick Club for details of Blackwood's correspondence with Dorothy Allhusen and Lady St Helier.

Bibliothèque publique et universitaire, Geneva, for Blackwood's correspondence with Ella Maillart.

The Harry Ransom Humanities Research Centre at the University of Texas at Austin for copies of Blackwood's correspondence with Appleton & Co., Stuart Gilbert, Louis Golding, Stephen Graham, A. A. Knopf, John Lane, Marie Belloc Lowndes, and Hugh Walpole.

The Henry E. Huntington Library for Blackwood's correspondence with W. Graham Robertson.

Hereford & Worcester County Record Office for Blackwood's correspondence with Sir Edward Elgar.

The Highgate Literary & Scientific Institution for Blackwood's correspondence with themselves.

Imperial War Museum for access to the reminiscences of Sir Ivone Kirkpatrick and the diaries of Major Kirke.

The John Rylands University Library of Manchester for Blackwood's correspondence with Basil Dean and Annie Horniman.

The Mander & Mitchenson Theatre Collection for copies of theatre programmes and supporting documentation and of a letter from Blackwood to Lance Sieveking.

The Moravian Brotherhood for access to documents in their archives on Blackwood's education.

The New York Public Library for Blackwood's correspondence with Anne Fremantle, W.T. Howe, Clara Huth Jackson, James B. Pinker and A.P. Watt.

The Public Record Office of Northern Ireland for copies of correspondence with Lord Dufferin from Sir Arthur Blackwood and Lady Kintore.

The University of Reading for Blackwood's further correspondence with Macmillan & Co.

Richmond Central Library for a copy of the letter from Maude ffoulkes to Douglas Sladen.

The Royal Society of Literature for copies of their correspondence with Blackwood.

The School of Slavonic and East European Studies at London University for access to Mary Bevan's unpublished memoir.

Sheffield City Libraries for Blackwood's correspondence with Edward Carpenter.

University of Toronto Library and Archives for copies of material relating to Toronto's history and for Blackwood's correspondence with Professor George Wrong.

Trinity College, Dublin, for Blackwood's correspondence with James Stephens.

Wellington College (Dr Heather Tomlinson) for access to their papers on Blackwood's education.

The State Historical Society, Wisconsin for Blackwood's correspondence with August Derleth and Richard Halsworth Rovere.

To all of the above and any I have overlooked my sincere and most grateful thanks. If there is anywhere where I may have inadvertently transgressed copyright please contact me care of the publisher.

Introduction

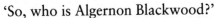

'So, who is Algernon Blackwood?'

I am asked that question from time to time. And when I explain that he was one of the twentieth-century's most creative writers of supernatural fiction, that he was an indefatigable traveller, that he was an extremely popular storyteller on radio and television – indeed he was on the first ever television programme – and that he was a secret agent during the First World War, people become interested. When I add that it was he who originated *The Starlight Express*, that he was a member of the magical order of the Golden Dawn and consorted with mystics and magicians, that he was acquainted with most of the literary establishment of his day, from Hilaire Belloc to W.B. Yeats and from Compton Mackenzie to H. G. Wells; that his work has inspired such composers as Sir Edward Elgar and Alec Rowley and such diverse writers as Stella Gibbons and Henry Miller, most people want me to reveal more.

I hope you do.

And I've hardly scratched the surface.

Algernon Blackwood was no ordinary writer. He was no ordinary person. Those who counted him as a friend revered him, and called him magical. They still remember him with affection and awe. Let me give you one example. Early in my research I interviewed Lady Vansittart. She was then in her nineties but as she remembered the first time she met Blackwood, nearly sixty years before, the age fell from her face, her eyes twinkled and for a moment she was thirty again. Anyone whose memory can achieve that, had to be magical.

When Stephen Graham first met him he said: 'I came into the presence of an unusual personality; some would call it weird, I would call it strange and elusive, rather unearthly.' Micheál MacLiammóir called him 'the high-priest of dreaming youth . . . a Chaldean sorcerer knowing no speech but that of the gods'. Maude ffoulkes, who 'discovered' Blackwood, said that there were three distinct aspects to his talent. He was an 'Interpreter of Children', an 'Interpreter of Nature' and, most supreme of all, he was the 'Interpreter of Super-Nature', rating him as the best of 'any writers of the day in any country'. H.P. Lovecraft called him 'the one absolute and unquestioned master of weird atmosphere'. More recently Jack Sullivan, in *The Penguin Encyclopedia of Horror and the Supernatural*, noted that Blackwood 'took large risks and sometimes blundered, but at his best he delivered a greater number of magisterial shudders than more refined writers in the genre ever attempted'. He added that 'masterpieces like "The Willows" and "The Wendigo" sustain an atmosphere of dread that no one has bettered.'

Blackwood left an indelible glamour of wonder over the people whom he met and produced some of the best supernatural stories and novels of the twentieth century. I first discovered Blackwood through the television series *Tales of Mystery* in the early 1960s. It was a few more years before I read his stories and became captivated by his unique approach to supernatural fiction. When, in 1976, I was compiling my *Who's Who in Horror and Fantasy Fiction*, and discovered how little had been written about him, the first urges of writing his biography stirred within me. Soon afterwards I came across a letter from Blackwood to a young writer, Ron Hall. It was written just two months before Blackwood's death. In it he admitted that all his books were 'more or less autobiographical'. When I read that, I knew I would have to write Blackwood's biography. I had to know more about the man who could see visions of Mother Earth in the Caucasus, who could experience the ancient past of Egypt engulfing him like a wave of time, who could sense the spirit world through his affinity with nature – a man who had the accumulated experience of centuries, yet who could still appreciate the world as through a child's heart.

I had not realized that my research would be spread over more than twenty years. I have frequently been diverted on to other projects, but Blackwood has never been far away from my thoughts. I knew the research was not going to be easy. Blackwood hated possessions. He was utterly nonmaterialistic. He kept virtually nothing. Almost every-thing he owned was kept in two holdalls. Unfortunately what other possessions and memorabilia he had kept were destroyed when his nephew's house, where he was staying, was destroyed by a direct hit during the Blitz in October 1940. I started with almost no information and built upon what I had. Thanks to the help of a wonderful array of individuals, who are acknowledged elsewhere, and thanks also to the discovery of surviving Blackwood letters and other unpublished documents, I was able steadily to piece his life together.

Or at least a fair picture of it. I doubt it will ever be possible to reconstruct Blackwood's life completely. Although he enjoyed the company of others, and delighted to be the centre of attention when telling stories, Blackwood was never happier than when far away in the wilds of the world. No one ever really knew him – perhaps Maya Knoop came closest, and she died before I was born. Blackwood only revealed as much of himself as he wished. In 1923 he wrote an autobiography called *Episodes Before Thirty*. As the title suggests it only covered the period up to 1899, when he returned to England from America. It concentrated on his life in Canada and New York throughout the 1890s, and he purposely avoided discussing his psychic experiences. As Blackwood's fame rekindled in the 1930s publishers beseeched him to produce a book about these occult experiences, or at the very least *Episodes After Thirty*. Blackwood steadfastly refused. All that he wanted to say about his beliefs and experiences was locked away in his stories for those with the right spiritual keys to unlock. Nevertheless, during the dark days of the Second World War Blackwood did make some notes for a second autobiography, but they never reached book form. He later cannibalized them for a few radio talks and magazine articles, but essentially kept the rest of his life and his occult adventures out of the public eye. This biography explores these, so far as I can, for the first time.

Knowing the real Blackwood can also be difficult. Different people saw different aspects of his personality. To some he was the deep and profound mystic with the air of an ancient Egyptian priest. This facet was known as 'Pan' or 'Starlight'. To others he was a delightful storyteller with a wonderful sense of humour as well as a sense of wonder, able to keep people spellbound with his rich voice and piercing blue eyes. This was the character affectionately called 'Uncle Paul'. To yet others he was an ancient child, innocent yet awesome. To others he was a fine athlete, an accomplished skier and tennis player. And to others who knew him in his final years he was a remarkably agile yet increasingly frail old man, whose eyes still betrayed a spirit of a thousand years.

I have tried to capture all these images and reflections of Blackwood. Although I cannot reveal all about him, I can reveal much, and bring together the first full-length biography of this remarkable man. I hope it will inspire further research so that an understanding of his life and work can be made more complete.

It seems such a shame that Blackwood and so many of his contemporaries no longer light fires in people's memories. Yet in their day they were the stars that brought light and life and fascination to the world. With this biography I want to rekindle those fires and show how much we have lost with the passing of generations. Blackwood's world was full of many amazing people. He encountered some of the most remarkable experiences you could imagine. His books contain some of the most overwhelming imagery and emotion you will ever experience. If I can recapture even just a portion of those in this book, I shall have achieved my aim.

Mike Ashley
August 2001

1

The Weight of Ages (1869–79)

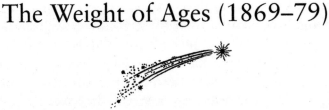

I

On 25 September 1949, a pleasant, warm Sunday evening, Algernon Blackwood made his way from the Savile Club, his second home for over forty years, to Oxford Street, then turned left into Regent Street to Langham Place and the august offices of the BBC.

He was instantly recognizable from his television broadcasts. Tall – six foot two inches, though stooping, thin and suntanned to a rich chestnut; bald, his face heavily wrinkled with a prominent, slightly hawkish nose and hypnotic blue-grey eyes. Friends likened him to an ancient Egyptian magician or a native American Indian. On this warm evening he wore his somewhat creased suit rather than his mackintosh, and shoes instead of his polished but well-worn hiking boots, but he still had his knapsack, a trilby pushed back on his head and sported a bright blue spotted bow-tie.

That evening Blackwood was to give a talk on the Home Service: 'On Being Eighty'. It was already scripted, but Blackwood never stopped improvising, so his mind continued to play with the topic. His theme for the talk was on certain goals that he had set himself – 'torches' he called them. At different times he had wanted to be a poet, a violinist, an explorer and mountaineer, and a holy man. Had he achieved those things? Had his life been a success, or were there ambitions still not satisfied?

Recent radio broadcasts had seen Blackwood in a reflective mood, whereas usually he looked forward, always fascinated in new developments, new ideas. Just the previous month he had given a talk,

'The Little Puzzles', on *Woman's Hour*, in which he mentioned how intrigued he had been when he learned about the planned new Observatory at Mount Palomar, in California. He mentioned it to H.G. Wells, whom he met in Cannes, enthusing about the new wonders of outer space that it would unveil. Wells responded, 'Why get excited about that?' Wells, the great scientific visionary, had grown sour and embittered in his old age, but Blackwood, the mystical visionary, remained fascinated and in awe. The wonders of the Universe, both the seen and the unseen, had taken Blackwood by the hand and the heart since his childhood, and they led him still. No matter how many 'torches' Blackwood felt had been his guiding lights, there had really only been one – Nature.

II

Blackwood was born on 14 March 1869. The young infant was at first named Henry after his famous great-grandfather, Sir Henry Blackwood (1770–1832) – the Algernon was added at his christening. He was born into a wealthy and very strict Victorian family, descended from and closely related to the nobility. Those upper-class connections would help him throughout his life, yet, at the same time, he would rebel against them. Blackwood was happiest when leading the simple life and for much of it he had little money – indeed, was often penniless – and mingled with tramps, criminals and peasants. Just like the explorer, one of his later ambitions, Blackwood would venture into unknown territory, escape from the everyday world and take risks, but he always had that lifeline back to comfort, good living and money. In effect, he had the best of both worlds, but it was not something he achieved easily. It took him nearly forty years – half his life in fact – to make that balance work, once he became a full-time writer.

Blackwood was the third of five children. His father, Stevenson Arthur Blackwood, then thirty-six, was a Clerk to the Treasury. He later became Secretary to the Post Office – and received a knighthood. Thereafter he was always known as Sir Arthur and, to avoid confusion with his eldest son (also called Stevenson) I shall refer to him throughout as Arthur. Blackwood's mother, Harriet, was of Protestant Irish stock, the Dobbs of Castle Dobbs, Carrickfergus. She had been married once before (at fifteen) to George Montagu, the 6th Duke of Manchester. Montagu was thirty-four years her senior, and this was his second marriage. He had had four children by his first marriage, already adults.

Needless to say, such a young wife caused quite a stir around court and she was always known, rather derisively, as 'Duchess Dobbs'. She was still only twenty when the Duke died, in August 1855.

Harriet had borne Montagu two more children: Sydney Charlotte (1851–1932) and George (1855–82). Algernon hardly knew George, who entered the Diplomatic Service and died in Washington DC aged only twenty-seven. But Sydney became a very dear relative. On 14 August 1873 she married Algernon Keith-Falconer, the son of Lord Kintore. He in turn became the 9th Earl of Kintore in July 1880. A newspaper report of the time describes Lady Kintore as 'a tall, fair woman, with charming manners. . . intelligent . . . with a pretty gift for writing verses; she has a kind heart and a ready helpfulness.' The same paper described Lord Kintore as 'one of the best shots in Scotland. His tall, strapping figure and good-looking face of the blond Scotch type have secured him the character of a handsome man and he is distinctly a favourite man in smart society.'

Their first child Ethel (known as Ettie) was born on 20 September 1874, when Blackwood was five. She was like a young sister to him rather than a niece. Often during his childhood, Blackwood and his family would visit the Kintores at their family home in Inverurie, Scotland. It was not long before Blackwood became used to the mountains, forests and wide-open spaces of one of Britain's last wildernesses – a far cry from the rigid discipline of his life at home.

When Arthur Blackwood married Harriet Sydney Montagu on 16 December 1858, he became stepfather to Sydney and George. They also had five children of their own: Cecilia Grace (known as Ceci), born 3 June 1862; Beatrice Lucy born 17 March 1866; and Stevenson Arthur (known as Stevie) born 30 August 1867. Then came Algernon himself and finally Ada Sydney, on 17 January 1871.

Blackwood's family connections are very complex. He said himself that he was 'overburdened with distinguished relations of heavy calibre'.[1] There are connections to Lord Dufferin, Governor-General of Canada, to Sir Henry Blackwood, a close friend of Horatio Nelson, and to Sir Richard Dobbs, Lord Mayor of London. They are covered in more detail in the Appendix (*see page 366*). Despite what many people believe, he was not related to William Blackwood and Sons, the Edinburgh publishers who, for many years, produced the world-renowned *Blackwood's Magazine*, even though the Blackwood family originated in Scotland, before the main branch settled in Ireland.

Blackwood was born at Wood Lodge, Shooter's Hill in north-west Kent, not far from the suburbs of London. Administratively it fell within the parish of Eltham, but it was closer to Blackheath. Wood Lodge was a significant property. Built shortly before 1800 it had been extended and developed until a surveyor's report, in the early 1800s, called it 'a situation superior to any within this Manor'. It stood in over thirty acres of land with rights over a further twenty-three acres of adjoining woodland. Originally the house was called Nightingale Hall, and the song of the nightingale was still heard there many years later. Wildlife abounded in the adjacent woods. The house had at least three sitting rooms, seven bedrooms, two dressing rooms, a brew house and stabling for six horses, and this was before it was enlarged by another tenant in 1860. Arthur Blackwood and his growing family moved there in January 1868. The 1871 census reveals that they had eight servants and a governess.

Wood Lodge is no longer standing. The property reverted to the Crown in 1916 when it was used by the War Department as an anti-aircraft unit. It remained unused for the next fifteen years, became dilapidated, and was pulled down in 1932.

It is just possible that Blackwood's earliest memory dates from those days. In his radio talk 'Minor Memories' he recalled that when he was just old enough to 'grip the lower bar of the nursery window' he saw the face of God. His parents spoke much of God but he had no idea what he looked like. The vision turned out to be a balloon sailing over Kent from Crystal Palace but it remained an indelible memory. [2]

Increased demands on Blackwood's father, with a greater number of evening engagements, meant that he often returned home late, and Wood Lodge was not conveniently situated near the railway station. In June 1871 the family moved to the Manor House, Crayford. This was the home that remained fixed in Algernon's memory. He lived there from the age of two till June 1880, when he was eleven. It was the home of his childhood, the home of the 'Starlight Express', and the house that appears in many of his stories.

Although Crayford was a growing industrial town with its brickfields and gasworks, the Manor House was just far enough north of it to feel rural still. It had been built in the Italian style in the 1820s on the site of a much older manor house. With some fifteen rooms on three storeys, it also had a meeting room on the ground floor where Blackwood's parents held fortnightly religious gatherings. Its grounds were not so large as at Wood Lodge, though there was easy access to the surrounding fields at the back (now a golf course).

The house made an indelible impression upon young Blackwood. In *A Prisoner in Fairyland*, where he disguises Crayford transparently as Crayfield, his narrator, Henry Rogers, reflects upon his childhood home.

> He saw the Manor House where he was born, the bars across the night-nursery windows, the cedars on the lawn, the haystacks just beyond the stables, and the fields where the rabbits sometimes fell asleep as they sat after enormous meals too stuffed to move. He saw the old gravel-pit that led, the gardener told him, to the centre of the Earth.[3]

The description continues, bringing alive the sounds and smells as well as the visual memories. Although the building is now an adult education centre owned by the local authority, the former bedrooms on the top floor remain essentially unchanged. The bars are still on the bedroom windows. There is still a giant cedar in the front lawn. There is no nearby gravel-pit, but there are still plenty in the area, huge quarries dug out of the ground to meet the ever-growing demand for roadstone and building materials.

Perhaps the most significant memory of Crayford is the seed of the Starlight Express. Algernon's father bought an old railway carriage as a present for his children and it stood at the bottom of the garden. Algernon discovered it when he returned home from a summer holiday. It instantly became his means of escape. In his imagination it took him to the stars.

The train reappears in *A Prisoner in Fairyland*, the book that formed the basis of the musical play *The Starlight Express*. Businessman Henry Rogers returns to the house of his childhood and stands, dreamily, in the garden absorbing the memories of the past.

> Then suddenly, looming against the field that held the Gravel-Pit and the sleeping rabbits, he saw the outline of the Third-Class Railway Carriage his father bought as a Christmas present, still standing on the stone supports that were borrowed from a haystack. The Railway Carriage had filled whole years with joy and wonder. They had called it the Starlight Express. It had four doors, real lamps in the roof, windows that opened and shut, and big round buffers.

It started without warning. It went at full speed in a moment. It was never really still.[4]

The Starlight Express took young Algernon off to Fairyland. He was not alone. With him were all the sprites and imaginary friends that he had created from out of the landscape. There was the Guard, of course, and the Tramp – which became something of an icon for Blackwood. An 'Eternal Wanderer' who could slip through the world and not be part of it. There was the Gypsy, the Creature of the Gravel-Pit, the Woman of the Haystack, the Laugher, the Sweep, the Dustman and the Morning Spiders. Whereas other boys might ally themselves to the great heroes of the world, explorers and adventurers, Blackwood's affinity was with the outcasts and everyday characters who appeared to have a freedom that Blackwood lacked, and a mysterious aura about them that seemed part magical.

Blackwood was always seeking to escape. If there is a memory that is stronger than the evocative gardens and nursery, it is the memory of his parents' religious zeal and of the frequent visitors who would pounce on the young boy and ask him 'Have you been saved?' The intensity of this religious fervour overpowered everything else in Blackwood's childhood, and it brings into focus Blackwood's father, whose influence on the young and sensitive Algernon was immense.

III

Stevenson Arthur Blackwood had been born at Rosslyn Lodge, Hampstead, on 22 May 1832. His own father, Arthur Johnstone Blackwood (1808–74), who had been Gentleman Usher to Queen Victoria, had not been especially religious and certainly imposed no strict religious regime upon his family. Arthur was a healthy and vigorous young man, given much to outdoor pursuits, especially riding. He enjoyed exploring the wilds of Hampstead Heath. He was educated at Eton and Trinity College, Cambridge, and later regretted that he was not more diligent at Cambridge, since he took every opportunity he could to abscond and go riding or rowing rather than reading. His mother, seeing that his studies were suffering, was quick to secure him a post as a Clerk to the Treasury in March 1852. Arthur had grown into a handsome youth, with a roguish manly charm. Known as 'Beauty' Blackwood, he was one of the most eligible bachelors in London.

Although he enjoyed the high life, he never gave into excesses and was held in check by his godmother, Charlotte Wright.

In March 1854 Arthur volunteered to serve with the Commissariat Staff in the Crimean War, where he was attached to the Brigade of Guards. He witnessed action in all the major battles, including Alma, Balaclava, Inkerman and the siege of Sebastopol. For most of the war he remained his usual worldly self, though always friendly and supportive of his fellows. However, as the war dragged on, he became steadily worn down, not just by the appalling disease and bloodshed he saw around him, but by a feeling of utter helplessness. There was so little he could do for the wounded and dying. His thoughts turned to God. Then came an overwhelming blow. His young sister, Ceci, to whom he was devoted, died in October 1855 aged only twenty. Arthur was heartbroken and railed against God for taking his sister away. Once his anger subsided he began to pray in earnest for her soul. From that moment he realized that he was not entirely helpless. He could at least help his fellow men come to terms with the horrors of the war and help the dying meet their Maker through the Scriptures. His good humour and tireless efforts were appreciated by the noncommissioned officers, who presented him with a silver statuette of a guardsman in recognition of his help and service when the War ended.

His religious conversion gathered pace rapidly upon his return to England in November 1855. In addition to his full-time work at the Treasury, Arthur helped organize a wide range of church and religious meetings and activities. He frequently lectured to gatherings such as the seaman's mission or other working men's establishments. This brought him into contact with the perils of drink and his talks turned increasingly to temperance, though he did not sign the pledge till 1878.

He became involved in the Mildmay Conferences, which were established by the Reverend William Pennefather at Barnet, North London[5], in June 1856. The purpose of these meetings was to bring together, on a nondenominational basis, devout Christians for study and discussion. It was at the first of these that Blackwood sensed his religious conversion, later stating that it was only then that 'the light of God streamed into my soul in all its fulness'.[6]

His own health suffered and he had a nervous collapse, complicated by a recurrence of rheumatic fever that he had had as a child. This laid him up for nearly a year, and that time was spent reading religious works. The illness left him with a permanently weak heart, but it did not stop his industriousness.

Through Mildmay and other gatherings Arthur Blackwood came into contact with many important and influential people. One of these was the Duchess of Gordon, widow of a former Marquess of Huntly. Her sister-in-law had been the first wife of the Duke of Manchester. The Duchess of Gordon, now in her sixties, continued to care for the Duke's second wife, Harriet Montagu, and her two young children at her home at Huntly Lodge, north of Aberdeen. Arthur occasionally ventured that far north to meet his friend Francis Keith-Falconer, the Earl of Kintore, who was another evangelist and temperance worker. His home at Inverurie was but a few miles from Huntly Lodge where, one day in the spring of 1857, Arthur first met his future wife. A year later they became engaged and married soon after on 16 December 1858. She was a kindred spirit, strongly religious and an ardent Christian. The couple became a strong team, and they attracted the attention of other evangelists.

Leading among these was Granville Waldegrave (1833–1913), the 3rd Baron Radstock, a distant relative by marriage. Over the next few years Blackwood and Radstock worked closely together and their two young families became well acquainted. Young Algernon would frequently play with Radstock's children, especially his younger daughter, Mary, who became an important friend in later years. An evangelical, Lord Radstock was for some years a member of the Plymouth Brethren. Arthur Blackwood was less fervent than Radstock, but no less committed.

In 1873 the Reverend Pennefather died suddenly, and the task of organising the forthcoming Mildmay Conference fell to Algernon's father, which he continued with for the next twenty years. Blackwood Senior held regular meetings throughout the Crayford area, speaking at Bexley Heath on Sunday evenings and taking open-air services on Crayford Bridge. He helped raise funds for a coffee tavern for the factory workers in Crayford to draw them away from the public houses. This was opened in April 1874 and here Blackwood Senior organized men's night school and Bible classes, Mothers' Meetings and religious gatherings. A memorial drinking fountain was erected to Blackwood Senior on Crayford Bridge, which is there to this day.

All of this was in addition to Blackwood's full-time work at the Treasury, which itself had become more involved and demanding, with the duty of preparing the estimates submitted to Parliament for approval each financial year. Young Algernon did not inherit his father's accounting skills, which passed to his brother, Stevie, who became an accountant. In October 1874 Blackwood Senior moved from the Treasury to the newly created post of Financial Secretary to the General Post Office, and this in turn led to his promotion as Secretary to the Post Office in April 1880, a position second only to the Postmaster General. At the same time he was made a Companion of the Order of the Bath. This honour was followed by the Knight Commander of the Bath in the Jubilee Honours in June 1887. From then on he preferred to be known by his second name and was always referred to as Sir Arthur.

Sir Arthur brought the same diligence and commitment to his work as he did to his Christian obligations. He travelled widely to secure postal arrangements throughout Europe and the Empire, and corresponded frequently in the Press about new postal arrangements. Among the new proposals that he saw through were the introduction of the parcel post and the postal order.

On occasions, when the American evangelists Dwight Moody and Ira Sankey toured Britain, starting in 1875, they stayed at the Blackwood home. Moody was too much for young Algernon to take. His powerful personality and hypnotic eyes frightened Algernon who avoided Moody for fear of being cornered and asked, 'Are you saved?' In his innocence, young Algernon found himself adopting the mood of his elders, accosting people (usually visitors or the servants) and asking if they were saved. But, as he later admitted, 'I never shared the beliefs of my parents with anything like genuine pleasure. I was *afraid* they were true, not glad.'[7]

This fear of hell and damnation was almost tangible in the Blackwood household, and young Algernon grew up torn by a terrifying dilemma – a fear that his parents were right and a fear that they were wrong. This severely dented his confidence. He grew up, quiet and unassertive. Above all it made Algernon feel perpetually guilty. If there was ever a hint that something had gone wrong, he would feel compelled to confess, even if he had committed no wrong. This manifested itself fairly early on when, at the age of twelve, he was sent to a private school in Sevenoaks in Kent. It was a school where his elder brother was already in attendance. Unfortunately young Algernon borrowed a school friend's poetry book without his permission and when accused of stealing it allowed his silence to prove his guilt. His father was called to the school, Algernon felt ashamed in his eyes, and at the end of term he and his brother were removed. This feeling of guilt never left Blackwood. Even as late as 1950, when Blackwood was well known as a television broadcaster, he became worried when a police officer kept watching him and followed him into the Underground. It was because he recognized him from television and was hoping to introduce himself, but during those few moments Blackwood was convinced he had committed a crime.

This guilt and perpetual doom permeates several of Blackwood's stories, but is most potent in 'The Damned'[8]. In this story a house, which had been occupied by a long series of ardent religious fanatics, becomes saturated with their passion and the souls of the damned, till every fabric of the house oozes oppression.

Despite the religious fervour of his parents and the sanctimoniousness of relatives and visitors, young Algernon had a comparatively happy childhood. He said as much in his radio talk 'On Being Eighty' even though he tempered it by adding that he had a perpetual dread of Hell every night he went to bed. He also remembers that he was 'frequently in tears about nothing except a vague horror of the practical world, full of wild fancies and imagination . . .'[9] But he did not fear his father. He called both parents 'genuinely saintly types', adding that for his father 'I had a special loving adoration, for he really *lived* his beliefs.'

IV

In 1880 the lease ran out on the Manor House at Crayford and rather than renew it, Blackwood Senior looked for another house nearer to London. He settled on Shortlands House near Bromley, in easy walking distance of the railway station. This was larger and more spacious than Crayford Manor, and had been renovated and extended only five years earlier. The grounds were still fairly extensive but the two previous owners had sold off several hundred acres for development and new houses were under construction nearby when the Blackwoods lived there. The house itself is quite striking with two semicircular bays at each wing, a verandah and an extensive conservatory at the back which looked over the fields down towards a series of ponds. It is difficult to assess the layout today because the house became a hotel for thirty years after the First World War and since 1950 has been a private school. Some of the original fixtures still remain, not least the beautiful oak staircase and the stained-glass windows on the stairs and landing.

They remained there for a decade. It was the last family home Algernon would know in England and in one of the first articles he wrote for publication, 'Christmas in England'[10], he drew upon his memories of Christmas there. He talks of gatherings at the village inn on Christmas Eve and of carousing and singing. The huge log fires at home, the decorations, carol singing and, if the weather allowed, sports and games in the snow on afternoon of Christmas Day, followed by parties in the evening. These are fond memories.

Of a more mystical nature, in *Episodes Before Thirty* he tells how he used to climb out of his window at night, down a ladder, through the kitchen garden and down to a pond in the lower field, where he would launch his boat and practise weird incantations and ceremonies. The garden was overgrown with trees, so very little moonlight or starlight penetrated the greenery and he believed he was surrounded by all manner of strange beings, perhaps tree dryads and fairies and water elementals. Sometimes he was accompanied by an elder sister, almost certainly Beatrice, who was then fourteen or fifteen. (Ceci was eighteen and unlikely to be interested in childish games.) Algernon says that this sister loved mystery and seemed to take on a different persona at night, 'more like a fairy being than a mortal', but during the day she reverted to being a dull girl. He used this strange transformation in a children's story that he wrote forty years later, 'The Water Performance'[11]. He also used it as the basis for a children's novel, with the working title *Rose and Ditt*, which he never completed.

Already Algernon's over-active imagination, together with his sensitive nature and fanciful daydreaming, was developing a mind that saw more than the normal senses perceived. Perhaps some of that fey Celtic outlook, inherited through the genes of his Irish and Scottish forebears, helped fuel the imagination.

Nevertheless, there was a common bond between father and son in their love of nature. Take the following passage:

> The approach of Spring was always hailed with delight. Winter he only endured; but when, after a long spell of East or North winds, gloom and cold, the wind would veer, even for a day, to South or West, he would return home from London, shouting, 'Hurrah! Wind gone to the South. Spring is coming!' . . . And when the soft green

began to appear, and the cuckoo's note was heard, and the blossoming of almond and cherry showed that Spring had come then the longing became irrepressible to get away where he could wander over moors and hills for miles and miles, or on the Surrey Hills, or through the fields and green lanes of Kent, or by the sea-shore in Devon and Cornwall.[12]

Now consider the following:

And when the Spring came round again with its charged memories of perfume and sight, and the singing of its happy winds; when the tree-spirits returned to their garden haunts, all flaming with the beauty of new dresses gathered over-seas; when the silver birch tree combed out her glittering hair to the sun and shook her leaves in the very face of that old pine tree – then Paul felt in himself, too, the rejuvenation that was going forward in all the world around him. He tasted in his heart all the regenerative forces that were bursting into form and energy with the spring, and knew that the pain and desolation he had felt temporarily in the winter were only spiritual growing-pains. . . .[13]

Those two passages could have been written about the same person. In fact the first was about Blackwood's father by a friend, and the second was by Algernon about Uncle Paul, the eponymous protagonist in his quasi-autobiographical novel *The Education of Uncle Paul.*

Blackwood's intense passion for the wonder and power of Nature infected him from an early age.

By far the strongest influence in my life . . . was Nature; it betrayed itself early, growing in intensity with every year. Bringing comfort, companionship, inspiration, joy, the spell of Nature has remained dominant, a truly magical spell.[14]

It began with such childhood expeditions as the nightly visit to the ponds at Shortlands. On his return he would be fascinated by the appearance of the house outlined against the night sky, flanked on one side by three large cedars.

I thought of all the people asleep in their silent rooms, and wondered how they could be so dull and unenterprising, when out here they could see these sweeping branches and hear the wind sighing so beautifully among the needles. These people, it seemed to me at such moments, belonged to a different race. I had nothing in common with them. Night and stars and trees and wind and rain were the things I had to do with and wanted. They were alive and personal, stirring my depths within, full of messages and meanings, whereas my parents and sisters and brother, all indoors and asleep, were mere accidents, and apart from my real life and self.[15]

Algernon had become detached from family life, dreamy, lazy. Yet his father was tolerant, perhaps seeing reflected in Algernon some of his own dissolute youth. Thankfully, their common delight in the natural world bonded them, when religion, study and work failed. When the two were on a walking holiday in North Devon in May 1888, Sir Arthur wrote to his half-sister, Lucy, saying:

I must tell you all about our walk when we meet. Never in my life have I had such a combination of perfect weather, lovely scenery and enjoyment of earth and sea and sky. It has been simply perfect. And A[lgie] such a pleasant, thoughtful and agreeable companion.[16]

Algernon was at his happiest and closest to his family when on holiday. Despite his father's gruelling workload, he ensured that the family had at least one holiday a year, and more usually two, even if sometimes work meant that he couldn't join them. The first holiday Blackwood remembered was in Kent, at Margate in September 1873. For Blackwood's father the holiday would be particularly poignant as it was the last time spent with his own father, Arthur Johnstone Blackwood. He was only sixty-five and appeared to be in robust health, joining his son for long walks, but three months later he was struck down with 'congestion of the lungs' – probably pneumonia – and died on 2 January 1874. Algernon makes no reference to this, although he was four and old enough to remember his father's grief. What sticks in his mind from that year was the *camera obscura* at Margate, which utterly fascinated him. Here was something that allowed him to remain hidden but view the world about him, something he would try to do for most of his life.

The family also enjoyed short boating trips. Sometimes these would be on the River Medway in Kent, but more often they were on the

Thames, usually at Whitsuntide, in May. One such trip was rowing from Medmenham, near Marlow in Buckinghamshire, to Windsor, having picnics on the river bank and camping out for a night or two. Blackwood became a strong rower and swimmer, copying his father's favourite sports (except for riding). They were both good at tennis and squash.

The best holidays, though, began in 1879, with their first extended holiday in Scotland, spending several weeks in the area around Loch Tay. In later years Sir Arthur availed himself of the hospitality of friends and enjoyed cruises around the Hebrides. Algernon always retained a strong affection for Scotland.

Yet despite these holidays and the relaxed companionship, Algernon was at heart a loner. He needed to escape from any reminder of the oppressive, guilty demands of the evangelist and the world of society, pomp and respectability, all of which pressed down on him with the sheer weight of ages.

> In times of trouble, as equally in times of joy, it was to Nature I ever turned instinctively. In those moments of deepest feeling when individuals must necessarily be alone, yet stand at the same time in most urgent need of understanding companionship, it was Nature and Nature only that could comfort me.[17]

Young Algernon was always out of step with the world around him. Although he did not openly rebel against his background he withdrew from it at every opportunity. At this time he had no way of expressing his feelings. This could have been when the first of those 'torches' that he referred to in his 'On Being Eighty' talk started in his mind – the desire to be a poet. A few years later, when opportunity presented, he began to write, and one of his first outpourings was a poem, 'Lines to a Dreamer'. It is reprinted in full in *Episodes Before Thirty*, so I won't repeat it here, but it contains two worthy lines. In the poem Blackwood shakes himself down and comes to terms with life. He realises that hanging around dreaming will not solve anything. Each individual has to take command of his own destiny. 'Stagnation means death,' he wrote. 'If you cannot advance you retreat.' But the only way forward is by learning from your own suffering.

Blackwood was learning one of the first hard lessons in life. If you want to achieve your ambitions you have to do it yourself, no matter what pain and agony you go through. But determination will yield results. It took Blackwood the first twenty years of his life to realise this, and the next twenty were full of further trials and anguish. It was a long, hard ladder to climb, but at least Blackwood was on the bottom rung.

2

Spirits Awaken (1880–87)

I

Blackwood's outlook on life did not blend well with his formal education. The private school in Sevenoaks, from which he was removed for apparently stealing a poetry book, was one of four or five 'horrible private schools', as he called them, that he attended at this time. How his father must have despaired.

In May 1883 Algernon was admitted to Wellington College at Crowthorne in Berkshire. This was a relatively new private school, which had become established under the authoritarian headmastership of Edward White Benson (who became Archbishop of Canterbury in 1883). All Benson's children were born at Wellington, including the authors Arthur (A.C. Benson), Frederick (E.F. Benson) and Hugh (R.H. Benson). Benson's tenure ran from 1859 to 1872. Although he had long gone by the time Stevenson Blackwood arrived in the summer term of 1882 and Algernon in the following year, he had left a legacy of a strict but free-thinking school. The new headmaster, Dr Edward Wickham, was more strait-laced than Benson, not given to his extremes of temperament, but at the same time not so forthright or so provocative. If anything, under him the school lapsed to more traditional public school lines.

Algernon did not blossom at Wellington. Among the few records that survive from the College's early years are his course results. The first at Christmas 1883 show that he was fourth out of twenty-seven in classics, divinity, English and French and third in physics. However by Easter 1884 he had dropped to sixteenth in classics, divinity and

English and was bottom in chemistry. Blackwood's own recollection was that he was good at Greek but poor at mathematics. He left at the end of the summer term of 1884.

Blackwood's education was suffering and drastic measures had to be taken. While his brother moved up to Trinity College, Cambridge, Algernon was despatched to Germany – to the School of the Moravian Brotherhood at Königsfeld in the Black Forest. He arrived there on a bright spring day in May 1885. Though he had enjoyed the outward journey and the wonderful enchantment of the Schwarzwald, as he approached the large, severe-looking building, he felt he was about to serve a sentence in prison.

The Moravians are a strict if pious evangelical sect of Protestants who believe strongly in following the teachings of the Bible, word for word, and in associated ritual and celebration. There were usually about eighty boys and sixty girls (the schools were segregated at either end of the village), mostly French – about a quarter were English. Upon arrival they were allowed three days in which they could speak their native tongues but from the fourth day they could only speak German. Any lapses into their own language resulted in half rations. Bedtime was at 8.30 p.m., rising again at 5.30 a.m., when they had just half an hour to get prepared before the first lecture. Anyone late was on half rations again.

Nevertheless, there was plenty of time for recreation. In addition to several breaks during the day for sports, they also went on regular hikes. Twice a year there were long camping holidays in the Black Forest.

This strict regime had a significant effect upon Blackwood. It bonded him with fellow pupils of his own age. This had not happened at his previous schools, whereas he later commented on the camaraderie of the Moravians. Blackwood kept in touch with the school for some years afterwards. The Brothers also practised equality. They followed the same discipline as the students. There was no 'us and them' or the 'holier than thou' feeling already imbued in Blackwood by his aristocratic and repressive home life. What Blackwood liked was that the school was not one that taught lessons by rote. The Brotherhood believed it important to develop a strong inner self, which required much meditation and reflection – 'real religion' Blackwood called it in *Episodes*. Finally it imprinted upon Blackwood a habit of asceticism. The meals were basic but nutritious, so although the students and

Brothers ate sparsely their meals were sufficient. Combined with the healthy air and exercise they were all fit. Blackwood remarked that there was scarcely any illness.

Though Blackwood might have rebelled against the strict discipline at first, the monk-like lifestyle appealed to him and it gave him greater command of himself in later years. His period at the Moravian School, for all that it lasted little more than a year, gave him more strength of character than any other education he underwent.

It seems slightly strange, therefore, that the one story in which Blackwood evokes strongly the Moravian Brotherhood appears, on the surface, to be negative. 'Secret Worship', one of the John Silence stories, does not name the school, but it hardly needs to. The description of it by the protagonist, Harris, is obvious.

> ... this school had left the imprint of its peculiar influence, and, though perhaps unknown to Harris, had strongly coloured the whole of his subsequent existence. It belonged to the deeply religious life of a small Protestant community (which it is unnecessary to specify), and his father had sent him there at the age of fifteen, partly because he would ... learn German ... and partly because the discipline was strict, and discipline was what his soul and body needed just then more than anything.[1]

Harris revisits the school which, in the story, is now in ruins, having been burned down by the villagers ten years before because of the school's wickedness. The Brothers, it seems, had turned to devil-worship, and so intense was their evil that a residuum continues and Harris falls victim to it.

Why should Blackwood, who admired the Moravians, make them devil-worshippers, something utterly alien to these devout disciples? The story builds on the idea that intense emotions can imprint themselves upon their surroundings – the same idea he used in 'The Damned'. In one sense, Blackwood was emphasizing the strict disciplinarianism of the Brothers which was so intense that it remained imprinted upon him after all else went. Because the story is essentially a horror story, it was easier for Blackwood to introduce devil-worship, which I think is a mistake. But a reason could be found for the idea. The area around the school was rife with legends. Stories of kobolds, dwarves and elves gave it an otherworldly feel. A short walk brought pupils out on to a plain where stood two pillars once used (so legend said) for hanging witches and evil-doers. The juxtaposition with the school easily blended into the story.

II

Blackwood returned home in July 1886. He was now seventeen, a maturing adult, but with an increasing belief in a wider world of religion that was not necessarily limited to Christianity. At the time he was still searching for an answer. He had no parameters against which to plot his world-view, but he knew there was more to it than the evangelical dogma of his parents. His father was surprisingly tolerant. Despite his religious fervour, he could see that young Algernon still mirrored his own youth, and trusted that he would grow through it. Antagonizing the boy would only repel. He could simply nurture.

But there was more. Blackwood's father was a true Victorian in more than one sense. He too wanted to learn and believed that through discussion and analysis one could demonstrate God's wonder in all its forms. Thus he was quite prepared to explore with Algernon all aspects of the world. For example, upon his return from the Black Forest, Algernon joined the family setting off for their holiday to Scotland. Most of the time was spent on the Isle of Skye during which they visited his father's old school-friend the MacLeod of MacLeod at Dunvegan Castle. It was during this visit that the idea was born in Blackwood that 'We humans are not the only beings on the planet'. His father told Algie that the MacLeods 'kept under a glass case a Fairy Banner stolen from the Fairies', but that Algie was not to laugh or pry.

Blackwood so wanted to believe. He later recalled that: 'The seed of enquiry was sown, doubtless, in fruitful soil, for my imagination was already blazing fiery trails about the planet, and he [Blackwood's father] probably thought fairies were less dangerous than enquiry into Spiritualism.' [2]

Blackwood's father was sure that his son would soon dismiss the idea of fairies, but he was unaware of the pantheistic view that even then was dawning on the boy. Algernon would not think of fairies as the little creatures depicted in nursery books. As his world-view developed he could consider fairies in the same way as elementals, as manifestations of the Earth-spirit. Instead of lighting a damp squib, Blackwood Senior had ignited an undying flame.

And there was more. Blackwood's father used to enjoy telling ghost stories – or rather 'queer stories' was his preferred phrase. These were stories that considered the unusual and had no rational explanation. Blackwood gave an example of one in his very last television broadcast, 'How I Became Interested in Ghosts'[3]. A man suffers from epileptic fits, and doctors cannot cure him. He consults a spiritualist who gives him a locket, which he must wear against his chest at all times and never remove it. Nor should he open the locket. He must simply trust in its power. It works. Over time the fits cease and the man feels cured. Eventually, however, curiosity wins out and he opens the locket. Inside is some extremely small writing, which he could read only with a magnifying glass. It said: 'Let him alone till he drop into hell.'[4]

This was typical of his father's 'queer stories'. They had to have a moral and a warning. This story, whilst it has a pleasant *frisson*, is clearly anti-spiritualist. 'He wouldn't have anything to do with spirits,' Blackwood commented. 'He was very religious in certain ways and wanted to warn me off that dangerous country.'[5]

So Blackwood Senior used ghost stories and legends to warn his son about the perils of dabbling with the unknown, without appreciating that he was cultivating an imaginative and sensitive mind instead.

To this enquiring mind was cast another line. Returning from Skye that September, Algernon found a copy of the *Yoga Aphorisms* of Bhagwan Shree Patanjali. The book had been left behind by mistake by one of his father's friends who was writing a brochure to warn England of these immoral Eastern teachings.* Blackwood found the book fascinating. Although he did not understand it all, he read it over and over again. 'A deeper feeling than I had yet known woke in me.'[6] He could see nothing evil in its teachings: quite the opposite. Indeed many complemented what he had been learning at the Moravian school. 'God is the One unique Personality, untouched by desire, affliction, action or its result,' states one aphorism. 'Devotion to God enlightens the soul, removes every obstacle,' says another. The book shows you how to focus on God by eliminating distractions from the mind in meditation. But what would have flipped Blackwood's attention is where this led. 'Mind attains peace when meditation produces extra-

---

* This was inspired by such incidents as the desertion of Charles W. Leadbetter who, in 1884, became the first Christian minister to proclaim himself a Buddhist. Leadbetter later became a prominent and notorious member of the Theosophical Society.

ordinary sense-perceptions.' 'Thus mind masters everything from the smallest to the greatest.' 'Instead of knowledge gained through evidence and inference, it brings direct knowledge of objects and their meaning in its entirety.'[7]

To Blackwood the book was his salvation. He felt he had discovered a 'get-out' clause to the formal religious dogma that had hitherto chained his life. In *Episodes Before Thirty* Blackwood lists a dozen or more books and tracts that he encountered which fuelled his conversion to Eastern wisdom and philosophy. He did not acquire these all at once. The majority of them he did not have for several years. His road to understanding took a while, but his father soon realized something was amiss and began to sermonise, but it did no good. Blackwood had found an escape route and he was determined to explore it.

Blackwood's education was still far from over. That autumn he returned to central Europe, this time to Bôle in French-speaking Switzerland, with the intention of learning French. He stayed at the home of a local pastor, Louis Langel, along with his cousin, Arthur Hobart-Hampden (1864–1952), who was a few years older, and could exercise some control over Blackwood. Bôle was only a small village and did not require a full-time pastor, so, in order to supplement his income Langel ran a small guest-house with his wife and daughter, and took in students to learn French. He also kept bees – around thirty to forty hives. Blackwood became interested in beekeeping and this planted a new seed – that of possibly running a small farm.

Blackwood also persevered with learning the violin. In his radio talk 'On Being Eighty' he mentions having a fine teacher while living in Switzerland. Evidently his father was paying for extra tuition besides the French lessons. Blackwood had a good quality Steiner violin, though apparently with a weak E string. Whereas other tutors may have given in to Blackwood's dreaminess, his violin teacher did not. 'He inflamed me', Blackwood recalled. 'Yet, despite the tyranny of practice and discipline I came to realize that any gift I had was mediocre, if a genuine gift at all.'[8] Nevertheless his tutor persisted, and succeeded in securing Blackwood a place playing second violin in the Berne Symphony Orchestra, presumably as part of a youth orchestra. Blackwood's memory of the occasion was that he literally 'scraped' through the ordeal, his teacher remarking that 'If we'd greased your bow nobody need ever have heard you!' Yet at one stage Blackwood had an ambition to be a violinist – it was one of his 'torches' – and his violin was his constant companion. He mentions it often in *Episodes Before Thirty* when, in moments of extreme depression, he would turn to his violin for solace. Moreover, people remembered his violin playing years later. John Macrae, President of the publisher, E.P. Dutton, met an old lady in 1935 who had known Blackwood in the 1890s. Macrae reminded Blackwood: 'Mrs Dodd informs me that you were, at the time she knew you, a very accomplished violinist.'[9] Memory may distort, and Blackwood was probably a better violinist than he was prepared to admit. He continued to play his violin throughout his life, and yet scarcely mentions it in later years.

Just as at Shortlands, Blackwood would venture out at night from the small guest-house, through the pine forests. Communion with nature was becoming like a drug to him. 'It was a persistent craving,' he admitted. Only alone with nature did Blackwood begin to experience a joy, even an ecstasy, which he never found in human relationships. He began to sense a spirit in the Earth, that everything around him was alive and that, if only he could find the way, he might communicate with it. It was this that drove Blackwood into further reading and searching for new experiences and techniques. It fuelled his life ever after. Every involvement that he had with mystical or esoteric studies and adventures in the wildernesses of the world, was aimed towards this escape from everyday life and a hope of communion with the powers of nature.

There were at least two other English boys at Langel's guest-house at this time – Percy Radcliffe and George Rainey. Both later became businessmen. Among Blackwood's few surviving papers was a letter to him from Percy Radcliffe written sixty years later, looking back on the time at Bôle.

> I wonder if you remember a long night walk we made, up through the forest by Bôle, on to the mountain. It was a night in June 1887, the even of Queen Victoria's Jubilee, and we proposed to celebrate it by climbing to the summit of the Tête le Rang to camp up there and see sunrise on the Alps. If you do recollect it you will remember that we left the Curé late in the evening, walking through the dark forest road up the village of Rochefort and then climbed for some hours reaching the summit of the mountain about midnight. I think you told us some ghost stories to keep our spirits up. On reaching the summit we made a fire and snatched a few hours rest and were then rewarded by having a magnificent view over the Alps.[10]

That vivid description is something we will encounter throughout the rest of his life: Blackwood, in the mountains or other remoteness of the world, close to nature and telling stories. Interestingly, there is a wood near this walk called the Bois Noir, which means Blackwood, and which was a pseudonym that Blackwood adopted for one of his early writings.

That very same day Blackwood's father received his knighthood, and I have no idea whether Blackwood already knew about that. He was always very proud of his father and, if he knew, it must have brought added wonder to that night's adventure.

When he was not studying, Blackwood was out exploring. He was able to write authoritatively about the region four years later in an article for the Canadian *Methodist Magazine*. In this he reveals not only his explorations through the mountains and along mountain streams, but also something less obvious. Describing sudden outcrops of rock, he goes on to say:

> ...the diligent observer may discover dark openings in the rock through which he may with difficulty squeeze himself. These are entrances to long and winding passages between the twisting strata which pierce far into the inerior of the mountain. We ourself have explored many hundred yards of these winding and tortuous caverns, and provided one keeps a clear remembrance of the different turns and twists of the passages, the journey, with a good lantern, is both interesting and instructive.[11]

These would become Blackwood's Star Caverns in *A Prisoner in Fairyland*.

Blackwood also sought out further esoteric books to expand his mind. Since he was now fairly fluent in both German and French he was able to read books in their original languages by many of the French, Belgian and German philosophers and poets, books which were not easily found in England at that time. He was drawn to the Symbolist poets, especially Paul Verlaine and Emile Verhaeren. Their fascination for evoking nature and depicting a past that continued to live and influence the present had strong appeal. He also liked the Romantic school, particularly Goethe, Schiller and above all Novalis, whose works created a beauty out of the past or legend. His favourite poet, though, was Shelley, not because he was another rebel against conformity but because his works explored those hidden forces throughout the Universe that could spread beauty and achieve wonder. His favourite work was *Prometheus Unbound*, which he knew by heart and often quoted.

His most profound discovery was the work of Gustav Fechner, who believed that everything, including the Earth, had a soul. Fechner, and his spiritual successor, the French philosopher Henri Bergson, who would soon be postulating the idea of racial memory, were like bread and milk to Blackwood. Their views began to build a structure which Blackwood could clothe with his own thinking.

By now he had discovered *The Bhagavad Gita*, which admirably supplemented the *Yoga Aphorisms*, and led him inevitably to other greater works of Sanskrit literature, especially the *Upanishads*. Through story and allegory the *Gita* provides a remarkable series of lessons for the improvement of the soul. Blackwood read these texts hungrily, again and again. The impression is of someone desperate to find the truth not solely for the truth itself, but in order to be as devout and as dedicated in his beliefs as his father was in his own. Blackwood loved and respected his father and so wanted his father to respect his own beliefs.

III

Blackwood returned from the Jura enriched in body and soul. Soon he was in discussion with his father about his future and a plan was devised. Algernon believed he might become a farmer and to that end his father suggested that, rather than try to establish a living in England, where increased industrialization was making farming difficult, perhaps he should endeavour to make it work in Canada, where there were ample opportunities and where Sir Arthur owned some land. It was agreed that while the rest of the family spent their summer holidays at Dalmally in Argyllshire, Sir Arthur and his son would visit Canada and explore the possibilities for Algernon's future.

The moment the Postmaster General learned of Sir Arthur's plans, what started out as a private trip became a quasi-official one. The Canadian Pacific Railway had been completed an amazing six years ahead of schedule in November 1885 and the first train to complete the full journey from Montreal to Vancouver had run just a year earlier in July 1886. The Post Office wanted to survey the line and explore its potential for conveying post, and here was a convenient opportunity.

The lead-up to their departure was hectic. No sooner had Sir Arthur ensured his family were safely ensconced at Dalmally on 27 July 1887, than he had to make the long journey back to Osborne, in the Isle of Wight, to receive his knighthood from Queen Victoria on 1 August. He had left strict instructions for Algie to meet him at Holyhead but, dreamy as ever, Algernon caught the wrong train and ended up in Liverpool. Sir Arthur was not amused. They set off on the *Etruria* on Sunday, 7 August. By the morning strong winds had whipped up the sea, and Algernon spent most of his day in bed, sea-sick. He had found his sea legs by the next day, though one of the passengers had died overnight and was buried at sea that morning. Otherwise it was an uneventful voyage and they reached New York that Saturday. Sir Arthur was not impressed by New York. 'Nothing in the town to attract and overhead railways and street trains very noisy. People the most commonplace and uninteresting I ever saw.'[12]

They soon escaped New York, travelling up the Hudson River to Albany and from there to Niagara Falls. Algie's past transgression was now forgotten. The young man had clearly come alive with the journey from New York. 'Algie a capital fellow traveller in every way,' his father wrote. They spent three days at Niagara, visiting the Falls twice and going for walks along the river. A chance encounter with an old contact diverted them briefly to the summer religious camp at Lake Chatauqua near Buffalo where Sir Arthur ended up presenting a small talk on his Christian work in England.

Sir Arthur was keen to make some headway on the matter of Algie's future and met the Minister of Agriculture in Ottawa, who arranged for a trip to an experimental farm a few miles outside the city. At this stage nothing was decided, but both Sir Arthur and Algernon were impressed at the industry and determination with which the sites were being prepared.

It was time to venture forth on the Canadian Pacific Railway. They left Montreal on 25 August in a comfortable sleeping carriage at the end of the train. Initially the views were 'exquisite', especially alongside Lake Superior but once they entered the prairie it became tedious. Nevertheless, on the night of 28 August, Algie had his first view of the Northern Lights. He wrote about it to his sisters:

I propped up my pillows and lay dreamily watching the landscape
as it glided past in the cold moonlight. I was, however, aware of a

certain 'light' in the sky, but it struck me as being nothing at all remarkable and I lay still, dreamily looking out. My perception of colour is not as strongly developed as it might be. But *suddenly*! as in the twitching of a nostril, the light shot across the sky forming a *huge semicircle* – red, yellow and gold – and at one end seemed to form a regular whirlwind of fire, circle within circle of ever changing streaks of light, and then from either extremity there shot down athwart the sky a brilliant flash or pillar of light, like the tail of a large comet, and then the whirligig part grew brighter and of a glorious fiery red and danced about shooting out long streaks of fire! *Then* (all this happened in a few seconds) I understood that I'd been watching an *Aurora borealis*![13]

In his excitement to tell his father the next few moments were like a farce. Algie bounced up out of bed, hitting his head on the upper berth. He put his trousers on back-to-front and in trying to put them on the right way round managed to bang his head twice more. With no socks or shoes on he hurried along the corridor, but the sudden lurch of the train propelled him through the curtains of another berth where he trod on someone's foot. He thought this belonged to someone he knew – a Mr Williams – but as he continued along the train he walked into Mr Williams and then realized the foot had belonged to an old lady. As he grinned rather inanely at Mr Williams, another lurch of the train caused his pyjama jacket to fly open. Gripping his trousers and trying to cover himself, Algie fled back down the corridor only to burst into yet another wrong berth, frightening another old lady, until he at last found his father.

Besides the humour is the comment about Blackwood's eyesight. Some friends believed he was colour-blind, especially to reds, which seems remarkable for someone who was so appreciative of nature. Even more surprising is the following, which he wrote many years later. 'I've never understood why pictures awaken no response in me for it is, I realise, an awful loss. I just look at them and see – nothing. Why poetry, music, colour – yes, colour – nature, etc., should bring ecstasy, while pictures leave me dumb and stupid, puzzles me always, but it is true.'[14] He was probably not severely colour-blind but marginally afflicted – I shall return to this later.

This trip was also Algie's first sight of the native North American Indians. His initial reaction was that they 'look so queer with their squaws living in tents'.[15] Algie spent most of his time reading, when he wasn't keeping his journal, or standing on the platform at the end of the train watching the world go by. 'I enjoy this trip more than I can say,' he told his sisters. Despite the monotony of the prairie, Blackwood was at home with the world around him. The scenery improved as they passed through the Rocky Mountains and they vowed they would spend more time there on their return.

They arrived at Vancouver on Thursday, 1 September. Sir Arthur was rather depressed. Not by the mere shanty town that it then was, but by the reckless and cavalier way in which they were clearing trees to make space for the shacks. They moved on quickly, taking the steamer to Victoria, a refreshing journey. There Sir Arthur was promptly besieged by reporters and officials seeking his help and advice on the need for Christian work in the vicinity. Sir Arthur agreed to stay on to deliver a talk at their local theatre on the Sunday. It gave them extra time to look over part of the island around Victoria and admire its beauty but also see some of the lesser sights, such as the Chinese quarter with its opium dens. By the end of their short stay, however, neither of them were feeling well, which Sir Arthur attributed to the sanitation of the town. They were thus delighted when their ship sailed in the early hours of 6 September, marking their first movement homewards.

At Vancouver they boarded the train. They had originally planned to spend more time on their journey home, leaving the train occasionally to explore. The extra time spent at Victoria reduced this opportunity. However, they did stop over at Glacier Hotel in the Rockies and revelled in the fact that for at least a day they were on their own. Surprisingly, Sir Arthur received a telegram to say that his stepdaughter and her husband, the Earl of Kintore, who were on a world tour, were on the next train heading westwards. The trains passed at Banff and they were able to meet briefly before the trains had to move on.

Their return journey was varied by stopping off at Winnipeg (on 10 September) and staying over at the home of Sir Donald Smith at Silver Heights. Smith, later the first Baron Strathcona, was a long-time friend of Blackwood's father and had been one of the benefactors of the Canadian Pacific Railway. The Sunday was spent at church, sightseeing and relaxing. The next day they inspected a new farm just outside Winnipeg and visited a herd of buffalo – but saw only two beasts.

They had planned to take the boat across Lake Superior to avoid continuing the train journey, but on their way by train to Thunder Bay the weather worsened and they heard stories of ships being wrecked on the lake. Nevertheless, they stuck to their plans and on the Tuesday (13 September) set off in the *Athabasca*, a 2000-ton ironclad steamer with about forty-five other brave passengers and a cargo of wheat. It was an extremely turbulent crossing. The swell was so huge at dinner that everything was thrown across the saloon, with food all over the floor, which made people feel even more sick. Sir Arthur and Algie remained unaffected and later, in a period of comparative calm, Algie even tucked into plum pudding. They surprised themselves at sleeping that night, although Algie joined in with a group of his own age who were attempting to sing various songs despite all being out of tune. Sir Arthur rearranged his mattress and bedding on the floor, whilst Algie attempted to set up a hammock, but that came to grief. They made it through the night and were treated to a remarkable sunrise. The weather calmed and by the time they reached Owen Sound and caught the train to Toronto, where they arrived on the 15th, it had turned into a beautiful autumnal day.

Algernon fell in love with Toronto. Sir Arthur was also impressed, calling it 'such a bright, clean, orderly and English-looking town'. They stayed there for a week. Time was spent exploring possibilities for Algernon's farming future. They visited an agricultural college at Guelph, but thought little of that. They became involved in judging at an agricultural show where Algernon amazed everyone at his knowledge of horses and cattle. Then they visited a prize-winning 100-acre farm just outside Agincourt, fifteen miles (twenty-four kilometres) east of Toronto. The place was a model of exactitude and best practice, almost sickeningly so. It would have been hard imagining Blackwood, no matter how committed he was, fitting into the discipline and routine required. The owner needed no extra workers at that moment, though noted that there were plenty of farms in the area which would take on people like Algernon (whom he called, rather condescendingly, 'your little boy').

By the end of their stay at Toronto, Sir Arthur was finding himself beset by requests for visits and public talks in his Christian capacity. He felt compelled to accept as many as he could, and the next few days were therefore spent on semi-official business in Ottawa, Montreal and Quebec. At Quebec (where they arrived on 23 September) they stayed as guests of Lord Lansdowne, then Governor-General of Canada, despite attempts to avoid his hospitality. Sir Arthur had known

Lansdowne when he had been a Junior Lord of the Treasury in 1869. Although Lord and Lady Lansdowne were very obliging and attentive there was little in common between them and the Blackwoods. Lansdowne could not sustain a conversation. In the end Sir Arthur admitted that 'if I had not told them ghost stories and every imaginable thing I could rake up, we should have sat twiddling our thumbs the whole evening.'

After Sir Arthur had delivered his talk at a YMCA gathering in Quebec that Sunday they left by train, heading east to Fredericton, New Brunswick. They found the whole area delightful, augmented by the autumnal colours of the trees. They spent two days checking out farms and then took a ten-mile (sixteen kilometres) drive to Kingsclear to inspect what Sir Arthur called 'the Blackwood Grant'. This was 800 acres of forested land that had been granted to Sir Arthur's father in 1837 by no less than King William IV. Unfortunately, in 1868 a mighty storm had felled most of the trees and soon after a forest fire destroyed the rest. Nothing had regenerated and it looked no more than a 'dismal swamp'. Sir Arthur vowed to dispose of it as soon as possible, though it remained in the family for another twenty years.

They travelled down the eastern seaboard into the United States to Boston, before catching the train inland to Northfield, arriving at the home of Dwight Moody on 30 September. Moody had to go to Montreal but he urged them to stay over. The Blackwoods took advantage of the beautiful weather for a walk along the Connecticut valley to Brattleboro', though got caught in a sudden downpour. They stayed in the area for three days, and Algernon found Moody much less of a daunting figure. At the end of their stay Moody took them to the station for the next leg of their marathon journey to New York and down to Washington.

Neither of them liked Washington but there was a serious reason for their visit. Sir Arthur's stepson, George, the son of his wife Harriet and her first husband the Duke of Manchester, was buried here. George had never known his own father, who had died when the boy was just eight months old. He was almost four when his mother had married Blackwood, and Sir Arthur had raised him as his own son. Algernon barely knew him. By the time he was three or four George had entered the Royal Artillery, where he became a lieutenant, and then joined the Diplomatic Service, and was posted to Washington. He was destined for a promising career, but died on 12 March 1882 of diphtheria. He was buried at Oak Hill Cemetery – 'a very pretty spot,' Sir Arthur noted. They paid their respects and returned to New York.

After two more days there, spent mostly on Sir Arthur's business duties, it was with great relief that they boarded the *Serbia* on the morning of Saturday 8 October for their journey home. The weather was fine for the first half of the voyage but by the Wednesday a terrific gale arose, with the wind so strong that it became almost impossible to stand on deck. Algernon spent the rest of the voyage below decks. They eventually reached Liverpool on 17 October and headed for home.

The extensive record put together by Sir Arthur based on letters and journals allows for a thorough study of this long expedition of ten weeks. It tells us much about the many official, unofficial and family connections the Blackwoods had in Canada and the extent to which Sir Arthur's reputation was known. This would be the saving of Algernon on many occasions when he returned to Canada. Sir Arthur clearly enjoyed Algernon's company and Algernon presented himself well on all official occasions, though otherwise he was still relatively immature. Algernon found it difficult to grow up. In some ways he never did, and that was one of his charms. But at this time it was going to be one of his failings. It was too easy for him to follow others and not set his own lead. And his inability to know where he was going would get him into all kinds of trouble.

3

Ghosts and Scholars (1887–89)

I

Life must have seemed dull to Algernon after his return from Canada. The wide-open spaces had called to him. The matter of his farming in Canada had been far from resolved, but they had explored its potential and made sufficient contacts for the future. It was now down to Blackwood to study, get his degree in agriculture at Edinburgh University, and make a go of it. Easily led, lacking in direction and not wishing to upset his father, Blackwood pursued this goal, even though he remained unsure of what he really did want.

His problem was deep-rooted, because what most interested Blackwood – exploring esoteric beliefs and communing with Nature (in an increasingly religious way) – was anathema to his father, and offered no financial security. Whilst Sir Arthur remained tolerant, it was only because he hoped Algernon would set his sights on the goal as a farmer, and that this should satisfy his love of nature. The concentration and effort to achieve this should (so his father must have hoped) rid Algernon of his temporary fad for Eastern religion.

On the surface that was easy to believe. Algernon was nearly nineteen. He had grown into a tall, slim, handsome young man, with much of his father's good looks and charm. His hair was fair, his eyes a penetrating blue which twinkled irresistibly when he smiled. He would have been a catch for any girl, but his natural shyness and lack of confidence made him avoid any meaningful contact with females. He still preferred the camaraderie of his former pupils, and he visited a reunion of his friends at the Moravian school in London on 12 January

1888, where he was able to tell them about his travels in Canada and plans for the future.

That Whitsun he and his father enjoyed companionship again on a walking holiday in North Devon, following the trails over Exmoor and the cliff-top walks around Clovelly, Linton and Ilfracombe. Sir Arthur had found his son a private tutor in Somerset who was going to prepare him for his days at Edinburgh University.

However, his father's connections were to open new doors. Whilst having no truck with spiritualism, Sir Arthur was interested in the valid scientific assessment of psychic phenomena. One of the senior clerks in the Secretary General's Department of the Post Office in London was Frank Podmore (1855–1910). He had worked at the Post Office since 1879, rapidly rising through the grades, and was well known to Blackwood's father. Podmore was one of the leading members of the Society for Psychical Research (or the SPR as it is commonly known). This was a serious organization, established by some of the most notable men in the land and devoted to the serious exploration of psychic phenomena.

The roots of the SPR can be traced back to a Ghost Club established at Trinity College, Cambridge in 1850 or so by the same Edward White Benson who became the first headmaster at Wellington College. The club rambled along for many years and attracted several people who would later be the principal lights in the formation of the SPR. Chief among these was Henry Sidgwick (1838–1900), who became Professor in Moral and Political Philosophy after his religious views were shaken by Darwin's theory of evolution. Sidgwick was a man of strong integrity and was held in high regard by all who knew him. In 1876 he married Eleanor Balfour, the sister of Arthur Balfour (1848–1930), who became Prime Minister of Britain in 1902. Benson was Sidgwick's second cousin and had married Sidgwick's sister, Minnie. Balfour had been one of Sidgwick's students at Trinity. Other students and later Fellows of Trinity College included Frederic Myers (1843–1901), who became a school inspector, and Edmund Gurney (1847–88), a noted scholar in music, medicine, law and experimental psychology.

The real driving force behind the formation of the SPR, however, was physicist William Barrett (1844–1925) whose particular interest was in telepathy, though it was then called 'thought transference' and was closely associated with mesmerism or hypnotism. He came to Trinity College in 1881 and galvanized Sidgwick's group into action.

Between them – Sidgwick, Balfour, Gurney, Myers and Barrett –the SPR was created in January 1882, with Sidgwick as its first president. These were all highly respected men – no charlatans. And early members attracted by the SPR were of similar stature – Lord Tennyson, William James, John Ruskin, W.E. Gladstone, Mark Twain and Charles L. Dodgson (better known as Lewis Carroll), plus eight Fellows of the Royal Society, including the later Nobel Prize winner Joseph Thomson.

Blackwood's father did not himself join, but it did not stop him being interested. Any work conducted by this group, especially if it helped debunk spiritualism, would have received his commendation. Thus, when time allowed, he would discuss matters with Frank Podmore. Podmore, together with Gurney and Myers, had already compiled a book of cases investigated by the SPR. This was *Phantasms of the Living* (1886) and it was a book that young Algernon found fascinating. It includes several cases that he adapted for his own stories. Perhaps the best known was a case reported by Lord Brougham (1778–1868) while at Edinburgh University in 1799. He had made a pact with a university friend that whoever died first should try to appear to the other. Brougham was one day relaxing in his bath when he saw his friend sitting on a nearby chair. The vision soon faded but he made a note of the occurrence. Soon afterwards he returned to Edinburgh, only to receive a letter to say that his friend had died in India. The core of the story is the same as Blackwood's 'Keeping his Promise'[1], also set in Edinburgh, where a dead friend keeps an appointment.

Podmore shared with Sir Arthur Blackwood reports that were being received by the SPR and agreed that if Algernon was interested he could join Podmore and Gurney in investigating certain cases – especially haunted houses. Blackwood makes little reference to this in his writings, though his last television talk, 'How I Became Interested in Ghosts', is more specific. Here he states that he received information on alleged haunted houses from Podmore via his father, but implies that he conducted these investigations on his own. However, a brief and very tattered typed note among his papers states that he usually undertook these investigations with someone else. Podmore is listed, as is the name of Edwyn Bevan.

In his last television broadcast Blackwood gave an account of the first haunted house he investigated. It was a lodging house in Kensington, London, in one of the streets that runs down from Knightsbridge to Montpelier Square. He does not give a date for his investigation other than it was a hot June night and that the play, *Dorothy*, starring Hayden Coffin, was running to full houses. *Dorothy* began its London run at the Gaiety Theatre on 25 September 1886. June 1887 is unlikely as Blackwood did not return from Switzerland until the end of that month and was soon whisked away to Argyllshire and on to Canada. June 1889 is also unlikely because Blackwood did not return from Edinburgh University until very late in the month. The most likely is therefore June 1888, since Blackwood returned from his private tutorials in Somerset in early June.

June 1888 has its own problems, however, as it was on the 23rd of that month that Edmund Gurney was found dead in a hotel room in Brighton. He had almost certainly killed himself.[2] Gurney lived in London at 26 Montpelier Square. It would be remarkable for young Blackwood, who was not a member of the SPR, to be allowed to investigate a haunted house on his own when the case was virtually on the doorstep of one of the SPR's founding members. Even if Gurney was too busy, Podmore was likely to be involved and the three of them may have met up at Gurney's home prior to the investigation. If this is so the investigation had to happen sometime in the middle of June 1888.

The facts of the haunting are as follows. The upper rooms of the boarding house were occupied by the landlady and two lodgers. All these, and others in the house, had seen the apparition of a tall thin woman, whose face was very sad, with marks of pain and suffering. The woman would cross the room and one of the lodgers saw her silhouetted against the window and then pass through the wall into the landlady's room. The landlady witnessed the woman come into her room. She screamed out, 'In the name of the Holy Trinity, what's troubling you?' In response the sad ghost raised her hand and sliced it across her throat where a mark was clearly visible. Then the ghost vanished.

Blackwood interviewed all the occupants individually to get their accounts of the hauntings, all of which agreed. He also went through the history of the house and discovered, from the local cemetery inspector, that fifty years earlier, an elderly lady had lived there, and that she had been found strangled in her bed, with a lot of money under the mattress. Blackwood then spent a night in the house alone. Although he heard noises, which he assumed must be mice, he saw nothing. In order that he did not begin to imagine things he took with him a copy of the *Pall Mall Gazette* and spent his time translating the editorial into shorthand, which he was then learning.

Because Blackwood was not a member of the SPR himself, no reports carry his name. Consequently, it is impossible to be certain just which houses Blackwood investigated or when. But we do know of one possible place, although once again the timing is complicated.

Through Podmore Blackwood learned of a haunting in a house in Brunswick Square, Hove, near Brighton. The SPR was not officially notified of this case until December 1890, by which time Blackwood had been in Canada for eight months, and it long confused me as to when Blackwood could have investigated it. When he wrote about this case in an article in 1948[3], Blackwood implies it was an early investigation. 'Eager to see a ghost with my own eyes,' he wrote, 'I was lucky enough to get advance notice of haunted houses the Psychical Research Society considered worth investigating.' He would not write in this way if it were an investigation of his later years. Although the SPR did not know of this house until December 1890, Podmore and Blackwood must have known earlier.

The individual who informed the SPR of the house was Ernest Westlake, a member. He can't have told Podmore earlier because he had only recently learned of the case. He was also told that the house 'had a great reputation for being haunted'. If so, then investigators in the Brighton area probably already knew about it. The most active SPR official working in Brighton was Edmund Gurney himself. Although he lived in London he was frequently in Brighton between 1883 and 1888 conducting experiments into telepathy under hypnosis. It would be surprising if he had not heard about the house and could have passed the information on to Podmore.

It is possible, therefore, that Blackwood investigated the house in Brighton before he went to Canada. This is the haunting that Blackwood later used for his story 'The Empty House'. A manservant in the house had been in love with a housemaid. She did not return his affections and in a moment of frenzy he chased her up the stairs and threw her over the bannister. This scene was repeated nightly.

The most surprising fact about Blackwood's investigation is that he visited the house not alone, but with a young woman. No one would think twice about that these days, but in the 1880s any decent young woman would be chaperoned. In 'The Midnight Hour' Blackwood says that originally he was going to visit the house with one of his sisters. However, at the last minute his sister pulled out. Once darkness had fallen the prospect seemed all too horrible. Blackwood then says that their 'hostess' would accompany him. He notes that 'my companion, my hostess, whom I knew slightly, was a youngish woman, gay, cheery, chatty'. In 'The Empty House' he converts the companion to an aunt, which seemed more proper. However, in a letter written to a friend in 1943, he confessed: 'No, it wasn't an aunt; it was a misguided, but charming lady, who had persuaded herself I should make a good husband, though such a thought had never even entered my head.'[4]

It might seem surprising that Blackwood, at nineteen or so, would be allowed by his father to visit a house with a young lady unaccompanied, assuming his father knew. This might be an argument for suggesting that Blackwood's investigation happened after he returned from Canada in 1899, when he was over thirty, but it does not square with Blackwood suggesting it was an early investigation of his or that he was conducting it on advance notice from the SPR.

Blackwood never saw the ghost, though he did hear a man's cough as they entered the house and stood in the dark hallway. But he did see something which stayed in his mind ever since, and which is the key episode in 'The Empty House'. He and his companion explored the house from top to bottom but found nothing. So they chose to wait in a small room at the top of the stairs, their only light a single candle. All was now silent except for the distant sound of the waves on the shore. As they waited Blackwood became aware that a wave of terror was overcoming his companion because he saw that her face had drained and had become the face of a little girl. 'It was a face masked by utter terror,' he wrote, 'its youthfulness somehow terrible'.[5] He realized that any sudden noise or activity in the house would cause her to faint with horror and the prospect of being found in an empty house alone with an unconscious woman would not be easy to explain. So, the investigation incomplete, he hurried her out of the house and took her safely home.

It was a lesson he exploited in several later stories. Sometimes what may be more frightening than the direct horror of seeing a ghost is observing the effects upon another.

Blackwood probably investigated other haunted houses at this time, but the likelihood of identifying them is remote. Nevertheless, he put his experiences to good effect and turned his hand to writing his first story, 'A Mysterious House'. It appeared in *Belgravia* for July 1889. *Belgravia* had once been a very sensationalist magazine edited by the notorious Mary E. Braddon but by 1889 its sales had fallen considerably and it was now a rather downmarket publication. It is unlikely to have been one Blackwood would have submitted his story to first. *The Cornhill* was the most respectable title at that time, and there was the rather more bohemian *Temple Bar*, which carried several ghost stories. For a first story the best one can say about it is that it is passable. It reads like the work of a young and inexperienced writer and it is possible, therefore, that the story may have been rejected a few times before it sold to *Belgravia*, which could mean it was written before Blackwood went to university.

Set in 1857, it is narrated by a man who is suddenly summoned to meet an old school friend, called Pellham, whom he has not seen for years. Pellham explains that he has bought a house in Norfolk only to discover that it had a reputation of being haunted. He remembered that his friend had been highly sceptical of the supernatural at college and called him in to help check the house over. There are several suitably atmospheric (if rather amateurish) creepy episodes, such as a window slowly opening of its own accord. As the night draws on Pellham begins acting strangely as if he has been possessed. At that moment the whole episode is revealed as a dream, a disappointing and unsatisfactory ending.

II

In October 1888 Algernon went to Edinburgh University. His brother Stevenson, who had already spent two years at Trinity College, Cambridge, joined him there. His transfer was probably in order to keep a brotherly eye on Algernon. His father must have been concerned that Algernon was in danger of wasting his life and it was important that he qualify and establish himself as a farmer.

It is interesting to compare the matriculation notes made by Algernon and his brother. Stevenson's handwriting is assured if a little hasty. Algernon's is immature and smudged.

Algernon was enrolled on the course in Agriculture and Rural Economy under Professor Robert Wallace. The components of the course included chemistry, botany, engineering, geology, veterinary hygiene and natural history. Some of these must have appealed to

Blackwood and yet he later wrote, 'My notebooks on Professor Wallace's lectures, crammed as they were with entries about soil, rotation of crops, and drainage, represented no genuine practical knowledge.'[6]

Instead he drifted away to what interested him more. He attended lectures on pathology, watched post-mortems, and generally fraternized with the medical students and lecturers. Two individuals in particular had a marked effect upon Blackwood.

The first he refers to simply as 'Dr H—,' who used hypnotism in his practice. He does not say whether this was a doctor in private practice or one of the lecturing doctors. In fact there were two Dr H—'s at Edinburgh and Blackwood would have known both of them. Blackwood states that the doctor's family were spiritualists and that his wife was a medium. This suggests Dr Robert Howden (1856–1940) whose wife was a medium and later became a member of the SPR. The chief drawback to Howden being Dr H— is that he did not marry until 1899.

Since Blackwood also talks about playing his violin together with the doctor's son, we must conclude he is referring to the other doctor, Dr David Hepburn (1859–1931), who was Howden's assistant. Hepburn's family was musical, and Hepburn himself was noted for his fine musical voice. Unfortunately, I have not been able to ascertain whether Hepburn's family were also spiritualists. Possibly Blackwood deliberately fused the two characters to avoid clear identification since both were alive at the time he wrote his autobiography.

It was Dr H— who taught Blackwood hypnotism. Blackwood refers enticingly to the doctor admitting him to 'private experiments in his study'. He also encouraged Blackwood to abandon his idea of farming and become a doctor. Blackwood visited the doctor's family and attended séances. Blackwood was impressed when the medium could apparently read his thoughts and at that time was gullible enough to accept it unswervingly, although the doctor warned him to be cautious. At one séance he was told he had been an American Indian in a recent past life and before that Aztec, Inca, Egyptian and even Atlantean. He was also told, by the spirit of an American Indian, that he would 'scratch', which was interpreted as becoming a writer.

Another influence was a fourth-year Hindu student, about to become qualified. There were several Hindu students at Edinburgh University at this time and it is difficult to be precise which one might have been such a close friend of Blackwood's. It was this student who helped Blackwood understand Patanjali's *Aphorisms*, and who instructed him in meditation and breathing techniques. They walked together for hours along the coast and up into the Pentland Hills where they could see the Forth Bridge being constructed. During these moments the student explored with Blackwood the mysteries of reincarnation and the potential for past lives. Blackwood states that he drew upon this individual in creating two of his fictional characters, John Silence and Julius LeVallon. The book *John Silence* is dedicated to 'M.L.W. the original of John Silence and my Companion in Many Adventures'. I had once presumed that this Hindu student must have the initials M.L.W. but there is no such name in the University Calendar or matriculation records. The university records note that a fellow student of Blackwood's was called Harvey Vaillant. He was twenty years old and was studying medicine. He had been born at Calcutta but raised and educated in Bengal. Further exploration revealed that there was an old colonial family in Bengal called Vaillant, the head of which was called William Julian Vaillant.

The story related in *Julius LeVallon* is highly autobiographical, and the section devoted to the period at Edinburgh University may reflect more truth than Blackwood was otherwise prepared to tell. Clearly Blackwood was close friends with someone he recreates as LeVallon, though in the book that individual is English (at least in his present incarnation) and not Hindu. In the book the narrator, John Mason (who is a thinly disguised Blackwood) meets again the character of Julius LeVallon whom he had befriended at his private school. They are bonded not by a simple friendship but by shared memories going back through countless past lives. Always highly imaginative and feeling disconnected from the current world, Blackwood delighted in the concept of reincarnation and karma. For a dreamer these beliefs were very convenient as it allowed him to become detached from his present existence and consider life on a more cosmic scale. He accepted that he may now be paying retribution for deeds in a past life.

In the Edinburgh section of *Julius LeVallon* there is an episode which has deeper connotations. In *Episodes Before Thirty* Blackwood states that he and the Hindu student 'made curious and interesting experiments together'.[7] He reveals no more, and one can't help wondering, therefore, if *Julius LeVallon* holds some secret. At one point in the story LeVallon involves Mason in an experiment. LeVallon believes that he has control over the elemental powers, in particular Wind and Fire, and he seeks to demonstrate this by re-animating a corpse. The experiment fails, though not without some drama.

There were two other people at Edinburgh University at this time whom Blackwood would come to know well in later years, and whom he might have met while he was a student. They were Dr J.W. Brodie-Innes (1848–1923) and Dr Robert W. Felkin (1858–1922). Felkin was a Lecturer in Tropical Diseases at the Park-place School, Edinburgh. This was part of the extra-mural School of Medicine, and was advertised in the University Calendar for that year. Brodie-Innes had a large and expanding law practice in Edinburgh and was on the law faculty as an occasional lecturer in Scots Law. A third person at Edinburgh University who also joined the Golden Dawn almost certainly knew Blackwood. This was Dr Andrew Aitken, Lecturer in Chemistry in the Faculty of Medicine who joined the Scottish Lodge of the Theosophical Society on 21 June 1890.

Both Felkin and Brodie-Innes were Theosophists. In fact Brodie-Innes was president of the Scottish Lodge of the Theosophical Society. They both became leading lights in the Hermetic Order of the Golden Dawn, a society established in order to pursue the studies of Hebrew Magic and the Kabbala. The first Temple, called the Isis-Urania, had been opened in London in March 1888, and news of this was announced in the Theosophical magazine *Lucifer*, which Blackwood could have seen as he was soon contributing to it. Brodie-Innes later established the Edinburgh Amen-Ra Temple of the Golden Dawn in June 1893.

The Russian-born founder of Theosophy, Helena Blavatsky (1831–91) had moved to London in 1887 amidst much publicity and her book, *The Secret Doctrine* (1888), soon followed. Blackwood had certainly read this book by 1890, and considering his growing need for books on Eastern wisdom, it is hard to believe that he did not acquire it soon after it was published.

The London Lodge of the Theosophical Society, which had been formed in 1883, has no record of Blackwood as a member during this period. This is not a total surprise. Blackwood would have been chancing his relationship with his father to join such an organization so openly almost on their doorstep. But in just the same way as he never joined the Society for Psychical Research, there was nothing to stop Blackwood learning about the organization's activities through theosophists. When Blackwood moved to Canada, he endeavoured to join the American Section of the Theosophical Society, but was in fact urged to help organize a branch in Canada. Yet even before that organization was chartered, Blackwood was contributing to the Society's magazine, *Lucifer* with 'Thoughts on Nature' in the December 1890 issue. This shows that he had access to Theosophical papers even when he was not a member.

What is more, a few years earlier, the Theosophical Society had been investigated by the SPR. The Theosophical Society had been established in 1875 in New York by Helena Blavatsky (who had emigrated there in 1873) and Henry Olcott (1832–1907). Blavatsky and Olcott later moved to Adyar in India where the Theosophical Society's headquarters were subsequently established. They left in charge in New York a young lawyer, William Q. Judge (1851–96), who would later be instrumental in Blackwood becoming a Theosophist.

Theosophy could be described as a synthesis of religion, philosophy and science. Its main object is to promote a universal brotherhood of humanity. To this end it encourages the study of comparative religion and the investigation of unexplained laws of nature. Blavatsky claimed that she was in touch with a number of Masters, who lived in remote parts of India and Tibet and who carefully guarded their secret knowledge passed down through the ages in their own reincarnations. One key tenet of Theosophy, which would have most appealed to Blackwood, was the Cycles of Evolution, which Blavatsky outlined in *The Secret Doctrine*. She told of a vast cosmic evolutionary plan in which divine potential is unfolded through a series of spiritual and material cycles. This grand scheme includes human physical, mental and spiritual evolution in which individuals determine the outcome through karma in each incarnation.

Many Theosophists in the 1880s believed that Blavatsky had been receiving instruction from the Masters, called the Brotherhood of Adepts. In some cases these instruction was received directly in physical meetings, but usually it was telepathic or, rather oddly, by letter. In 1884 Henry Sidgwick met Blavatsky and Olcott and wanted to know more about the psychic phenomena that Blavatsky claimed. He set up a committee consisting of himself, his wife Eleanor, Edmund Gurney, Richard Hodgson, Frederic Myers and Frank Podmore. In November 1884 Richard Hodgson went to India to investigate Blavatsky's claims. He spent three months studying the letters and other documentation and eventually concluded that the letters were fraudulent. This report remained controversial and it was not until 1986 that the SPR refuted Hodgson's original report and maintained that the case was not proven. Blavatsky denied such claims, but accepted that some forgery may have been conducted by her assistants in India, Alexis and Emma Coulomb. The Coulombs became the scapegoats, and Madame Blavatsky emerged, blemished but intact.

The important point here is that Blackwood would almost certainly have discussed Theosophy with Podmore and that even though some aspects of it had been discredited, its basic creed still held true for him. Moreover, the fact that it had been investigated by the SPR meant that, so far as Blackwood's father was concerned, it had been tested and found wanting and therefore was likely to be a harmless fad that Algernon himself would soon dismiss.

All this suggests that even though Blackwood did not join the Theosophical Society before he left for Canada, he was reading Theosophical material and mixing with other Theosophists informally whenever he could.

Blackwood's days at Edinburgh University, therefore, did everything that his father must have feared. Instead of devoting himself to agriculture, Algernon lost interest and turned to pathology, hypnotism and esoteric studies. The hope that his elder brother would keep an eye on him had not worked because Stevie had been taken ill. He had not returned to Edinburgh after the Christmas break. Indeed concern grew about Stevie's health and in February 1889 he was sent to South Africa in the hope that the climate would improve his strength. This left Algernon alone to do as he wished. Algernon must have been desperate for his alternative studies to work, because he had now so distanced himself from his father's convictions, that he knew he would have to be as sincere about his beliefs in order to assuage his father. It must have been a wary Blackwood who returned home from Edinburgh in July 1889.

4

Northern Lights (1889–92)

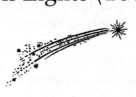

I

Sir Arthur Blackwood needed all the spiritual strength he could muster during 1889. In addition to the pressure of his official work, plus an ever-growing demand for his Christian work, he was worried about his elder son's health and his younger son's dismal record at university. Algernon had come home that July a complete failure in his agricultural studies. 'I knew nothing',[1] he later confessed. To add insult to injury Algernon had been spending his time studying esoteric wisdom and Eastern religions. His father must have believed his soul was lost. How he must have despaired. Yet pressure of work probably limited his chances to do anything. He wrote to a friend, 'Oh! when will this pressure cease? I seem almost bewildered with the drive – drive – drive of work of all kinds.'[2]

Soon after Algernon's return from Edinburgh they each went their separate ways to find some peace. His father took a four-day cruise on the *Ormuz* during a Review of the Fleet by the German emperor at Spithead. At the same time Algernon headed off to Switzerland.

He had been issued with his own passport on 23 August. He was twenty years old, and the world was his. He took the steamer from Harwich to Antwerp, and then by train through Brussels, Luxembourg and Basel to Chur. He arrived in pouring rain, but that did not worry him. He felt, 'like a deer set free'.[3] His plan was to walk from Chur, over the Splügen Pass and down to Lake Como in northern Italy, setting himself a target of about thirty miles a day. Even in good weather that was a difficult target, considering the terrain. In the rain it was quite punishing. None of this worried Blackwood. 'My clothes were soaked through, but my life seemed to have mingled with the wild forces around me and no bodily discomforts could affect me.'

The first day brought him to the village of Splügen. The next took him over the Splügen Pass to Chiavenna, and the third brought him to Cólico on the shores of Lake Como. He then took a steamer to Bellagio where he spent an idyllic evening listening to the sound of violins being played against the dramatic backdrop of the Chiavenna mountains. After such an energetic three days he took it easy, taking a whole week to cut across land to Lugano and then to Stresa at the south of Lake Maggiore. There he became involved in a regatta at which the Queen of Italy was present. His journey then took him over the Simplon Pass to Brig, where he spent a night in a hospice run by monks and played with the St Bernard pups. The final leg of his walk was over the Gemmi in a blinding snowstorm, and into the Bernese Oberland at Kandersteg and finally to Thun.

This walk of several hundred miles took him three weeks. He had rain, sun and snow, but he later wrote, 'there is no such thing as *bad* weather. All weathers to me are glorious – all kinds of weather speak to me with penetrating voices full of meaning and power.' To Blackwood this was part of merging with Nature, almost a religious experience. This was the first marathon walk he had accomplished on his own and it fired his desire for more. Blackwood's spirit was now unleashed and it would be impossible to contain it again.

II

Returning home in mid-September, Blackwood joined his family on holiday in Scotland. They had spent the first few weeks at Killin, by Loch Tay, but at the end of September went on a cruise to Skye. They returned to London in October.

Blackwood did not return to Edinburgh. Instead his father insisted that the plans for Canada must go ahead as discussed, though in the light of Blackwood's failure at Edinburgh, Sir Arthur decided options must be kept open. If farming was not possible, maybe a job on the Canadian Pacific Railway? Blackwood was doubtless as dissolute as ever. There is no record of what he did over the next few months, though I suspect he continued to read more of his esoteric literature, go for extensive walks and investigate one or two haunted houses on behalf of the SPR.

Also of great concern to Blackwood and his family was the news received from South Africa on 10 December 1889 that his brother, Stevie, was seriously ill. He had been travelling to Natal when he had been taken ill in isolated territory, far from medical aid. Thankfully, the next mail brought news that Stevie was in good hands and recuperating. Nevertheless, it was decided to bring him home as soon as spring arrived. In February it was agreed that Beatrice would travel to the Cape to collect him. Sir Arthur accompanied Beatrice as far as Madeira before returning home. Such worries took their toll on Sir Arthur who, though still only fifty-seven, was finding his excessive workload draining his strength. His weakened heart from the rheumatic fever in his youth added to the problem. And as if he did not have enough to concern him, that same month an offer came to move to a smaller house at Great Amwell in Hertfordshire. With Algernon moving to Canada and Stevie hopefully setting up in business when he returned home, Sir Arthur no longer needed such a big house.

Some work had to be done at Great Amwell before they moved, and this was not completed before Algernon was ready to leave for Canada. On 18 April 1890 Sir Arthur accompanied his son to Euston station and set him on the train for Liverpool. Whatever passed between them, they were the last words of his father's that Algernon ever heard. He would never see him again. He also missed the return of his brother who did not get back to England until 12 May, just as the family had settled into Great Amwell. Blackwood had spent his last days in a family home. In fact he would never again have a home he could really call his own.

Blackwood left Liverpool on the *Aurania* and arrived at New York five days later. He caught a train to Toronto. In his pocket were three letters of introduction to officials on the Canadian Pacific Railway. Blackwood chose to post only one, to Sir George Stephen in Montreal. He received a pleasant acknowledgment and was informed that the official he needed to see was currently away on business, but he would contact Blackwood upon his return.

Blackwood's father had given him an allowance of £100 a year, the equivalent of around £7,000 today. Useful, but insufficient to live on. The rest of his capital was due once he was established. Blackwood found lodgings at 29 Elm Street, which was conveniently central to the town. A further letter of introduction took him to the Temperance and General Life Assurance Company – his father knew the President, George Ross, through his temperance activities. The company had been founded in 1886 and had recently moved into new offices on the corner of Yonge Street and Colborne Street. Here Blackwood was employed as a general office boy at no pay. His only recollection of it was that he licked stamps all day. It was hoped that he might learn the insurance trade and possibly bring business from England to Canada. It was a forlorn hope. Blackwood had no business sense at all, and little hope of gaining any. With no additional money coming in, the insurance business was for him a dead end.

Then a letter arrived from the Canadian Pacific Railway, together with an invitation to the society gathering of the year – a race meeting followed by a ball. If Blackwood played his cards right, his future with the CPR should be assured. This, of course, assumed that Blackwood had any social acumen at all. But shy, immature, inexperienced and nervous, Blackwood failed miserably. At the ball, the CPR official (whom Blackwood calls Mr T—) introduced Blackwood to his sister, expecting that he would ask her to dance. Such a step hadn't occurred to Blackwood and after a few moments' embarrassing silence, Mr T— whisked his sister away. Little wonder then that when Blackwood presented himself for interview the next day, Mr T— kept him waiting and then informed him most peremptorily that there were no vacancies. Salvaging what he could of his dignity, Blackwood left, the door to his most promising opportunity well and truly shut.

To supplement his remittance, Blackwood turned to giving French lessons at fifty cents a sitting and he built up a small but steady clientele. It all helped him make contacts in the city. Despite his shyness he was affable and friendly. The Chief Justice of Ontario was Sir Thomas Galt (1815–1901), another friend of his father's. Blackwood came to know one of his daughters and through her was introduced to William Withrow (1839–1908), editor of the *Canadian Methodist Magazine*. Blackwood refers to Withrow as a 'pleasant old gentleman', though he was only fifty-one when Blackwood met him and was younger than Blackwood's father. But Withrow appeared old – he had a long white beard and pottered around in a frock coat and slippers, muttering to himself like some absent-minded professor. But he had an astute mind and shared some interests with Blackwood. He had travelled extensively throughout Europe, and had been the Professor of Ethics and Metaphysics at the Wesleyan Ladies' College at Hamilton.

Blackwood served as Withrow's secretary and personal assistant – the shorthand he had been learning now proved helpful and Withrow taught him how to type. Withrow dictated short essays and features for the magazine, but at times his mind would run ahead of himself and Blackwood had to remind him of the subject matter under discussion, or correct occasional errors. They had a good working relationship, so much so that even when Blackwood announced he had become a Buddhist, Withrow kept him on board – though they never broached the subject again. Thereafter Withrow paid closer scrutiny to the material Blackwood was preparing for the magazine, but he appreciated Blackwood as a good worker.

Blackwood did the copy-editing for the magazine, wrote short filler material, and was allowed to contribute an occasional article. Some of these were anonymous, so there may be more unattributed material in the magazine. The first to carry his name was 'Christmas in England' in the issue for December 1890, followed the next month by 'Memories of the Black Forest' and 'About the Moravians' in the February 1891 issue. Blackwood was able to draw upon his travels and education to produce readable and interesting essays. They gave Blackwood experience at writing, even though he still felt he had no leanings in that direction.

Blackwood received a wage of four dollars a week that, along with the money from his French lessons, increased his income by about 50 per cent. This level was reasonably comfortable. Yet to Blackwood it was still marking time. He had to establish himself as he meant to go on – in the farming business.

Through the clerk at the bank where his allowance was deposited Blackwood got to know a local dairy farmer, Arthur Cooper. He ran a small but unprofitable farm at Islington, six miles west of Toronto. There were just him, his sister and his ageing mother. At the time Blackwood believed the idea to go into partnership with Cooper had been his own, but he later became convinced he had been set up as a naïve greenhorn. They signed a simple document to confirm their partnership, dated 23 December 1890. It says nothing about the financial and legal responsibilities between them.

The feedback to his father must have shown that Algernon was at last making progress. Holding down a regular job with the *Methodist Magazine*, he now had a solid enterprise in which to invest. His father was prepared to send the rest of the capital. Blackwood received $10,000 (or about £2,000) – today equal to around £130,000. Lacking any business sense whatever, he invested it all in the partnership rather than holding some back. At first it seemed a sound move. Trade profited. The milk was regarded as the best in Toronto. New machinery was acquired. New farm buildings. Further staff. New milk carts. Trade was so brisk they could not fill all the orders and began buying milk from neighbouring farms. For a few months at least Blackwood must have felt on top of the world. An office was established at 291 College Street, and Blackwood moved in there, living over the premises.

Then it all went sour – literally. No one understood why the milk turned sour, and they could not rectify the problem. Trade dropped rapidly. Everything collapsed. Although Cooper was an experienced dairy farmer, Blackwood knew nothing about the business and could do nothing. Within six months the partnership was dissolved. The dairy herd and equipment were sold. Cooper kept the farm, which had not been part of the partnership, though his business was lost. Blackwood was able to recoup about $3,000 (£600).

At the time it was a bitter blow to Blackwood, more because he had disappointed his father than because of his failure. Nevertheless, it impressed upon Blackwood that he and business were not suited.

III

To his friends Blackwood must have seemed a victim of circumstance. He could still hold up his head in the exalted circles in which he moved. It's easy to get the impression from *Episodes Before Thirty* that Blackwood was near the poverty line in Toronto, and getting poorer by the minute. But during the early days of the Blackwood and Cooper partnership he was a successful local businessman and lived the life of one. He refers in passing to 'dinner parties' and 'influential business friends'.

Although he generally skirts over these other activities, Blackwood was able to dine out on the reputation of his father and Lord Dufferin, and still had important contacts in Toronto. In addition to Sir Thomas Galt, Blackwood got to know publisher Goldwin Smith (1823–1910) and his private secretary Arnold Haultain (1857–1941). Smith was born and raised in England, and was a Professor of History at Oxford until 1866. He came to Toronto in 1871, married a rich widow, and established himself as a focus for art and culture in the city at his home in The Grange. This was a large house set in 100-acre grounds to the west of the city, and is now part of the Art Gallery of Ontario. From here Smith published two magazines, *The Week* and *The*

Bystander, of which Haultain was editor. Haultain used to visit Blackwood in the early hours of the morning at the Dairy and the two of them would walk under the stars and watch the sunrise. Haultain bought a couple of poems from Blackwood for *The Week*: 'The Song of the Sea' and 'Lines to a Dreamer'[4], both published under the pen name Du Bois-Noir. Blackwood was experimenting with his early desire to be a poet. He had also fallen under the spell of Walt Whitman, a poet who, like Shelley, had struck a chord with Blackwood's naturist spirit.

Blackwood also talks of his friendship with George Wrong (1860–1948), Professor of History at Toronto University, whom he calls a 'sterling, sympathetic man'[5], and who would remain in touch with Blackwood for many years, visiting him later in England. Not only did Wrong provide Blackwood such moral and financial support as was needed – he was like an elder brother – but they also shared much stimulating and intellectual discussion. Blackwood later recalled vividly the first lunch he had at 'Mr Blake's', when he and Wrong talked philosophy. Blake was Edward Blake (1833–1912), Wrong's father-in-law who had been Premier of Ontario in 1871. He and his brother Samuel had established an eminent Toronto law firm, which doubtless informally advised Blackwood as his life spiralled into financial chaos.

If Wrong provided the intellectual succour and Haultain the literary escapism, Blackwood's spiritual needs were met by a group of Theosophists he befriended. In *Episodes* Blackwood relates that he became acquainted with a 'mystical minor poet' who had developed his own spiritual perspective on life and had managed to blend this in with his everyday existence, where he worked in the family cement business. The poet was Albert Smythe (1861–1947) who had converted to Theosophy when he met William Q. Judge on a transatlantic crossing in 1884. Fired with enthusiasm Smythe did what he could to promote Theosophy in Toronto by distributing leaflets around the city.[6] It was this that brought Blackwood into contact with the Theosophists. He probably met Smythe in the late summer of 1890, and it was probably soon after that he told Dr Withrow he was a Buddhist.

His introspective article, 'Thoughts on Nature' was published in the Society's magazine *Lucifer* for December 1890. Quoting poetry (Shelley) and describing his deep affinity with nature, Blackwood states that these glimpses of the world 'can only be appreciated and therefore thoroughly enjoyed by the Theosophist.' He also quotes from *Magic, White and Black* by Franz Hartmann, which had been published by the Theosophical Society. Clearly Blackwood regarded himself as a Theosophist even though he had not officially joined the organization.

It was not until January 1891 that Blackwood wrote to the Theosophical Society in New York seeking membership. The response, dated 26 January, came from William Judge, who suggested that Blackwood become a Charter member of the proposed Toronto Branch. Blackwood was admitted to the Toronto Branch of the Society on 17 February, though the Branch was not officially granted its charter until 25 February. It's one of the oldest surviving charters of the Society in North America and one of the last to be signed by Helena Blavatsky, who died three months later.

The meetings were held at the home of Emily H. Stowe and her daughter. These were two enterprising women active in female emancipation. Dr Stowe (1831–1903) had been the first woman school headmistress in 1852 and the first woman doctor to practise in Canada in 1867. She had been refused entry to the University of Toronto because she was a woman. So she qualified in New York and persisted in practising medicine in Canada despite threats of imprisonment from the Ontario College of Physicians and Surgeons. She was not granted her licence in Canada until 1880. Her daughter, Augusta Stowe (1857–1943), also faced similar opposition but became the first to undertake her complete medical training in Canada and become the first woman to graduate in medicine in 1883. Soon afterwards she married fellow graduate Dr John B. Gullen and became Demonstrator of Anatomy at the new Women's Medical College.

In 1891 Emily Stowe's husband, John, died and Emily went to live with her son, Frank, on Spadina Road next door to her daughter and her husband. Emily Stowe also owned an island in Lake Muskoka, which later came to be called Stowe Island. She spent much of her time there after John's death, and Blackwood would later stay there.

In the character of Albert Smythe we see something that would later shape Julius LeVallon. Blackwood tells us that Smythe believed that his soul had existed for ever and would never cease to exist. He also said that for Smythe 'the world was a schoolroom, a place of difficult discipline and learning, and the lessons he was learning were determined logically and justly by his previous living and previous mistakes'.[7] LeVallon existed by the same approach.

Smythe's first volume of poetry, *Poems Grave and Gay*, was issued in 1891. They are close to the true Celtic visionary poems of W.B. Yeats and George Russell (better known as Æ). Though Blackwood called his poetry 'poor in form', he went on to say that it has 'the elusive quality of genuine mystical poetry, unearthly, touching the stars, and wakening in the reader the note of yearning for the highest things'.

Blackwood also refers to a woman, over sixty, who was always dressed in black. Though substantial in frame she looked 'ethereal'. She claimed that she had continuous consciousness, so that even when her body slept her spiritual self continued to function. She would enthrall Blackwood with her accounts of her spiritual travels at night. She had a way of telling a story that Blackwood would later adopt – one of leaning back passively into a chair and lowering the voice and then suddenly projecting herself and her voice in an explosive moment which shocked the listener. This lady was Mrs Mary E. Day MacPherson, a columnist for the Toronto socialist newspaper, *Labor Advocate*.[8] She had joined the Aryan Branch of the Theosophical Society in New York in December 1887 and returned to New York in 1892, meeting up again with Blackwood when he moved to New York.

Though Blackwood was now in contact with many like-minded souls, his interests were not wholly fulfilled by the group. He loved to swap stories and ideas with people. While he was still running the dairy farm he met a farmer from Texas who told the following story. One winter's night this farmer's younger brother, Jim, went out in the snow to collect water from the well, 150 yards away. He never returned. Footprints in the snow went halfway to the well at which point were the two pails he'd taken with him. There were no other footprints. Jim had vanished, though the farmer fancied he could hear his cry for help. Blackwood used the idea in this story "Entrance and Exit" and later retold it as a radio talk "Strange Story of a Texas Farm Disappearance".[9]

At the outset Blackwood was secretary of the Branch, but that role was soon taken over by Dr Augusta Gullen. Upon joining the Theosophical Society he had been quick to order the primary texts – *The Perfect Way* by Anna Kingsford and Edward Maitland and *Esoteric Buddhism* by A.P. Sinnett. He also obtained *The Mysteries of Magic* by Eliphas Levi from the London Branch of the Society. Along with Hartmann's *Magic, White and Black*, and Blavatsky's *Isis Unveiled* and *The Secret Doctrine*, these were the key books to understanding Theosophy, and remained Blackwood's constant companions over the next few years. As spring arrived, Blackwood preferred to be out among the woods and stars than closed in a meeting room.

Hartmann's book had a special appeal. Almost its opening words would have struck a chord with Blackwood, so closely do they reflect his own outlook.

> If you doubt whether there is any such thing as Magic, and if you desire any practical illustration about it, open your eyes and look around you. See the world, the animals, and the trees, and ask yourself whether they could have come into existence by any other power than by the *magic power of nature.*[10]

You need look no further than the following passage, also in the introduction to Hartmann's book, to see the basic belief that fired Blackwood's own experiments and studies over the next ten to twenty years and which features so strongly in his fiction:

> The Life or *Will* in nature is a magician, and every plant, animal and man is a magician, who uses this power unconsciously and instinctively to build up his own organism; or, in other words, every living being is an organism in which the magic power of life acts; and if a man should attain the knowledge how to control this power of life, and to employ it consciously, instead of merely submitting inconsciously to its influence, then he would be a magician, and could control the processes of life in his own organism.
>
> Magic is that science which deals with the mental powers of man, and shows what control he may exercise over himself and others. In order to study the powers of man it is necessary to investigate what Man is, and what relation he bears to the universe, and such an investigation, if properly conducted, will show that the elements which compose the essential man are identical to those we find in the universe; that is to say, that the universe is the *Macrocosm*, and man – its true copy – the *Microcosm*.

Hartmann continues at length discussing what Blackwood came to live and breathe. Blackwood believed that there was a unity between all creation, which existed in harmony. The relationships between all aspects and projections of Nature could be perceived by humans provided they were in tune with that harmony. Too many humans were out of tune, either by imbalanced emotions arising from everyday stress and angst, or because of the overwhelming suffocation of civilization, which had a cumulative effect of distorting the balance with Nature. Blackwood held the view that by withdrawing from this oppression of civilization and by refocusing on the harmony in Nature you could become aware of the earth spirit and of the true spirit of Nature. He expressed this view time and again in his nature articles and it was most noticeable in his recent essay, 'Thoughts on Nature':

> As the darkness of the night slowly merges into the first streaks of the sunrise lights, the beholding spirit seems to leave its own plane of consciousness and to enter that of the surrounding nature-life, to commune, indeed, with the potencies which, above and behind all natural phenomena, render them beautiful, mysterious or weird. Then, too, we seem to be in perfect sympathy with the 'unknown' (not the 'unknowable') which gives to all such beautiful scenes their wonderful life and high spirituality. Then it is that the spirit understands intuitively the expressive voices of the trees, and is more susceptible to the sweet cadences of the song of the stream . . .[11]

Blackwood again quotes Hartmann in his next article, the rather presumptious 'Notes on Theosophy' in the March 1891 *Lucifer*, written under the alias 'Du Bois-Noir'. To Blackwood, as to Hartmann, Theosophy, in its exploration of the spiritual power of humankind, was a science not a religion. The 'supernatural' was not something magical or unnatural, in the superstitious sense. Everything was 'natural', but mankind could no longer see the whole. The world-view of mankind had become diminished, and thus the only way to see the whole was to step beyond the everyday world into the 'super-natural'. It was simply an extension of everyday consciousness.

Although Blackwood would later experiment with drugs to achieve this higher awareness, he did not think that this was a suitable or even a workable approach. Higher awareness had to come from within. It was a state of mind that came from self control, through meditation and special exercises. It was easier if this meditation was conducted away from the urban nightmare of humanity. Thus we will find Blackwood at his most potent and most imaginative when he is in the great wildernesses of the world. It was from out of the wilderness that came his greatest stories, whilst it was from the suffocation of humanity that came his more depressing horror stories.

Blackwood was so keen to discover more about this self-control that he asked as early as January 1891 for more information about the Esoteric Section of the Theosophical Society. Judge, obviously cautious of a neophyte, said: 'I will answer your question respecting the E.S.

after you are admitted a member of the Society.'[12] The E.S. had been created by Helena Blavatsky in London in 1888 as a specialist group within the Theosophical Society devoted to the study of the occult and magic. The group always met behind closed doors and was sworn to secrecy, so much so that even years later members who had long since disassociated themselves from the group still would not discuss it.

Judge kept Blackwood at bay over the E.S. In response to a further enquiry in December 1891 Judge said: 'Before going further into the matter of the E.S. I should like to know your motive in desiring to enter it. It should be clearly understood that this School was founded to help the T.S. and to promote practical altruism, its members being all expected to work to these ends.'[13] The subject is not mentioned again in letters and it was probably not until Blackwood met Judge and others in New York that he was accepted into the inner sanctum.

Although Blackwood would appear a 'dreamer' to others, someone who was out of joint with reality, he was actually the opposite. He was striving to be in tune with the 'reality' of the world. Unfortunately for Blackwood it would be many more years before he could find that freedom and escape through his writing.

IV

After the dairy failure Blackwood relied on his French lessons for additional income during the summer of 1891. He also began violin lessons and continued to contribute the occasional article to the *Methodist Magazine*. Professor George Wrong was a staunch friend during these days. 'I remember borrowing $50 from you, and your surprise when I repaid it,' he reminded Wrong years later.[14]

During the summer he travelled back to Niagara, arriving there on 16 August.* He captured these moments in an introspective piece, 'From a Theosophist's Diary'. It is one of those rare moments when

---

* Blackwood visited Niagara on at least one other occasion. He refers in *Episodes* (p. 130) to having seen the Toronto photographer, Samuel Dixon, cross the Falls on a tightrope. It was a baking-hot day. He also refers to a 'broiling summer day' in his radio talk 'The Fear of Heights' (*The Listener*, 6 November 1947). Blackwood also says 'I was running a small hotel in Toronto at the time.' However, Dixon crossed the falls twice (6 September 1890 and 17 July 1891), both times before Blackwood's period with the hotel. I believe that Blackwood's memory is of the September 1890 event.

Blackwood bares his soul. When he looked back over these years in *Episodes Before Thirty* he was far more cautious, saying that he 'would leave unmentioned of set purpose those inner activities which pertain to the intimate struggles of a growing soul. There is a veil of privacy which only in the rarest cases of exceptional value should be lifted.'[15]

In this highly personal essay[16] Blackwood describes himself as 'three parts a corpse' and talks about the 'untold misery and despair' that he had suffered previously as he struggled to conform to the demands of a Christian God whom he saw as capricious and despotic – an extension of a human being. He shivered over the thought of the Hell that Christianity had created and to which would be consigned the souls of so many 'struggling, weeping, despairing human beings'. His thoughts suggest the self-destructive image of Hell. 'The immeasurable despair that swept over my soul as I felt I could never love such a God, that I could never be frightened into heaven, and that therefore my only alternative lay in the blazing tortures of a localized volcano, where I should live forever in death.'

But he moves on. Four days later, after an evening at a ball at Cobourg, he strolls down to the lake and skims a stone over the surface. His mind considers how each leap of the stone is a new life, until eventually the stone finds its own *nirvana* in the depths of the lake. And he considers the force that was first applied to the stone to send it spinning through its series of lives.

Blackwood now became acquainted with another emigrant from England, though of Dutch descent, Johann Kay Pauw. (He calls him John Kay in *Episodes*.) Pauw ran a small sports shop. Blackwood was a keen tennis player whilst Pauw had been a heavyweight boxer. Pauw was the eldest of four children. He had been born in Timperley in Cheshire on 1 October 1866. His father, Klaas Pauw, was a well-to-do merchant. Blackwood believed Pauw had been to Oxford, though there is no record of him there.[17]

Pauw sympathized with Blackwood over the loss of the dairy farm and enquired whether he would be interested in investing what was left of his capital in a hotel. The sports shop was not that profitable and Pauw had decided to cut his losses. A hotel, known as the Hub Café, on the corner of Colborne Street and Leader Lane, which was owned by Billy Bingham, had become run-down and seedy. It was up for sale at a knock-down price. Pauw's enthusiasm ran away with him and infected Blackwood. He was in a dreadful dilemma. On the one hand he wanted to redeem his reputation over the failure of the farm. On the other, he felt he had already betrayed his family enough. With the strong temperance beliefs of his father the idea of running a bar seemed just too traitorous. Pauw convinced him, saying that his father need never know. They would trade as the Hub Wine Company. So Blackwood added deceit to his growing list of indiscretions. And of course Blackwood's father did learn of the venture though one of his evangelist contacts in Toronto. Apparently Sir Arthur called Algernon's brother, Stevie, into his study and told him that Algie's soul was lost and that he had gone to Hell.

Blackwood says that the Hub Wine Company opened for business the same week that 'Lines to a Dreamer' appeared in *The Week*. That was 9 October 1891. However the Toronto *World* did not report the sale of the Hub Café until 26 November, and even then noted that extensive improvements needed to be carried out. It reported their intentions to make the Hub 'the most attractive, respectable and comfortable hotel in Toronto'. It was fitted with electricity and developed to allow for social events and dinners. They placed a large photograph of Lord Dufferin above the lunch counter as guarantee of the bar's respectability and named the two bars the House of Commons and House of Lords. They employed a local restaurateur, Albert Collins, as their business manager.

Once again business was brisk at the outset and they made good money. It was a long day. Blackwood was up in time to visit the market at six a.m. for provisions, and the bar did not close until eleven p.m., or even later for private functions. Blackwood was glad that Pauw liked officiating at these functions, giving vent to his theatrical bent by reciting Henry Irving monologues. Sometimes Blackwood would play his violin for the clients, often accompanied on the piano by a regular client and good friend, an energetic Frenchman whom Blackwood called Louis B.

Blackwood soon realized he had made a mistake. The Hub became a 'prison' to him. He hated the close suffocation of humanity, the smell of drink and cigarettes, the uninspiring conversation. He yearned for escape. What few hours he could snatch would be to the lakes or nearby woods, and that was not as easy during the dead of winter. As soon as the spring came Blackwood wanted out. In what was the only sensible business decision he made in the first twenty-six years of his life, Blackwood assigned his share of the Hub Wine Company to Pauw. I doubt that Blackwood made this decision on his own. Lord and Lady Kintore were passing through Toronto at this time and it was more likely to be their advice. Lady Kintore gave Blackwood $20, which was then all the money he had, but was all he needed to escape to Lake Muskoka. The split was effective from 5 May 1892. Blackwood heaved a huge sigh of relief. It was as if a massive burden had been taken from his shoulders. And none too soon.

It was already apparent that the business was starting to fail. No one really knew why. Blackwood believed their business manager was creaming off the profits, or at least had his hand in the till. Pauw gave it his best shot, but debts mounted. At length it passed into the hands of a receiver. Pauw and Blackwood did a moonlight flit. Although friends had been supportive in the Hub's last days, it now looked like they had something to hide. So far as Blackwood was concerned, he was safe. The debts were no longer in his name. Pauw, however, had creditors after him.

A lawyer friend – probably one of the Blakes – offered them the facilities of an island that he owned in Lake Rosseau. Pauw and Blackwood left in the early hours of the morning of 24 May 1892. Louis B— drove them in a wagon and horses at top speed (more for the sense of the dramatic than out of necessity) away from Toronto, avoiding the main station, and out to a small station to the north. The train took them round Lake Simcoe up to the town of Gravenhurst, and from there they set out across Lake Muskoka. There were actually three lakes, Joseph, Rosseau and Muskoka, which form a letter Y, and their island was at the conjunction of the Y. The mainland was about a mile-and-a-half to the north. The island was ten acres in area, irregularly shaped, full of bays and deep pools. It was covered in pines with a small central hill and a ridge running east-west. Blackwood and Pauw would sit at the western end watching the sunset, or the eastern end watching the sunrise. There was a small hut on the island for cover, though they often slept out under the stars. The researches of John Robert Colombo have identified this island as one now called, rather appropriately, North Bohemia Island. They fished and hunted and otherwise wanted for nothing.[18]

Occasionally friends visited them. It was well known where they were. They had not really escaped the creditors. Everyone thought they would return in the winter.

Now Blackwood had a golden opportunity to steep himself in his esoteric studies. He also toyed with the idea of writing. In addition to a few articles for *The Methodist Magazine* and *Lucifer*, he thought it would be fun to write about life on the island. He told his half-sister about it.

> I am writing a funny account of it – some of the situations indeed have been irresistible. I have a camera and have many illustrations, comic, interesting and otherwise. It is my wish and intention to publish it. I see no reason why it shdn't sell well – for the district is unknown and unwritten and full of wild beauty and lonely loveliness. I may ask your influential aid to give me a letter to a publisher – for Father, in his well meant narrowness – sits on my scheme.[19]

Blackwood's father had, in fact, been encouraging Blackwood to take the only honest course and return to Toronto, get a job, and re-establish himself. Blackwood felt cut off from his family, his half-sister, Sydney, being his only real contact.

Blackwood's book was never published. He probably lost it and forgot all about it because in *Episodes* he says: 'It never occurred to me to write even a description of our picturesque way of living, much less to attempt an essay or a story.'[20] He did maintain a scrapbook, which contained a wealth of interesting photographs, but that was destroyed when his home was bombed in the Blitz in 1940.

Gradually autumn touched the island. Blackwood and Pauw knew they would have to leave, but they decided not to return to Toronto. If they were going to establish themselves it had to be in the United States, and nowhere better than New York. On 12 September 1892 they packed their bags and caught the steamer to Gravenhurst where the train would take them to New York. For Blackwood the last few months had been a 'fairy-tale' existence, but ahead of him lay the darkest days of his life.

5

The Depths of Hell (1892)

I

Blackwood and Pauw arrived in New York on 13 September 1892. They had just $60 between them. They found lodgings at 41 East 19th Street in the Gramercy district, just one street away from the birthplace of Theodore Roosevelt. They were cheap lodgings, but they did not have to pay rent in advance, and no questions were asked. Their landlady was a German Jew, Mrs Bernstein, whose husband, Adolphe, ran his own small café orchestra.

New York frightened Blackwood. He was ill prepared for it. The sheer size, noise and bustle of the city, the unpredictable, seething mass of humanity, especially the refugees and immigrants, unnerved him. Easily led, Blackwood had followed his one friend, in the belief that he could make something of himself. Pauw decided to look for work in the theatre, whilst Blackwood thought he'd become a journalist.

The next day Blackwood headed down to the offices of Harper's in Franklin Square, at the time one of the best known and most prestigious magazine publishers in America. He was fortunate to secure a meeting with Richard Harding Davis (1864–1916), then the managing editor of *Harper's Weekly*. Davis, though only five years older than Blackwood, was confident, vibrant, entrepreneurial, full of life. Blackwood was shy, uncertain, immature. Davis must have wondered what to make of Blackwood. Here was a young man who looked fit and healthy, had been burned chestnut by the open-air life, and already had some interesting experiences worth telling. Yet when Davis asked Blackwood what he had written, Blackwood said nothing.[1] He made no mention of his articles for the *Methodist Magazine*, or of the humorous account of his island life. Little wonder that Davis smiled to himself and showed Blackwood the door. But he didn't throw him out. He introduced him to the editor of *Harper's Young People*. Blackwood remembered the name as Storey, but he was Alfred Butler Starey, an Oxford graduate. He joined Harper's in 1880 and became editor of *Harper's Young People* in 1885. A few months after this meeting Starey caught typhoid fever and died on 8 August 1893 aged thirty-four.

Blackwood took an instant dislike to Starey, even though he was English and had known Blackwood's father when he had worked at the Post Office. Starey gave Blackwood a test assignment. A cargo of wild animals had arrived for the New York Zoo, in Central Park. Blackwood set off to interview the various keepers and ship's crew and composed a short item while sitting in Trinity Church in Lower Broadway. Blackwood brings out some interesting points about how animals get sea-sick and how this may be overcome, and other anecdotes about individual animals. He took the item back to Starey who accepted it but with no show of enthusiasm. It was eventually published a month later as 'A Cargo of Wild Animals'[2], and Blackwood received $10, but no further assignments.

Blackwood put no further effort into finding more work. He simply waited to hear from Starey. Pauw was likewise having no luck finding any acting work. However, he had met a Shakespearean actor called Bob Mantell, who was going to be a significant catalyst in Blackwood's life, on two counts.

The first count arose as a result of a cricket match, a 'momentous match'[3] Blackwood called it. Mantell was captain of an actors' cricket eleven, the Thespian Cricketers, and had arranged a match for the next day (15 September) against the Staten Island Cricket Club. Unfortunately Mantell had another engagement and other thespians had pulled out, so he was desperately trying to find others to play. Blackwood and Pauw agreed.

The match was a walkover for the Staten Island Club. They won 191 to 85. Blackwood scored the most runs for the Thespians – 19, with Pauw getting a respectable 10. But that was not the significance of the match. What was 'momentous' for Blackwood was that the match introduced him to a young man who would for a while become his closest friend and then his worst enemy. In *Episodes* he calls him

Arthur Glyn Boyde, but Blackwood believed his real name was Arthur Glyn Bigge. Identifying the real Bigge has been difficult. He had created his own personal history built up from more than one relative. From data in later newspaper reports it seems certain he was George Arthur Bigge, cousin of Lord Stamfordham and the son of George Richard Bigge, who had been a prison chaplain in Guernsey at the time of his death in 1886.

This smooth-talking, charming, charismatic man quickly worked his way into Blackwood's confidence. In England the Bigges were a well known, banking family from near Morpeth in Northumberland. One of them, Arthur John Bigge (1849–1931), was at that time Queen Victoria's Private Secretary, and remained in that capacity to Edward VII and George V. He was made Baron Stamfordham in 1911.

Bigge was twenty-nine. Blackwood later learned he had run away with the widow of a recently deceased army major. He soon abandoned her. Shortly before he met Blackwood he had been working at a local stables, but had left after becoming involved with the employer's niece. He then befriended the English artist Lynwood Palmer (1867–1941). Palmer was already becoming well known for his paintings of horses, for which he later gained a significant reputation. Palmer took Bigge under his wing and lent him money, but soon realized that Bigge was a confidence trickster and threw him out.

Bigge loved to play the English gentry. He wore fine clothes, a frock coat and sported a monocle, and was a real 'charmer'. He had a good tenor voice and was a fine organist. He won the confidence of Dr Putnam, pastor of the Baptist Tabernacle on Second Avenue. He had such a charismatic personality that he found it easy to borrow money from people. He also found his way into the theatre, joining E.H. Sothern (1859–1933) in the Lyceum Company as an understudy in *Captain Lettarblair* and *The Disreputable Mr Reagen*. That was how Bigge knew Mantell and ended up at the Thespian cricket match.

Blackwood knew none of this. He found Bigge delightful company. More to the point Bigge was streetwise and showed Blackwood and Pauw how they could get free meals and get the best deals in pawnshops. Bigge was earning a small fee as an understudy, but claimed he was waiting to hear when he would start a major job at the Rockaway Hunt Club. Bigge joined Blackwood and Pauw in their lodgings and for a few weeks all was fine.

In the meantime, thanks again to Bob Mantell, Blackwood had been introduced to the playwright Cecil Clay (1846–1920), an English gentleman, who clearly knew the City well[4]. Clay gave Blackwood an introduction to William Laffan, the publisher of the *New York Sun*. *The Sun* was arguably the most influential paper in New York. It had been founded in 1833 and established a reputation for its sensational but strong human interest stories. In its early days it had not been averse to publishing the occasional hoax story, which boosted its circulation dramatically. Although the paper had become rather tamer under proprietor Charles A. Dana, who purchased it in 1867, *The Sun* still enjoyed placing a humorous and often exaggerated slant on its stories, and loved scandals.

The offices of *The Sun* were in an unimposing old building on the corner of Park Row and Frankfort Street in downtown Manhattan. Just five storeys high it was dwarfed by the surrounding buildings. It was cramped, noisy and out-moded, but at the same time exciting, lively and vibrant. *The Sun* frequently employed bright young men, straight out of college, so that its reporting was topical, popular and fresh.

Laffan was a bluff Irishman from Dublin who had become a major figure in the newspaper world. In 1887 he launched an evening edition of *The Sun*, which became even more popular than its morning parent. Laffan agreed to give Blackwood a trial as a reporter and referred him to the *Evening Sun*'s managing editor, William McCloy (1859–1940). Blackwood was employed at $15 a week. At the same time Pauw was offered work in a touring company to start shortly, also at $15 a week. At last, after only three weeks in New York, things were starting to look up.

II

Blackwood reported for duty on Monday, 3 October 1892. As a test, McCloy asked him to write a piece 'From Methodism to Running a Saloon'. The piece was never published, but it got Blackwood writing. He was sent on two assignments that afternoon and made a mess of both of them. On the first he couldn't find the person to interview. On the second – a suicide – he could find no reason for the man taking his own life. After he'd filed his story he discovered rival papers had the full story – the man was a gambler with huge debts.

Blackwood expected to be fired on his first day. But he was on trial and still learning. The following Monday he was assigned to cover the

Tombs Police Court. This dark, forbidding place built in a mock-Egyptian style, was where prisoners were detained prior to trial. Blackwood had to file his story by ten o'clock each morning, so it was always a quick check through the records to find the more interesting arrests and then to try to get the basic facts from the prisoner and police. There was no *sub judice* restriction on reporting at that time. Each day he would run through the latest cases coming to trial. Then he would move on to the courts themselves and report on the trials. He would even interview condemned prisoners just prior to their execution. Most vivid in Blackwood's mind was talking to those men condemned to the electric chair. This was still new and few understood it. Hanging or shooting, they understood. Blackwood found himself explaining how the electric chair worked to the very people who hours or days later would become its next victim. Years later he would remember their faces. 'I could do without these memories,' Blackwood wrote, 'but they never fade. I can still see the twitching features, the forced smile, the pleading expression as when they peered at me through the bars of their cell.'[5]

Blackwood got to know some of the prisoners quite well and, through his interviews, formed an opinion about their guilt or innocence. Blackwood was still very impressionable at this time and easily led, but he learned quickly. He later concentrated his experiences as a court reporter into one story, 'Max Hensig' published in *The Listener*. The story is told by Williams, a reporter for the *Vulture*, who is covering the trial of a German doctor, Max Hensig, accused of murdering his wife with arsenic. Hensig is acquitted, but thereafter Williams believes he is being stalked by the doctor who has a phial of bacteria capable of causing death with a scratch. Blackwood was nearly 100 years ahead of the time with his study of a serial killer and stalker. The story was based on the case of Carlyle Harris, a medical student who poisoned his wife with morphine. *The Sun* began reporting on Harris's appeal on 20 November 1892 through to his final statement and his execution on 8 May 1893. There were over fifty individual reports, some of significant length. Of particular interest is a letter written by Harris himself and published in the *Sun* for 19 February 1893. A similar incident arises in 'Max Hensig' where one of the reporters says to Hensig:

> But, you know, in New York the newspapers try a man as much as the courts, and we thought you might like to make a statement to the public which we should be very glad to print for you.[6]

Blackwood may himself have prompted the letter.

It is unfortunate that none of Blackwood's journalism carries his name, so it is impossible to be sure which items in the *Evening Sun* are his. It is only when it can be confirmed from his own testimony that we can be certain, and even then it is not straightforward. In *Episodes*, Blackwood tells how in the second week of his apprenticeship a lion escaped from a local circus and took refuge in a stable where it killed a horse. Although in *Episodes* he recounts the events as all happening in one day, they stretched over two. What's more the episode happened on 27 October 1893, a whole year after Blackwood began on *The Sun*[7]. It shows that Blackwood's memory of dates is unreliable, a problem we shall encounter again*.

During November 1892 life for Blackwood became almost unbearable. Towards the end of October he developed a poisoned abscess in his side, resulting from when he struck a rock while diving into the lake during his Canadian retreat. He was unable to work and no money came in. Bigge's income was irregular. He spent some time as a model for local artists or playing the organ at the local church. Pauw's acting tour of Ontario was delayed until the middle of November, but the first few weeks were a failure and no salaries were paid. The troupe continued but audiences did not improve.

Blackwood was more-or-less bedridden with increasing pain and debility arising from his abscess. He was delirious at times and with virtually no food. He ate dried apples followed by hot water so that the food reconstituted inside to give a feeling of repletion. During mid-November he spent a few days away with Bigge at Far Rockaway to recuperate, otherwise he was confined to his lodging room.

During this delirium ideas for stories came to Blackwood. 'A Suspicious Gift' features three men living in a third-floor back room. Only the narrator, Blake, has a job, as a reporter in the police courts. He writes stories at night and is presently writing an autobiographical story about his experiences in Canada. A visitor arrives with a parcel. He will not say whom it is from but insists that Blake give him a

---

* For example, see *Episodes*, p. 5, where he says that they arrived in New York towards the end of October. In fact it was the middle of September. That date was not corrected in any reprinting of the book even though it clearly contradicts the accurate reference on p. 90 to 'some ten days to a fortnight had passed and October . . . had come' and on p. 10 to 'it was now past mid-October'.

receipt. Blake's amazed to find that the parcel contains $10,000. He's naturally suspicious but is desperate for the money. He agrees to take it but feels he needs a witness. He goes to fetch the lodger upstairs only to discover that he has been murdered. There is blood everywhere and money scattered throughout the room. In a panic, Blake rushes downstairs to accost the visitor but he has gone. Blake has blood all over his hands and at that moment the police arrive.

It has been inspired by an actual incident. One day Blackwood found a parcel in the hall addressed to him. It had been left by a messenger boy and gave no indication who it was from. Inside was a big silk stocking full of food, small items of clothing and an envelope containing $100. Despite enquiries he never discovered who his benefactor was.[8]

The opening of 'A Case of Eavesdropping' also owes its origins to these long, lonely hours. It's full of self-recrimination on the part of Blackwood's fictional alter-ego Jim Shorthouse, who appears in several stories.

> Jim Shorthouse was the sort of fellow who always made a mess of things. Everything with which his hands or mind came into contact issued from such contact in an unqualified and irremediable state of mess. His college days were a mess: he was twice rusticated. His schooldays were a mess: he went to half a dozen, each passing him on to the next with a worse character and in a more developed state of mess.[9]

He adds later:

> About the age of twenty-two . . . his father's purse and patience had equally given out, and Jim found himself stranded high and dry in a large American city.

So Jim Shorthouse seeks work as a journalist. All Blackwood's stories contain kernels of personal experience, but those that arose from his New York days are the most painful.

The delirium also gave birth to the idea that there is a crack in time between today and tomorrow, an imperceptible crack but one that, in the right circumstances, you could slip through into a paradise. There you could see all the beautiful wonders of the world, but magnified 1,000 times, so that you could see the winds come alive, for instance. This idea stayed with him for years and formed the basis of *The*

Education of Uncle Paul, where the chapter on the wakening winds includes some of his most imaginative writing.

Blackwood was unable to afford a doctor but one of his anonymous benefactors called in a German doctor who lived along the street. This was Otto Huebner, who became a close friend of Blackwood's over the next year. It was also at this time that visitors began to tell Blackwood that Bigge was a crook and that Blackwood needed to look out for himself. Blackwood did not believe them, but over time, and with nothing else to do but lie in bed and brood, he began to watch for the little clues that gave Bigge away.

Blackwood was able to earn a little money by translating stories from the French paper *Le Courier des Etats Unis*. They published one every Monday and if it were of special merit, Blackwood would translate it for McCloy. Previously Blackwood had not received extra money for these, but now he was not otherwise employed, McCloy paid $5 a story. It's difficult to identify these stories. Their source is not disclosed because they were effectively being pirated. One possibility is 'The Story of the Frightful Scarecrow' in *The Sun* for 20 November 1892. It tells of a woman who made a scarecrow but dressed it in fine clothes. A tramp exchanges his old rags for the scarecrow's. Just then the police appear and to avoid being caught the tramp takes the place of the scarecrow. After that he creeps away, much to the shock of the landowner who sees her scarecrow walking up the road. A tramp story such as this would appeal to Blackwood.

Blackwood continued to produce these translations while on his sick bed. Bigge took them down to the *Sun* offices and returned with the money. On one occasion, when Blackwood had done five such stories, Bigge returned with only $10, saying that McCloy had rejected three. Only later did Blackwood discover that Bigge had been paid for all five, but had pocketed the rest.

One day Blackwood noticed torn up in his bin a letter from Pauw referring to money he had sent plus a blank cheque bearing an attempted Blackwood signature. Although still weak, Blackwood confronted Bigge, who admitted only so much and profusely apologized. Blackwood accepted the apology though admitted that his faith had been dashed. He had become devoted to Bigge, and now had no idea whom to trust. Over the next few days he heard further stories about Bigge borrowing money from friends to help Blackwood, though Blackwood had seen none of it. Bigge had been spending money on food, drink and his lady friend, the dancer Pauline Markham.

By the end of November Blackwood was feeling well enough to get out for short periods. He attended a Theosophical Society meeting at Chickering Hall on 2 December with Bigge to hear Annie Besant deliver a talk on 'Death, and After?' Blackwood met Alexander Fullerton, the Society's treasurer, at that meeting and introduced him to Bigge. Clearly Bigge was his usual charming self as in a letter the following day, Fullerton referred to him as 'that nice Mr Bigge'.

At this same time the Bernsteins moved their lodging house to 19 Lafayette Place. They remained there for a little over a year before moving back to East 19th Street, although further along at number 106. In *Episodes* Blackwood refers to this move as happening later, but it shows that he was well enough to move at the start of December. The location was better for Blackwood because it was closer to the Astor Free Library and the Mercantile Library, where he spent many hours.

The relationship with Bigge steadied for a week or two, and then deteriorated rapidly. Blackwood was visited by his friend, the banker and sportsman August Belmont[10]. He had learned of Blackwood's plight and, despite Blackwood's protestations, left Blackwood with $32[11]. When Bigge returned they decided how to apportion the money. Bigge took $10 with him to pay the landlady and the rest was left in a desk drawer, including money to pay Dr Huebner. Blackwood later discovered Mrs Bernstein had not been paid, and when Otto Huebner called and checked in the drawer, there was no money. Bigge had taken it all, and vanished for four days.

The last straw came in the second week of December when Blackwood wrote several letters to his family and found that Bigge had not posted them but instead had stolen the stamps. There was a final showdown. Bigge left, and Blackwood decided to press charges.

It was not going to be easy. Blackwood was up against the corruption of the Tammany administration. New York had suffered from this for many years – some might say benefited. Whether by bribery or extortion, the New York political administration, especially the police, gave patronage to those who paid the most. Those with nothing, or who opposed Tammany, found little protection. Blackwood certainly could not afford to bribe the police to help him. His only advantage was that he knew the police and that the *Sun* was an avid pro-Tammany paper. Bigge, to his advantage, knew New York better than Blackwood and knew where he could hide. Blackwood managed to secure the help of Detective Lawler who agreed he would arrest Bigge, but only if Blackwood brought him in. Blackwood had to find him.

Huebner insisted in accompanying Blackwood. They must have looked a strange pair. Blackwood, tall, emaciated, gaunt, and with staring blue-grey eyes, dressed in a thin jacket, vest and trousers (everything else had been pawned, and Bigge had stolen Blackwood's overcoat). Huebner, forty years older, of average height but appearing shorter because he stooped, white hair and moustache, thick glasses that magnified the size of his eyes, a big slouch hat, and who walked slowly with a limp. After two weeks the old doctor, addicted to morphine, was in a state of physical collapse. They gave up the chase.

Pauw returned for Christmas and learned the truth of events for the first time. On an impulse, on 27 December[12], Blackwood set out again and this time walked straight to Bigge. Blackwood wondered if it was predestined. He instinctively followed a route that took him along Eighth Avenue towards Madison Square Gardens. There, on the corner of 28th and Eighth Avenue he saw Bigge with a heavy-set male companion, both slightly worse for drink. They went into a bar. Just as Blackwood was about to follow, two policemen appeared. Blackwood told them his story and they agreed to arrest Bigge if Blackwood brought him out.

With a courage he never knew he had, Blackwood marched into the bar, straight up to Bigge and clapped his hand on Bigge's shoulder to arrest him. Bigge couldn't believe it to begin with, but Blackwood's manner convinced him. Suddenly he wilted. His large companion threatened to strike Blackwood but took no action.

Blackwood told Bigge that if he came quietly he would charge only petty larceny, otherwise it was forgery. It worked. Bigge complied. Blackwood handed him over and Bigge was marched off to the nearest police station. Blackwood was exhausted and though he meant to fill in the complaint sheet for a theft of $25, which was the limit for petty larceny, he forgot and completed it for the $32 that Bigge had stolen from the drawer. As a result Bigge was charged with grand larceny and was bound over for the Grand Sessions instead of being dealt with by the local magistrate.

Bigge pleaded guilty at the Grand Sessions on 29 December, but sentence was not passed until 6 January. The recorder received several character references on behalf of Bigge, pleading clemency, but they carried little weight. Bigge had wronged too many people of sufficient status, and all appeared in court. These included the artist Lynwood Palmer, the author Richard Harding Davis, the actor E.H. Sothern, and the banker August Belmont. Bigge was sentenced to two years at the penitentiary on Blackwell Island. Bigge was released after eighteen months. Blackwood saw him soon after but Bigge made himself scarce. He saw Bigge ten years later in London and again he hastily vanished.

III

The episode of Blackwood and Bigge raises several important issues. Blackwood's autobiography, *Episodes Before Thirty*, revolves around it. His account of his relationship with Bigge takes up the best part of 120 pages out of 300. He even reproduces several letters Bigge wrote him from prison. Why?

The most obvious answer is that it is a good story, and Blackwood was at heart a storyteller. He was never comfortable talking simply about himself. And yet there was so much else in Blackwood's life during these years. Blackwood had to cut 30,000 words from his first draft to make it of commercial length, but he could easily have saved some of that wordage by editing down the Bigge episode and he chose not to. When he wrote to his half-sister about the book he said, 'I had strange bed-fellows in those days, and I omitted, of course, lots of other experiences in the book.'[13] So, why did he omit other experiences and yet concentrate so much on this one?

This was a traumatic experience that haunted him for years. Here, at one moment, Blackwood discovers a new, deep friendship. Within two months it is turned savagely on its head. Blackwood, ill, weakened, poverty-stricken, has to haul himself off his sick-bed and track down and arrest a man, in an alien city. And then, inadvertently, he charges him with grand larceny and has his friend put away in prison for two years. Despite all that Bigge had done, Blackwood still felt as if he had betrayed him. Some guilt clearly remained. Was this then therapy to cleanse his conscience by writing a complete account?

The episode was traumatic in other ways. Before Bigge, Blackwood had been carefree, blunted by the failure of the dairy and the Hub, but not despondent. He had picked himself up and carried on with his life. And he did again after Bigge. But then it was a different Blackwood.

The combination of his illness and his confrontation with Bigge had taken Blackwood to the rim of Hell. It was his darkest moment. There would be plenty of hard times ahead, but nothing ever again as bad as this. It rocked his faith in humanity. It tested his beliefs. He felt he must be paying retribution through karma for some major misdemeanour in a past existence. If he could work it through then he could redeem himself and regenerate a new karma for the future.

By writing at length about it Blackwood also relived it. He says several times during his account how real it all seemed. The lodgings were more real than where he lived later. Watching Bigge in his room seemed but a few moments ago. And reliving it allowed Blackwood to confront it and come to terms with it. Blackwood wrote his autobiography at the time he had encountered the teachings of Gurdjieff, and his need to relive and explain these events was part of his therapy to rid himself of guilt that still haunted him.

There is also the less significant but no less pertinent question about Blackwood's sexual orientation towards Bigge. Blackwood no doubt chose his words wisely, and one has to interpret them sensibly. So, what does Blackwood mean when he wrote, 'My attachment to him deepened into affection.'?[14] Or when he writes, 'I watched Boyde's face, as he slept calmly beside me in that narrow bed, his expression of innocence and kindliness increased my feelings of gratitude, even tenderness towards him.'[15] And later, when Pauline Markham visited Blackwood, why did she ask Blackwood to 'give him back to her'?[16]

The whole episode bears the hallmark of an affair and break-up between two lovers. That was certainly the intensity of the emotion on Blackwood's part. Dr John Nesfield, who knew Blackwood for the last thirty years of his life, had also questioned Blackwood's sexuality. He believed that Blackwood's upbringing had caused him to repress his natural heterosexuality, as if any yearning of the flesh was sinful, with the result that he could only feel close to men[17]. Throughout his life Blackwood knew many homosexuals, though this did not mean Blackwood was homosexual himself. Frank Podmore was known to be homosexual, and there was even a scandal in the Post Office in 1889 with the revelation that several telegraph boys were found in a male brothel in London. It would be difficult to imagine Blackwood's father did not know about this. There were several other homosexuals in the Society for Psychical Research including Arthur Sidgwick (the brother of Henry), F.W.H. Myers and John Addington Symonds.

Blackwood knew all of these at one time or another. Also, Alexander Fullerton of the Theosophical Society was allegedly homosexual – certainly he was charged in later years with relationships with a young boy.

In later years, however, once he overcame his shyness, Blackwood attracted women like bees to honey, although he preferred to remain celibate. As a true mystic, Blackwood removed himself from physical pleasure. Soon after he had completed *Episodes*, he wrote to the young explorer Ella Maillart, in which he said: 'I knew I must not marry, so when passion sometimes came to cloud my deeper intuitive judgment, I left always.'[18] He explored this view in more detail in *The Education of Uncle Paul*, his most autobiographical novel. Having returned to England from years abroad, Paul Rivers reflects about his life.

> Of women, of course, he knew little or nothing; to him they were all charming, some of them wonderful . . . They stood closer to God than men did, he felt, and the depravity of really bad women he explained by the fact that when they did fall they fell farther. The sex-fever, so far as he was concerned, had never mounted to his brain to obscure his vision.[19]

Blackwood's shyness and repressive upbringing made him feel awkward with girls, whereas he was comfortable in the company of young men. Blackwood also related to a more imaginative, artistic and creative temperament of whatever gender.

His fear of rejection and his sense of shame drove him to seek the company of those he could regard as father figures or fellow siblings. His immaturity caused him to become devoted to these friends in a way that might appear to be homophilic but which was more agapemonitic, a brotherly love. He found himself drawn closer to Bigge than any other man. Bigge, on the other hand, was a philanderer. He had already run away with one man's wife, and had entered into romances with at least three women in the previous few months.

Bigge's betrayal and desertion marked the point at which Blackwood suddenly grew up. He would still make mistakes – plenty of them – but he was more in command of himself. But from then on I believe he became asexual. He continued to enjoy the company of men, and steadily became more comfortable among women, but he repressed any sexual feelings as deeply as he could.

By 1893 Blackwood the Boy had virtually disappeared. Blackwood the Man and Blackwood the Mystic were now in the ascendence.

6

Dreams and Illusions (1893–95)

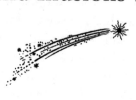

By mid-January 1893 Blackwood was sufficiently restored to health to resume work as a full-time reporter with *The Sun*. Although he now had a regular income, it was still difficult to make ends meet. He and Pauw continued to lodge together, at 19 Lafayette Place, and occasionally others stayed with them, free of charge. There was a down-and-out whom Blackwood calls Calder. Blackwood suspected he might be another Bigge and threw him out after a day or two. He then felt guilty – and still felt guilty writing about it in *Episodes* thirty years later. Then the ebullient Frenchman, Louis B—, their friend from the Hub Café days, turned up, having left his wife and newborn child at home. He stayed with Blackwood and Pauw until the summer.

Louis added nothing to the finances and was often a drain on them, but he was always exciting company. Apparently, with Blackwood accompanying him on his violin, Louis would often sing in a high falsetto, and Pauw would join in with a deep bass, well into the early hours, much to the annoyance of fellow boarders. They would sometimes conduct a mock 'black mass', cavorting around a candle-lit 'faun' dressed in odd garments. It was surprising that Mrs Bernstein retained them as lodgers, especially as they always owed her money, but for some reason she liked them.

Blackwood's life settled into a routine. He worked every day at *The Sun*, mostly in the police courts, but undertaking such other assignments as arose. He also gave occasional violin lessons. In the evenings, if he wasn't at the free library, or at a Theosophical gathering, he would visit friends, or suffer the company of Pauw and Louis in their flat.

Sunday was his day of escape. No matter what the weather, Blackwood headed to the Bronx Park. This was before it became a zoological gardens. Although not as large as Central Park, which was nearer – it was little more than a square mile – it was wilder and less frequented, and was a haunt of artists because of its unkempt beauty. Over time Blackwood went as far as building a small lean-to hidden under the bushes by an outcrop of rocks within earshot of the trickling Bronx River, which here was little more than a shallow stream. These moments of solitude and meditation gave Blackwood the spiritual regeneration he needed and allowed him to cope with the pressure of life in New York.

Blackwood was fortunate in that, during 1893, two of the most notorious murder cases of the 1890s occurred. Besides the Carlyle Harris case, already mentioned, was the more famous one case of Lizzie Borden. She was arrested on 12 August 1892 charged with the murder of her parents in Fall River, Massachusetts, having allegedly killed them both in their sleep with an axe. The case had been headline news since the murder on 4 August. She was indicted before a Grand Jury on 2 December 1892. The full trial took place in New Bedford, Massachusetts from 5 to 20 June 1893. The main reporter for *The Sun* was Julian Ralph, later a notable *Daily Mail* reporter in the Boer War, but Blackwood was also present and even interviewed Borden at some stage. Though she was acquitted, Blackwood had formed his own opinion about her guilt, for, in *Episodes,* he states that he believed she killed her parents. When Blackwood wrote that (in 1923), Lizzie Borden was still alive (she died in June 1927) and she could, presumably, have taken action against Blackwood had she known.

There were a few other memorable moments. An unqualified doctor was found to be running a home for the insane at Amityville on Long Island. The Health Authorities were going to raid the place at dawn. Blackwood found the episode distressing, especially as all the inmates were hauled out of the home as well as the staff, and an impromptu hearing was carried out by a local magistrate in a nearby barn. Blackwood believed that many of the inmates had once been perfectly sane but had been locked up just to be out of the way. There was also the bizarre experience of reporting on a dance held for deaf-mutes, where the only sound was that of a big drum to keep time and the shuffling of feet, plus the nonstop fingering of sign language.

One bright moment happened during 1893 with a visit by Lord Kintore. Kintore was Governor-General of Australia, but periodically returned to Britain, usually via America. He called in at the *Sun* offices to find Blackwood, who was out, so left his card. It raised Blackwood's status considerably in the eyes of his fellow reporters to see such an illustrious relative. Kintore treated Blackwood and Pauw to dinner at the Brevoort House hotel on Fifth Avenue, noted for its cuisine, and Blackwood dined sumptuously. He remembered that meal many years afterwards.

Perhaps the last item of note during 1893 was Blackwood's interview of the great actor Henry Irving. Irving had arrived in New York on 26 August as part of his North American tour with Ellen Terry, and Blackwood hastened to interview them in their special train. Also present was Irving's manager, Bram Stoker. Stoker had yet to write *Dracula*, but had already published several books and stories.

Interesting though these assignments were, they were the exceptions. Blackwood found most of his work tedious, and he turned to writing other items when he could. Because none of the *Sun*'s articles are signed, it is impossible to say which are Blackwood's. There was, for instance, a long series of nature articles, which ran throughout 1893 and it is hard to imagine that Blackwood did not contribute to these. There were also travel articles and one of these, 'The English Tourist'[1], is worthy of comment.

It is a scathing and rather amusing piece about the slovenliness of the English tourist when on the continent. The author decries the fact that although the English upper class is courteous and respectful when on tour, Europe is being overrun by the 'lower classes of society' and 'small town people' who 'make themselves conspicuous by their bad manners and bad clothing and generally disreputable appearance'. Blackwood expresses an almost identical view at the start of 'Ancient Sorceries'.[2] Elsewhere in the article the author talks about rising early, to get the best of the day, and being greeted by the 'tinkling of a thousand cow bells'. Exactly the same phrase appears in 'The Messenger', where the first person narrator has climbed up into the mountains at night to witness the dawn.[3]

We can identify one piece by Blackwood because he refers to it in *Episodes*[4]. This was 'He Tried Hasheesh', in the *Sun* for 11 June 1893, which reports the experiences of a young doctor who had experimented with hashish a couple of weeks earlier. Blackwood states that he took it purely to earn the extra money for the newspaper item, and not for his own indulgence. But it brings us back to the subject of drugs, and that in turn takes us back to Dr Otto Huebner.

Blackwood frequently visited the doctor's home, in East 19th Street, where they would talk philosophy or play music. Huebner was a mentor and father figure to Blackwood, a forerunner of the even more mystical Alfred H. Louis. Huebner's wife, Anna, was about twenty years younger than he, and their daughter, Elsa, was seven. The doctor hardly earned enough to keep food on the table, but a little extra money came in through his wife's work as a dressmaker.

Huebner had been born in Prussia but had left home following family problems and become a naturalized American. He worked for years at the local piano factory, saving enough money to study medicine, and eventually qualified in around 1875. His practice was not very successful. He even operated on his own leg, and complications left him with a limp. He sought relief from pain in morphine and became an addict.

Blackwood witnessed the change that came over the doctor after taking morphine, turning him from an irritable, moody old failure, into a tender, genial being. The doctor saw Blackwood's fascination and gave him a weak dose. Blackwood stated that the effect was remarkable. Within three minutes he was in a 'state of absolute bliss'.[5] Huebner administered an injection every night for the next month, from mid December 1892 to mid January 1893. Perhaps because the dosage was small Blackwood never became addicted, unlike the doctor. Once his health had improved by mid January he visited the doctor less often, usually weekly, and the injections ceased.

The experiment with hashish, or cannabis, was totally different. It was a one-off, thankfully for Blackwood, because if his account is true, it almost ended in his death.

In the article the 'young doctor' takes a few 'hasheesh pills' on Saturday afternoon. Nothing much happens so he takes another. Still nothing happens so he goes to his local barber. Then the drug kicks in. Suddenly everything is exaggerated. The barber becomes a giant and his razor an axe. Scared witless by seeing the axe being brandished at his throat, the 'doctor' runs from the barber's. In the street everything is vast. Telegraph poles reach the sky. People are giants. Buildings are suffocatingly huge. He tries to run home, but the streets have increased in length and he becomes exhausted. Behind him he is aware of a glow and finds a volcano has erupted and lava is flowing towards him. He struggles on. When he reaches his apartment the steps are almost too high to climb. He finally makes it to his room. He lies on a mattress and his friends place another mattress on top of him on which they lie to hold him down. At first he rebels but then falls asleep. He dreams he is in Spain and travelling around the world. He makes it to ancient Rome where he meets Ovid and they walk to Egypt. There they are attacked by the sultan's bodyguard who beheads Ovid and chases the 'doctor'. The 'doctor' is about to leap out of a window when his friends, who had thought he was asleep and had got off the mattress, just save him in time. An old doctor (clearly Huebner) is brought in, but the 'young doctor' has to stay in bed for two weeks.

Blackwood probably wrote the account while recuperating, so counting back two weeks suggests the experiment happened on 27 May 1893. This date fits in remarkably well, for once, with Blackwood's recollection, since he refers to the experiment 'when May came'.[6] There is no reason to doubt the account, but it suggests that Pauw and Louis were only just in time to save Blackwood jumping through their third-floor window.

Blackwood never became addicted to drugs – although he smoked cigarettes regularly. He was addicted to nature and that gave him all the escape and heightened sensations that he needed. But he drew upon the experience in several of his books. The best known is in 'A Psychical Invasion', the first of the John Silence stories. Here a young author, Pender, known for his humorous stories, hits a writer's block. He takes cannabis because he has heard it will heighten his humorous perception. Nothing happens for a while and he falls asleep only to wake to the sound of his own laughter. But then he becomes aware of a presence in the house: a feeling of utter evil. According to John Silence, taking the cannabis has increased his awareness of the vibrations of the world about him and made him cognisant of an evil influence that remains in the house.

He also refers to the experience in *The Centaur*, where he comments that in ancient times people's senses were less specialized: 'that perception came to them in general, massive sensations rather than divided up neatly into five channels – that they felt *all over* so to speak, and that all the senses, as in an overdose of haschish, become one single sense'.[7]

In late September Blackwood took two weeks' holiday in Canada, at Haliburton, in northern Ontario. On the last day he was staying with a friend of the family at the St John's Presbyterian Church in Hamilton, Ontario. It was here that the news reached Blackwood of his father's death. Sir Arthur had died on 2 October 1893 when his heart finally failed him. He had not relaxed his overwhelming workload, and was returning from official business in Germany when he collapsed at Rotterdam and barely survived the trip across the North Sea. He died late on Monday night at the Great Eastern Hotel at Harwich, aged sixty-one.

Blackwood's first response was to run into the woods for solace. He already felt guilty at having let his father down and at not redeeming himself sufficiently in his father's eyes. Now all chance of that had gone. His father had died believing Blackwood's soul was lost and that he was a failure. There was, of course, nothing he could do. It was even too late to return to attend the funeral.[8] Blackwood simply returned to New York, and tried to get on with his life, ever regretful.

In his later stories Blackwood sometimes turns himself into a father figure, certainly the avuncular father he wished he had but never knew. There is a telling couple of moments in the poignant story of childhood imagination, 'The Other Wing'[9]. It is the story of a young boy, Tim, who lives in a large Victorian house. He has grown up with the belief that during the day dreams hide in 'the Other Wing' and only emerge at night. Then one night he notices a corridor he has never seen before, the Nightmare Corridor to the Other Wing. He goes down it with much trepidation but as he passes through the door at the far end he is greeted by a kindly old man whom he remembers as his father's grandfather from pictures he had seen. It is, of course, all a dream, and suddenly the kindly old man becomes his father, wondering why Tim is in his study so early in the day. He hugs him and all is well. Later in the story, the kindly old man reappears and this time warns Tim of a fire. Tim wakes the household and saves everyone. However, in the process, a valuable old walking cane is lost and Tim's father scolds him for losing it.

These two images clearly contrast the father Blackwood wanted with the one he knew. Blackwood had loved and revered his father. At times they had been close in their love of nature, but Blackwood's esoteric interests forced them apart. Blackwood came to think of him

as distant – 'something of a stranger'[10]. Now the chance for recon-
ciliation had gone for ever.

II

Back in New York Blackwood settled into a daily routine. The state
elections that November saw a surge in popularity for the Republicans
who claimed they would root out Tammany corruption. A committee
of inquiry under Senator Lexow was established in January 1894 and
ran through to September. Blackwood reported regularly on the
committee for *The Sun*, gaining a major insight of the Tammany
organization.

Blackwood's financial position improved slightly. Louis had
returned home. Pauw had a regular job as a financial broker in the
Exchange Place banking district. Blackwood also decided to do some
modelling for local artists. This was something Bigge had done for
extra cash, and in *Episodes* Blackwood maintains that he followed
this up once he was well enough in November or December 1892.
However, Blackwood also notes that the first pose he did, for one
of Charles Dana Gibson's cartoons, was of a down-and-out actor
against a hoarding with a joke about a bill-board and a board-bill.
That sketch appeared in *Life* for 16 November 1893, and is unlikely
to have remained unused for a full year. Since Blackwood talks
about the thrill he had when he saw it, I would imagine this was
the first.[11]

Blackwood posed for a few other artists, including William Smedley
and Rufus Zogbaum of *Harper's Magazine* and, of course, Lynwood
Palmer, with whom Blackwood remained friendly. Blackwood does
not mention whether he also modelled for Robert W. Chambers (1865–
1933). Chambers became a well known novelist but began his career
as an artist and shared a studio with Gibson, both doing work for
Life. Blackwood must have met Chambers at this time, though there
is no evidence of a friendship. Soon after Chambers began work on
several original works of weird fiction, starting with *The King in Yellow*
(1895). This is a series of connected stories about a possible real King
in Yellow who has worked behind the scenes through the centuries to
influence the progress of mankind. It's a strangely theosophical theme
that would have delighted Blackwood.

But it was Gibson whom Blackwood posed for mostly, because
Gibson paid for a full afternoon's sitting even if he only wanted his

model for an hour. Gibson (1867–1944) would soon become famous through the creation of what became known as the 'Gibson Girl', the idealized, fashionable, modern girl.

It was around this time that he first met Angus Hamilton (1874–1913), newly arrived from England and a young reporter on the *Sun*. Blackwood calls him a 'lovable fellow' but also notes that when Hamilton was 'in the money' and held dinner parties, neither Blackwood nor his cronies were invited. Hamilton was the son of an army captain in the 2nd West India Regiment, who was a cousin of the 7th Baronet Hamilton of Silverton Hill. His father had died young, when Angus was only five, and his mother, who was an actress, had married the playwright and actor Arthur Wing Pinero (1855–1934). He therefore had both aristocratic and literary connections.

Hamilton had taken lodgings above Blackwood's and would sometimes pop down to share an evening with him, Pauw and Louis[12]. Some evenings, if the mood took him, Blackwood would tell stories. He must have had a fund of tales and anecdotes from his newspaper assignments and his haunted house investigations, yet he maintains he still had given no thought to writing them down as stories and selling them. It was Hamilton who enthused about them and asked if he could write them up, convinced that they would sell. Ten years later Hamilton was instrumental in Blackwood becoming an author, but for the moment Blackwood showed little interest.

As spring returned to New York, in 1894, and dreading the prospect of another claustrophobic summer, Blackwood looked for a new escape. It came one Sunday as he was venturing to his hideout in the Bronx Park when he read in his newspaper about the gold fever erupting in the Rainy River area of Ontario. He recalls that it was in late April that gold had been found, but in fact such reports had been surfacing for some while. The real buzz began when a prospector, George Davis, was panning for gold on Little American Island in Rainy Lake in July 1893 and found sufficient for the word to spread. Shanty towns sprang up all over the area. The biggest was Rainy Lake City, which was incorporated on 17 May 1894 by the Rainy Lake Improvement Company of Duluth, with an 'instant' population of around 400.

It was almost certainly this news that Blackwood read about and immediately he resolved to go gold prospecting. He gathered around him a party of hopefuls. There was an engineer called Paxton who had just lost all of his money in a financial investment. Then there was the son of the Hamilton clergyman, whom Blackwood calls simply

R.M. This was Reggie Moreton (1869–1929), who was quite a colourful character. He was an insurance broker and a good amateur boxer. Family legend has it that he could punch a hole in a door. Moreton used to run boxing classes in the church hall on Sundays and a local pastor took exception to this. Moreton challenged the pastor to a fight and the subsequent squabble hit the local headlines. Moreton decided to vanish for a while, and the opportunity to join Blackwood was ideal.

Blackwood arranged train passes with the *Sun*, promising McCloy he would send back news stories. They pooled their money and set off by train for Duluth in early May. Pauw missed the train. Blackwood makes the point it was the last time he ever saw him, but in fact they met up again upon his return.[13] Moreton had apparently been out celebrating the night before so was stone-cold drunk and had to be thrown on to the train at Hamilton.

Blackwood was in his element, escaping New York and heading towards the lakes and forests. It's strangely incongruous to realise that in his bag was a revolver, which he had picked up at the Tombs. It's hard to imagine Blackwood with a gun, but he kept it for years. At Duluth they acquired provisions and a canoe – Moreton had brought a tent – and a guide. He was a half-breed called Gallup who was morose the whole trip and liked to frighten the men into thinking, that once they got there, the prospectors would have it in for them, because they were posh Britishers. He also took them by a longer route, so he gained several extra days' payment. Their provisions ran out, but they were able to fish and hunt. Blackwood did not worry. The journey down the Vermilion River was magical to him. 'Everything sparkled, the air was champagne; such a winding river of blue I had never seen before.'[14] They sped through the rapids, trying to keep pace with Gallup in his small canoe. Despite his illness and frequent lapses in diet, Blackwood was strong, lean and healthy. And his spirit was alive again.

He thought about the forests that stretched without interruption five hundred miles to the north, and reflected that 'somewhere in the heart of that old forest the legendary Wendigo . . . had its awful lair'. It was not this trip, but one four years later, that provided the real inspiration for Blackwood's famous story, 'The Wendigo'. Yet the exhilaration, the experiences and the sheer excitement of this journey were all shades of darkness and light, mystery and magic that Blackwood would use to colour his stories in later years.

What remained with Blackwood on this journey, apart from the pure joy of being out in the wilderness, was the need to watch his back. They were convinced that Gallup was going to lead them to renegades who would slit their throats, and became very nervous when on the eighth day he abandoned them. But nothing happened. Gallup was having a reunion with friends. They were also warned of a murderer called Morris, and he was the very man who befriended them at Rainy Lake.

Upon arriving at Rainy Lake in the middle of May, they were disappointed to find that there was no loose gold to be panned. It was all trapped within rocks of quartz, which had to be mined and crushed. It required expensive machinery. The journey had all been for nothing – in the material sense. In the spiritual sense, Blackwood felt it was worth more than gold.

They spent six weeks at Rainy Lake, until they could stand the mosquitoes no longer and realized they needed to get home before the weather turned. They left just as a typhoid epidemic broke out and there was no doctor in the town. With no money and no ready transport, it was a long trek back to New York. They sold their canoe, as the prospect of fighting their way back up the rapids was too appalling, and decided to follow the portage trail. To Blackwood's horror, who should join them on the return trip but none other than the murderer Morris and his two cohorts.

The weather changed and it poured with rain. This slowed their progress and they had to walk through thick forest, as the trail at times was non-existent. The first night they spent in a ramshackle hut that they found deep in the woods. Moreton said he would keep watch but fell asleep. Blackwood remained awake. During the night he saw Morris move stealthily towards Moreton. Blackwood watched silently. Then he realized Morris was only covering Moreton's head to shelter him from the rain dripping through the roof. In fact Morris proved to be wonderful company and never once lived up to his murderous reputation.

They spent the summer working their way along the shores of the Great Lakes and eventually back to New York. Blackwood never did file his newspaper reports. It transpired that they had gone at the wrong time. A year later gold was found a few miles away along the Seine River and this was easier to access. Prospectors poured in and for a while the area boomed, but it was all over by 1901. Blackwood did not return.

III

Back in New York at the end of October, Blackwood found new lodgings at East 21st Street. It was these lodgings that inspired the story 'A Case of Eavesdropping'. Blackwood regularly heard the Germans in the room next to his muttering all night and yet never once saw them. The Bernsteins had moved to another boarding house at 106 East 19th Street, and Blackwood would join them there the following year.

Blackwood had no desire to go back to the routine of police court reporting so tried his hand at freelancing, placing stories and fillers with as many of the New York papers as were interested. This makes it all but impossible to trace anything he wrote at this time, since none of the items are signed and he makes precious few references to the pieces he submitted.

Blackwood met up with Pauw again. Pauw had at first moved with the Bernsteins but then found new lodgings over the river in Pelham Bay Park. He still worked occasionally at brokerage in Exchange Place but he was also tempted by the theatre and had found a place in a company run by a Canadian actor, J. H. Gilmour. They were touring New York State with the play *Jim the Penman* by Sir Charles Young. Gilmour gave Blackwood the part of a prison warder and took him on at $15 a week.

Blackwood's role involved him trying to stop Gilmour escaping from prison. By the end of the first week, however, Gilmour and Blackwood were at daggers drawn over the leading lady, Bettina Gerard. Gilmour was mad about Bettina, but Bettina had turned her eyes towards young Blackwood. On the seventh night of the tour, Blackwood a little worse for drink, tackled Gilmour rather more realistically than previously. It turned into a full fight, much to the audience's appreciation. Blackwood had the better of Gilmour until the end when Gilmour knocked him semi-conscious. There was thunderous applause, but that was the end of Blackwood's run with the company.

Blackwood always felt that he had no talent for the theatre, certainly not as an actor, and not really as a writer. He needed others to rework his well crafted stories into the structure of a play. But none of this stopped Blackwood's fascination for the stage. He loved the theatre and, in his later years, it became a significant part of his life.

Blackwood continued to meet interesting, usually slightly strange, individuals – often outcasts. The deepest, most spiritual friendship he had was with Alfred H. Louis (1828–1915). Louis had once been a lawyer of repute and a prospective parliamentarian in England, but, by the time Blackwood met him, Louis was a drop-out from society. Yet those who knew him were captivated by his magic. Blackwood called him 'some ancient prophet, some mysterious priest'.[15] The renowned Chicago society hostess Cornelia Lunt (1843–1934), who knew Louis in her twenties said 'No one she had ever known talked as Mr Louis talked and none wrote so beautifully.'[16] She was advised by her sister not to see Louis again, and she regretted that till the day she died. The author 'George Eliot' (1819–1880), who knew Louis at her Sunday salon in St John's Wood in 1876, was sufficiently inspired to base the character of Mordecai, the Jewish mystic in *Daniel Deronda* (1876), on him[17]. The emerging American poet, Edward Arlington Robinson (1869–1935) took even greater inspiration, developing an entire narrative poem, *Captain Craig* (1902), around the character of Louis. And when Maude ffoulkes, Blackwood's first editor, met Louis in his final years, she called him 'one of the most singular people I have ever met'.[18]

Louis's spirit touched many people and left a profound mark on them all. Blackwood said that Louis knew no bitterness, and perhaps he had found time to forgive, but his face would grow dark at the mention of the British Prime Minister W. E. Gladstone. Louis had distrusted Gladstone and made it known. As a consequence, Gladstone had Louis ostracized. That blighted Louis's parliamentary life thereafter. A promising lawyer with a penetratingly astute mind, Louis found himself a wanderer. He spent some years practising law in America, returning periodically to England. Louis had married in his youth and had a young child, though I have no idea what became of mother and child. Though born a Jew, Louis was baptised into the Church of England and later turned to Catholicism before reverting to his original faith not long before his death.

By the time Blackwood met him, he was about sixty-six, down-and-out, and his mind was starting to go. Louis saw in Blackwood a fellow free spirit who soared above the mundane world. Between them they would talk for hours – or rather Louis talked and Blackwood listened. They would sit on park benches under the stars, by the river side, even in a warehouse wharf, where they would sip olive oil and eat sparingly of dried apple rings. Louis lived in a small, unkempt garret at 33 East 8th Street, near the East River. 'The whole universe lies in this room, or just beyond that window-pane,' he once told Blackwood, ' for here past and future meet and all dreams find completeness'. Louis did not literally mean that room, he meant each human being. Our past and future lies in us, and only we know the way to fulfil our dreams.

With Louis, Blackwood's soul was among the heavens. At his heart Louis was a poet. He had sold over a dozen poems to *Harper's Magazine* in the 1870s. It was the poet in Blackwood as much as the mystic that responded to Louis. Louis became the father that Blackwood had lost. Even more he became the father that Blackwood had wished for and never known. Louis would not suffer fools. He had mood-swings and outbursts that kept Blackwood on his mettle, but he was also a mentor, guide and soul-mate. It is thanks to Louis that Blackwood began his upward struggle back into the world. After his meeting with Louis, Blackwood's life measurably improved. He regained the self-respect that he had lost. He gained a confidence in himself that he had never had. It did not stop him being foolish and reckless at times – Blackwood loved the spirit of adventure too much for that – but it was now within a sphere of self-control and responsibility that Blackwood had hitherto ignored.

Louis remained close to Blackwood, or as close as he could be to anyone, for the next twenty years. Blackwood helped look after him in his final days back in England. He dedicated *Episodes Before Thirty* to him. Blackwood also composed the mood story 'The Old Man of Visions'[19] about Louis. It is only when you know the relationship between Blackwood and Louis that this story comes to life. It relives Blackwood's discovery of Louis, transplanted to London, and shows the birth of a spiritual affinity. At the heart of the story is one man's personal vision. In Louis's philosophy 'no true dream can ever be shared' and any attempt to share that dream means the dream is lost. In the story the narrator tells a friend about his 'Old Man of Visions' and with that the Old Man is lost and never seen again.

In like ways Blackwood would share only so much of his life, of his experiences, of his visions. His stories are his expressions of wonder. But only so much. All else is silence for fear that the magic is lost.

There were two other people who entered Blackwood's life at this stage who are worth mentioning. The first he called Mrs Kent, though that was not her real name. She was a wealthy widow, though the wealth had not come from her husband, but from her sister, who was married to the owner of Florida Water. Mrs Kent's husband had been a successful businessman, in real estate, but a slump during the 1880s led to a drop in profits and the stress of work caused him to have a mental decline. One day he broke down and tried to strangle his wife. A psychiatrist was called in and Mr Kent was admitted to the Bellevue Hospital for the Insane.

What happened next was one of those queer stories that Blackwood loved to recount. Mr Kent had been married before and had a son to whom he was devoted. The son lived apart from them and Mrs Kent had never met him. Then she read in the newspaper that the son had committed suicide. She knew that if her husband read this news it might turn his mind completely. She advised the ward doctor who assured her that Mr Kent had seen no newspapers. Yet she learned that her husband had suddenly become increasingly violent and kept asking about his son. His sudden change in temperament and his questions about his son had started at the time of the son's suicide. The husband never calmed down and died a few weeks later.

Mrs Kent lived at the respectable Chelsea Apartments on West 23rd Street. Blackwood visited her often, much to the annoyance of the lady's sister who believed that this English reprobate, half the age of Mrs Kent, was only after her money. Mrs Kent, however, who was lonely, appreciated Blackwood's company. She was a Swedenborgian, following a religion developed from the thinking of Emmanuel Swedenborg, who believed that the physical world was a manifestation of the spiritual one. Blackwood accompanied Mrs Kent occasionally on visits to the Church of the New Jerusalem on East 35th Street, but he refused to join the sect. He did not hold the same spiritualist beliefs.

Nevertheless, they would talk frequently about their religious views and Mrs Kent grew fond of Blackwood – so much so that she wished to adopt him as a son. Blackwood refused, since his own mother was still alive. Neither did he want further filial ties. He wished to remain free and unencumbered. His rejection of her proposal did not sour the relationship. Indeed, Mrs Kent would continue to visit Blackwood when he returned to London, and was involved in a strange psychic vision, which I shall recount later.

The other friend whom Blackwood encountered during this period was another outcast from Britain and he nearly landed Blackwood in gaol. His name was William Hamilton Henderson, but Blackwood refers to him simply as Brodie. Henderson was a Scot who claimed he was an illegitimate son of the Duke of Hamilton. He was at one time also a broker in Exchange Place and probably met Blackwood through Pauw. At the time Henderson lived in East 22nd Street, just a couple of blocks from Blackwood's. Henderson set himself up in the perfume trade, selling eau-de-cologne to many of the big stores. The business was profitable. Blackwood had helped Henderson out one day by ejecting a guest who had overstayed his welcome at Henderson's apartment. In return Henderson offered Blackwood a business partner-ship. Henderson was essentially illiterate and needed Blackwood's education. Blackwood found himself earning $10 a week on top of his journalism and his violin teaching, and feeling rather comfortable.

Then, just as with Bigge, friends began to warn Blackwood that Henderson was a rogue. The main warning came from a rather sinister character whom Blackwood calls Von Schmidt, and whom Blackwood believed might have been a blackmailer. He never did find out what Von Schmidt did, and even wondered if Henderson might be one of Von Schmidt's victims.

Blackwood later learned that Henderson had stolen the eau-de-cologne formula and that the trade had become suspicious. Henderson moved his clothes and prized possessions into Blackwood's apartment, whilst at the same time making great show of the purportedly expensive items still in his flat. Blackwood became suspicious of Henderson's motives, especially when Henderson took Blackwood and others out to dinner one evening and became increasingly nervous. When they returned home they discovered Henderson's rooms on fire, and his 'precious' possessions destroyed.

There was talk of arson, and Henderson and Blackwood found themselves up against the Fire Marshal, James Mitchel. Mitchel was out to prove himself. There had been many arsons in New York, and Mitchel had been asked to resign by the Republicans (as part of their Tammany sweep) because of allegations of corruption. A new fire marshal had been appointed but Mitchel refused to go. He was determined to root out the culprits. Blackwood was convinced that, even though he was innocent, he would be found guilty of being an accomplice and sent to prison.

Fortunately for Blackwood a fellow reporter on the *New York Times*, called Mullins, was interviewing Mitchel to get his side of the case[20]. Mullins was certain there was an opening for Blackwood on the *Times*, so when Blackwood appeared before Mitchel, he made it clear that he was about to become a *Times* reporter, and the last thing Mitchel wanted was further scandal over a simple accident. Blackwood suggested that he would be only too pleased to help Mitchel out if he picked up news of suspicious fires in his job as a reporter.

Blackwood got away with it, but more by luck than design. He never saw Henderson again, although the rogue stayed in the perfume business in New York. He even cropped up in the news again four years later when he disappeared for a few days in May 1899 only to turn up in hospital. But by this time Blackwood was back in England and well clear of Henderson and all the other colourful New York reprobates who had threatened to drag him into the gutter.

7

The Road to Recovery (1895–99)

I

Mullins's hope that Blackwood would soon have a job on the *New York Times* was not an idle dream. The opening was there, but Blackwood needed to wait a few weeks. He remembered those six weeks as 'the most painful and unhappy of all my New York days'.[1] He had no regular employment, his free-lance work had dried up, and his friends, all except Old Louis, were away.

He could not even afford his lodgings and became a vagrant. He spent the days at the Free Library, lunched with Louis, usually on olive oil and dried apples or rice, and slept either under the trees in Bronx Park – though it was a long walk there – or on a bench in Central Park. Blackwood writes little of this period, and it was probably painful to remember. He had his beliefs to sustain him spiritually and his friendship with Louis. Despite all the hardships he had gone through, this was his loneliest and most trying. There is little wonder that Blackwood came to venerate the Tramp figure, which features strongly in his children's books, because he had known many and been one.

When the confirmation of the post on the *New York Times* came, in September 1895, Blackwood could hardly believe it. With it came a salary of thirty-five dollars a week – a fortune. He had never earned so much before. He was so used to living frugally that he became fearful of losing money and began to save. In later years he always gave the impression of being poor, even when he had money, because he was so fearful of spending it and having none again.

Blackwood remembered his eighteen months at the *New York Times* with 'nothing but pleasure'.[2] He was working with top quality men who became good friends. He could afford to dress properly and eat good food. He also had a variety of interesting assignments, though his hours were long. He started at ten in the morning and could still be working at midnight.

On 12 December 1895 Rector Ahlwardt, a member of the Reichstag Central Party, was to give a talk at the Cooper Union Hall. Ahlwardt was notoriously antisemitic and Blackwood was sent to meet him off his steamer from Quarantine to advise him to be cautious. At the following meeting Ahlwardt's speech caused an uproar and he was bombarded with eggs by the audience. Blackwood covered the events. Theodore Roosevelt was, at that time, the Commissioner of Police and he refers to Ahlwardt's visit in his *Autobiography* (1913). He recalls that in order to minimalize Ahlwardt's impact he assigned forty policemen to protect him – every one of them Jewish.

Blackwood was sent to cover a series of lectures by Lyman Abbott on 'The Theology of an Evolutionist'. Abbott (1835–1922) was pastor of the Plymouth Congregational Church in Brooklyn but was better known as editor of *The Outlook*, a highly respectable family magazine. Abbott was known for his provocative views. He had a sharp, astute mind capable of delivering a complex speech at a fast pace and yet hold an audience riveted. Every Sunday, from 8 March to 3 May 1896 Blackwood honed his shorthand to keep track of Abbott's multi-stranded talk and then abridge it to fit into the column for the next day's paper. It was always a rush, and extremely tiring, but Blackwood was fascinated with Abbott's ideas and welcomed the challenge. Sometimes he became too absorbed in the talk and found he hadn't kept up with his notes. Abbott's theme of upholding fundamental Christian beliefs but interpreting them in the light of theories by Huxley, Darwin, Tyndall and others, was something that appealed to Blackwood's philosophy. He believed that religion and science were two sides of the same coin, and that one had to explore one's beliefs with a scientific exactness in order that they could be proven and upheld.

Later Abbott paid Blackwood the compliment of telling Charles Ransom Miller, the editor of the *New York Times*, that when anyone asked him if his talks were available in print he referred them to the *Times'* summaries which, he maintained, were better than he could do himself[3]. As a consequence Blackwood received a $5 a week rise.[4]

Whether this change in fortune affected Blackwood's attitude about his fiction, but a story under his name, 'The Story of Karl Ott', appeared in the October 1896 issue of *Pall Mall Magazine*. This highly prestigious London magazine was financed by the American millionaire William Waldorf Astor and was edited by Lord Frederick Hamilton, son of the Duke of Abercorn and distantly related to Angus Hamilton. Although *Pall Mall* had appeared in the wake of *The Strand*, which established the vogue for highly illustrated magazines of popular articles and fiction, *Pall Mall* was in a class of its own. It was flamboyant, championed art nouveau, and was more closely allied to the bohemian literary and artistic movement of the 1890s than the other popular magazines.

'The Story of Karl Ott' is not typical of the stories Blackwood came to be known for. It is set in Switzerland, at Niederwald in the Valais Alps, and tells of a local young man, a pastor's son, known for his obstinacy, who falls in love with a young English lady. The girl enjoys his company but does not return his love, even after he saves her little dog when it strays too close to a precipice where cliffs fall away to the Devil's Rocks. Then Karl discovers the girl is returning to England. They go for one last walk together but he cannot bear to be parted and in one last embrace they fall together over the precipice to the Devil's Rocks. It reads more like a retelling of a local story Blackwood may have heard on his travels. It lacks the passion of his later work. I suspect that 'The Story of Karl Ott' was one of those stories that Hamilton copied down and, through his connections, had been able to sell for Blackwood. Yet it still did not encourage Blackwood to turn to writing.

Blackwood probably spent his summer break in 1896 back at the Muskoka Lakes. In his article, 'Summering in Canadian Backwoods'[5], he refers to the summers he spent there. He also states that his stays around the lakes have sometimes been 'with tent and canoe, sometimes in the greater luxury of the hospitable island-homes,' and that these were 'among the pleasantest memories of many years spent in Canada'.

One short story emerged from his Muskoka experiences. This was 'A Haunted Island', published in *The Pall Mall Magazine* for April 1899. It is set 'on a small island of isolated position in a large Canadian lake, to whose cool waters the inhabitants of Montreal and Toronto flee for rest and recreation in the hot months'. The narrator remains in a sizeable cottage [6] on the island after the main party returns to Montreal. All is well but on the tenth day the narrator begins to find the room oppressive and develops an uncontrollable desire to leave. Unable to re-enter the room, he sleeps downstairs. That night he witnesses two Indians who canoe quietly to the island and with utmost stealth enter the house and go to his bedroom. He hears a thump and they drag something downstairs. In a flash of lightning he is horrified to see that they are dragging his own dead and scalped body. Needless to say, the next day he leaves the island.

Blackwood was travelling further afield now. One of his newspaper assignments was to visit the home of Dwight Moody, his father's evangelist friend and the man who had so frightened Blackwood in his childhood. Moody was now nearing sixty, and his health was deteriorating. Blackwood went to write an article about Moody's work with schools and hospitals. While there he chose to confirm with Moody an incident that he had related long ago to Blackwood's father. It's another of those strange events that so intrigued Blackwood. Apparently, many years before while in Liverpool, Moody had been on his way to a meeting when, for no reason, he suddenly had the urge to cross the road. Some while later he was at an evangelist meeting when a man jumped up to proclaim that he was 'saved'. This man then confessed his sins, which included admitting that he had once intensely hated Moody, so much so that he planned to kill him. He followed Moody one evening down the street with his knife in hand and was almost ready to strike when, for no reason, Moody suddenly shot across the road. This action saved Moody's life, but Moody never knew why he had done it.

During this period there had been considerable changes in the running of the New York Theosophical Society. The years following the death of Helena Blavatsky in 1891 had been turbulent ones with conflict among the leadership hierarchy. W.Q. Judge was elected President in January 1892 after Henry Olcott resigned due to ill-health, but pressure was brought upon Olcott to reconsider. There were those who did not trust Judge and in 1894 Annie Besant brought charges of deception against him. The case came before a Theosophical Society hearing in London in July 1894, where the charges were dropped, but Judge's name had been tarnished among many members. Conflict continued and in April 1895 Judge chose to secede from the parent body establishing an independent Theosophical Society in America.

Just a year later, on 21 March 1896, Judge died of Chagres fever, a few weeks before his forty-fifth birthday.

Judge was succeeded as President by E.S. Hargrove. More controversial, however, was Judge's successor as head of the Esoteric Section. This was the comparatively unknown Katherine Tingley (1847–1929). She did not join the society until October 1894, but soon became close to Judge. Blackwood could have known her earlier. In the winter of 1892/3 she had established a Do-Good Mission on the East Side to help victims of a strike. The mission continued to help any destitute and poor, and Tingley strove to do further humanitarian work among the sick and orphaned. Blackwood could well have availed himself of Tingley's soup kitchen during his bleaker moments.

Within two years Tingley succeeded Hargrove and gained complete control over the society. She remained head of the Esoteric Section, but her interests were in social reform and welfare. She developed a new site for the American Society at Point Loma near San Diego, California. She wanted to create a new society built upon utopian principles. The land was acquired in 1897 and there were several schools and artistic academies established from 1900 onwards.

It is strange that Blackwood did not show interest in this development, but he was evidently becoming disenchanted with the organization. Though he continued his studies, his membership seems to have lapsed until he returned to England.

II

By the end of 1896, after sixteen months on the *New York Times*, Blackwood became footloose again. Despite the security and variety of his work Blackwood did not like to feel shackled for too long. One day he found himself seated in a train next to the businessman and philanthropist William Earle Dodge (1832–1903). Dodge had known Blackwood's father because of their shared interest in Christian work. Blackwood had visited Dodge on his first visit to New York with his father in 1887 and their paths had crossed a couple of times since. When Dodge enquired after Blackwood's well-being, Blackwood mentioned how keen he was to change his job. Dodge made an appointment to see him. Nothing seemed to come of that meeting and weeks passed by, then Dodge called for him again. Dodge had secured Blackwood a job as private secretary to the banker James Speyer on a salary of $2000 a year. Although that was the same salary he was getting from the *Times* it was for less hours: eight to two daily.

Speyer was only eight years Blackwood's senior, but came from an entirely different world. Although born in New York, he had been educated in Germany and France and had entered the family banking business in 1883, becoming a partner in the New York branch in 1885. His work kept him extremely busy. Blackwood's role was more of a personal manager than private secretary. Speyer was a bachelor, and needed someone to look after his estate. So, in addition to dealing with Speyer's daily correspondence and, in theory, his books (though Blackwood had no head for figures so a clerk was brought in to do that), Blackwood looked after the supervision of Speyer's town and country houses, his staff and horses and his various charity interests. Although there was plenty of work, and Blackwood needed to keep on his toes, he found he could handle it comfortably. The free afternoons and evenings (except on special occasions) gave Blackwood plenty of time for reading and going for long walks.

Blackwood travelled regularly between Speyer's New York home in Fifth Avenue (it transferred to 257 Madison Avenue upon Speyer's marriage in November 1897) and his grand country estate called Waldheim at Scarborough-on-Hudson near Ossining, thirty miles north of New York. From there Blackwood could have time exploring the Catskills and longer breaks further north in the Adirondacks.

Blackwood also accompanied Speyer on occasional trips. Although he does not name them, I am sure that Speyer and his fiancée are the couple referred to in Blackwood's article 'A Spiritualist Camp in New England'[7]. One September (almost certainly 1897), Blackwood and his colleagues were staying in Connecticut, near New London, when they learned that there was a summer encampment of spiritualists nearby. Although Blackwood had ceased his practical acquaintance with spiritualism several years before, he was still curious. He found the people uninspiring, illiterate and ready for any opportunity to earn a dollar. Whilst their beliefs may have been genuine, this gathering lacked the heart-felt fervour of others he had known. Nevertheless, he paid a medium a visit and discovered that his spirit guide was an American Indian called Black Hawk.

Blackwood's story, 'The Strange Adventures of a Private Secretary in New York'[8] owes its origin to this period, but it is one of his weakest pieces. It's another of his Jim Shorthouse stories. Here he works for businessman Jonas B. Sidebotham, who has fallen out with former partner Joel Garvey. They haven't seen each other for twenty years. Garvey is trying to blackmail Sidebotham. Shorthouse is entrusted to take certain documents to Garvey's remote house at the far end of Long Island and bring them back safely once Garvey has removed his signature. Sidebotham warns Shorthouse that Garvey will try to steal the documents. Thereafter it becomes a routine, even melodramatic gothic horror story. Shorthouse at first finds Garvey quite congenial, but he is delayed and has to stay the night. Garvey has odd eating habits – he eats raw flesh only – and the implication is that Garvey is a werewolf. He has as his servant Marx, an old Jew. The story is unforgivably antisemitic, very uncharacteristic of Blackwood, who had a high opinion of Jews. The story continues through the usual gothic stereotype of hidden chambers, sliding walls, eyes peering through paintings. It even has overtones of *Dracula*, with Shorthouse being trapped in his room and seeing things through the window, similar to Jonathan Harker at Castle Dracula. *Dracula* had been published in England in June 1897, and Blackwood could have read that edition before the American one issued two years later. The story reads like a routine exercise in horror that Blackwood would tell at house parties in the firelight – in fact, it really only works that way. He never wrote another like it.

Blackwood was present at the wedding of James Speyer and Ellin Lowery, which took place on 11 November 1897 at the bride's home at 32 West 35th Street. Blackwood liked to think he had played his part in bringing the happy couple together[9], though Speyer had known her for several years. Ellin Lowery (1849–1921) was twelve years older than Speyer and her first husband had died in 1892.

Through Ellin, Blackwood got to know her nephew, John Dyneley Prince (1868–1945). Since 1892 Prince had been Professor of Semitic Languages at New York University. He would go on to become a New Jersey senator (from 1910 to 1913), and State Governor. He later became a diplomat, serving as Minister to Yugoslavia from 1926 to 1933. Blackwood and Prince became firm friends and kept in touch with each other for many years.

III

Prince's main interest was in languages and during the 1890s he was undertaking a study into the language and beliefs of the native Americans, especially the Algonquin tribe. When opportunity allowed Prince took trips into northern Canada, to study local Indian life and folklore. Blackwood joined him on at least one such expedition in October 1898[10]. This inspired five stories[11], including one of his greatest, 'The Wendigo'.

The primary purpose of the trip was to hunt moose. Prince's wife, Adeline[12], was a keen huntress even though in her later years she took over from Ellin Speyer as head of the New York Women's League for Animals, which ran the Ellin Prince Speyer Animal Hospital. It may also seem strange to think of Blackwood, such a keen lover of nature, hunting animals. But Blackwood was imprinted with the mores of his day, when wild animals were accepted as fair prey for the hunter, whether for food or as trophy. Blackwood appreciated the interaction of animals and nature, but was not an ecologist. He had no qualms about hunting animals or felling trees, though his mood mellowed in later years.

The party consisted of Blackwood, Prince and his wife, plus two woodsmen from the Adirondacks and a half-breed Indian guide called Hank. They travelled from Montreal on the Canadian Pacific Railway to Mattawa, and from there by canoes and portage to Lake Cogawanna where they pitched camp. They used this site as their base and set off for a day or two at a time in groups of two, tracking moose. Blackwood tells of following a moose trail up to Garden Lake, ten miles north, where he eventually shot his first (and only) moose. It must have been a huge beast as its horns were fifty-two inches across with twenty-eight points.

They arrived at Garden Lake at sunset and as they quietly paddled across the arm of the lake 'the moon rose over the ridge of forest and silvered a picture of fairy-like enchantment such as I have never seen equalled. It was peace beyond telling . . . .' They had the forests and lakes to themselves and the animals. They encountered no other humans. At night the forests would come alive with the sound of wildlife. 'Everything is awake and moving. Yet, how silently,' he observed. They might hear the splash of an otter, the patter of a mink across stones, the occasional fish jumping in the lake, or the sound of deer drinking. Other animals might snuffle around their tent – skunk, porcupine. Some nights they would hear wolves howling. Blackwood was enthralled by the spell of the area.

One of the stories arising from this expedition was no more than a reworking of a local legend, 'How Garnier Broke the Log-Jam'.[13] It tells of a novice woodsman, Jean Garnier, who proves his manhood by risking his life and breaking a log-jam on the river.

The origin of the second is more complex. On the train journey to Mattawa they had met another moose-hunting party including a lawyer from Albany. That party set off in another direction and in such a vast territory there was no reason their paths would cross again. On their last day Hank noticed a movement far out on the lake. They realized it was the lawyer paddling a canoe with a branch. By the time he reached them he was exhausted but no one could stop him talking. Over and over he related how he and his guide, Jake, had been crossing Garden Lake. They hit a rough spell and the canoe capsized. The water was so cold that they could hardly move. The lawyer struck out for a small island clinging to the upturned canoe. When he got there and looked for Jake, his guide was nowhere to be seen. Neither Blackwood nor Prince believed the story. The next day as the main party returned to Mattawa Halt, Hank and another guide made off to Garden Lake. Blackwood later heard that they found the body of Jake near the island with his head bashed in. Blackwood was convinced that the lawyer had murdered him. The lawyer shared Blackwood's tent that last night and told Blackwood not to listen if he talked in his sleep. As the man stared into his face Blackwood believed he was about to spend the night with a murderer. The man's face haunted Blackwood for years. He turned the experience into the story 'Skeleton Lake'.

By this period in his life Blackwood was regularly telling stories around the camp-fire[14]. In his collection *Pan's Garden*, Blackwood notes at the end of each story where it originated. The note after 'The Destruction of Smith'[15] states simply 'Hank's Camp'. Maybe there were other Hanks on other trips, but this story is peculiarly suited to this expedition. It is set, unusually, in Arizona. Blackwood never visited Arizona, but in this case that isn't significant. It's about a man and his town. Ezekiel B. Smith had discovered oil in Arizona and staked his claim. Around his oil-well grew the town of Smithville. It was his town – his child. The narrator and his guide, Hank, encounter Smith on a hunting trip. Smith had been a giant of a man, but now he is a shell of his former self. He is struggling to get back to Smithville where his wife is dying. In fact Smithville is dying. The town has been such a child of Smith that it has become a projection of himself. He has provided it with life. Now, the spirit that was Smithville is collapsing and, in its last moments, that spirit returns with such an almighty force to Smith himself that the concentrated power kills him.

This story has many elements in common with 'The Wendigo'. It even has a moment of intense similarity as 'A shrieking city, it seemed, fled past us through the sky'[16] – just like the spirit of the Wendigo passes overhead. In both stories Blackwood is looking at primeval forces, spirit forces. Whilst in 'The Wendigo' that spirit emanates from nature, in 'The Destruction of Smith' it comes from a man – the very essence of life. This theme clearly appealed to Blackwood. We will return to it again and again – the relationship between Man and the forces of the world about him.

While telling stories at base camp, Blackwood and Prince would talk about the legends of the area, and none more potent than that of the Wendigo. This was an ancient Algonquin legend. The Wendigo was a spirit, as much bear as man, which ate human flesh. It was believed to exist deep in the forest. No one who saw the Wendigo lived to tell the tale. In the way that legends mutate, some spoke of the Wendigo more as an air-spirit than in any physical form. Blackwood drew upon the latter, building into it beliefs drawn from his Theosophical studies. He envisaged the Wendigo as the embodiment of the spirit of the wild north. Blackwood was himself captivated by this spirit which set his soul on fire. He perceived it as a form of wind-walker, a state achievable by a Yogi by intense meditation. If a human spirit can form a wind-walker, or *keshara*, what would the wind-walker of the Earth spirit be like? – the Wendigo.

For several years after this expedition Blackwood lived with that image of the Wendigo, as Nature personified, and his subconscious played with it, shaping it, moulding it. Eventually, ten years later, snowbound in a wooden cabin near Champéry, with a blizzard raging outside and the wind threatening to tear the cabin to splinters, the story took shape.

'The Wendigo' takes place exactly where Blackwood and his friends travelled. There are five characters. Head of the party is Dr Cathcart, a psychologist interested in hallucination. With him is his nephew, Simpson, a young Scottish divinity student, and a French-Canadian, Joseph Défago, a morose but imaginative woodsman. The Défago family was well known in Champéry in Switzerland – the name can still be seen in street names and locations. There was a guide called

Hank Davis – the real name of Blackwood's own guide – and an Indian called Punk.

Having established base camp, they split into two parties and Simpson and Défago strike out to Fifty Island Lake. As they head north Défago becomes increasingly nervous about the forest and this affects Simpson. Both feel that the forest is listening to them, watching their every move. They camp for the night. Défago quakes all night, huddled up against Simpson. As light dawns there is a sudden sound outside, a 'soft, roaring voice close outside the tent, overhead rather than upon the ground, of immense volume'.[17] The voice cries the name of Défago, and the Canuck, unable to withstand the call, rushes screaming from the tent and vanishes. Simpson hears the cry of the voice dying into the distance along with the anguished cries of Défago.

Simpson tries to follow Défago's tracks. He sees Défago's stride getting larger and larger and alongside it prints of some beast of unimaginable size. Simpson eventually finds his way back to Cathcart. The Doctor tries to bring the voice of reason to the situation, saying that Défago had implanted the idea of the Wendigo in Simpson's mind and that this was therefore all part of a waking dream. As they search for Défago, though, Cathcart's view changes. He believes the Wendigo is the Call of the Wild and that Défago has become consumed by it. Suddenly they hear a rush of wind and a cry. Hank cries out for Défago to come back and there is a sound like a heavy body falling and crashing through the trees. Then Défago is before them, but not the Défago they knew. He is as if some vampire has sucked away his spirit.

In 'The Wendigo' Blackwood wrote the equivalent of his signature tune. He spelled out his own life experience. Blackwood had sold his soul to nature. He had seen and heard the Wendigo and was now its slave. But with Blackwood there was one vital difference. The Wendigo had rejuvenated Blackwood. The Wendigo may have meant that Blackwood was lost to the civilized world – he was never really ever a part of it again – but it was not the Wendigo that had sucked Blackwood dry. New York had done that. Blackwood's Wendigo was mankind. It had taken him away for nearly ten years and finally spat him out for his return to England. But he was lost to the world. Nature had claimed him now, and always would.

The Quebec trip was Blackwood's last major expedition in Canada. By the time he returned to New York he was becoming homesick. A few months earlier, at the end of April, the Kintores had passed through

New York at the end of an extensive tour through South and Central America. Hearing of their travels Blackwood felt he was becoming confined in North America. He had seen many wonders of the New World, but now he yearned for the Old World. He wanted to see Switzerland again and explore other countries. Old Louis told Blackwood he should see his mother again before she died. It was a timely message. Lady Kintore's eldest son, Ian, had died the previous August aged only twenty. It was a poignant reminder of mortality. Blackwood was talked into believing he had redeemed himself. He had a respectable job and had overcome his problems.

Moreover Speyer needed a different kind of manager now. His wife was looking after the town and country homes, so Blackwood's work there had diminished. Speyer had become a senior partner in the family bank, and he needed a more senior financial manager, which did not interest Blackwood.

Blackwood had considered joining Roosevelt's Rough Riders in June 1898 as they embarked for Cuba in the Spanish-American War. Everyone advised Blackwood against it. It seems strange to imagine that Blackwood would even consider going to war, but it was the spirit of the age, and seemed more heroic than sensible. However, he caught a severe bout of typhoid fever and was seriously ill for much of the summer, by which time the Rough Riders heroics were over. The journey to the Canadian wilderness was doubtless adequate compensation, but it was clear that throughout 1898 Blackwood was ready to move on.

He had saved enough money to pay for the journey back. Kintore promised he would secure work for him when he returned. There was also a possibility of work arising with a colleague, James Hatmaker, whom Blackwood had met through the banking business, and this would develop in a year or two. Blackwood also felt he might be able to turn his hand occasionally to free-lance writing. He produced a few literary review columns for the *New York Times* under the heading 'About Bookmen' and he sent ahead of himself the story 'A Haunted Island' to *Pall Mall*.

With these sales and the promise of more work Blackwood took the plunge. He left New York on the *S.S. Cymric* on 22 February 1899, waving goodbye to Old Louis at the harbour. Nine days later Blackwood saw the outline of Ireland form on the horizon. 'The sight of it was a hundred times more poignant than he had imagined it

8

Magical Moments (1899–1903)

I

It's easy to imagine the tears of joy as Blackwood was welcomed back to the bosom of the family – a genuine 'return of the prodigal'. The homecoming may well have been how Blackwood described it in *The Education of Uncle Paul*, where Paul Rivers (a thinly disguised Blackwood) feels shy, awkward, embarrassed, and it requires the homely naturalness of his kin to set him at ease.

Blackwood had not seen his immediate family for nine years. His mother, though only fifty-four, looked a good ten years older. She deeply missed her husband, and the strain of his loss and keeping the family together had taken its toll. She lived at Parkfield, at Harrow in Middlesex (now in North London). Of his three sisters, Ceci was thirty-six and already looking middle aged, and Beatrice, whose thirty-third birthday was on 17 March, had gained considerable weight. Only Ada, who at twenty-eight still acted young and spritely, did not seem to be touched by the pressures of life.

Algernon's brother, Stevie, now thirty-one, was in poor health. The illness that had struck him down before Algernon went to Canada, had left him bronchial and weak chested. It showed in his face, which was thin, drawn and prematurely lined. He was working as a company secretary in the City and lived at Gillingham Street, near Victoria.

And of course Algernon himself had changed considerably. He had always been thin, tall and gangly. He had gained some weight since his lean years, but always remained gaunt. His hair was receding with male-pattern baldness. His skin was heavily freckled and was well weathered due to his regular outdoor life.

Blackwood would certainly have visited his father's grave at Kensal Green cemetery in West London. Who can tell what emotions this stirred. It had been over five years since his father had died, and Blackwood had moved on. He had survived New York. He had made good to some extent. He was what he was. No one was going to change Blackwood now.

Blackwood found lodgings first at 5 Langham Chambers, near Portland Place, and then at 37a Sussex Street in Belgravia during 1900, before settling at 28 Halsey Street near Cadogan Square from 1901. It was close to his sister, Beatrice, who lived in Moore Street, which backed on to Halsey. It was also close to the Berkeley Hotel where the Kintores stayed when in London. Algernon met them regularly because he adored his half-sister and particularly her two daughters, Ettie and Hilda Keith (now twenty-four and twenty-three) who had been his life-line through correspondence during his darkest days.

Initially it was one long round of parties, renewing old acquaintances, and settling into a new life. The Kintores, when in London, were great theatre-goers and Blackwood joined them regularly. There were also frequent dinners at the Carlton Club or the Bath Club or the Berkeley Hotel. Blackwood found himself back into the social calendar.

What also cheered Blackwood was that his friend from Toronto, George Wrong, came to London for a week, as part of his extended holiday in Europe. He arrived on 9 June 1899 and took lodgings in Chelsea. Blackwood took him on a tour of the City and, on the 15th he accompanied Blackwood to see his mother and then went for a long walk in Richmond Park. Wrong noted in his diary about the 'interesting conversation'.

This exhilarating honeymoon period lasted for several months. The horrors of New York steadily receded into a dream, but they never went away. Almost immediately upon his return Blackwood began to write a memoir of his experiences. They later served as the basis for *Episodes Before Thirty*, but they no longer survive. Some of them he shaped into separate articles, which he sold to a few magazines. 'A Spiritualist Camp in New England' went off to *Macmillan's*, ''Mid the Haunts of the Moose' to *Blackwood's* and 'Summering in Canadian Backwoods' to *Longman's*. These are still essentially reportage with a strong personalised element, but they are a far cry from the writing he would soon turn to. He also wrote a few additional book columns for the *New York Times*, including one on Kirkcaldy and another on Matthew Arnold.[1]

The urge to write gradually took hold. Perhaps now that he was back in comparative safety among those he loved he was able to relax the shutters he had built around him in order to survive in New York. With those shutters open Blackwood found the 'accumulated horror' of those years starting to leach out. It became a 'habit and delight to spend my evenings composing yarns on my typewriter, finding more pleasure in this than in any dinner engagement, theatre or concert'.[2]

Hilda noted in her diary on 21 January 1900 that she 'went to Algy's rooms with him and he read me his new story. Full of imagination.'[3] Several stories were completed by now. It may have been 'A Case of Eavesdropping', which he sold to *Pall Mall Magazine* (December 1900), or 'The Listener', which was written in 1899 according to an annotated copy that survived in Blackwood's papers. 'The Listener' is one of Blackwood's best early stories. It is interesting, biographically, because its opening probably reflects Blackwood's life at that time. Even the dates may be relevant. It is told in diary form and begins on 4 September with the narrator having at last found suitable rooms. He states his income was £120 a year, far less than the £400 a year Blackwood had been earning in New York, but close to the £2 a week he claimed he was paid in the City. Of most interest is that he records his work:

> articles; verses for the comic papers; a novel I've been 'at' for three years, and concerning which I have dreams; a children's book, in which the imagination has free rein; and another book which is to last as long as myself, since it is an honest record of my soul's advance or retreat in the struggle of life. Besides these, I keep a book of poems, which I use as a safety valve and concerning which I have no dreams whatsoever.[4]

This closely parallels Blackwood's work. The articles I have already listed. I know of no published poems from this period, though Blackwood was frequently writing verse, some of which appeared in his later novels. The 'record of my soul's advance' was probably the scrapbook and account that he kept of his New York days and which eventually formed the basis of *Episodes Before Thirty*. The novel could be *A Flying Boy* (the original of *Jimbo*), to which I shall return shortly.

As for the children's book, I suspect that was something called *The Children's Secret Society*. This story had been submitted to the publisher John Lane in July 1900 but by October he had heard nothing. His sister Ada, who had helped with its transcription from shorthand notes, enquired after it, only to learn that John Lane had returned it but it had been lost. Blackwood was anxious to trace it, not only because the original shorthand notes had been destroyed, but because an Edinburgh publisher had shown interest. He placed an advert in the newspapers and thankfully the lost manuscript was found. However, it must also have been rejected by the Edinburgh publisher (he does not say which one) as the book never appeared. It's possible this story was an early version of *The Education of Uncle Paul*, as that involves an initiation into a children's secret society.

Unlike Blackwood the narrator of 'The Listener' has few family connections and is alone in the world. But like Blackwood, he is afraid to give his imagination too much rein, for fear of the horrors it might unearth. The narrator is alone in his lodgings except for the landlady and her family. Over time he finds the rooms becoming disagreeable. Blackwood takes us slowly but cautiously over the threshold into the mental and physical disintegration of the narrator as he falls prey to the ghostly presence in the house.

At this same time Blackwood completed *A Flying Boy* which, as *Jimbo*, became his fourth published book. Jimbo is a young and imaginative child. He has a brother and several sisters, though the only one to take a prominent part is his sister Nixie. Jimbo's father, a retired colonel, believes that Jimbo requires special attention and employs a governess, Miss Lake. On land adjoining his father's estate is an old, empty house, that Jimbo believes is haunted, not by ghosts but by 'bad things'. Miss Lake, pretending to join in the child's imagination, develops the horrors of the Empty House saying that in charge of all these things is the 'Inmate of the House' who may one day capture Jimbo and hold him prisoner. This frightens the wits out of Jimbo. One day while out playing Jimbo is tossed by a bull and knocked unconscious. In his delirium he believes he is trapped in the Empty House. He undergoes a series of adventures, always menaced by the Inmate and the Bad Things until the governess comes to his rescue. The only way to escape from the house is to fly. He still faces many perils but at last summons the strength and courage to fly from the house and return home. With that he awakes and all is well.

Blackwood later stated that the characters of Jimbo and his sister were based on children he once knew. Jimbo reappears in later novels, and I believe he is then based on the child of one of Blackwood's cousins, whom I shall discuss later. I believe the original Jimbo is a childhood development of Blackwood's alter-ego Jim Shorthouse.

The novel is full of subtexts. In his childhood Blackwood was trapped in a deeply religious house, trapped by an evangelistic fervour that allowed him no self-expression. In Toronto he was trapped in business, by the failing dairy and the failing hotel. The hotel was a major millstone. He hated the concentration of humanity, and it went against his original temperance principles. New York was the greatest pit of all. There Blackwood sank to the depths of despair out of which he had to struggle.

At the start of Jimbo's entrapment he finds himself torn between two figures. There is the dark, cowled Inmate of the House, sinister and fearful, the personification of Fright. And there is the governess, Miss Lake, his ultimate saviour. Shades of Blackwood's own evangelical terrors are obvious, but there are other comparisons. Blackwood was himself constantly torn between these opposing factions. On the one side was the rebellious Blackwood who wanted to explore the unknown, including its dark shadows. On the other was the family figure of Algie, who never wanted to harm people and always liked to help. Then again there was the young Blackwood who had never really wanted to grow up. In many ways Blackwood never did. He remained a 'Peter Pan' at heart. He did not want to lose his childhood wonder and innocence, but he was being pulled into adulthood, pulled into a world he was ill equipped to face. Then there was the man who needed to earn a living but was forced into work that he seldom enjoyed whilst Blackwood wanted to be in the wilds of the world, escaping from everyday toil and as free as the birds.

All of these tensions feature in *Jimbo*. The child enters the Gallery of Memories, which seems to go on for ever, and the sheer weight of memories drags him down. In fact everything threatens to drag him down and hold him to Earth: the fear of failure, the memory of the past, the association with things around him. To fly he has to free himself from all these things (which was part of Blackwood's Theosophical instruction) and concentrate on escape and freedom.

Blackwood began to submit *A Flying Boy* to publishers. It was rejected by fourteen publishers before Macmillan bought it in 1909. Little wonder then, that with this manuscript constantly being returned over the next few years, Blackwood saw little point in collecting together any of his stories for submission as a book. He wrote them for relaxation and his own amusement. Writing was therapeutic, and even if there was no financial gain, it gave him considerable satisfaction. Only a very few were submitted to magazines. In addition to 'A Haunted Island' and 'A Case of Eavesdropping', both published in *Pall Mall*, he had a typical boys' story, 'The Last Egg in the Nest' published in the *Boy's Own Paper*.[5] The remainder just accumulated in a cupboard.

II

Upon returning to London Blackwood had secured a job courtesy of Lord Kintore. It was a job in the City with a company promoter, akin to his work as a private secretary. Blackwood had no interest in it at all, and viewed his employers as swindlers – probably because he never understood business and financial practices. He only ever regarded the job as a stop-gap. His wage was a meagre £2 a week. He was waiting for James Hatmaker to establish his business, but that was taking a little longer than planned.

In the meantime Blackwood indulged himself. In June 1900 he began another of those vagabond holidays, one that would inspire perhaps his greatest story, 'The Willows'.

On 6 June 1900 he and Wilfrid Wilson (1875–1957) left London bound for Donaueschingen in the Black Forest. Their canoe had been sent ahead by freight and they followed by train with a gypsy tent and such limited equipment as they needed. Wilson was a tall, strong man, six years younger than Blackwood[6]. He was a man of private means, descended from the wealthy banker Christopher Wilson (1765–1845) of Abbot Hall and Rigmaden Park in Kendal, in the English Lake District. I am not sure exactly how they came to know each other. Mary Jennings, Wilson's housekeeper from the 1940s and 1950s, believed they had met in Canada, as a branch of the Wilson family lived in Ontario. Wilson, in any case, travelled widely. Wilson's elder sister, Julia, had married Rear-Admiral Edward Inglefield[7], who had been involved in the relief of Khartoum and whose father was the famous Admiral Sir Edward Inglefield (1820–1894). The Wilsons and Inglefields had probably been known to the Blackwoods for some years, because when Hilda Keith refers simply to 'W. Wilson' in her diary in June 1900, she doesn't need to note who he was.

It had been their intention to do the full journey to the Black Sea, but they soon realized that that was too ambitious. Their progress was slow, hindered first by weeds and then by a series of rapids and weirs. They made it to Imendingen by the end of the first day and Kallenberg the second. The locals all thought they were crazy, convinced they would never make it even as far as Ulm in such a flimsy canoe, though it was a very graceful and easily controlled craft. Nevertheless, Blackwood had underestimated the power of the rapids and rather than risk the canoe in the more turbulent waters they carried it over the rocks. Their first downpour came at the end of the third day at Sigmaringen. They sheltered under an overhanging cliff. The next day the rain-swollen river was running fast. Although it meant they travelled fast it also made the rapids and weirs more dangerous. At Riedlingen the force of water was such that they fell while carrying the boat across the weir, but thankfully with no serious damage. They made it to Ulm the next day, 13 June, camping just outside the town.

They stayed at Ulm for a week before they set off on 19 June. The Danube, joined by the Iller in full flood, carried them along at a fast pace. They braved the rapids at Neuberg and the whirlpools at Ratisbon, and even shot the weir at Pleinling. It was all good *Boy's Own Paper* adventure. Another week brought them to Passau and a few days later to Vienna. By now it was early July and Vienna was packed and hot. Neither Blackwood nor Wilson relished the idea of spending more than a couple of days in lodgings.

Disaster struck as they came to leave Vienna. As they were loading their canoe it was caught in the current and swept away with all their provisions and equipment. The canoe crashed into a row of barges and turned over, and their goods floated away. Some sank irretrievably but thanks to the quick action of the bargees and townsfolk with boat hooks and poles, most items were saved. Alas, the canoe's bow was smashed. Fortunately a local carpenter was able to repair the boat in a few hours and they were soon scudding along the river into the wild and lonely countryside towards Hungary.

Beyond Pressburg (now Bratislava) the Danube splits into three streams and the main channel, heavy with water, had flooded wide. As they were swept along they had to avoid many side channels and lagoons into which water was foaming. They also had to avoid many low, sandy, willow-strewn islands, some of which the water almost covered. The power of the water was so strong that Blackwood expected the islands to be swept away.

This was the territory of 'The Willows'. Soon after their return from the trip Blackwood wrote about it in 'Down the Danube in a Canadian

Canoe'[8]. Through this it is possible to see how closely 'The Willows' follows Blackwood and Wilson's trip. Blackwood is the unnamed narrator whilst Wilson is transformed into a Swede. Seeking camp for the night they land on one of these willow-strewn islands, about an acre in size. They had already heard legends about these islands, and another man who passes them in a boat gives the sign of the cross. Undeterred they make camp. The wind continues to gust so that there is a constant roaring through the branches of the willows. The wind keeps the sky clear of clouds and later the full moon rises. The narrator begins to feel the isolation of the place as if it is a frontier with an alien world, 'a world tenanted by willows only and the souls of willows'. He becomes convinced that they are trespassers on the island and that the spirits are against them.

They eventually settle down for the night but the narrator is woken after a couple of hours. Climbing out of the tent he sees the shapes made by the tracery of leaves and branches against the sky. The more his eyes adapt he becomes aware that there are swirling, shifting shapes forming a great writhing column rising from earth to sky, a vortex of beings. 'I seemed to be gazing at the personified elemental forces of this haunted and primeval region,' he reflects in awe.

As the night continues the narrator finds himself buffeted and invaded by the powers of the place. The next day they find the canoe has been damaged. It takes all day to repair it and they have to face a second night on the island. Now the powers, feeling twice invaded, double their force. All night the travellers face the onslaught of the primeval powers and it is only by great strength of will that they survive. The next day they find the body of a peasant at the edge of the island. They suspect he too must have strayed too close to the vortex of power and had been dealt with.

Blackwood focuses on the power and psychology of a single location and suggests what would happen if this place, isolated and far away from civilization, had become a frontier between our world and another. In 'The Psychology of Places' Blackwood mentions how one of his companions on his travels always went through a ritual-like process when establishing camp as if to appease the gods. He also warned against ever camping on the edge of anything, because this is a frontier between forces.[9] How would the guardians of that world treat us? What would they be like? – powers beyond our comprehension, living at a different rate of vibration, and only discernable at the intersection of the two worlds.

How much of this was simply imagination? Blackwood's years of meditation and study had heightened his awareness of nature and the world beyond our normal comprehension. In his article about the trip, written six years before the story, he recalled:

> About sunset the clouds broke up momentarily and let out a flood of crimson light all over the wild country. Against the gorgeous red sky a stream of dark clouds, in all shapes and kinds, hurried over the Carpathian mountains, and when we went to bed a full moon cast the queerest shadows through the tossing branches.

That night Blackwood's sensitivities were drawn to that image and his mind created a story of two individuals helpless against the growing anger of an alien world.

All critics hold this story in high regard. E.F. Bleiler says that it 'is one of the classics of supernatural fiction; in the opinion of some it is the finest single short story'.[10] Jack Sullivan brackets it with 'The Wendigo' and acknowledges that Blackwood had created 'at least two authentic masterpieces'.[11] H.P.Lovecraft ranked it alongside Arthur Machen's 'The White People' as the finest tale of supernatural horror ever written.

The story's potency comes from the fact that Blackwood could draw it from life. He lived and breathed that story because he was there, and had experienced such otherworldliness. The power is in real life. His imagination clothed it in sensations of awe and wonder.

Although 'The Willows' was not completed until six years after this expedition, the experience lived with him and must have grown in the imagining. That the experience came within two years of the events that inspired 'The Wendigo', his other acknowledged masterpiece, shows that by now Blackwood's spirit was sharply attuned to the majesty of Nature and was storing images and experiences that would soon flow from him in a torrent.

III

It was soon after his return from Hungary, and while he was still chasing the lost manuscript of *The Children's Secret Society* that Blackwood turned to a real Secret Society, the Hermetic Order of the Golden Dawn, courtesy of his acquaintanceship with W.B. Yeats.

When Blackwood had returned from America he registered his membership with the London Lodge of the Theosophical Society. He was officially accepted on 5 May 1899. The London Lodge was almost autonomous and was presided over by Alfred P. Sinnett (1840–1921), who was vice president (under Olcott) of the International Theosophical Society. Annie Besant was a frequent visitor. Yeats was also a member, though his enthusiasm had waned. Yeats was more interested in the study of magic, and the Esoteric Section of the T.S. had not satisfied this. He found the Hermetic Order of the Golden Dawn more instructive and was initiated into that Society in March 1890.

Through Yeats, Blackwood discovered the work of George William Russell (1867–1935), better known under his alias Æ (derived from Æon). Russell was a true mystic. He was also a Theosophist. He was the hub around which the literary Celtic renaissance revolved. Upon encountering this movement Blackwood remarked: 'My breathless dog, Imagination, broke the leash and dashed off full speed into the unknown.'[12]

The record is silent on Blackwood's activities in the London Lodge, but since it was only a little over a year before he was initiated into the Golden Dawn it is likely that he undertook intensive studies in the society's Esoteric Section.

The purpose of the Golden Dawn was to study the occult sciences, especially Hebrew magic and the Kabbala. Ellic Howe (1910–91), an authority on the Golden Dawn, conjectured that it had been established as a deliberate counterpoint to Blavatsky's Theosophical Society, which was based on Oriental wisdom. The Theosophical Society had encouraged the study of Eastern occult sciences, but not as a primary aim. It was only through the establishment of the Esoteric Section in the society that these studies gained prominence. The Golden Dawn, on the other hand, was solely for the study and practice of Western hermeticism.

The origins of the Hermetic Order of the Golden Dawn centre around three individuals. It began with Dr William Wynn Westcott (1848–1925), a Freemason and student of the occult who in 1887 acquired a purportedly ancient manuscript written in cipher. The origin and authenticity of this document would later be called into question, just as with Blavatsky's letters from the Masters, and it was never fully resolved. Shrouded in mystery, and made all the more arcane by Westcott's later references to Secret Chiefs and long-dead magicians, the document was one that held strong appeal for those not wishing to ask too many questions.

Westcott devised a series of rituals, based on descriptions in the cipher manuscript and established a succession of grades through which the student could progress by study and examination. Upon entering the Order one was dubbed a 'neophyte' and, if deemed worthy, was initiated into the Zelator grade. One could progress, if successful, through Theoricus and Practicus to the Philosophus Grade. This was the highest grade in the First or Outer Order.

Next in importance was fellow Freemason (and fellow Rosicrucian), Samuel Liddell Mathers (1854–1918). Together with Dr William R. Woodman (1828–91), who was Supreme Magus of the Rosicrucian Society in Britain, these three became the Chiefs of the Isis-Urania Temple of the Golden Dawn, which was founded in London in 1888. Woodman played no major rôle in the Golden Dawn's activities and, though Westcott was its founding father, it was Mathers who was the driving force throughout the 1890s.

With his wife-to-be (married 1890), Mina Bergson (1865–1928), sister of the philosopher Henri Bergson, Mathers became a formidable power within the Order and devised a second series of rituals for the Second or Inner Order. Members of the Inner Order were the adepts. Mathers never held down a regular job, relying instead on the patronage of others to enable him to pursue his occult studies. His chief patron was Annie Horniman (1860–1937), daughter of the famous tea merchant, until he fell out with her. Most people fell out with Mathers after a while. He was self-centred and despotic, ruling the Golden Dawn like some military command.

Further temples were opened at Weston-super-Mare and Bradford in 1888 and Edinburgh in 1894. This last, known as the Amen-Ra Temple, was under the control of John W. Brodie-Innes. In 1894 Mathers moved to Paris where he established the Ahathoor Temple.

Membership in the Golden Dawn grew rapidly during the 1890s. In addition to Yeats and his close associates Florence Farr and Maud Gonne, other early members include Constance Wilde (the wife of Oscar Wilde), Violet Chambers (later Violet Tweedale), A. E. Waite, Allan Bennett and Robert W. Felkin.

Probably the most notorious member of the Golden Dawn was Aleister Crowley (1875–1947). He joined in November 1898, when he was twenty-three, but he made rapid progress through the grades to Philosophus by May 1899. He expected to progress beyond this into the Inner Order but was delayed. There were time restraints initiates had to comply with. Moreover, the London Temple had doubts about Crowley's intentions and were uncertain about admitting him to the Inner Order. Already Crowley was undergoing extra-curricular instruction from one of the Order's adepts, Allan Bennett. Crowley's friendship with Mathers, however, enabled him to be initiated as Adeptus Minor in the Paris Temple in January 1900. The London Temple refused to ratify this. This infuriated Mathers. He chose to undermine the London Temple by suggesting that the authenticity of Westcott's original documentation was subject to doubt. The London Temple split into those who were loyal to Mathers and the greater faction who opposed him. Mathers was threatened with expulsion.

Furious, Mathers sent Crowley to the headquarters of the Inner Order at 36 Blythe Road in Hammersmith. This was the start of what has been called 'the Battle of Blythe Road', which happened in April 1900. Crowley sought to take over the headquarters. Although he gained access and held it for two days (17th to 19th) the combined might of the London adepts, led by W.B. Yeats and Florence Farr, succeeded in his ejection, and the matter was taken to court. The end result was that Mathers was expelled from the Golden Dawn and this effectively brought an end to the original Order.

Yeats now rebuilt the Golden Dawn. He was elected as Imperator of the Isis-Urania Temple in April 1900 and a new hierarchy was established with Florence Farr and Annie Horniman. Soon after, Mathers, along with his supporters, established a rival Isis Temple in London in May. Crowley, in the meantime, set off in high dudgeon, to Mexico, via New York. Allan Bennett, who was in poor health, also left England for Ceylon.

This was the background only months before Blackwood joined the Order. It was Yeats who introduced Blackwood to the Order and he was initiated on 30 October 1900 at Mark Mason's Hall in Great Queen Street, Holborn. The ceremony was masonic in structure. Blackwood was blindfolded, dressed in a loose-fitting ankle-length black robe, tied at the waist with a triple-stranded black cord, and with red sandals on his feet. He was then led by a cord bound round the right wrist and held by his guide. This is representative of the initiate as the soul of the dead being led into the Hall of Truth by Anubis. As Blackwood was led into the temple, water was splashed on his hands and robe, as purification, and incense wafted around him. He was led to the altar where, kneeling, he took his oaths of secrecy and fraternity. He was then paraded around the temple before the blindfold was removed. Then three adepts took Blackwood through a series of questions and answers designed to explore his commitment to the Order and to begin the purification of his spirit. It was a fairly lengthy ceremony lasting about an hour. Only then was Blackwood formally adopted into the order, receiving his magical name. Blackwood chose *Umbram Fugat Veritas*, which means 'Truth puts the darkness to flight'.

Once initiated Blackwood began an intense series of studies, which ran through most of the next two years. The Neophyte Grade concentrated on astrological studies and the significance of the four elements, the Hebrew alphabet and the Kabbala. Only when he had passed an examination to assess his understanding was he allowed to progress to the Zelator Grade. This must have kept Blackwood well occupied. His niece Hilda Keith noted in her diary for 21 December 1900 that she 'Felt in the dumps. Waited for Algie after [tea] but he never came.'

Having risen to the Zelator Grade Blackwood undertook further studies, this time focusing on alchemy and the detail of the Hebrew Alphabet. Blackwood commented on this briefly in his radio broadcast, 'The Little People & Co.' in 1948. 'Among other things it entailed a knowledge of the Hebrew Alphabet, whose endless correlations contained a complete system of Hebrew Magic.'

Blackwood progressed as far as the Philosophus Grade, which was the highest in the First Order. By then he probably knew more about the Western tradition than he wanted. His interest had always been in the mystical aspects of the Kabbala and this he had satisfied. He chose not to progress beyond the First Order and become an adept.

Blackwood had joined the order almost a year after Arthur Machen (1863–1947), who was initiated in November 1899. Either Machen did not take his studies as seriously or he was less interested, as he did not progress beyond the Practicus Grade. It is likely that Blackwood and Machen studied together for some of this period, yet he could never be called a close friend of Machen's.

Interestingly, Machen did not warm to Blackwood's work either. During the 1920s, Vincent Starrett recorded this comment by Machen about Blackwood:

> I have met him a number of times in certain esoteric circles. He is a most interesting and amiable man. There is some difference perhaps in our approach to our subject matter, although I realize that we are lumped together by the reviewers. Tennyson, you remember, says

'the cedars sigh for Lebanon,' and that is exquisite poetry; but Blackwood believes the cedars really *do* sigh for Lebanon and that, Starrett, is damned nonsense![13]

Blackwood and Machen are the two best known authors of the supernatural who were members of the Golden Dawn. Whilst Machen used the results of his studies in some of his fiction, most notably in the novel *The Hill of Dreams* (1907), it was not so overt as in Blackwood's work. Blackwood brought the knowledge learned from the Golden Dawn to several novels, in particular *The Human Chord* and *Julius LeVallon*, and in the story collection *John Silence*, as well as several individual short stories.

The earliest of these was 'With Intent to Steal'. It's a first-person narrative by a man slightly younger than Blackwood. The only other character in the story is Jim Shorthouse, though this is not the incompetent, accident-prone Shorthouse of the earlier stories. It's a man of about fifty, who has travelled the world and is vastly experienced. He is, in fact, a precursor to John Silence. Even the initials are the same, as is the description of the man, with his personal magnetism, his suntanned face and his black beard. The story reveals that a black magician had escaped capture by hanging himself in an old barn, but his spirit returns periodically to prey on the living. Shorthouse tries to exorcise this spirit but nearly falls victim to its power but for the narrator intervening. Throughout the story Shorthouse discusses the occult and uses such phrases as 'elsewhere and otherwise'. This is a term Blackwood employed often, including as the title of a story. It refers to another plane or dimension hidden from normal human awareness but where spirits or other powers may be found.

There is an interesting passage where Shorthouse illuminates how he came to terms with his past and reflects Blackwood's own anxieties.

> Until a man has deliberately turned and faced for himself the fiends that chase him down the years, he has no knowledge of what they really are, or of what they can do. [. . .] Until you have faced these emotions . . . and made them your own, your slaves, you have no idea of the power in them – hunger, that shows lights beckoning beyond the grave; thirst, that fills with mingled ice and fire; passion, love, loneliness, revenge, and – *fear*.[14]

Although it has not been possible to identify the specific background to this story, there is no reason to doubt that Blackwood could have been involved in an episode of this kind. Since his return to England he had continued his unofficial investigations of haunted houses on behalf of the SPR. One such early investigation was of Brockley Court, twelve miles west of Bristol. The case had been reported to the SPR in September 1900 and an official investigation was carried out in January 1901. Blackwood's name does not appear in any of the SPR files, and I suspect he investigated it separately soon afterwards, as he mentions it in a draft note for a radio talk. The Brockley Court case did not feature the spirit of a black magician but of a white monk, with eyes of fire, that would drag the unwary from their bed.

Blackwood's scribbled note mentions that he investigated Brockley Court with Edwyn Bevan. Bevan (1870–1943) was the son of evangelist parents, like Blackwood. Blackwood knew him before he went to Canada. Bevan's sister Gwendolen had married Ian Keith-Falconer, the brother of Lord Kintore in 1884, and the strong family ties of the Blackwood/Kintore families would have brought them together on several occasions. It's likely that Bevan accompanied Blackwood on earlier investigations. Despite his strong Christian background Bevan was noted for his liberal outlook on life. He was described by his *Times* obituarist as having 'a most unusual beauty of character spreading its unconscious influence' and of having 'a quite striking fairness of mind'.

While Blackwood had been in America, Bevan had excelled as a scholar. He could talk French, German and Italian fluently, and knew Greek, ancient Egyptian, Latin, plus some Hebrew and Indian tongues. Having obtained his degree in 1892 Bevan spent a year travelling in India and another year at the British School of Archaeology in Athens and also in Egypt.[15] Bevan became recognized as one of Britain's greatest Hellenists. He wrote extensively on the ancient Greek world as well as on Christianity. Somehow he managed to merge these two passions without conflict. On 25 April 1896 he married another of Blackwood's childhood friends, Mary Waldegrave, the daughter of Lord Radstock. Edwyn and Mary Bevan were close friends with Blackwood in the years immediately after his return from New York. From 1901 they lived at Banwell Abbey in Somerset (just a few miles from Brockley Court). Blackwood often visited them there.

A second story, 'Smith: an Episode in a Lodging-House', draws on detail from Blackwood's Golden Dawn studies. It is told in Blackwood's most straightforward style – that of a storyteller, a doctor in this case, recounting a past experience. His story is set in Edinburgh when he was a medical student and concerns Smith, the man who has the room above his. Smith is a short, thick-set man of about forty-five, with a large head and shoulders but small hands. His eyes were also large and strangely luminous. Smith talks to the doctor about his knowledge of Hebrew and borrows the doctor's rare Hebrew Treatise, going unerringly to it on the bookcase. Smith was clearly studying ancient Hebrew wisdom. The doctor explains that:

> The words he asked me to pronounce for him were probably 'Words of Power' which, when uttered with the vehemence of a strong will behind them, were supposed to produce physical results, or set up vibrations in one's own inner being that had the effect of a partial lifting of the veil.[16]

One of Blackwood's earliest studies, and one that keenly interested him, was the subject of vibrations. It formed the basis for his novel, *The Human Chord*. The following, which comes from a Golden Dawn ceremonial textbook, echoes Blackwood's commentary almost exactly:

> Certain names or 'Words of Power' when properly vibrated or intoned attract certain energies which are associated with them. A technique known as the Vibratory Formula is a method by which divine names and words are spoken forcefully and with authority in a 'vibration.'[17]

The doctor becomes sensitive to powers around him and is eventually drawn to Smith's room. He forces his way in. At first he feels the room is full of people, or at least 'beings'. There is a circle drawn on the floor, complete with curious designs, which is smoking and filling the room with clouds. Smith is cowering against the wall. The doctor helps Smith back into the circle where, 'by the power of his voice, behind which lay undoubtedly a genuine knowledge of the occult manipulation of sound,' Smith controls and then dominates the powers that he has unleashed.

This episode is remarkably similar to one purportedly experienced by Aleister Crowley at his flat at 67/69 Chancery Lane in London in 1899. Crowley recorded that he had left the flat one evening after an experiment during which he had summoned up forces. When he returned he found the room in total disarray and 'semi-materialized beings marching round the room'.[18] The description of Smith could well fit Crowley, apart from the age. If there was anything anyone remembered about Crowley, it was his sinister, overpowering eyes, his large head and powerful shoulders.

Both 'With Intent to Steal' and 'Smith' were written within a few years of Blackwood's initiation into the Golden Dawn. Both were first published in *The Empty House*. Two other stories also date from around this time, although in terms of book publication their first appearances were many years apart. 'The House of the Past' was first collected in *Ten Minute Stories* in 1914 but had been published ten years earlier in *The Theosophical Review* (15 April 1904). It is an evocative mood piece taking place in a dream which takes the narrator to an empty house, rather like *Jimbo*. The house is full of memories, not just of this life but of past incarnations, and the narrator realizes that he has to face these ancient memories and atone for past actions. Blackwood reworked much of this into 'The Insanity of Jones', which first appeared in *The Listener* in 1907. Jones is Mr Ordinary. He is contemptuous of psychic research and has no interest in Theosophy. Yet he is aware that he has lived past lives. He also becomes intuitively aware that the manager at the office where he works was someone he had encountered in a past life. As the story progresses Jones meets a man who is a reincarnation of an old friend called Thorpe, and Thorpe takes Jones, as in a dream, to the House of the Past, where he becomes aware of a past life in which the manager had murdered Jones. Jones takes retribution in this life. To normal humans, Jones is seen as mad and a murderer.

Blackwood's association with the Golden Dawn was doubtless affected by a scandal that rocked the organization soon after he joined. This was the Horos affair, and it takes us back to the origins of the Golden Dawn. Following the discovery of the Cypher Manuscript, Westcott claimed that he had made contact with a German Rosicrucian adept, Fraulein Sprengel who was, purportedly, chief of a German occult order called Die Goldene Dammerung. Sprengel had authorized Westcott to found an English branch, and thus the Golden Dawn was born. Later Westcott revealed that Sprengel had died in 1891, but there were those who came to suspect that Sprengel might still be alive, assuming she had existed at all. Over the years there were several attempts to trace Sprengel, especially by Dr Felkin, but all to no avail.

In 1899, Mathers met an unsavoury American couple who went by the names of Madame and Theo Horos.[19] To Mathers's surprise, Madame Horos whispered to him that she was really Fraulein Sprengel. Mathers was completely duped. He encouraged their activities and, at length, they settled in London and established the Order of Theocratic Unity in 1901. There was little, if any, theocratic purpose to their Order. It was a means whereby Theo Horos (then thirty-five) could obtain young girls for his own sexual gratification, aided and abetted by his wife (then fifty-two), who took pleasure through voyeurism.

Mathers had by now come to his senses but was still considering how best to deal with the Horoses when the law caught up with them. They were arrested on 20 September 1901 when one of the victims brought charges of fraud. Three weeks later another victim, Daisy Adams, brought charges of procurement and rape against Theo Horos. When the case came to court, the tabloid press revelled in it, holding up to ridicule the rituals within the Horos's Order. Since these had been appropriated from the Golden Dawn the connection was soon made and the members of the Golden Dawn were made to appear sordid. Several members left the Order.

In a futile attempt to salvage its reputation the Golden Dawn was renamed the Order of Morgenröthe (the German equivalent) in June 1902. At the London Temple Yeats stood down as Imperator and was succeeded by Dr Robert Felkin, but it was followed by another leadership struggle. At its annual general meeting in May 1903, when Brodie-Innes expected to be elected head, A.E. Waite seized control. After months of bitter wrangling the society split in two. The original organization under Felkin and Brodie-Innes became the Order of the Stella Matutina, whilst Waite established the Independent and Rectified Rite (later the Holy Order of the Golden Dawn). It was reconstituted in July 1903. Both Machen and Blackwood followed Waite into his new order, though by now both were losing interest[20]. Machen was later very dismissive of the Golden Dawn. 'As for anything vital in the secret order, for anything that mattered two straws to any reasonable being, there was nothing of it, and less than nothing,' he wrote in his autobiography[21], adding 'the society as a society was pure foolishness concerned with impotent and imbecile Abracadabras'. Blackwood agreed. When he reviewed Machen's book he said, 'His opinion of a certain Secret Society he once belonged to for the study of alleged magical things is justified, both in its contempt and humour.'[22]

Blackwood treated it more like a club where he was able to meet like-minded individuals and discuss esoteric subjects. Contact with the Golden Dawn had given him a new network of acquaintances. He remained friends with A.E. Waite and others such as W.B. Yeats and the artist William T. Horton. There were also new members, such as Edith Sawyer and her husband William Harcourt Sawyer, who joined in 1909. William rapidly rose through the ranks to become an *adeptus minor* in January 1910. Edith was the daughter of an evangelical friend of Blackwood's father, George Hanbury, and it must have been satisfying to Blackwood to win over this childhood friend.

The Road to Freedom (1903–08)

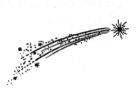

I

It does seem slightly bizarre that two of Britain's greatest writers of supernatural fiction, Algernon Blackwood and Arthur Machen, should be connected by dried milk. The Golden Dawn connection is logical – but dried milk?

With Machen it was really malted milk – Horlick's in fact. A.E. Waite, when not spending time planning to take over the Golden Dawn, was the London manager for the Horlick's company. He managed to talk the firm into issuing a magazine. This was not a house or trade journal, but a formal 'popular' magazine along the lines of *The Strand* or *Pall Mall*. *The Horlick's Magazine and Home Journal* first appeared at Christmas 1903, dated January 1904, and has some grounds to claim it was the first English magazine of fantastic fiction and the occult. Apart from Waite's own extensive contributions, it ran stories and features by Evelyn Underhill, Edgar Jepson and Arthur Machen. Virtually all of this was occult or supernatural. In fact it ran Machen's much eulogized short story, 'The White People' (January 1904) and serialized 'The Garden of Avallaunius' (July to December 1904), which was later reprinted as *The Hill of Dreams*. Alas, the magazine was not to the public's taste, and it folded after eighteen issues in June 1905.

Since Waite knew Blackwood well at this time and Blackwood was starting to write short fiction, it is surprising that he contributed nothing to the magazine. Even though he had already published four supernatural stories in magazines, he was not pursuing obvious markets.

Maybe Blackwood felt he should not be contributing to a rival market, for at that very same time he was also managing a dried-milk company.

The seeds for this had been sewn in New York. When he was private secretary for James Speyer, Blackwood inevitably met other private secretaries, and he became friendly with the private secretary to Cornelius Vanderbilt, James R. Hatmaker (1866–1930). One of Hatmaker's duties was to check out promising young inventors and acquire rights to their inventions. Through Blackwood he met Alfred Louis who advised Hatmaker on patent law. Around 1898 Hatmaker entered into discussion with Dr John Augustus Just (1854–1908), a chemist in Syracuse who believed he had mastered the process for producing powdered milk. Scientists had been experimenting with this for years but doctors and scientists believed that many of the essential salts and vitamins in milk were destroyed in the process. Hatmaker, though, believed he was on to a winner, but was not yet in a position to risk large-scale production.

When Blackwood returned to England it was with a view to developing an English branch of Hatmaker's organization. That opportunity arose in 1903. Cornelius Vanderbilt had died in September 1899. Hatmaker had benefitted substantially under his will (by $10,000). This helped provide the working capital to develop the business and undertake the necessary tests. Furthermore Hatmaker became engaged to a rich divorcée (they were married in November 1903). The Just–Hatmaker company was established in New York for the production of dried milk. A patent was granted in England in March 1903 and that November Hatmaker established a company in Leadenhall Street, London, to import dried milk into England and Europe. Hatmaker, who settled in Paris with his new wife, set up further outlets in France and New Zealand.

It was now that Hatmaker brought Alfred Louis back to England, as he valued his legal mind. Blackwood found him lodgings in Great Russell Street, opposite the British Museum. It was a delight to have his old mentor back with him, even though he was more irascible and less forgiving. Louis's legal mind was still sharp, though the years of deprivation was taking its toll on his health. After only a few months in England he yearned to be back in New York, missing his contact with the circle of artists and poets. He had far fewer friends in England and far too many sad memories. Nevertheless he remained, and continued to serve as Blackwood's spiritual guide for many more years until his mind went.[1]

The original managing director of the Dried Milk Company, Albert Martin, stepped down on 3 March 1904 and Blackwood took over. Considering that Blackwood was particularly inept at business and had failed twice in past undertakings, it is surprising that Hatmaker should trust him in this enterprise. It is true that Blackwood was now older and wiser, on the eve of his thirty-fifth birthday. Also, for the past year, Blackwood had been one of the directors of the Atlantic Club Syndicate, a company set up in February 1903 to promote and assist companies with connections on both sides of the Atlantic. Although short-lived (it was wound up in April 1904) it may well have been via this syndicate that Hatmaker was able to develop his company in Europe. More significantly, Hatmaker's enterprise was established on considerably better financial and business grounds than anything Blackwood had been involved in before. Hatmaker had done his groundwork. He had the finances, the distribution network, and the contacts. Blackwood just had to run the London business. In fact he had the equivalent job to Waite's at Horlick's.

Business blossomed. There was plenty of work to be done in establishing the product's name and identity and Blackwood was responsible for overseeing the promotion and advertizing as well as distribution and development of the business. Hatmaker had a good idea for a gimmick to promote dried milk.

There were those who believed that dried milk was not so nutritious as full-fat milk. Hatmaker wanted to disprove this. In 1906 he bought a young weaned colt, called Azote, and reared it solely on dried milk, plus some hay for roughage. It worked. The horse gained 825 pounds in weight in the 533 days since it was weaned, apparently a record at that time. Veterinary inspection showed that the horse was fit with good strong bones. Hatmaker decided to enter Azote for several of the classic races of the 1908 season, including the Grand Prix of Brussels, the French and English Derby, the French Grand Prix and the English St Leger. The horse ran only once in England, at the 1908 Derby on 26 May. Unfortunately the press reported the horse as something of a 'freak', which it was not. It began as a 200–1 outsider and unfortunately finished next to last. After that Hatmaker ran the horse only in France, where it did moderately well. It was retired after the season. But Hatmaker felt he had proved his point, and interest in dried milk increased. In fact his (or Just's) process for producing a skimmed-milk powder by drying skimmed milk over cylinders is still called the Hatmaker process to this day.

It was at this point in 1908, as the business was becoming established, when Blackwood decided to leave. Hatmaker went on to earn a fortune and died a wealthy man. Blackwood may well have mused in later lean years over whether he should have remained with Hatmaker. But Blackwood had at last seen the light. By 1908 he was a published author, gaining a reputation, though it was only by luck rather than design that this happened at all.

II

The initial burst of writing that affected Blackwood upon his return from New York lasted about two years. We know that he had already written 'A Haunted Island' before his return. Soon after he wrote 'The Listener' and 'A Case of Eavesdropping', and probably also 'The Empty House', 'Keeping His Promise', 'A Suspicious Gift', 'Max Hensig', 'Skeleton Lake' and 'The Strange Adventures of a Private Secretary in New York'. His experiences in the Golden Dawn inspired 'With Intent to Steal' and 'Smith', but I suspect these were not written until 1903 or later. His studies within the Golden Dawn would have absorbed much of his spare time for most of 1901 and 1902. Similarly running the London branch of the Dried Milk Company would also have eaten into his time from March 1904 onwards, for at least a year. During 1902 he wrote 'The Last Egg in the Nest' and towards the end of 1903 he wrote 'The House of the Past' and possibly 'The Wood of the Dead', inspired by his hiking in the West Country.

At Christmas 1903 Blackwood entered a story contest. The January 1904 issue of *Pearson's Magazine* announced a 'Storyette' competition for stories of between 1,000 to 2,000 words to be submitted by the end of February. (Rather oddly the magazine gave the deadline as February 31st.) The first prize was £10, the equivalent today of about £650. Blackwood's story was not typical of his work, but is typical of *Pearson's* lighter stories, especially for women. 'Testing His Courage', subtitled, 'the story of a quaint device' is a romance, and a story with a twist. Julia Mansfield is something of a feminist. She is in love with Mark Lister but is taken aback when he states his love for her. As he is about to leave for India, though, he believes he could not propose marriage. Julia reciprocates her love but says that Lister must prove himself by seeking permission from Julia's guardian, her gruff old aunt. Lister visits the aunt who refuses permission on the grounds that he would not have enough money to support her. Lister still professes his love and is about to write to Julia to see if she will still marry him without her aunt's allowance when the aunt reveals herself as Julia in disguise. It was all a test and Lister passes.

Blackwood did not win but was a runner-up and received £5. His story appeared in the September 1904 issue. This should have given him confidence to submit further stories, but apart from selling 'How Garnier Broke the Log-Jam' to the *Boy's Own Paper*, nothing else of significance appeared at this time. He may have sold a few slight stories. Ten years later, when John Murray assembled *Ten Minute Stories* from material Blackwood sent him, Blackwood discovered to his horror that they had used some early weak stories which he could not bear to see reprinted, and actually paid to have them removed. These stories were not identified, and may have been brief items syndicated through provincial papers.

Other stories later collected in *The Listener* were also completed around this time, certainly before 1906[2]. These include 'The Woman's Ghost Story', which reads as though it were written from direct experience from one of Blackwood's psychic explorations. This tale of a haunted house is related by a woman, and looks back at an investigation carried out some years before. 'In those days I was interested in psychic things,' the narrator says, as if she has moved on. Blackwood had, in a sense, also moved on by 1905. He was no longer regularly investigating haunted houses for the SPR. The woman visits a lodging-house, which she is told is haunted by the ghost of a woman who was murdered. When she arrives she meets a man whom she first thinks is the caretaker. She soon realizes it isn't and discovers that it is in fact the ghost of a man who became misanthropic, shut himself away in the house and killed himself. The spirit, which pervades the whole house and is thus everywhere at once, is desperate for someone to show it sympathy and compassion and thus release it from the world. The woman embraces the ghost and thereby exorcises it.

Both 'Testing His Courage' and 'The Woman's Ghost Story' are written from a woman's perspective. A further story, 'Miss Slumbubble – and Claustrophobia', is also told by a woman. It's a brief story about a woman who finds herself in a train carriage with the ghost of a suicide and who begins to feel suicidal herself. This female perspective could simply be because Blackwood was associating more closely with women now and, if so, there was one particular influence.

Mrs Kent, the widow whom Blackwood had met in New York, continued to visit Blackwood most summers after he returned to England. Sometimes she would stay at a hotel but usually Blackwood found her lodgings near him, in Moore Street. He saw Mrs Kent most evenings for dinner where they would continue the discussions they had years earlier on matters spiritual. On one occasion their discussion turned to astral travel and the possibility that an individual's astral self might meet another's whilst the body was asleep. They decided to set themselves a challenge whereby that night, as they fell asleep, they should concentrate on each other and see what happened.

As Blackwood tells the story[3], he returned to his rooms in Halsey Street, where he found a letter from his sister asking for help. He sent an immediate response that so distracted him that he forgot about his promise to Mrs Kent. He only remembered the next day when he visited her. Before he could explain his reasons for forgetting, Mrs Kent described her experience. Apparently in her dream she had struggled to contact Blackwood but without success. There was always a dark figure that blocked the way. She made one last effort, actually calling out his name in her dream. Then she heard a response, apparently from this dark figure, saying 'There's no good looking for him, because he's with his sister'. Blackwood suggested this may be an example of telepathy, but it remained in his file of 'oddities'.

There was one other oddity that Blackwood remembered. At that time Blackwood believed strongly in reincarnation, but Mrs Kent did not. Blackwood felt that because of his natural affinity with the outdoor life he may, in a former life, have been a Native American, or Red Indian as they were then termed. They reached no agreement despite an evening of friendly but at times heated discussion. By ten o'clock Blackwood got up to leave but as he headed towards the door he heard a noise behind him. He turned to find that Mrs Kent had risen and was calling out to him in a language he did not understand. As she came closer he realized she had taken on the form of an Indian squaw. It unnerved Blackwood and he hurried from the house, visibly shaken. It was two days before he next saw Mrs Kent, and he chose not to mention the incident. Yet when he arrived she immediately told him that the other night, as he left, he had made a strange sound as if he were ill. Mrs Kent had risen from her chair to help him, but as Blackwood turned at the door, he was no longer the same man. He was the same shape and height but now was the figure of a Red Indian.

When Blackwood came to write about this forty years later[4] he was uncertain how much he had embroidered his memory of the occasion, but he was still convinced something of this nature happened, and again put it down to telepathy.

These visits to Mrs Kent most evenings must have given rise to many ideas for stories, and it's possible that those he wrote from the female perspective originated in discussion with her.

In August 1905 Blackwood made another journey down the Danube.[5] This time they travelled in a flat-bottomed punt, 20-feet long by 3-feet 6 inches wide, which held four. This was not suitable for taking down the rapids from the river's source, so the journey was a more sedate one from Ulm to Budapest. Thankfully this time some of the photographs that Blackwood took survive as they were published alongside his articles[6]. One of these shows Blackwood manfully steering the punt with a long pole. His feet are bare, his trouser legs rolled up to his knees and his shirt sleeves up to the elbows. Even in black-and-white the picture shows how bronzed he is. What's left of his hair clings to the back of his head. Thankfully the pictures also reveal his travelling companions. They are clearly Wilfrid Wilson and Edwyn and Mary Bevan.[7]

The trip was not so eventful as the earlier canoe adventure, though again the wilderness between Bratislava and Komárno captured his imagination. It was on this trip that they found three drowned bodies in the river, one of them lying on a shingle bed, cast up by the flood waters. He refers to these drowned bodies in 'The Willows', which suggests that he did not complete that story until after this journey.

III

It was a chance meeting which now changed Blackwood's life for ever. Early in 1906 Blackwood was hailed in Piccadilly by his old friend Angus Hamilton. He hadn't seen Hamilton in twelve years or so since their days on the New York *Sun*. Hamilton's reputation had soared. He had been a noted war correspondent for the London *Times* and the *Pall Mall Gazette*, throughout the Boer War. He sent the despatches from the siege of Mafeking. He became a Reuter's correspondent on the Balkan problems in 1903 and the Japanese conflict with Russia in 1904–5. So important had been his reports that when he returned home in 1905 King Edward VII asked to see him in a private audience.

He had written a popular book on Korea and another on Afghanistan, which was to be his best-selling book.

Hamilton returned with Blackwood to his new lodgings at 31 Moore Street, which were also the London lodgings of the Bevans. They chatted over old times and experiences and Hamilton enquired whether Blackwood had kept up his short story writing. Blackwood revealed a cupboard full of manuscripts. Hamilton borrowed about a dozen to read.

Blackwood thought no more of it. Hamilton soon headed off to China for Reuter's and Blackwood probably thought that was the last he'd seen of his stories. Needless to say he was rather perplexed when, some weeks later, he received a letter from Eveleigh Nash expressing a wish to publish the stories in book form, and asking Blackwood to come and see him.

Unbeknown to Blackwood, Hamilton had sent the stories to Eveleigh Nash with a strong recommendation. Nash was a comparatively new publisher. He had formerly worked as a literary agent and then as adviser to the publisher Archibald Constable before setting himself up in business in 1902. Nash sent the stories to his reader Maude ffoulkes (1871–1949). She remembered the occasion well.

> That winter was memorable for me, inasmuch as it marked my discovery of the work of Algernon Blackwood under rather trying conditions of life. I was in the throes of a violent influenza cold when Eveleigh Nash asked for an opinion of a typescript, entitled 'The Empty House'. . . I was half inclined to leave it unread until I was better, but when I glanced down the first page I paused breathless, because it was suddenly borne upon me that this was the work of a genius![8]

She goes on to say that she was entranced, the cold forgotten, as she read every word. Her imagination had become so heightened that she almost screamed at the sound of her own sneeze, and kept the light on all night.

She hurried to see Nash the next day with great enthusiasm. She told Nash he must publish this book, 'because it will be a long time before you will ever meet with another Algernon Blackwood'.

Blackwood was at first annoyed that Hamilton had submitted these stories behind his back. Then he was alarmed at the thought of having a book in print. Blackwood visited Nash at his premises, then at 32

Bedford Street, off the Strand in Covent Garden. In due course a contract appeared, dated 24 September 1906. Nash agreed to pay Blackwood £25 for the exclusive right to publish the book in Great Britain, Ireland, its Colonies and Dependencies. Payment was due on publication, which was set for 24 November. This was a rather meagre advance, the equivalent today of around £1,600, but Blackwood was a new author and thus regarded as a risk. Moreover, Blackwood was none the wiser, and still somewhat shocked that anyone should publish a book of his. In the end he earned far more. The first print run of 750 copies sold out quickly. It was reprinted and started to earn royalties. There was also subsidiary income from colonial sales, and the book continued to be reprinted throughout his lifetime.

Blackwood owed a considerable debt to Angus Hamilton, yet he does not record ever seeing him again. Hamilton travelled widely as a reporter. In 1913 he unwisely decided to go on the lecture circuit, in the United States – unwise because although he had a fascinating wealth of stories and anecdotes, Hamilton was a nervous man with a stammer. This became all the more aggravated when, as soon became apparent, his tour was a failure. Tragically, Hamilton killed himself by cutting his throat in a New York hotel room on 14 June 1913. He was thirty-nine.

The cover of *The Empty House and Other Ghost Stories* was rather eye-catching. Bound in olive-green cloth with gilt lettering, it featured a ghostly figure outside an empty house with a 'To Let' board. We have already encountered all its contents.[9] Appearing just before Christmas it sold well. The Edwardian period saw the heyday of the English ghost story. Hilaire Belloc used this background as the basis for a long review of *The Empty House* in *The Morning Post*.

> Here on the table is a book of such a sort as does from time to time appear, making, one supposes, no particular pretence to fame, and yet exceedingly well done, because it is instinct with this national power, and everyone who has a shelf for the horrible in his library will welcome it and give it its place.[10]

The Academy had been one of the first to note the book's merit, calling it 'one of the best books of "horrors" since the appearance of Mr Bram Stoker's *Dracula*,' adding that 'it is the convincing manner in which they are told which compels admiration'.[11] *The Bookman* noted that:

They are written so vividly and with such plausibility of circumstance that these most supernatural incidents wear a matter-of-fact vesture of reality and are the more ghostly and the more grimly impressive because of their every-day surroundings.[12]

Praise followed praise, with *The Spectator* devoting a whole column to the virtues of the book. The degree of negative criticism was minimal. Blackwood was doubtless being oversensitive when he later remarked that 'What I may call left-handed compliments . . . flew wildly across a barrage of "faithful criticism".[13] Blackwood was encouraged. Deep down he must have been amazed. For the first time in his life he had done something that was a success and was appreciated. It had required someone else to act as a catalyst. Years later Blackwood reflected on the little things in life and wondered just what might have happened had he not been in Piccadilly at that moment and been seen by Angus Hamilton. Upon such minutiae do entire worlds revolve.

Nash was sufficiently satisfied with sales to commission a second volume. There were certainly already enough completed stories to assemble one without too much trouble. The contract for the next book of ghost stories, *The Listener*, again only offered an advance of £25, but the first royalties came through that autumn (1907) for the sales of *The Empty House*, which must have encouraged Blackwood further.

Blackwood began to consider his fortunes. Other changes were afoot. His mother's health, which had been delicate for many years, declined rapidly. She became diabetic. She spent most of her time at Ore, just outside Hastings, up on the cliffs near Fairlight, where the bracing sea air is still invigorating. This had long been a favourite place where she and Sir Arthur had spent many holidays. Their first son Stevie had been born there. Now the family gathered about her again. She passed into a diabetic coma and died on 30 May 1907. She was seventy-two.

Her estate was divided equally between her children. The estate had dwindled in the fourteen years since her husband's death as there had been so many family demands upon it. Algernon's share amounted to around £300 (today equal to about £20,000). Although not significant, it was more money than he had had since he squandered his father's remittance in Canada.

Blackwood now had a scent of freedom and you feel that one by one the ties around him were coming loose. Even his interests in the Theosophical meetings and the Golden Dawn were waning. The reputation of the Theosophical Society had taken a further knock in May and June 1906 with the revelation of possible child abuse by Charles W. Leadbeater, one of the society's foremost figures. It caused a number of people to dissociate themselves over the next few years, including A.P. Sinnett and Blackwood's friend G.R.S. Mead. Mead formed the Quest Society in 1908 of which Blackwood was a member.

His appearances at the London Lodge of the Golden Dawn also dwindled. Ellic Howe found the following reference in a letter from Robert W. Felkin to J.W. Brodie-Innes dated 2 March 1909, where Felkin wrote: 'With regard to Blackwood I have not seen him for years but he still works with S. R. & Co.'[14] S.R. stood for *Sacramentum Regis*, the motto of A.E. Waite.

If he needed any more encouragement, it came with the publication of *The Listener* at the end of November 1907. Once again *The Academy* led the critical response: 'Mr Blackwood has gone far towards fulfilling the promise of his earlier work and has given us something that deserves more than a passing notice.' The review, as did many that followed, highlighted 'The Willows' as being something special, where 'Mr Blackwood really shows what he is capable of'.[15]

Blackwood was on his way. He departed for a winter break in the Swiss Jura with a growing euphoria.

IV

Blackwood now gave serious thought to his next book. He tells us that the stories began as separate studies of various psychic themes, but Eveleigh Nash suggested he group them together under a common character and work on a 'bigger canvas'. Thus for the first time he attempted a unified volume. It was the real start of his writing career.

The character Blackwood created was originally called Dr Stephan. It was only later that the name John Silence was invented. This was when the book was complete and Blackwood, Nash and Maude ffoulkes were having dinner at Nash's home in Park Street near Grosvenor Square[16]. Nash was clearly uncomfortable with the name Stephan. Over dinner they cast about for a new one, and Nash suddenly said to Maude ffoulkes, 'Didn't you have some ancestor or other with the name of Silence?'[17] They settled on the name at once.

Blackwood had not set out to write a series of stories about a psychic or occult detective, but this arose naturally around the need to have a common link. However, this meant he had to rework some of the stories he had already written to include the Doctor, whereas he is central to the later ones. This gives you a rough sequence to the order in which the stories were written, which is useful to see the character's evolution. I believe that 'Ancient Sorceries' and 'Secret Worship' were the earliest written. Silence does not really have a strong role in either of these – he's just grafted on to the story in a final revision. We know that 'The Camp of the Dog' was the last to be finished because Blackwood said as much in his radio talk 'Two Holidays'[18]. That leaves 'A Victim of Higher Space', 'A Psychical Invasion' and 'The Nemesis of Fire' which were probably written all together (and probably in that sequence) during the winter of 1907/8.

The character of John Silence is most clearly introduced in 'A Psychical Invasion', which is the first story in the book, but a more composite picture grows as the stories develop. Some of the description helps us identify the real individual behind John Silence. The character is a clear development of the Jim Shorthouse of 'With Intent to Steal'. He is introduced as a man of independent means, an eccentric, who has chosen to become a doctor but is more interested in spiritual and psychic affliction than physical problems. He had undergone five years of arduous training during which time he disappeared from the everyday world. He was past forty, was sparely built, with gentle and worldly brown eyes. He had a close-cut beard, an almost translucent skin and delicate features, but an air of grim determination. Overall he has an aura of calming authority. You are safe in his presence, and he is spiritually strong even though he does not look physically strong.

The original edition of *John Silence* contained only five stories. 'A Victim of Higher Space' was dropped at the last minute because it was considered weak. It is closer to Blackwood's original idea of a discussion on psychic matters – in this case transportation through the dimensions, 'elsewhere and otherwise'. I suspect this story was the first Blackwood tried to write featuring the character (then Dr Stephan) and it remains more theoretical than practical. It presents Silence almost as a psychic Sherlock Holmes with his assistant Barker as a rather weak equivalent of Watson. Barker is dropped from the other stories. In both 'The Nemesis of Fire' and 'The Camp of the Dog' there is a more developed first-person narrator, just like Watson, called Hubbard[19]. These two stories were the last to be written and the ones that fit best the psychic detective model.

'Secret Worship' was discussed in Chapter 2, and 'A Psychical Invasion' in Chapter 5. 'Ancient Sorceries' is set in France in a small town where the inhabitants have a secret life. The whole town has become affected by a witch cult whereby they appear to turn into cats and witches at the time of the sabbat. 'The Nemesis of Fire' is set in an English country manor house that is under attack from a fire elemental brought to England with an Egyptian mummy. 'The Camp of the Dog' is a werewolf tale set on a Swedish island.

Every one of these stories is based on impressions gained by Blackwood at various locations. 'A Psychical Invasion' is based on a haunted house in Putney. Its key element, that of drugs causing the taker's consciousness to expand to become aware of an evil spirit, was based on Blackwood's experiment with cannabis in New York. 'Ancient Sorceries' came to Blackwood when he hiked through Laon in France one summer. Blackwood was entranced with the atmosphere of the town when he stayed at the Auberge de la Hure, and particularly by the presence and attitude of the local cats. 'The Nemesis of Fire' is set at Rempstone on the Isle of Purbeck in Dorset. This was the rented home of Edwyn Bevan, himself an Egyptologist, and where he had brought certain Egyptian antiquities. 'Secret Worship', is based on the Moravian School in the Black Forest. 'The Camp of the Dog' is almost certainly set on the island of Ängsholmen[20], forty miles north of Stockholm. Here Blackwood was one of a party of six who rented the island for a month during the late spring of 1908. In addition to Blackwood this party included Edwyn and Mary Bevan, the Bevan's gardener, and Edwyn's cousin and his wife.

So who was John Silence based on? Blackwood dedicates the book 'To M.L.W. The Original of John Silence and My Companion in Many Adventures.' Many people have assumed that the original John Silence has the initials M.L.W. and that, because of Silence's background, M.L.W. must have been someone in the Golden Dawn. Yet the surviving membership records of the Golden Dawn list no one with those initials.

We are after someone who was his 'companion in many adventures'. This person had to know Blackwood well, and to have shared many of his experiences over some of the last twenty years. Blackwood only ever dedicated books to people who were close to him. The real M.L.W. has to be near at hand. As further proof that this person was a close friend, his previous book, *The Listener*, had also been dedicated to M.L.W., though with no additional comment. This eliminates two individuals who have been suggested as M.L.W. The author Margaret L. Woods (1856–1945) and the HM Commissioner of Prisons Maurice Lyndham Waller (1875–1932). Woods inscribed the dedication of her novel, *The Invader* (1907) as 'by their grateful and affectionate friend, M.L.W.' Waller was a member of the Savile Club when Blackwood joined on 31 March 1908. At that time he was attending séances and had several psychic experiences. But there is no evidence that either of them were close friends of Blackwood or shared in his adventures. Neither did Waller know Blackwood before 1908 to warrant the dedication in *The Listener*.

There was one person close to Blackwood who also fits the description of John Silence. A man who was a first-class honours student, who had travelled the world including India and Egypt, and who shared many adventures with Blackwood, from investigating haunted houses, to punting down the Danube, to camping on a Swedish island. And this man was also a member of the Savile Club and had been one of Blackwood's proposers. This was Edwyn Robert Bevan.

However, Bevan's initials are clearly not M.L.W. Nor by any ingenious cryptography could you make them so. But there was another companion of many adventures who shared them with Bevan and Blackwood, ever since childhood – Bevan's wife, Mary Waldegrave. It is unfortunate that Mary appears to have no middle name, certainly not on any official documentation, nor do I know of any pet name of Blackwood's. She was almost always called Daisy. Yet she remains the most likely candidate.

There is no doubt that the Bevans were close to Blackwood for many years. Blackwood's esoteric studies and Bevan's knowledge of ancient Egypt brought together two intertwined threads that prompted ardent discussions about subjects they shared in common.

Also of relevance is that Mary Bevan's cousin, Guy Marston, who actually owned Rempstone, was interested in the occult and was training as a neophyte for the Golden Dawn though was never initiated. He was a friend of Aleister Crowley and invited Crowley down to Rempstone in May 1910, along with Crowley's new mistress, Leila Waddell and their friend, the mystic Victor Neuberg. They conducted a ceremony that purportedly invoked the demon Bartzabel. It consisted of Crowley's chanting and Neuberg's dancing accompanied by Waddell on her violin. Marston was so fascinated with the ceremony that he suggested it be performed publicly, without the final invocation. The idea appealed to Crowley and he developed the ceremony as a series of seven rites, called the Rites of Eleusis. They were first performed publicly before a paying audience in Victoria Street, London in August 1910[21]. Blackwood did not attend this performance as he was in Switzerland.

I do not know whether Marston held other ceremonies at Rempstone prior to Crowley's in 1910, or whether the Bevans or Blackwood were at any time involved. There is no reflection of this in 'The Nemesis of Fire'. The house described in 'The Nemesis of Fire' is a combination of Rempstone and the Bevans' former home at Banwell Abbey. The location, including the Twelve Acre Wood and the stone circle, and the general picture of the house, all fit Rempstone. The name Rempstone itself is believed to be derived from *Roundstone*, referring to the stone circle. However, the underground tunnel featured in the climax to the story is at Banwell Abbey. Mary Bevan wrote about it in her reminiscences as follows.

> It had an underground passage communicating with the beautiful chapel which was just outside our grounds, a little 13th Century chapel, an ilex, supposed to be eight hundred years old – altogether a fascinating and romantic abode, which I shall never cease regretting that we sold. During our time there, in spite of the odd stories told about our predecessors, we never heard or saw anything supernatural. Then, when some Americans bought it, they were so impressed by the 'spirit of evil' in it, that the wife threatened to divorce her husband unless he gave the house up.[22]

William James, the American philosopher and brother of the author Henry James, and a leading light in the SPR, stayed at Banwell Abbey. Both he and his wife firmly believed the place was haunted.

What is strange is that neither Edwyn nor Mary Bevan makes any reference to Blackwood in their writings. There was little opportunity for Bevan to do so in his books, but Mary did compile a set of memoirs. It was never published, but a copy survives. Called 'Odd Memories of an Ordinary Person', it runs for sixty-five typewritten pages. Although it mentions the Dufferins, her father's evangelism, and their holidays, it never once mentions Blackwood. It does go into detail about the holiday on the Swedish island that she describes in almost the same words as Blackwood, and yet she does not mention him. It seems that by the time Mary came to write this, in 1927, she and Blackwood had become distanced. It is a shame that no Bevan archives have survived, which might have revealed more.

The character of John Silence was not the first occult detective in fiction. The idea of a specialist investigator of the occult had been developing in Victorian fiction since the time of Samuel Warren's *Passages from the Diary of a Late Physician* as far back as 1833. Interestingly that investigator was also a doctor. The idea was given greater impetus by the creation of the S.P.R. and the growing interest in spiritualism. Joseph Sheridan Le Fanu introduced the character of Dr Martin Hesselius as a link between stories he had written and later collected as *In a Glass Darkly* (1872). But the first authentic ghost hunter in fiction was Flaxman Low, created by the mother-and-son team of Kate and Hesketh Prichard (writing as E. and H. Heron). He featured in a series of stories run in *Pearson's Magazine* during 1898–9 and published as *Ghosts* in 1899. The series had been well received, as it was given the atmosphere of 'true' stories.

Unlike the Prichards, whose stories are deliberately sensationalised and full of pseudo-occultism, Blackwood brought an authenticity to his stories, and John Silence emerges as a real character, just like Sherlock Holmes. In fact the stories appealed to many of the Holmes fans as well as the growing number of devotees of weird fiction.

Nash could see the potential in the book and the character and decided to give it major promotion. When Nash received the final copy for the book at the end of May 1908 (two days after the Derby in which Azote ran) he offered an increased advance of £40, but with the usual royalty arrangement of 10 per cent up to 750 copies and 15 per cent thereafter. He added that he planned to advertize *John Silence* on the buses. Five weeks later he wrote again to Blackwood, mentioning a major poster campaign, and revising his offer. The £40 stood but the royalties were now 10 per cent on the first 3,000 copies sold rising to 15 per cent thereafter. He added, 'I shall require to sell about 3,000 copies to financially justify my advertizing experiments.' Blackwood suggested an all-round royalty of 10 per cent if the advance could be increased to £50. Nash agreed. This shows Blackwood's continued lack of confidence in potential sales. For the sake of an extra £10 up front, Blackwood lost out to several hundred pounds in royalties over the years.

John Silence was published in 16 September 1908. On that day the horsedrawn omnibuses in London carried posters announcing the book.

There were also over 200 posters on hoardings all around London. They all depicted the mysterious Doctor looking out of a window over a darkened city with the slogan, 'JOHN SILENCE – the Most Mysterious Character of Modern Fiction'. The campaign featured the largest illustrated book poster to appear on hoardings in England at that time. It demanded attention and it worked. The first printing of 3,000 copies sold out by Christmas, earning Blackwood royalties of £90, the equivalent today of almost £6,000. It went through many further reprints, remaining in print throughout Blackwood's life. It was also the first of Blackwood's books to be published in the United States, by J.W. Luce in Boston on 20 March 1909. There was also a pirated American edition from Brentano's the following year.

The book not only gained Blackwood a public and a reputation as an author, it also gained him some notoriety as a 'black magician'. Soon after the book appeared a distant relative (I've never been able to identify who) circulated a story that Blackwood was involved in black magic, and that he was involving children in a sacrilegious ceremony with candles and holy water stolen from St Paul's Cathedral. Blackwood had to resort to the law to curtail these libels, but apparently pirated editions circulated for some while. The allegations were doubtless no more than the retaliation of a distant relative, proud of Sir Arthur's reputation and saddened by the son's fall from evangelical grace. They were probably by someone with no knowledge of the Golden Dawn other than what circulated by gossip and rumour. Whatever it was, it did Blackwood no harm. No doubt then, just as now, a little notoriety helped boost sales.

In fact, as his fame grew, Blackwood found readers contacting him – or John Silence – for help or comfort. Blackwood was not always in a position to respond, although he did follow up some of the more interesting cases. He was no longer interested in haunted houses or ghosts, but cases of psychic affliction intrigued him. Unfortunately, there is very little record of which cases he did undertake. Most of these are in later years when he felt more competent in dealing with individuals. The following is an intriguing example, made all the more frustrating in that half the letter is missing. It bears no year but simply 'May 28th' (probably 1909 or 1910), and came from a man from Christchurch in Hampshire.

> Does 'Dr Silence' still exist? & if so where & how can one reach
> him? I have vital intense need of some such seer & psychic worker

& it is very urgent. You say the original is 'M.L.W.' Please *do* bring me into professional touch with him. Only to one deeply skilled in hypnotic & will-power, & the forces of the unseen . . . [*page missing*] The average clairvoyant is worse than useless. As an utter stranger to you I make this appeal. In your kindness let it not be for nothing & please quickly.

If Blackwood responded to a letter he would sometimes scribble in shorthand on the back what he intended to say, but this one has nothing. It is odd though that this letter survived among Blackwood's papers when he usually destroyed them. It suggests he may have pursued it, and it may have even provided an idea for a future story.

In another letter a Cornish woman, who signed herself simply L.W., wrote directly to 'Dear John Silence' saying that she felt an affinity with him and hoped someday to meet. She wondered whether until that day, they could meet telepathically and set aside 10.00 p.m. every night in the hope of hearing from him. As the letter carried no address there was no other way of contacting her.

Even though there is no follow-up to these letters they open the door just a crack into Blackwood's growing public persona. His works were a comfort and inspiration to many.

John Silence made Blackwood's name and reputation. It is still the book he is best remembered for to this day. Most important of all it gave Blackwood freedom. Freedom to travel, to write, to enjoy life. For Blackwood life really did begin at forty. And with that freedom the last remaining shutters were removed.

By one of those bizarre coincidences that dictate the direction of life, just three days before the publication of *John Silence*, John Just, the inventor of the dried-milk process, died. Hatmaker used this as an opportunity to reorganize[23], and Blackwood took that as his chance to break free of the business. There was nothing now to hold him back. With his mother's passing, he had no further filial responsibilities. He had no contractual obligations to Hatmaker. The next five years would see Blackwood produce the most remarkable body of supernatural fiction ever written.

10

The World of Uncle Paul (1908–10)

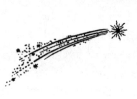

I

Before Blackwood left for Switzerland for the winter, he set a few wheels in motion. If he was serious about earning a living as a writer, he needed to make sure not all his eggs were in one basket. Income from books is sporadic. If he sold one new book a year plus royalties on past books he might gross £100 a year, though more likely average £60–£70. He needed a more regular income for day-to-day expenses, and what better than to sell stories to the magazines and newspapers.

London proliferated with fiction magazines at this time. The premier title was *The Strand*, but there were many others including *Pall Mall, Pearson's, The Royal, The London, The Windsor* and *Lady's Realm*. Blackwood's sister Ceci had sold a couple of stories to *Lady's Realm*[1]. Most magazines paid around five guineas for a short story (equal to about £340) or up to ten guineas for longer stories. Newspapers paid two or three guineas for a short story or sketch. If Blackwood sold about one story or article a month, he could almost double his writing income, and he was likely to sell more than that.

Blackwood had previously sold a few stories to *Pall Mall* and he placed a fourth with them, 'The Kit-Bag' (December 1908). It's similar to the stories in *The Listener*. The story is set in Bloomsbury, where Alfred Louis had his lodgings. The narrator is Johnson, a counsel's private secretary, who is relieved to get away after a murder case so he can go on holiday to the Swiss Alps. Johnson goes back to his rooms in Bloomsbury to pack, and a big canvas kit-bag is sent over. Johnson fancies he hears shuffling sounds, then catches quick glimpses of someone on the stairs, and sees the kit-bag move. It transpires he has been sent the wrong bag. This was one that the murderer had used to stuff the dismembered body in.

As he planned to live abroad, Blackwood needed an agent in Britain to market his stories. He approached London's premier literary agency, A.P. Watt in Norfolk Street off the Strand. Their formal agreement was signed in May 1909, but Blackwood probably consulted them before he went to Switzerland in January. The arrangement was that Watt's would handle all Blackwood's 'literary work', but not his 'journalism', which he would deal with direct. Blackwood anticipated writing regular articles and sketches for newspapers and could liaise with these specific markets himself. Watt's had the harder task of securing sales to the more prestigious magazines.

Blackwood secured two major markets that would carry most of his short pieces over the next few years. One of the leading evening papers in London was the *Westminster Gazette*, a highly influential Liberal paper edited by John A. Spender (1862–1942). Angus Hamilton had been its special correspondent in 1904. It ran a short story every day, sometimes, two, and enjoyed the occasional unusual story. Blackwood started his fourteen-year relationship with them with 'The Secret', published in the edition for 7 November 1908. In later years Blackwood regarded these stories as hackwork, just bread-and-butter stories – he usually got two guineas per story (now about £125) – and most do not compare with his inspired work. Yet they reveal another side of Blackwood – the storyteller who can create an amusing episode or anecdote out of a wisp of puffery. 'The Secret', for instance, takes place in a London restaurant where the first-person narrator meets a friend. This nameless friend is always vague, forgetful, hesitant, dreamy. It takes ages for him to get to the point. In this story he has a wonderful idea for a play, which he tells the narrator, whom he swears to secrecy. Needless to say, the play's never written, because the friend forgets all about it.

Two other early stories are worth a note. 'Stodgman's Opportunity' (5 December 1908) is Blackwood's observation on the dullness of 'civilized' man. Stodgman is a writer totally lacking in imagination. He can produce technical articles with the minutest detail but is oblivious of the wonders about him. On a train journey he dreams that the train is about to take him out of this world into another. He wakes, and though he tells this dream to others, in the most boring way imaginable, he has no idea what to do with it and forgets about it. An Irish author who heard the story uses it for a wonderful story called 'The Night Journey' which Stodgman reads and wonders how people get their ideas. Interestingly, the dream story is a little like what would eventually become *The Starlight Express*.

'The Story Mr Popkiss Told' (24 December 1908) was one of those queer stories that Blackwood enjoyed so much, ideally suited as a fireside Christmas tale. Mr Popkiss is taking a train into Surrey when he becomes aware of a train running parallel to him. The train compartment is empty, just like his own, except for one man. He realizes the other man is himself. His double warns him to leave the train. This he does at the next station and discovers that the train crashes a few miles further on, with fatalities.

Later in 1909 Blackwood developed his other regular market, *Country Life*. He used this upper-class society magazine more for his mood pieces and nature stories, such as 'Pines' and 'Clouds and Mountains'.

Before his agreement was finalized with A.P. Watt, Blackwood dusted off his unsold manuscript of *A Flying Boy*, now retitled and revised as *An Imaginative Boy* and sent it to Macmillan's. He was delighted to find that Frederick Macmillan was keen to publish it. This all happened at breathtaking speed. Blackwood submitted the original typescript on 16 November 1908. Macmillan's made their offer on 27 November, subject to a few revisions. The contract was signed on 30 November. Blackwood submitted his final copy on 3 December and the page-proofs turned up just before Christmas. Blackwood worked on the proofs over Christmas, returning them on 27 December. The book was published in February 1909. After eight years of trying and fourteen rejections, *Jimbo*, as it was finally retitled, took flight like a dream. The critics loved it. 'I have rarely read a book that has given me such unqualified delight,' wrote Sidney Dark in the *Daily Express*. '*Jimbo* is a delicious book,' concluded E. Hallam Moorhouse in the *Daily Chronicle*, adding, 'and one that should be read by all who long at times to escape from this working-day world, into a region of haunting and half-remembered dreams.' Even the reviewer in the *Times Literary Supplement*, who disliked the title, felt that it was a 'prose-poem' where 'the reader will find evidence of a fine imagination'.

Jimbo remains a delight and is one of Blackwood's forgotten treasures. It is dedicated to A.S.B., which were the initials of

Blackwood's younger sister, Ada Sydney Blackwood. Blackwood remained close to Ada all his life, and only she, of all his three direct sisters, retained a youthful spirit at heart. *Jimbo* is a wonderful demonstration of how to overcome the trials and anguish of a childhood where expectations upon the child are far greater than the child believes they are capable of. It's a message as relevant today as ever.

Blackwood must have felt extremely pleased with himself as, in early January 1909, he took the boat-train out of Victoria heading for Folkestone and the Continent. His escape was complete.

II

Blackwood settled at Bôle in the canton of Neuchâtel in the French-speaking Jura. He had loved this place since his youth when he stayed with Pastor Louis Langel to learn French. Many of his old friends were still there, including the pastor. Also here were his cousin, Arthur Hobart-Hampden, with his wife Henrietta and their children. Arthur Hobart-Hampden (1864–1952) was the grandson of the 6th Earl of Buckingham. Arthur's father, Charles, had married Lucy Wright (1828–1913), Algernon's aunt and his father's half-sister.[2] Arthur had married Henrietta Fetherstonhaugh (1865–1916), pronounced Fanshawe, from a Protestant family in Wicklow, Ireland.

They stayed most of the time at a small *pension* or boarding house run by the village postmaster Fritz Grether and his wife Olga (who became Madame Jequier in *A Prisoner in Fairyland*). It was renowned for its conviviality and good food. Life was relaxed and entertaining. It was also cheap. Blackwood could live there for just five francs a day. The *pension* occupied the upper two floors of the house, with the ground floor being the post office. Blackwood had a room at the top that overlooked the village and the surrounding Jura hills. It was right next door to the church. From his window Blackwood could watch the hustle and bustle of village life. If the weather allowed he would sit in the garden and play with his cousin's children.

Blackwood never really had a routine. He would spend some part of each day writing, but did not let this get in the way of enjoying life. Every day he would venture out somewhere, either for a walk to Lake Neuchâtel, or up through Rochefort into the mountains, or through the gorge of the little river Areuse. Everywhere to Blackwood was a delight.

Blackwood was also a fine skier. He had learned in his youth but had not had much opportunity to practise until recently. Skiing was becoming very popular among tourists bringing in whole new waves of British and Americans as the mountains opened up with the railways. Blackwood had been among the first wave of these. He was experienced and could teach people, though he never did that professionally. He would on some occasions act as a guide and take people on particular routes, but he kept the favourite ones to himself. 'The poetry of ski-running has yet to be written,' he wrote within a year of settling in Bôle. Ski-ing gave Blackwood even more freedom, the closest he could get to flying.

> The analogy of flying . . . seems to me a far truer one than that of the dipping and rising of a boat. The motion is even, undulating, sinuous; and the effect of taking a new slope suddenly must be surely akin to what a bird feels when its stretched wings know the pressure of a new air-current from below. The earth seems to lift one up; then, as the slope curves over, to recede again and carry one with it.[3]

Except for the years of the Second World War, Blackwood went skiing every year for the next forty. He was fit, agile and supple. Everyone has said how excellent Blackwood was at doing the sudden telemark turn-and-stop. Those who knew Blackwood in Switzerland all have the same memories. He would take you far up into the mountains, to the special snow-fields and slopes that he knew. He would dig a pit in the snow, and fill it with twigs and pine cones. He always insisted that sandwiches and snacks were wrapped in greaseproof paper as he would use this to begin the fire. He would tell a story while you sat around drinking hot tea or soup. Then he would lead you on a downhill ski. Not always fast – it wasn't a race or an exhibition. The point was to become as one with nature as gravity took you silently over the snow and back down towards the valley.

By the time Blackwood returned to the *pension*, usually for a hot soup or a meal, it was often late afternoon. He would deal with his post, and spend the evening writing or chatting with friends.

More often, of course, Blackwood was on his own, and it was while in the mountains, sometimes in a cabin, or sometimes just out in the rocks, that he would produce his daily quota of writing. Inspiration struck Blackwood when he was as one with the world, and his best work would be written – at least that first magical draft – in some remote area, usually high up in the mountains. A short story or sketch for *Westminster Gazette* or *Country Life* could easily be dashed off in one of his lunch time reveries in the mountains and typed up later. He kept a notebook in which he would sketch out a story or a chapter during the day as he wandered through the hills and forests. One day Blackwood lost this notebook and with it all his story notes. That night, he dreamed he saw his notebook lying just beneath the surface of a small stream. He remembered this in the morning and after a moment's reflection recalled the spot. After several hours he found the place and there was the notebook. Somehow his subconscious must have noticed the pad fall, even though it had not registered on his conscious mind[4]. Just two or three brief stories or sketches a month kept him in food and rent. During 1909 he completed such minor stories as 'Entrance and Exit', 'A "Trunk" Call', 'The Invitation', 'The Lease', 'Faith Cure on the Channel' and 'Up and Down', all for *Westminster Gazette* plus several mood pieces for *Country Life*.

Blackwood's main work, during the the first half of 1909, however, was to finalize his quasi-autobiographical novel, then still entitled *Between Yesterday and Tomorrow* but soon to become *The Education of Uncle Paul*. It is one of only a handful of books that Blackwood dedicated to fellow spirits rather than to individuals: 'To all those children between the ages of eight and eighty who led me to "the crack"; and have since journeyed with me through it into the Land "between yesterday and tomorrow".' This then was not a children's book, but a book about how children view the world and how an adult, who has not lost that childhood imagination, can share that perception.

The Education of Uncle Paul follows the transition of Paul Rivers as he returns to England on a year's sabbatical after twenty years as a woodsman for a lumber company in America. He is now forty-five and has inherited a fortune from his aunt. Unlike Blackwood, Rivers is an orphan with a younger sister. Like Blackwood, Rivers is a loner with a spiritual affinity for nature. He is shy, since he seldom had the company of people, and this makes him wary of his return as he has no idea how to mix with people and feels his child-like innocence will be interpreted as immaturity. These same tensions had festered in Blackwood's mind for years before he returned to England, but now he had recognized the benefits of his life.

> It never occurred to him that in this simple thrill that Nature still gave him he possessed one of the greatest secrets for the preservation

of genuine youth. . . For with the majority, such dreams die young, brushed rudely from the soul by the iron hand of experience, whereas in his case it was their persistent survival that lent such a childlike quality to his shyness, and made him secretly ashamed of not feeling as grown-up as he realized he ought to feel.[5]

Paul's widowed sister, Margaret, has invited him to come and stay at her house in Dorset. Paul feels shy and clumsy but this is soon overcome by his sister's welcome. She leads him to the Gwyle wood, an area that she finds damp and chilly but was somewhere her husband, Dick, had loved. Paul feels himself coming alive there. The pine trees, the wind, all talk to him. 'The wood is full of whispers', he says. Paul discovers that one of the children, Nixie, also loves the wood and often plays there.

There are three children (plus a young baby, who scarcely features in the book). The eldest child is Nixie (real name Margaret Christina). She's about ten, with golden hair, like sand, whom Paul instantly sees as some kind of water sprite, 'a creature of the elements'. Her younger brother is Jonah (Richard Jonathan), who's about eight, and a little unsure of himself. The youngest is Toby (Arabella Lucy), who is cheeky and audacious.

Nixie, Jonah and Toby were based on real children whom Blackwood knew, but unlike the children portrayed in *A Prisoner in Fairyland*, these are more composite. He drew chiefly on the younger children of his cousin, Arthur Hobart-Hampden. Nixie was Aileen, Jonah was Vere (a future Earl of Buckinghamshire), and Toby was Lucy. Aileen was the most spritely, and Blackwood adored her. There was an elder brother, Arthur, who was sixteen and away at school. There may be some of Arthur in Jonah, since Arthur had only been five when Blackwood had returned from America, and had first worked on this book (which I believe began life as the now lost *The Children's Secret Society*).

Paul's sister, Margaret, could well have been based on Blackwood's elder sister Beatrice. Although she had never married and had no children, there is a melancholy about her that hangs over Margaret in the story. Beatrice had failing health and lived some of the time in Cannes, in the south of France, where the climate was more suitable. She had lived close to Blackwood in London but, since their mother's death, had moved to a farm at Breamore, near Salisbury. Elements of that farm may also feature in *Uncle Paul*.

There is an immediate affinity between Uncle Paul and Nixie and the novel explores their growing relationship. Paul undergoes an initiation into the children's world of make-believe and 'aventures'. This makes him unbelievably happy because now he has a world in which he can express himself in his innocent way without being ridiculed. This 'initiation' delights Paul more than any formal initiation into a secret society. The Golden Dawn and the Theosophical Society may have opened doors for Blackwood to worlds of ceremony and arcane lore, but this paled into insignificance compared to the world of childhood, which is the greatest treasure of all. As Blackwood grew physically older, so his mind and imagination retained the purity and innocence and, above all, wonder of childhood.

Now initiated into their circle, Uncle Paul is allowed to join the children on their 'aventures' and the first is one of the most exciting in all of Blackwood's fiction – the Vision of the Winds. Nixie and Paul sink through the earth in their dreams and find themselves in a lost primeval dream-forest before the dawn. Their consciousness feels absorbed by the trees. As dawn approaches so the winds begin to rise and they take the form of multi-coloured ribbons that seem to hang beside the trees but with the coming light rise and stream out. Warmed by the rising sun these winds change colour so that they watch a chorus of coruscating streamers greeting the sun.

The episode is vividly described. It could be interpreted as a drug-trip. Blackwood certainly had achieved heightened awareness on drugs, as we have seen, but he also stated that after his experiment with cannabis he never touched drugs again. Blackwood did not need such aids for his visions. After twenty years affinity with Nature, Blackwood's awareness was enhanced simply by his close association with the elements. There would have been countless nights when Blackwood watched the world awake around him with the dawn. He would have sensed the rising winds, heard their chorus and imagined their brilliance. The ability to think in colours and sounds was part of the initiation required for the Golden Dawn in order to increase the acuity of the senses. Through association, Blackwood could conjure up the image of a colour in relation to a smell or a sound.

We know that Blackwood's colour perception was not highly developed – he wrote as much when he saw the Northern Lights for the first time. This is not to say that he was colour-blind, although there were those who believed he was, but that his awareness of colour was abnormal. It could be that Blackwood experienced synesthesia. This is a condition where sensory perception may shift so that sounds are seen as colours or smells as shapes.[6] During his delirium in New York in the winter of 1892 Blackwood might have temporarily suffered from this, as it was then that he first described seeing the winds 'changing colours as they rose and fell, attached to the trees, in tenuous ribands of gold and blue and scarlet. . .'.[7] Apparently a number of mystics have shown signs of synesthesia, including Helena Blavatsky, Frederic Myers and Annie Besant. Gustav Fechner, whose work Blackwood studied, had also conducted experiments into *farbenhoren* ('colour-hearing').

Later in the novel Rivers reflects on what is happening to him. 'By a curious process known only to the poetic temperament, he passed on to *feel with* everything about him – as though some portion of himself actually merged in with the silence, with the perfumes of trees and garden, with the voice of the little tapping leaf.'[8] This ability to dissolve one emotion or sense with another was the basis of the education of Uncle Paul. It inspires Paul to write a poem called 'The Winds of Inspiration', a rare example of Blackwood's poetry.

The story continues through other sensual adventures culminating in the journey through the crack at midnight to the land between yesterday and tomorrow. It's a place of dreams, where time continually renews itself and where things, emotions, opportunities, moments that came and went and were lost can be rediscovered. Here live the ghosts of broken things waiting to be found and mended. In Blackwood's world the 'Crack' is available to anyone who has the right temperament – or better still, the imagination. As people grow old they lose their childhood innocence, and lives become more complicated. Through the 'Crack' they can recover that innocence and make the world a simpler and better place. However, you have to be 'thin' to get through the crack, which means you can only escape there in those moments when your soul is not burdened by life's complications. 'Every one's thin somewhere,' Nixie tells Uncle Paul, meaning there are those moments of supreme happiness when you can transcend the mundane world.

Perhaps the most remarkable aspect of *Uncle Paul* is that what reads superficially like a children's book is really a deep mystical adventure. Because he appeals to your innocence and the simple things in life Blackwood is able to reform life's basic building blocks into an alternate view of what he calls 'the Realities'. This is the term Blackwood always used for that part of the world which is beyond our everyday understanding but which controls and guides our existence. What we term God is an aspect of the Realities. They are what we may believe of as supernatural, but which are the engines of the world.

As a consequence even when tragedy strikes, Blackwood is able to show this as a wonderful new 'aventure'. Nixie falls ill and dies, but Uncle Paul is able to meet her again through the 'Crack', only this time she has become a true elemental spirit, and she continues his education by bringing him a greater understanding of the Realities. Death is not simply the Final Adventure, it is the most Wonderful Adventure of all.

Uncle Paul is so enchanted with this heaven 'through the Crack', that he writes a book called *Aventures of a Prisoner in Fairyland*. A few years later Blackwood did write that book, at a time when the world needed dreams, when it was riven apart by an approaching world war. But Blackwood himself would have a lot more 'aventures' before he produced that book and its aftermath, *The Starlight Express*.

At one point in *Uncle Paul*, Rivers meets Joan Nicholson, the niece of his sister's dead husband. Paul finds an affinity with Joan and though he doesn't fall in love with her, he enjoys her company and her work. She works for a charity looking after 'lost children' and Paul throws himself into a new life working for abandoned and destitute children. The references to 'lost children' inevitably brings comparisons with the immortal play *Peter Pan* by J.M. Barrie. Both stories are about captured and eternal youth, and the spirit of *Peter Pan* recurs in many of Blackwood's books. It had first been performed at the Duke of York's Theatre on 27 December 1904 and has been performed somewhere every Christmas since. Blackwood was a great theatre-goer and would have seen the play from the start, though curiously he never wrote about it.

The Education of Uncle Paul was published by Macmillan's on 16 November 1909. The critics were fascinated by the book. Although most reviewers found the character of Nixie a little hard to believe, that did not stop them recommending it. *The Standard* commented that at present Blackwood's imagination has 'no rival at all for strength, sincerity, and poetic vision'. Perhaps most fascinating of all is that this was the first book of Blackwood's read by C.S. Lewis, though he did not discover it until 1916 (when he was seventeen) when he borrowed it from the library. It turned him instantly into a fan of Blackwood's work, which he read avidly over the next few years.[9]

III

Blackwood spent the first half of 1909 in Switzerland. His base remained at Bôle but he travelled around the country to Champéry, Neuchâtel, down to Lac Leman (or Lake Geneva), his favourite lake, and even as far afield as Kandersteg. He returned to England some time in July and spent the summer with the Bevans in Dorset before returning to Bôle in December. Throughout 1909, once he had finished *The Education of Uncle Paul* he produced around twenty stories and short articles. Most of these would form his next collection *The Lost Valley*, which Eveleigh Nash published in June 1910 though some, like 'The Man who Found Out', published in *The Lady's Realm* for June 1909 did not appear in a collection until *The Wolves of God* in 1921. Blackwood was now producing more material for the magazines than the book market could accommodate.

Most of these stories draw inspiration from where Blackwood is travelling, so many are set in Switzerland. Others are inspired by people Blackwood knew. The book is dedicated 'To D-M-J and other old friends at Bôle, 1887–1910', showing that ideas came from fellow villagers over the years.

The best example from this period is 'The Man who Played upon the Leaf'[10]. This story is transparently autobiographical. It is little more than a sketch, a mood piece, which Blackwood is able to spin out to over 6,000 words through a spell-binding creation of atmosphere. It is set in Bôle where the narrator is sitting in the garden café of the village inn. He is in conversation with two locals, Louis Favre and Jean Grospierre. Both were real people whom Blackwood knew from his earliest days at Bôle after his return from America. Grospierre was a local pastor. Favre (1822–1904) had been a professor at the University of Neuchâtel, and lived at Boudry. He was fascinated by local tales, and this story is almost certainly based on a local character who travelled between the villages playing a clarinet. The narrator hears in the distance a thin, wailing tune which he first takes to be the wind, until Favre tells him it is Perret, the man who plays upon the leaf. The narrator falls under the spell of Perret who is Pan's disciple and pied piper and whose tunes call to the spirit of those who love nature.

'The Strange Experience of Phillip Ambleside'[11] is set in the Valais Alps, probably at Kandersteg, where Blackwood visited in May 1909. It is a tale told to him by a visiting chaplain. Normally a fairly mundane and uninspiring individual, Ambleside is suddenly overwhelmed by a strange feeling that he is not alone, even though there is no one within miles as he climbs far up into the snow-fields. Somehow this mood leads him in a direction he had not intended. Ambleside encounters the tracks of others, which he follows. He is directed down a dangerous slope where he discovers a sealed envelope containing a lock of hair. Just before this discovery he has a sudden vision of a face within the rock. He puzzles over this lock of hair and it is only later that he overhears an argument between a young betrothed couple where the girl feels the man has lost interest in her, because he has lost the lock of hair. Ambleside is able to restore the envelope to the man and reunite the couple. He ponders why fate chose him to conduct this seemingly minor deed, and whether the child of this couple may prove to be an important individual who will carry out the purpose of the Deity.

'The Occupant of the Room'[12], set in Champéry, is a rather more traditional ghost story about a hotel room haunted by the spirit of a suicide. 'The South Wind', also set in Champéry, written a few months later, is a strong mood piece about the south wind heralding the arrival of spring.

The crowning achievement of his work at Champéry, however, was 'The Wendigo'. He records that he wrote it in a mountain hut above Champéry with the November winds crashing among the pine-forests. He could have written it in either November 1908 or November 1909. He records that he was inspired to write it when a friend, recently returned from Labrador, told him about a family who had moved out of a lonely valley because they had been scared stiff by the Wendigo. He does not identify this friend, but the reference to Labrador suggests it was one of the missionaries from the Moravian Brotherhood.

Two stories at this time both relate to twins. 'The Lost Valley'[13] is set in the Jura, near Bôle, in 1900. It tells of two brothers who are totally devoted to each other. Both fall in love with the same girl, and one decides to sacrifice himself for the other. On one of his travels Stephen stumbles into the 'lost valley'. This is a valley of legend where the souls of suicides go. In the valley Stephen encounters Mark, though later finds that Mark has killed himself. Stephen is never able to find the valley again.

In 'The Terror of the Twins'[14] Blackwood explores the prevalent idea that twins share a soul. The bond between Edward and Ernest is strengthened because their father had wanted just one son and heir, so he always regarded them as one child, and maintained they would inherit as one when they reached twenty-one. The father had died by then but his desire takes form for as the men reach twenty-one so their personalities fuse. Ernest shrinks until he is but a shell, while Edward's strength doubles.

'The Eccentricity of Simon Parnacute' is one of Blackwood's transcendental allegories. It is about a retired professor who, released after years of academia, at last becomes aware of the world about him. He finds affinity with the freedom of the birds and releases a caged bird. He fears, thereafter, that he will be caught for this 'crime' (typical Blackwoodian guilt), and catches a fever. During his delirium he meets the World Policeman (a typical Blackwoodian image) who, delighted that Parnacute wishes to free trapped creatures, takes Parnacute on his own flight. The story is a rather laboured parable, but has a moving ending when it is discovered that Parnacute has died. His body was his cage but his spirit is now free.

'The Man from the "Gods"' involves another dream sequence. Le Maistre has written a fairy play, complete with music, but the actors and musicians do not seem capable of performing the piece to the standard Le Maistre expects. He falls asleep in the theatre and has a vision of an extended form of himself performing the music at its best.

Le Maistre is almost certainly based on the artist and dramatist Walford Graham Robertson (1866–1948). Robertson was a fascinating character who had been friends with Oscar Wilde and was involved in the artistic revolution of the 1890s. He was also devoted to his dogs one of whom, an old English sheepdog called Portly, was the source of the name for Kenneth Grahame's baby otter in *The Wind in the Willows*. Robertson was of the same fey spirit as Blackwood. Robertson had written a fairy play called *Pinkie and the Fairies*, which was first performed at His Majesty's Theatre in London in December 1908[15].

Writing to Robertson in 1911 Blackwood said:

> Often I think of our delightful days together, the music, the teas, talks, work, sitting for portraits, the dreaded company nights, and all the rest. For me it was an ideal life. . .[16]

This reminiscence suggests a long-time friendship. Surprisingly Graham

Robertson's autobiography, *Time Was*, makes no reference to Blackwood and it is not clear how and when they met. Blackwood referred to Robertson as 'Father' in his letters as if Robertson was taking over the role of Alfred Louis as Blackwood's main mentor, even though Robertson was only three years his senior.

There was one other link with the theatre at this time. The dramatist Louis N. Parker (1852–1944) was overwhelmed by Blackwood's *John Silence*, which he read soon after publication. Parker, who was born in France of an American father and an English mother, had once stayed in Laon and related strongly to 'Ancient Sorceries'. He arranged to meet Blackwood to discuss the possibility of bringing some of Blackwood's work to the stage. Parker had already successfully adapted W.W. Jacobs's highly atmospheric short story 'The Monkey's Paw' in 1903. Despite several experiments Parker had to admit that Blackwood's work was too atmospheric and otherworldly to adapt to the stage and they had to admit defeat. The idea was sown with Blackwood though, and he would subsequently become heavily involved with the theatre. It would be over thirty years before Parker and Blackwood were able to dramatise Blackwood's material, this time for radio.

One other story is worth mentioning. 'Old Clothes' is a story of a haunting and of reincarnation and is one of Blackwood's best. A young girl, Aileen (the name of Hobart-Hampden's eldest daughter), has an over-vivid imagination. Her mother worries about her but her uncle, George (who narrates the story), believes she will grow out of it and that it's best to humour her. She tells him of a friend called Philip who talks to her and tells her sad stories. She then reveals that Philip is her Uncle George – that one has been reincarnated as the other. Some months later the girl and her mother move to an old house in Norfolk. When George next visits them he finds that Aileen knows the house intimately and has become morbidly attracted to a stretch of wall. The girl takes on certain obsessions but eventually comes to reveal a past life when she was Lady Helen and her lover was Philip. She was betrayed and bricked up in a wall. Sometime later when the house is renovated the skeleton of a girl is found incarcerated behind the wall.

IV

December 1909 found Blackwood back in the Jura for the season. There had been a heavy fall of snow in November and there was another in March, making this one of the better ski seasons for some years. Blackwood's output of stories decreased, not only because he was enjoying himself (and after such a productive period had sufficient funds in the kitty) but also because he was concentrating on his next novel, a complete change from *The Education of Uncle Paul*.

This was *The Human Chord*, which may be seen as his one complete hermetic novel arising out of the Golden Dawn. There are later stories drawing upon his learning and experiences (one of which, 'Sand', rates among his best and is almost of novel length), but *The Human Chord* stands alone among his books.

The story is built around the long held cabalistic belief that to know the true name of something is to possess it. Everything on this Earth has a true name, which is seldom the common name we know it by. In order to avoid being controlled by another everyone or thing hides its real name. For that reason the true name of God is never revealed but is spelled only by its consonants, the tetragrammaton YHVH. Although we may pronounce it as Yahweh or Jehovah, neither is the true name.

Retired clergyman Philip Skale believes he can recreate that true name. He brings together a select group of four individuals who have perfect pitch. One of these is Robert Spinrobin, who tells the story. Spinrobin, like Blackwood, is one of life's failures who, at twenty-eight, is earning a meagre salary as a financial secretary in the City. He responds to an advertizement that leads him to a house tucked away in the Pontwaun Hills in Wales. There he meets Skale's niece, Miriam, and the housekeeper Mrs Mawle. Together with the eccentrically dressed clergyman, they possess the four notes in the human chord. Skale has a deep bass voice, Spinrobin a tenor, Miriam a soprano and Mrs Mawle an alto. Skale has also captured other sounds in jars that are needed for the final invocation.

Skale explains that everything is the result of vibrations. 'All sounds create their own patterns,' he tells Spinrobin. 'Forms, shapes, bodies are the vibratory activities of sound made visible.'[17] This was a basic tenet of the studies in the Golden Dawn where vibrations and sounds are the basis for invocations. To know the real names of the demons and elementals and to be able to reproduce that sound is to have control over those spirits. Skale demonstrates by playing an E-flat, which is Spinrobin's perfect note, on a violin and showing the pattern this creates in sand.

The novel contains many wonderful moments. Blackwood explores the sensations Spinrobin experiences when Skale reveals his true name.

Spinrobin discovers that by manipulating vibrations Skale can make himself invisible and could at any time be spying on them. Spinrobin also experiences the effects of one of Skale's experiments in pronouncing just part of the One True Name, when the world seems to shift.[18] This makes both Spinrobin and Miriam nervous about the final invocation, so that when that moment comes, in a superbly powerful climax, the equal of almost anything Blackwood wrote, all does not go according to plan.

The Human Chord ranks high among Blackwood's work. It draws from his direct experience and is written with authority and passion. He believes in what he is writing, and is able to create sensations of otherwordliness that escape many other writers. Blackwood takes the world we know, shifts it slightly out of synch, and manages to take us with him.

Blackwood returned to England in April having sent *The Human Chord* on in advance. He met with Frederick Macmillan on 23 April. From subsequent correspondence it suggests that Macmillan was cautious about the novel. Perhaps he felt the esoteric nature of the book would turn readers away. He asked Blackwood to write a special introduction, but Blackwood felt that unnecessary, though Macmillan did eventually squeeze a 500-word summary out of him to use in the book's promotion. What is most suggestive is that Macmillan proposed that the book be published on the basis of 'half profits'. This means that there is no advance and no royalties in the usual sense, but once the book has broken even with the publisher, Blackwood then receives 50 per cent of all future profits. It was a not uncommon approach among publishers at the time but was used mostly when the publisher felt the sales were questionable. If the book was a runaway bestseller Blackwood would be the winner but it was a case of waiting.

Blackwood accepted the offer, and recommended it to Watt's. He must have been fairly confident in the book, especially as Macmillan's had just paid over £100 (equal to about £6,000 today) on account of the first earned royalties on *The Education of Uncle Paul*.[19]

The Human Chord was published on 18 October 1910 and was well received. Critics had come to expect something unusual and stirring from Blackwood. Ever since *John Silence* he had been a name to watch. Only Aleister Crowley, reviewing in *The Equinox*, complained that it was merely a copy of Edgar Jepson's *Number Nineteen*. There are indeed similarities – both involve a magician who is seeking to summon a major power (though in Jepson's case it's a dark lord) and his niece who falls in love with the narrator. But Blackwood's book was finished before Jepson's was published, and what similarities there are, may be no more than coincidence[20]. Blackwood would not take much heed of Crowley's comments, since neither was enamoured of the other. But it is worth remembering that it was only a few months since Crowley had conducted his experiments at Rempstone. I suspect Crowley saw something of himself in the book and was jealous that Blackwood could create something so moving without at least giving some glory to Crowley. This is reinforced by Crowley mentioning Somerset Maugham in the same review. Maugham had caricatured Crowley as Oliver Haddo in *The Magician* (1908), which Crowley had resented. Possibly Crowley saw something of himself in Philip Skale.

That may have been Blackwood's intention but, by the time of Crowley's review Blackwood had moved on. During the summer of 1910 he went on an expedition that would transform his writing and lead to the most intense period of creativity he would ever experience.

11

The Peaks of Inspiration (1910–11)

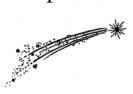

I

There was panic in the air in May 1910. Halley's comet had returned after its 76-year orbit of the sun and there was the inevitable talk of doom and destruction. The death of Edward VII on 6 May further fuelled the flames. Three years later Sir Arthur Conan Doyle recaptured this panic in his novel *The Poison Belt* (1913), where most human life on Earth is destroyed after the Earth passes through a poisonous cloud in space, much like the comet's tail. The Earth passed through the tail of Halley's comet on 18 May 1910. It certainly did not wipe out the Earth's population, but it may have inspired some.

Blackwood watched the comet in the pre-dawn hours from the deck of a small Mediterranean steamer. He had left London at the end of April and travelled by train down to Marseilles where he caught the boat that was to take him to the gates of Eden.

The first part of the journey was fairly routine as the boat clung to the coast, exchanging tourists at Naples, Catania (in Sicily), Athens and Smyrna (now Izmir, in Turkey). By Constantinople (now Istanbul) most of the tourists had gone and only twenty or so more 'serious' passengers remained as the boat chugged along the southern shore of the Black Sea towards Batoum (now Batumi) in Russian Georgia. Within sight of Batoum, Blackwood daydreamed about Jason and the Argonauts, who followed this route to Colchis, and of the Caucasus mountains and Ararat, the traditional cradle of the human race, where Noah's Ark is said to have landed after the Flood.

Customs at Batoum were rigorous and Blackwood had to smuggle his pistol and camera through wrapped in old clothing. Had they discovered them he could well have been expelled, or certainly heavily fined. But Blackwood felt he needed his pistol – the same one he had acquired from the Tombs seventeen years before – because Batoum had been and still was a hotbed of revolutionary activity. Eight years before the twenty-two-year old Georgian revolutionary, Koba, had organized strikes in Batoum and gone underground like some Robin Hood figure. During this period fifteen people died. Koba was arrested and sent to Siberia from where he escaped, returned to Batoum and took on the name of Stalin. Four years before the British consul had been gunned down, while just two years before, a bomb had exploded, killing the wife of a Russian general and resulting in mayhem, as Cossack warriors charged down the main street slashing at anyone in sight. Most recently a Greek doctor had been kidnapped and found murdered and almost every month there were killings of one kind or another. Blackwood was warned never to go for walks alone.

While at Batoum, Blackwood, under instruction from a local copper-mining engineer, took a trip with three Turkish escorts along the valley of the river Tchorokh (now Coruh) into what was then still Russian Armenia (it was returned to Turkey in 1918). He likened the Tchorokh to the Danube, because of its rapids and wide-open stretches. At points it was then the fastest flowing river in the world and is renowned today for its white-water rafting. Blackwood sped down the river in a *caiouke*, or flat-bottomed boat. His destination was Mount Triall, a 3,000 metre peak, deep in the Lesser Caucasus. He climbed this through forests of rhododendron and azalea in the early hours before dawn, much to the amazement of his escorts, who fell asleep at the first point they stopped. Blackwood continued with the porter, though the escorts soon found him again. He had reached sufficient height to see the sun rise over the distant Caucasus, turning the mist in the valleys to deep purple and setting alight the dark blue of the Black Sea to the west, dotted with white sails. He reached the summit and, while his guides fell asleep again, he drank in the 'magical beauty' of the scene that was soon to be descrated during the First World War.

After returning to Batoum, Blackwood took the slow train to Tiflis (now Tbilisi), a journey of 200 miles. He delighted in the beauty of the scenery as the train trundled along the coastline before turning inland and climbing steadily through the wooded valleys and hills, seldom exceeding twenty miles per hour. After thirteen hours they arrived at Tiflis by night, the lights of the town merging with the stars. By day he found the town rather disappointing, especially where it was being modernized. Over the next few days, however, as he explored the town, he grew to like its mysterious diversity. The sheer multitude of cultures and languages in Tiflis near numbed the brain, as all were intent upon their vigorous trading. It was like Babel, and Blackwood felt himself being drawn further back in time.

> There is nothing in this great unstained land to remind you of anything you ever saw or knew before. The modern world drops away in a single leap – silently. You step back, not a few centuries, but into some half-imagined childhood world where anything and everything becomes possible of belief. You forget your age, your past, your stupid little limitations, and run back through this brilliant coloured atmosphere into a time when the world was young – very young.[1]

Blackwood was fascinated by the Georgians themselves – often huge and bear-like with massive shoulders, many as tall as Blackwood. Always friendly, pleasant, delighted to talk (though Blackwood knew only a smattering of Russian), Blackwood also found they had a child-like innocence, as if they too were children of the deep past catapulted unprepared into the present. At one point in his musings he found himself comparing Ossetians and Georgians to centaurs dressed, as they were, in their *bashliks* and *bourkas*, which cloak them from their neck down over their horses' haunches. The land and people made him acutely aware of the juncture of legend and reality, past and present.

In *The Centaur* there is a powerful passage where Blackwood rails against so-called technological progress which is destroying the old-world magic for the sake of speed. Although written in 1910, his message is as relevant and topical today.[2]

Blackwood spent most of June in Tiflis and the surrounding area. From Tiflis he headed north along the old Georgian Military Highway in a *telega*, a horse-drawn springless cart, to Vladikavkaz. The journey took him several days, with a dozen changes of horses and drivers. Blackwood found the outgoing journey delightful. The Caucasus from the south was full of flowers, delightfully wooded valleys and dramatic views, dominated always by the towering pyramidal peak of Kazbek at over 5,000 metres.

He stayed at Vladikavkaz for a week, exploring the area and surrounding valleys. This is the spot that would be his gateway to the

Garden of Eden in *The Centaur*. It's a strange locale, as the northern stretch of the Caucasus is far less attractive than the southern approach, with many severe cliffs and escarpments unbroken by trees and vegetation.

Blackwood returned to Tiflis by bus in the almost indecent haste of twelve hours. It was a daunting journey with the bus often perilously close to sheer precipices. The bus had been running for less than a year with the idea of opening up the area for tourists. Once again Blackwood found himself jerked from the days of legend to scientific progress. His whole experience in the Caucasus had been of gradually perceiving an ancient world of legend through the veils of a blinkered, commercialised world. It was this mood that stayed with him for months.

He returned to Batoum at the end of June and took the steamer back to Marseilles. Unfortunately, just after the steamer had left Inebolu, on the last stop before Constantinople, a passenger fell overboard. Although the steamer stopped to rescue him, his heavy clothing became waterlogged and he sank, unaware of the purpose of the life-buoys being thrown to help him. It cast a sombre mood over the return journey and caused Blackwood to reflect further on how the modern world was affecting cultures, and how the old-world beauty and charm were being lost in the march for progress.

II

Blackwood was back in London by late July, but had no plans to stay for long. On 10 August he left London for Ste Croix in Switzerland. He remained in Switzerland for a couple of months, returning to London in October. Writing to Macmillan's over the final arrangements for *The Human Chord* he said, 'I find this an admirable place to work, among pine forests on the high Jura plateau, a most excellently managed little hotel with a few French families and no noisy tourists.'[3]

Blackwood was eager to write. He had returned from the Caucasus 'charged with a thousand storms of beauty and wonder'.[4] But he found that he could not write about it. The impact of the place had overwhelmed his creativity. He began *The Centaur*, with the idea of exploring how a primitive being could survive from the earliest days of the world complete as a separate and almost forgotten offshoot of evolution. He got so far and no further. It was necessary to file it away and wait for inspiration.

Apart from a couple of travel articles, Blackwood wrote only two short stories at this time, and both are worth mentioning. 'The Singular Death of Morton'[5] is his only traditional vampire story, though it only just acknowledges convention. The eponymous Morton shares a name with Blackwood's old goldfields friend, Reggie Moreton. Morton is described in the story as a 'big man', though that's all. Blackwood had remained in touch with Moreton, who now lived in London, with his wife Mary Beresford.

The second story from this period is full of connections, and introduces us to one who would become Blackwood's soul-mate for the next ten years. 'The Empty Sleeve'[6] tells of two brothers, John and William Gilmer, who collect violins. These are so precious that they allow only one person to play them, a Jew called Hyman, and then only because they want to hear the beautiful sound. They wince at the sight of another touching their violins. Hyman loves the violins and hates the restrictions on their use. He projects his spirit body, in the form of a large cat, inside the brother's apartment where he reforms in human shape and plays the violins while the brothers are out. One day he is nearly caught and the brothers stop his services. Hyman tries again. John Gilmer becomes aware of his presence as a giant cat, and attacks it with a sword, severing one of the limbs. When they next see Hyman they notice he has lost an arm.

It must have been about this time that Blackwood met the two brothers Johann and Andreas Knoop, Russians who had inherited the title *baron* from their father, Ludwig. Johann Knoop (1846–1918) was immensely wealthy. He collected violins and kept them under lock and key, forbidding anyone to play them. His father had established a giant cotton mill at Narva, on the borders of Russia and Estonia, and this developed into Russia's most important textile manufacturing industry. Johann travelled throughout Europe and the Mediterranean in connection with the textile business. He had homes in London and Paris and opened a sanatorium in Egypt at Helwan. At that time Helwan had a growing reputation as a health spa and was patronized by the rich and famous. The Knoops spent most winters in Egypt.

Johann Knoop had become entranced by a young violinist, Maya Stuart-King (1875–1945), whom he had seen performing with a quartet in Vienna. Maya – her real name was Mabel but she was never called that – had apparently run away from home when she was eighteen or so and gone in search of her godmother, who was a German princess.

She took with her her most treasured possession, her Stradivarius violin. Knoop's first wife had died and he sought out Maya as a governess for his child, Ludwig. Romance blossomed. The two were married in England, at Haslemere, Surrey, in July 1899, followed by a full Russian Orthodox ceremony. They settled in England, first at Tunbridge Wells in Kent, and then at Wadhurst, on the Kent–Sussex border, where the Baron had acquired a large house. Unfortunately, the romance does not seem to have long survived the wedding. Knoop apparently treated Maya like his other treasures and she became little more than a prisoner in his 'castles'. He confiscated her violin, incorporating it into his collection, so that Maya was not able to play it. The overriding desire to have access to it is only too obviously translated into 'The Empty Sleeve'.

Just when Blackwood first met Maya remains something of a mystery. Stephen Graham[7] relates how they met on a Nile cruiser, owned by the Baron. If true, and since we know for certain that Blackwood knew Maya by the summer of 1911 it would suggest they had met earlier in Egypt, and Blackwood denies having been in Egypt earlier than January 1912. If 'The Empty Sleeve' is based on the Knoops, Blackwood must have known them at least by the summer of 1910, to allow him time to write the story and *The London Magazine* to publish it, just before Christmas 1910. Blackwood could have met them on his trip to the Caucasus. Knoop would have had plenty of trade and business around the Black Sea and Blackwood could have encountered them at any of his ports of call. Maybe Maya's recollection of meeting Blackwood on a steamer related to the Black Sea steamer not the Nile.

Blackwood met Stephen Graham (1884–1975) on 4 November 1910. He was the son of the editor of *Country Life*, Anderson Graham. Remarkably, Stephen Graham had been in the Caucasus at the same time as Blackwood and was writing a book about his experiences, *A Vagabond in the Caucasus* (1911). Their mutual interest brought them together and they arranged to meet at the Savile Club. Graham's account of that first meeting is typical of many.

> I came into the presence of an unusual personality; some would call it weird, I would call it strange and elusive, rather unearthly. [. . .] His face was all that mattered. He was a tall man, but his face glowed as he spoke, though his eyes looked inward all the while. He had a long percipient nose, and that was his unusual feature. It moved

about like a dog's nose, scenting the plates, the waiter, the air we breathed, myself. He believed there was a sixth sense which some of us were on the verge of using. It made him aware of the past history of a room and of the spiritual atmosphere which clothes a person like the cloak of a ghost. He had a rapid power of imagination and could tell a haunting original story at the drop of a hat.[8]

It was whilst visiting Stephen Graham during December 1910 that the inspiration returned to Blackwood and dispelled his writer's block. He was in Graham's flat during a suffocating London fog when through the window came the sound of a street beggar playing a penny whistle like the Pan Pipes. The sound conveyed Blackwood back to the Caucasus. In that moment the floodgates opened, and stayed open for two years, whilst he produced his most imaginative stories.

He recreated that moment in 'Imagination', one of his squibs for the *Westminster Gazette* (17 December 1910). It tells of a highly imaginative author, William Jones, staying at his brother's flat, who finds his inspiration blocked half way into a story about a centaur. He could not conceive how a man, containing this instinctive spirit, would look. Setting the story aside he reads the paper only to find a visitor at the door. A man enters who appears larger than life, massive, just like the Georgians Blackwood had met. He has come as in a dream to reveal to Jones a centaur-man. The brother returns home, the image fades, but the block has gone.

Another story probably written at this time, though not published for a couple of years, was 'A Man of Earth'[9]. This features an incident in the Caucasus where the narrator, having made friends with a mining engineer near Batoum, ventures into the mountains to visit a new mine. He is nearly killed by a landslide. The implication is that the native Ossetines can draw upon the power of the earth-spirit to save their land.

Blackwood did not immediately throw himself into completing *The Centaur*. He was working on two books. The other was *Julius LeVallon*, which he had started soon after finishing *John Silence*, and which he had struggled with for two years. He was closer to finishing *LeVallon* than *The Centaur*, so he returned to that. *Julius LeVallon* was really the first half of a two-part book. Blackwood had wanted to know what a true child of Nature would be like, a child born by the power of the elementals. But to do that he had to explain how such a child came about, and that was *Julius LeVallon*.

We have already encountered part of this book, because its early chapters drew upon Blackwood's school and university years. It was probably those parts that Blackwood had completed. Julius LeVallon is a man who has complete memories of all his past incarnations. Thus, when he meets John Mason at school, he remembers the first time they had met in a previous life aeons ago, a time LeVallon calls the Temple Days. This was a time of true Nature magic when the humanity of that time was in harmony with the elements, the stars and the sun.

> The elements were an expression of spiritual powers. To be in touch with them was to be in touch with a Whole in which the Earth or Sirius are, after all, but atoms. Moreover, it was a conscious Whole. In atoms themselves he found life too. Chemical affinity involved intelligence.[10]

In those days they had other names – Concerighé and Ziaz – and there was a third, a girl, Silvatela. The three had revelled in each other's company and under the influence of Concerighé (LeVallon) had conducted certain experiments. At one point they are able to undertake astral travel, leaving their shells in the Hall of Vacated Bodies. Concerighé attempts to summon the elemental powers through Ziaz's empty body, but Ziaz's astral self returns and the experiment is aborted. However the powers of wind and fire had been released, and remained uncaged. Over the millennia Concerighé had searched for his soul mates Ziaz and Silvatela in order to repeat the experiment and recapture the elemental powers. In the first half of the book he had found Ziaz. By the second half he has found Silvatela and married her. They live in the Jura at Bâle (a thinly disguised Bôle), where they await the birth of their first child. LeVallon summons Mason to join them. In the Swiss valley he feels the elemental forces are more potent.

The climax of the novel is one of Blackwood's strongest. The three souls unite and LeVallon summons the powers of wind and fire. There are parallels to the climax in *The Human Chord*, and it may well have been the completion of that novel that left Blackwood bereft of a conclusion for this. Newly inspired, though, *Julius LeVallon* is a remarkable achievement. The experiment goes wrong and the forces are channelled not through LeVallon but his wife, and into the unborn child. That is where the book finishes.

Triumphant at its conclusion Blackwood wrote immediately to Graham Robertson.

I really must tell you that this morning at 11.30 a.m. I finished, after two years' work on and off, the first half of Julius LeVallon. Mrs LeVallon has given birth to a fine, queer boy, fierce child of Wind and Fire. I don't care two straws if it's never published; the writing of it has been to me pure joy; and especially these later scenes when in trance she remembers and reports the scene in the Chamber of the Vacated Bodies and the great temptation which seduced us all three so long ago.[11]

That last phrase suggests that Blackwood, Robertson and another had discussed this idea some while before. Certainly *Julius LeVallon* owes much of its source to Blackwood's experiences in the Golden Dawn, and his affinity over the years with the powers of Nature. Part of the character for LeVallon was drawn from his Hindu student friend at Edinburgh University and the idea behind this story may well have originated that long ago.

It's likely, however, that Maya Knoop provided the final inspiration. It would explain why, when this book was eventually published, five years later, it was dedicated 'To M. S.-K. (1906)'. M. S.-K. was her maiden name, Maya Stuart-King. The reference to 1906 is harder to explain. One might think it was when Blackwood first met her, and perhaps they did briefly without becoming friends. 1906 was the date of Blackwood's first book, which Maya may have read, so the date could refer to their first 'spiritual' meeting.

It is strange that Blackwood did not seek publication of *Julius LeVallon* straight away. Possibly he felt he needed to complete the second half first, though in his letter to Robertson he says: 'And so now I return to our old Centaur till he's finished. Then, a long way off yet, the second half of Julius.' So he did not anticipate writing the second volume immediately and it was another ten years before that book, *The Bright Messenger*, was finished.

When he wrote to Macmillan just a week later, he refrained from telling them what books he was working on, as they were still some way from completion, but he hoped to have a book ready for the autumn. Clearly he was not about to reveal the completion of *Julius LeVallon*. It would be nearly five years before Blackwood mentioned the book to Macmillan and only then because he felt honour-bound to offer it to his first editor, Maude ffoulkes, to whom he had promised the book when she was still with Nash. In that letter (dated 3 January 1916), Blackwood stated he had only recently finished the novel, so he may have returned to it, despite his triumphant conclusion on that Monday morning in February 1911. Blackwood's relationship with Nash had changed. Despite the continued success of *John Silence*, Blackwood now regarded Macmillan as his primary publisher and that they should get first refusal on his work. It was because Blackwood felt it his duty to keep his promise to Mrs ffoulkes that, *Julius LeVallon*, arguably the best of all of his novels, remained unpublished for five years.

III

Having finished *LeVallon*, though, Blackwood now put all his soul into *The Centaur*. It is easy to understand why this book was so difficult to finish and why Blackwood needed all of the inspiration he could command. It was to be the favourite among his novels, because it best represented all that he was trying to achieve, but it is a complicated message and one that requires tremendous effort from the reader to appreciate. Maybe that makes it a flawed masterpiece, but masterpiece it still remains. It is unlike any other work in the field of supernatural or mystical fiction.

The basic concept behind the story is derived from the theories of Gustav Fechner: that the Earth is a living, sentient being – literally Mother Earth. All living things on the Earth are part of her collective being. She in turn is part of the collective consciousness of the solar system, and that in turn is part of the collective consciousness of the Universe, and so on up to the total omniscient consciousness, which is God.

Blackwood believed that spirits were projections of the human consciousness. In like vein the Mother Earth could project her own consciousness and this took the form of the Gods of Old. The growth of civilization has caused the Earth to withdraw her consciousness and these ancient Gods have thus faded, surviving only in those remote and 'unstained places', as Blackwood called them, where they are still perceived by the local folk and worshipped.

Blackwood's idea was that his hero, O'Malley, would meet a primitive man, a survival from the Earth's ancient past, who has not been encumbered by modern traits or civilization. This does not simply mean a primitive *human* being, but also a primitive *spiritual* being, one who has remained attuned to the Earth's consciousness. He calls this being an *urmensch*, meaning literally 'primeval man'. Because O'Malley is also sympathetic to nature he is aware of the greater glory of the *urmensch*, and through contact with them his eyes are opened to the Old World. Travelling to the Caucasus, he first experiences this wonder on board the steamer, where he meets the *urmensch*, but once in the Caucasus O'Malley falls under their spell. He follows Blackwood's route, along the Georgian Military Road to Vladikavkaz, and then via Alighir and Oni deep into a remote Imerethian valley. Here O'Malley and his 'leader', the *urmensch*, continue uphill, above the tree line, deeper into the Earth's own consciousness. Gradually his senses become aware of shapes and forms around him, but still his mind is not quite in tune. Then they reach the top of the peak. The glamour of the Old World closes about him and the spiritual Garden of Eden appears.

There follows a transcendental spiritual experience, which is impossible to describe. It is the peak of Blackwood's writing and a major literary achievement. If it falls short of a masterpiece it is because Blackwood is struggling to describe an out-of-this-life experience with the mundanity of our daily language. He is bound by his physical limitations. Even so the book is potent.

Blackwood admitted his own limitations. 'The theme, of course, is far beyond my powers,' he wrote to a friend, 'but it flames in me with such pain that I MUST get it out as best I can'.[12]

Blackwood continued to work on *The Centaur* throughout the spring and summer. He returned to England in April with the death of his sister Beatrice. She died of cancer at Lansdowne Grove House, a nursing home in Bath, on 23 April 1911. She left her personal effects to her brother Stevie. Blackwood received £250 (now the equal of £15,000), with the rest left in trust to her sisters.

The few stories Blackwood completed at this time do not seem unduly influenced by Beatrice's death. 'The Prayer'[13] may seem the most obvious. Interestingly it features a character called O'Malley, showing that Blackwood could not separate himself from his spiritual traveller. He and his friend Jones are fellow medical students. O'Malley acquires a drug that allows them to see thoughts, which look like tiny shooting stars. They see an especially powerful thought that hovers like a halo above people's heads before moving on, working its power. They trace the thought back to its origin and find it comes from an elderly invalid who spends all day in bed praying for the good of the world. 'The Prayer' is actually the first seed of *A Prisoner in Fairyland*, which is all about a network of good thoughts, and the story stands as a bridge between that and *The Centaur*.

'The Golden Fly'[14] also dates from this time. In *Pan's Garden* Blackwood reveals that this was written at his sister's farm at Breamore, south of Salisbury. It's a mood piece where a suicide draws strength from seeing a small fly surviving, and realizes he can call upon Nature as his god to reinvigorate him in moments of crisis.

'Two in One'[15] may have been inspired by the impending marriage of Blackwood's brother to Kate Abbott, though the story, about a young couple who appear to be two aspects of the same reincarnated spirit, also casts shadows of Maya and Blackwood. Stevenson Blackwood and Kate Abbott were not married until 11 December that year (1911). Kate was half Stevie's age, just twenty-two, the daughter of a master builder from Dorset. Blackwood was not at the wedding. He was already back in Switzerland by then.

While still in the West Country Blackwood had the idea for 'Accessory Before the Fact'[16]. It may even have been suggested by his brother as the narrator, Martin, is an 'accountant on holiday', a hiker. He finds himself unaccountably lost and is attacked by two tramps, apparently German spies in disguise. The attack turns out to be a premonition, a dream, of a real murder that happens the next day. Martin had received a warning meant for someone else. This is the first story in which Blackwood gives any indication of his feelings for a possible German invasion, though it was a subject that had been occupying the press for some years.[17]

IV

After a few days in London, Blackwood visited his friend Graham Robertson at his home at Sandhills, at Witley in Surrey, to discuss plans for *The Centaur*. It was his desire that Robertson should illustrate the book. It was not practical for Robertson to provide illustrations throughout the book, but Macmillan's agreed that he provide a design for the cover and the end-papers. It depicted spirits deep in a mountainous valley, being welcomed by a group of centaurs. In fact it's the only formal representation of centaurs in the entire book for, apart from a couple of allusions, Blackwood does not mention them at all.

Macmillan's had seen Blackwood's draft of *The Centaur*, and their reader had suggested some revisions in order to strengthen the character and motivation of O'Malley. Blackwood continued to work on this and generally strengthen the story during July and August 1911 when he was staying at the Sussex home of Johann and Maya Knoop. The Knoop Brothers had originally lived in Tunbridge Wells during their visits to England but in November 1903 Johann Knoop acquired a large house situated to the south of the village of Wadhurst on the Kent and Sussex border. The house had been substantially rebuilt as a mansion in 1884. Standing in comparative seclusion in woods on a south-facing hill, it overlooked the Kent and Sussex Weald with one of the most beautiful views in the south-east.

Those who recalled Baron Knoop remembered that he was an invalid in his final years and that all of his life he had been something of a hypochondriac. Despite his wealth he was seldom happy and spent much of his time in seclusion. Maya, on the other hand, though petite, was full of life, a bundle of energy, always laughing and gay. She was headstrong and delighted in organizing things. She oversaw the refurbishment of South Park and set about establishing the gardens, no doubt helped by Blackwood. Blackwood was always working in people's gardens, usually helping felling trees and clearing undergrowth. Although Knoop was apparently unsociable, he must have given in to his wife's desire to have friends and guests at South Park. Stephen Graham recalls that the Baron would not allow visitors to stay overnight, and they usually stayed at a local village inn. Blackwood nevertheless firmly stated South Park as his forwarding address during the summer of 1911.

Blackwood casts a gloomy picture of Knoop as the character of Samuel Franklyn in 'The Damned', where he acknowledges that Franklyn/Knoop was respected by many because of his philanthropy but distrusted by those of an artistic temperament who could not conform to his exact cut-and-dried world. Knoop and Blackwood lived in two opposing worlds. Knoop's rigid stoicism and Teutonic temperament may have reminded Blackwood too much of his own evangelical youth.

There is a poignant description of Maya that Blackwood wrote to Stephen Graham a few years later.

> Ah! She is a great soul and gives her life away for others as naturally
> as flowers give their perfume, while in her private life – I can say
> this to you, my dear fellow, she has daily cruelty and pain to bear

that few other women could endure for a month, let alone years and years.[18]

These potent emotions helped spark Blackwood's creativity. Even as he completed his final polish on *The Centaur* he was at work on some of his best short fiction.

'The Man Whom the Trees Loved' is a 26,000-word novella. Though started at Holmesley Lodge it was probably finished at Sandhills. It features an artist called Sanderson, clearly based on Graham Robertson. Sanderson has a skill for painting trees, bringing them alive, imbuing each one with its own personality. This skill is admired by David Bittacy, who commissions Sanderson to paint a cedar tree from their garden in the New Forest. Bittacy's wife, Sophia, comes from a strict evangelical background and though she understands her husband, she feels he loves trees more than her. She accepts, or more accurately, suffers Bittacy's fancies rather than appreciates them. Bittacy believes that trees have a psychic sentience and that a forest has a collective consciousness, with which humans could have an affinity if only they tried. The story follows the harmonization of Bittacy with the great forest until one day his wife realizes that the man she has married is now only a shell and his spirit has merged with the forest.

The story was finished in late June or early July. Blackwood was impressed when Watt's sold it to *The London Magazine* for £60 (the modern equivalent of £3,600). By then Blackwood had already seen this as one story in a volume projected for Macmillan's for the following spring, but he did not propose the idea to the publisher until October, by which time he had worked on further stories. He saw the book as a unified whole, exploring his belief that there is a relationship between human beings and Nature.

This is the book that became *Pan's Garden*, though for a long while it had the working title *The Man Whom the Trees Loved*, and appears under that name in some advance publicity. Macmillan's agreed to publish it again on the half-profits basis, and also agreed for Graham Robertson to illustrate it. This time Robertson provided a one-page sketch for each story.

Over the last year Blackwood had produced two masterpieces – *Julius LeVallon* and *The Centaur*. The same stimuli that had inspired those works was still craving for an outlet. The earliest story in the collection is 'The South Wind', written in January 1910 as a mood piece heralding the arrival of spring, and a suitable harbinger for the collection. At that stage Blackwood had not fully considered the idea of an holistic volume of nature stories, as there are stories in *The Lost Valley* which would have worked better in *Pan's Garden*, and vice versa. Take 'Special Delivery'[19]. That is a companion piece to 'The Strange Experience of the Reverend Phillip Ambleside', and was written at the same time. It features another curate, Meiklejohn, who has a premonition of disaster while staying at Le Guillaume Tell inn at Bôle, where Blackwood occasionally stayed. Likewise 'The Return'[20] is really a reworking of 'Keeping His Promise'. Where this story differs is that, rather than have a tangible ghost, the narrator is visited by the mood and vision of beauty. Blackwood had moved from the spiritually mundane to a glorious transcendence.

The earliest story which may have been composed consciously for this volume of nature stories was probably 'The Sea Fit'[21]. The idea came to Blackwood while staying in Dorset with the Bevans in September 1909, though it was written some while later at the Haven Hotel, across Studland Bay in Poole. A great storm gathers over the bay, watched by a group of men who have come together for Easter. One of these, a Norwegian with a Viking temperament, hears the call of the old Norse gods in the storm and follows them to his death (or transmogrification).

Blackwood continued to work on the book till March 1912, when he completed 'Sand', so the stories span this phenomenally creative period of two-and-a-half years. The next he wrote specifically for the book was probably 'Clairvoyance'[22]. It was written while he was staying at the Knoops. The story even portrays a thinly disguised Johann Knoop as the nonpsychic 'elderly man in the corner' who contributes nothing to the discussion, and Maya as the childless 'potential mother of the world'. Maya loved children, but was unable to have any by Knoop. The woman is unable to stay in a room because she feels it is haunted. The nonpsychic man spends a night there and becomes aware of the spirits of unborn children. The story is a poignant image of an unhappy couple and an unfulfilled woman.

Maya is present in spirit in most of the stories in *Pan's Garden*. When the book was published in July 1912 it was dedicated 'To M. S.-K., who made with me these little paths across Pan's Tangled Garden'.

'The Transfer'[23] was written at Sandhills. It is one of Blackwood's few stories narrated by a woman, the governess of a young girl and her brother, Jamie. Jamie is scared of his Uncle Frank, a man who has tremendous vitality, which he seems to draw from others. In the rose garden of their house is a patch of land upon which nothing will grow. One hot day when Uncle Frank visits he collapses upon this patch of land. Thereafter Uncle Frank's strength fades, but the patch of earth blossoms. Years later Blackwood told psychic researcher Peter Underwood that there had been an original to 'Uncle Frank', though he did not reveal who[24]. Nevertheless Baron Knoop again springs to mind.

'The Heath Fire'[25] was also written at Sandhills, remembering an especially hot September day when the sun sparked off fires on the dry heathland that adjoins Witley at Thursley. It's a clear companion piece to 'The Sea Fit'. A group of men are drawn together. One is O'Hara, recently back from Batoum, with the 'Black Sea fever'. O'Hara ventures up onto the heath where he witnesses the fire elementals of the Earth responding to the call of the Sun.

Several stories are set in Switzerland. 'The Glamour of the Snow'[26] is comparable in mood to 'The Lost Valley'. Hibbert is a sensitive soul, conscious of three worlds – the civilized world of the English tourists, the pastoral world of the local villagers at Champéry, and the mystical world of Nature. He becomes attracted to a woman who nearly lures him to his death. 'The Attic'[27] is a later story and one that shows the transition to Blackwood's next book, *A Prisoner in Fairyland*, upon which Blackwood began work at the end of 1911. It's important because it is the first story that uses the nickname Pan, by which Blackwood became known to his close friends, and it refers to locals whom Blackwood knew in Bôle. The attic is a room over the carpenter's workshop. In real life it was a spare room rented by Blackwood's cousin and used as a study. He kept his books and pipes there and would spend many an hour simply reflecting on life. In the story the attic is haunted by the spirit of a suicide, Petavel, a userer, who hanged himself a century before. The spirit is released one night, through prayer and through the channel of a cat. The story is so minutely described that you feel you are there.

In addition to the 26,000-word 'The Man Whom the Trees Loved' there are two other novellas in *Pan's Garden*, of even greater length, 'The Temptation of the Clay' and 'Sand'. These three alone would make a substantial book. 'Sand' was squeezed into the book at the last moment, and I shall discuss it in the next chapter. 'The Temptation of the Clay' is set on a farm in Sussex. Blackwood had found it difficult to finish and may have worked on it over some time. Even when finished he still referred to it as a failure[28]. The main character, Dick Eliot, is another sensitive mystic who wasted his young adult years travelling the world, married and then returned to England to settle in a home that they both loved even though it was too large and unmanageable. After twelve years the wife dies and Eliot lives on on his own.[29] He had grown to love the Place, as they called it, and the two of them had poured so much love into the land that it has almost come alive. He wants to protect it to cherish her memory, but he is also poor and does not know how he can afford to keep the land. At that point into his life comes Mánya Petrovski, the fourteen-year-old child of his widowed sister, and a spirit of Nature. Her Russian father had been subject to 'violent tempers'. Parallels with Maya and Johann Knoop are clear. Mánya becomes the spiritual guardian of the Place, whilst Eliot is inflicted with commercialism. He finds valuable white clay on the land and believes he can make a profit by mining the clay and using that money to continue to support the Place. The Place, however, using Mánya as its agent, will not let him. Despite devious tactics, the Place rises up and rejects Eliot.

The story is a fitting conclusion to the book because it is in complete contrast to 'The Man Whom the Trees Loved', which opens it. In that story Nature had welcomed and absorbed the spirit of Bittacy. In 'The Temptation of the Clay', Nature rejects the spirit of the man who had turned to financial gain. Blackwood's early ecological message is only too clear. Capitalism is the enemy of nature, and the Earth will reject those who attempt to despoil it.

V

The Centaur was published on 10 November 1911, once again dedicated to M. S.-K., this time as a 'rare type of being: an intellectual mystic'. The book received considerable critical acclaim, even from the normally cautious *Times Literary Supplement*, which recognized the complex concept that Blackwood was seeking to explore, and that the reader is carried 'on the crest of a succession of shimmering waves of language, extraordinarily intense and sincere'.[30] *Country Life* singled it out as their 'Book of the Week', whilst *The Bookman* called it 'the masterpiece of the new romantic movement,' adding, 'It is quite the best thing that Mr Blackwood has yet given us.'[31]

Such reviews must have pleased Blackwood. He regarded the book as the closest to his own personal outlook. A few years later he told critic and devotee, Robb Lawson, 'Most writers hold their own test of the value of their readers. Kipling, I am told, regards his exquisite story "They" as the touchstone of the readers whose approval he cherishes most – so when readers tell me they like *The Centaur*, I know they have passed my test.'[32]

But even more rewarding to Blackwood was the response he received from new and leading literary lights. Praise came from the young poet Siegfried Sassoon, the Irish author James Stephens, the philosopher Edward Carpenter and the great Irish mystic Æ (George Russell). Æ was very excited. A few years before Æ had produced a painting based on a mystical vision he had of a centaur on the sacred mountain Ben Bulbin. He was keen to discuss Blackwood's own mystical experience. They did not get to meet until after the war, but Blackwood's memories of that meeting are worth noting now:

> Æ set the mind ablaze. That my 'Centaur' was his theme doubtless flattered my vanity, but, apart from that, his rolling words were a whirlwind, a tornado, that rushed me back into the fabulous grandeur of the Caucasus where Prometheus still lay defying the Furies and the vulture and the Argo pointed its silver prow towards Colchis. My memories of that region became alive again, the pretty valleys of Galway faded out. [33]

Perhaps the most immediate delight was praise Blackwood received from the author, socialist and craftsman Edward Carpenter (1844–1929)[34]. Carpenter had set up a smallholding at Millthorpe near Sheffield in Yorkshire in 1882. Like Blackwood he was a disciple of Nature. He showed how compatible these views were in several books that caught the public mood of the time and acquired a cult status, especially *Towards Democracy* (1883), inspired by the *Bhagavad Gita*, and *Civilization: Its Cause and Cure* (1889). Blackwood had devoured these books and taken them to his heart, even quoting from the latter at the head of Chapter 2 of *The Centaur*.

Carpenter wrote to Blackwood on 3 January 1912 saying, in part, 'You must have had a severe attack of "Earth-passion" to be able to write that & describe it so graphically.' Carpenter hoped they could meet some day. The letter found Blackwood in Bôle and he responded immediately. 'I'm sure you cannot know how pleased I was to read your letter, for I owe so much of my love of the Earth to your own interpretation of her, and any little inspiration I may have has certainly filtered with me through channels opened by "Towards Democracy" many years ago.'[35] He added, 'This "Earth-passion" is very strong in me, and always has been, and I spend very little time in cities.'

Carpenter is one of those unjustly forgotten individuals of the Victorian and Edwardian period. His thoughts, like those of William Morris and others of the Arts and Crafts Movement, did much to engender a public respect for the simple life and fuelled the interest in socialism. Eventually this would change the political and social structure of Britain. Blackwood brought a mystical perspective to this. His books, especially *The Centaur* and *Pan's Garden* contributed to a greater awareness of the Old World magic.

But even Blackwood recognized that it was not easy to turn around the so-called advancement of humanity. At the end of *The Centaur* O'Malley vows to return to the West to lecture on his experience and give his message to the world. But it all ends in failure. The world is not prepared to listen. Eventually a solution comes to him.

> 'I've begun at the wrong end,' he said; 'I shall never reach men through their intellects. Their brains to-day are occupied by the machine-made gods of civilization. I cannot change the direction of their thoughts and lusts from outside; the momentum is too great to stop that way. To reach their hearts, the new ideas must rise up from within. I see the truer way. I must do it *from the other side*. It must come to them – in Beauty.'[36]

This was the conclusion that Blackwood had reached some while before. He had to find a way to spread beauty throughout the world, and there could be no better way than through the hearts and minds of children.

It was time for Uncle Paul to take control of the Starlight Express.

12

The Spell of Maya (1912–13)

I

After the longest time spent in England for several years, Blackwood hurried back to the Jura in October 1911, polishing the final stories for *Pan's Garden*. He wrote to his friend, Mrs Lamont[1], at the start of December, that he was now 'established abroad for my winter of work & skiing', but in fact it was a poor season. There was more snow in Scotland than in the Jura, causing Blackwood to report in *Country Life* on 'Failure of the Swiss Winter Season'.[2]

Nevertheless, it gave Blackwood more time to write and travel. He said to Mrs Lamont that, '[I] am busy upon the book that "Uncle Paul" wrote – "The Aventures of a Prisoner in Fairyland", for my mind turns instinctively, and by way of relief, to something lighter. *The Centaur* was very hard work indeed.'[3] And not just *The Centaur*. To have written that and *Julius LeVallon* and most of *Pan's Garden* over the last twelve months should have been enough to leave anyone exhausted.

Yet the creative spark had not yet dimmed. It was at this time that he completed 'The Messenger', 'The Attic' and 'The Destruction of Smith'. This last story, which owed its origins to Hank's Camp, thirteen years earlier, at Lake Cogawanna, also owed something to the same muse that inspired 'The Temptation of the Clay'. Both stories consider how an individual's soul can be absorbed by Nature, just as Blackwood's had been by the Caucasus, and soon would be again by the Egyptian desert.

But you can also sense the start of a transition in Blackwood's work. Having pursued the macrocosm in *The Centaur*, Blackwood now

Harriet Sydney Blackwood, Blackwood's mother, soon after her husband's death.

Sir Arthur Blackwood, Blackwood's father, soon after his marriage.

Wood Lodge at Shooter's Hill, where Algernon was born.

Blackwood's sisters, Ada, Beatrice (top) and Cecilia, and his brother Arthur (bottom).

Young Algernon when
he was about 4 or 5.

Blackwood in his late teens
on holiday in Scotland.

Mr Saunder's House at Wellington College. Algernon is third from the left at the back. His brother, Arthur, is seated third from the right in the front row.

Offices of the New York Times in 1893 at the junction of Nassau Street and Park Row, New York.

Alfred H. Louis around 1908.

Edwyn R. Bevan, part of the
inspiration for John Silence.

Maude ffoulkes,
Blackwood's first editor.

The cover of the first edition of John Silence
showing the enigmatic doctor.

Blackwood being helped to the summit of a mountain in the Alps by
Freddie Dufferin in 1925.

Blackwood punting down the Danube
in August 1905.

The church and pension at Bôle where
Blackwood lived from 1908–12.

Blackwood with Sir Edward Elgar studying the score of *The Starlight Express*.

Blackwood reading to Lena Ashwell and children at rehearsals for *The Starlight Express*.

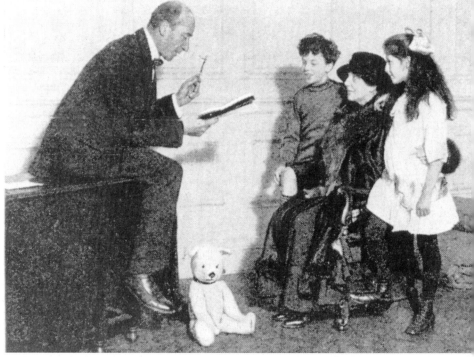

Maya Philipson at Encombe in 1923.

Encombe at Sandgate, Hythe in Kent in 1923.

Blackwood with Sinclair Lewis, John Drinkwater and the Ainleys in 1921.

Blackwood with Vincent Nesfield in Switzerland in 1949.

Blackwood dancing with Cornelia Lunt the Empress of Britain in 1933.

What was left of Algernon and Patrick's home after the bombing during the Blitz. The two were saved by the sausages in the air-raid shelter.

Happier times after the war. Blackwood relaxing with his nephew Patrick and Patrick's wife Ellen in Switzerland.

Blackwood proudly displaying his CBE which he received in 1949.

focused on his own personal microcosm. 'The Attic' had marked the start of this followed by the sketch 'In a Jura Village'⁴, which would later be worked into *A Prisoner in Fairyland*. At this stage it is no more than a reflection. The narrator (clearly Blackwood) sits in his attic room in Bôle and looks out over the village at dusk, commenting on the people, the sounds, his memories and, above all, how little seems to change here whilst the rest of the world falls over itself to race ahead.

'The Whisperers'⁵ is a similar piece. The narrator (again Blackwood) is in Bôle, in the attic room, trying to write. But the room is suffused with images and sounds, 'whisperers'. He later discovers that his cousin had only recently emptied the room of hundreds of books, unread for too long. The books' spirits had become restless.

Eventually Blackwood did settle and *A Prisoner in Fairyland* took shape. This is the book promised by Paul Rivers in *The Education of Uncle Paul*. There, through the magic of childhood imagination, Paul had been taken through the 'crack' between yesterday and tomorrow into a timeless land of faëry.

> And to all who – since childhood – have lived in Fairyland and tasted of its sweet innocence and loveliness, comes sooner or later the desire to transfer something of these qualities to the outer world. Paul felt this more and more as the days passed. The wish to beautify the lives of others grew in him with a sudden completeness that proved it to have been there latent all the time.⁶

Uncle Paul's desire to 'beautify' the world through his stories was the same spiritual mission that O'Malley had set himself in *The Centaur*. *A Prisoner in Fairyland*, therefore, becomes the culmination of these efforts.

We are introduced to Henry Rogers, a successful businessman now just turned forty, whose early life reflects Blackwood's own but whose financial status is more of a dream. Able to retire from the management of his companies, and draw income as a director, Rogers withdraws from active business life to allow more time for himself. Lured by the beauty of a spring day he visits the haunts of his childhood, and back to his home at Crayfield. Here he sees again the railway carriage his father had given him as a birthday present and which he christened the Starlight Express. His mind's eye is filled with the many characters his imagination had created – the Dustman, the Lamplighter, the Sweep, the Woman of the Haystack and others – and he remembers too the huge Net of Stars he had made in order to catch stardust, and the Caves of Lost Starlight where the stardust collected. Soon he becomes a prisoner of childhood memories and the fairyland of childhood surrounds him.

Rogers invites himself to join his cousin, John Campden, in Switzerland. Campden (the name thinly disguises Arthur Hobart-Hampden) is a writer, living with his wife and three children in Bourcelles (a name that Blackwood contrived from the neighbouring villages of Boudry and Corcelles, but which is unmistakably Bôle). Campden has become tired and drained by years of supporting a family. He gets easily confused – 'wumbled' the children call it. He is not wealthy, but it is a happy and well bonded family. He too used to have childhood dreams of the Star Caves, something he must have shared with his cousin when they had visited Switzerland as children, though he can't now remember. He spins stories to his children of the Starlight Express and the Net of Stars. One night, before 'Cousin Henry' joins them, the children have a dream where they leave their bodies, join the Starlight Express and see the Star Caves.

The children are Jane Anne (or Jinnie), aged sixteen; Monkey, a twelve-year-old girl whose baptismal name has been forgotten, and Jimbo, aged ten. These are the exact same ages of the Hobart-Hampden children Aileen (Nixie of *Uncle Paul*), Lucy (Toby of *Uncle Paul*) and Vere (Jonah of *Uncle Paul*). Jinnie, although more adult, is still the spritely Nixie, and the one most keen to please Cousin Henry when he arrives. Needless to say, once he does he soon becomes wrapped in their 'aventures'. In their dreams the children travel to the Star Caverns where they collect stardust to sprinkle over people and 'unwumble' them. The effect is most noticeable on Father, who finds he can write again and begins his story about the Star Caves, in which Cousin Henry appears as Orion, the Mighty Hunter.

The constellation of Orion is one of the most prominent in the night sky. In Greek mythology, and in the stars, Orion is perpetually pursuing the Pleiades, seven sisters whom Zeus changed into stars. The eldest and most beautiful of the Pleiades was Maia, who is also the brightest of the Pleiades constellation. Maia was the mother of Hermes, the messenger of the Gods. To the ancient pre-Roman inhabitants of Italy, she was a divinity of spring. Maia is thus full of life, bright, sharp, fulfilling.

Towards the end of *A Prisoner in Fairyland*, the family is visited by a Countess from Austria. Petite, charming and alluring, she too has childhood memories of escaping in her mind away from her authoritarian father into a world of star caverns and stardust. Henry Rogers falls instantly in love with her, believing that they had met somewhere before, maybe in dreams. The book ends with Orion and Maia together. Beauty has returned to Henry Rogers's world and he is now a total captive of Fairyland.

Despite the beauty of Blackwood's theme, the book is overlong and repeats its message too often. It suggests that Blackwood did not want to leave the novel. He was delightfully at home here, a prisoner in his own fairyland. He was living a story set in his own world, with all of his close friends and family, and the tale could have spun out like a daily soap opera, spreading love and happiness as it went. As he told Stephen Graham, 'Here I have forests & children. What more can a man want?'[7]

The trouble from the reader's point of view is that this begins to pall after a while. It becomes too saccharine. *A Prisoner in Fairyland* is a charming book, which benefits from a second reading if you can survive the first. Its charm comes from knowing the people and places described and understanding their relationship. It would have meant most to Blackwood's close circle of friends. The further you drift from Blackwood's time and world, the harder it is to capture the heart of his desire, that the world be covered by a network of strong, positive, good thoughts which enrich people's lives.

The book can seem over sentimental today. When *Prisoner* was published, on 27 May 1913, critics themselves could not make up their minds. Most were supportive. 'A supremely beautiful book,' wrote the *Daily Express*; '. . . in many ways the most beautiful of all Mr Blackwood's remarkable achievements,' said *The Globe*; 'it is the finest he has yet given us,' said *Country Life. The Times Literary Supplement* was more cautious. '. . . the idea itself is more fantastical than imaginative, which is the book's weakness'.

Yet a few years later authorities such as Stewart M. Ellis were regretful of such books. Although he rated Algernon Blackwood alongside M.R. James as the two writers who stood out as specialists in the art of the ghost story, he was sorry that Blackwood had ventured into the groves of pantheism and metaphysics. 'I would sacrifice all the Starlight Expresses and Centaurs and Men that the Trees Loved for some more stories in the style of "A Case of Eavesdropping", "The Listener" and "Secret Worship".'[8] Evidently Ellis had become too wumbled and was not sympathetic to Blackwood's aim of bringing a little beauty back to the world.

In his review in *The Quest*, G.R.S. Mead made an interesting observation. He liked the character of the Countess and wished she had been introduced to the book earlier. The Countess is, of course, Maya Knoop and the book is, once again, dedicated to her as that 'little mouse that, lost in wonder, flicks its whiskers at the thunder!' Maya's charming and eccentric personality took a hold over Blackwood as he worked on the book, making him her 'prisoner'.

II

On 15 January 1912 Blackwood left for Egypt to visit the Knoops at their hotel and sanatorium in Helwan[9], about fifteen miles south of Cairo. At the time Helwan was a fashionable health resort due to its local mineral-water springs. Its qualities had been discovered in the 1870s and it soon became the exclusive resort for the wealthy. The Khedive Tewfiq built a vast winter palace that later became the Tewfiq Palace Hotel. There were also the Grand Hotel and the Al-Hayat. The Knoops developed the Al-Hayat around 1900 originally as a sanatorium. Johann's son Ludwig (always called Ludi) had suffered from tuberculosis but had been cured, and as a token of gratitude Knoop opened the sanatorium and later developed it into the Hotel Al Hayat. It soon gained the reputation as one of the most luxurious hotels in Egypt.

When Blackwood first visited Helwan he did not stay at the Al-Hayat. Perhaps he needed to keep at arm's length from Baron Knoop. He booked in at the Tewfiq Palace Hotel – no doubt all paid for by the Baroness. Blackwood described this first visit in a piece for *Country Life*.

> My windows in a cool and airy building, formerly a vice-regal palace, with spacious halls, wide, lofty corridors, and palms that rustle endlessly in a shady garden, look forth to the Pyramids across the strip of brilliant vegetation where the Nile meanders with its freight of sweeping, pointed sails that rise like great wings of birds from the very ground. And from another window, facing south and east, I can see the sun rise over the Arabian wilderness of sand. [. . .] And

when the moon comes up behind the dim Mokattam Hills and the fragrant Desert air blows across my writing-table, it is difficult to believe that the stately building is not a tent and that the stirring of the mosquito curtains round the bed is not the flapping of its canvas sides.[10]

Blackwood could not find a more ideal location. He soon did all the tourist spots around Helwan – the pyramids, the cemetery at Memphis, the temples of Thebes, the Sphinx by moonlight, though he found these 'disappointing' compared to the majesty and mystery of the desert. What captivated Blackwood was Egypt's timelessness or, more accurately, accumulation of time. 'Its very endlessness,' was how Blackwood described it. 'Egypt *is* endless and inexhaustible; some hint of eternity lies there, an awareness of immortality almost.'[11]

Although Blackwood was part of the rich society at Helwan, and thus was drawn into the social engagements, plus playing tennis, golf and dining with the Knoops and other rich guests, there were also opportunities to escape. Trips down the Nile, walks into the desert, exploring ridges and gullies – especially at night. Egypt was fascinating by day, but by night the mystery of the desert deepened.

Last night, on going to bed, I went out on to the balcony to close the shutters. The stupendous apparition of it stood upright – as it were, on end – against my very face, reaching to the stars as well as to the far horizons.[12]

Blackwood spent a couple of nights in the desert at the Wadi Hof gorge an hour east of Helwan. Sleeping in a sleeping-bag during the day, watched by jackals and vultures, and awakening at night to absorb the sensations, he wrote that 'the desert soaked down into him'. He could feel the primevalness of the place, and that he could almost be on another world. But most strongly of all was the sense of eternity, 'world without end'.

It was that intensity of Egypt's past that stimulated him. Some years before he had started a story called 'Sand', set in Egypt. He told Macmillan's that he had been unable to finish it until he had experienced the desert first hand. 'Sand' is a powerful novella of the occult, a throw-back to the John Silence stories and *The Human Chord*. The narrator is Felix Henriot. Driven out of London by the winter, Henriot visits Egypt and stays at Helwan. This part of the story is totally autobiographical, even to the point of standing on the hotel balcony and feeling the desert rise up before him.

Henriot meets an odd Englishman, Richard Vance. Henriot can hear music and chanting coming from his room. Later he sees Vance with a woman, his aunt, Lady Statham, whom Henriot is convinced has control over Vance. Statham is an elderly lady, her face 'wore centuries'. He is drawn to them and becomes part of their circle, though he later reflects it was not of his volition. He was chosen to take part in their experiments. Henriot is required as a witness, to describe the events and to capture an image of the shape and form of the being that is summoned. For Lady Statham intends to evoke the very spirit of ancient Egypt itself. The invocation takes place at Wadi Hof, and Blackwood's description as the past comes to life and the desert rises up into enormous cliffs of time through which the ancient spirit returns to the world is among his most powerful writing. Hereward Carrington later cited 'Sand' for the graphic description of an invocation that was similar to one he had witnessed.[13] Once again, though, the experiment has fatal consequences and ends in failure.

'Sand' was the first of Blackwood's stories inspired by Egypt. He completed it in only a few weeks, in time to include in *Pan's Garden*, sending the story to Graham Robertson for illustration at the end of March 1912.

III

It was during March 1912 that Blackwood met the German poet Rainer Maria Rilke (1875–1926). Maya Knoop had decided to accompany Blackwood back to Switzerland en route to England. I have found no evidence that the Baron accompanied them, and if this seems strange, the evidence of Stephen Graham in his autobiography suggests that Blackwood and Maya were often together without the Baron.

In July 1911 Rainer Rilke had sent Maya a copy of his translation of *Le Centaure*, a prose poem by the French poet Maurice de Guérin (1810–39), written in 1835. The translation was dedicated to Maya in thanks for the help and support she and the Baron had given Rilke that winter. Always with a weak constitution Rilke had spent a month at the Knoop's Helwan sanatorium during February and March. Blackwood was already aware of Guérin's poem, but no doubt interest was restimulated when Maya showed him Rilke's translation during his stay in February 1912. Maya had come to know Rilke through his wife, the young sculptress Clara Westhoff. The Baron had commissioned work from Clara and after Clara and Rilke's separation, Clara had visited the Knoops at Helwan.

On their trip back from Egypt Maya decided to introduce Blackwood to Rilke. Rilke had been staying at Duino Castle, just outside Trieste (at that time part of the Austro-Hungarian empire), where he was the guest of the Hapsburg Princess Marie von Thurn und Taxis-Hohenlohe. He had become footloose again and was considering heading for Vienna, but instead went for a few days to Venice. There he met Maya and Blackwood, at the Grand Hotel. Blackwood's only memory of the meeting was that they spent a few hours in a gondola. It seems the conversation was wholly in German and Blackwood later stated that while he followed it easily, he felt unequal to contributing much.[14] Clearly the discussion was entirely between Maya and Rilke. It was about books and poetry and life in general. There was nothing about mysticism or Eastern philosophy, otherwise Blackwood recalled he would have contributed. Maya mentioned Blackwood's own book *The Centaur*, which raised Rilke's interest. Unfortunately the lack of a German translation and Rilke's inability to read English meant he could not read the book.

The exact date of the meeting is not known. Rilke wrote to Princess Marie about it on 29 March, and Blackwood was back in Bôle by the 30th. He says that the Baroness 'passed through here quite hurriedly,' so it was clearly just a fleeting visit, and they could have reached Switzerland the following day. But Rilke was not the best of correspondents, often delaying writing letters so the meeting may have happened several days earlier. Rilke's recollection is more detailed.

> Just think who was there, too? Blackwood in person. Dear Lord, Princess, these coming men look like Arctic explorers or lion-hunters – they are right. At last it is being discovered that one needs such an outfit for this métier of writing. What's more, he is now doing three books at a time, the beast, and still has masses of time left to enjoy the pleasantest of leisure. All the same, in the short time we had, we got on well together, that is to say we both looked at each other in genuine amazement.[15]

The apparent familiarity with Blackwood at the start of that letter originally made scholars think Rilke had met Blackwood earlier. Eudo

Mason of Edinburgh University concluded that they had met when Rilke was at Helwan the year before[16] but Blackwood had previously denied that, stating categorically that he only met Rilke the once. It is more likely that Maya had mentioned Blackwood to Rilke following his translation of Guérin's poem and that Rilke had discussed this with the Princess.

Evidently the Baroness gave Rilke a copy of Blackwood's *Centaur*, but Rilke, unable to read it, had passed it to the Princess. She read it twice, and was effulgent about it in a letter to Rilke in May 1912.

> I am reading *The Centaur* again, and once again I am experiencing that same extraordinary sensation which I had the first time: it is something calling and sounding – something wonderful – not clearly expressed, on the contrary, as though someone were stammering out a message – and yet, or perhaps for that very reason . . . O *Dottor Serafico*, we must read it together![17]

Rilke's reaction was:

> Dear Princess, what you said about Blackwood's *Centaur* made me prick up my ears – that he finally managed this test makes everything possible. I'm really impatient to read him with you.[18]

Maya Knoop continued to send Rilke copies of Blackwood's books, which he duly forwarded to the Princess. She must have read several of the books to Rilke, perhaps in an abbreviated paraphrased translation, but enough for Rilke to know what the books were about, because ten years later he referred to *The Education of Uncle Paul*. This was in a letter to Balthusz, the young son of the artist Baladine Klossowska. Balthusz's birthday was on 29 February, and Rilke told the boy that his birthday was hidden in this land in the crack between yesterday and tomorrow. He hoped he could peep through that crack in his sleep provided he didn't disappear into it altogether.

There is no evidence that Blackwood's work in any way influenced Rilke, though it is possible the meeting, and the enthusiasm of the Princess for *The Centaur* encouraged Rilke in his work. Early in 1912 Rilke had written his first *Elegy* of Duino and then he hit a moody, dry period, but his sojourn in Venice seemed to inspire him and he began work on his second Duino *Elegy*. Perhaps Maya, if not Blackwood, had helped that inspiration. Stephen Graham said of her that 'she was one of those women who allow a man to shine'.[19]

IV

Back in Switzerland Blackwood promptly mailed 'Sand' off to Graham Robertson to illustrate, wrote to Macmillan to advise them the story was en route and knocked off a quick squib for *The Morning Post*, 'Egyptian Antiquities', a nonfantasy set on board the Marseilles–Alexandria steamer and looking at the commercial fakery in fraudulent 'antiques'.

With Maya present, Blackwood was inspired and threw himself into completing *Prisoner in Fairyland*. 'Something had lit the world,' is how he describes it in *Prisoner*. 'Something had lit his heart.'[20] And so it was. If Blackwood was ever in love, at least by his way of thinking, this was the closest he ever came. Stephen Graham thought so too. 'Algernon Blackwood fell under her spell,' he wrote. 'A love-affair began and lasted the rest of his life, though without physical expression. . . She was his inspiration and they were inseparable.'[21]

A Prisoner in Fairyland is the book that it became because Blackwood had found his own spiritual fairyland. It is probably true to say that Blackwood was never happier than he was during 1912 and 1913. His books were being received and reviewed favourably, and earlier ones were being reprinted. He did not have much money but he had sufficient for his needs and now had a patroness in Maya. His life at Bôle was a delight, almost like Shangri La. And he had a spiritual companion. His dedications to Maya tell their own story. Why, we might ask, is *The Promise of Air* simply dedicated 'To M. S-K. (1913)' unless that year held a special significance in their growing relationship.[22] In *The Extra Day* he calls her 'You Extra Being in an Extra Day', whilst in *The Wave* she is 'Egypt's Forgetful and Unwilling Child'.

Although *A Prisoner in Fairyland* is a beautiful story, it is highly self-indulgent, and maybe we can excuse Blackwood that since he was in a seventh heaven when writing it. More than a fairy story, he had written a love story. Although he always regarded *The Centaur* as the best book he had written, *A Prisoner in Fairyland* remained closest to his heart, as we shall see with his continuing desire to keep it before the public as *The Starlight Express*.

Blackwood and Maya returned to England in May. Maya returned to the Baron at South Park, whilst Blackwood stayed with friends in London. It was not so easy to stay at his brother's as it had been before Stevie married. With no London flat any more Blackwood needed to draw upon his growing circle of friends for a place to stay when he was in England. This only ever once seemed to be a problem, when Stephen Graham's wife Rosa would not let Blackwood stay at their country cottage. But that was after the war.

Blackwood did not plan to stay in London for long. It gave him an opportunity to check publishing details with Macmillan's and to catch up with friends. This was when he at last met Edward Carpenter and, for the first time, Hilaire Belloc (1870–1953).

Blackwood had corresponded infrequently with Belloc for at least the last couple of years and probably longer. It had been Belloc's essay-review of *The Empty House* that had helped boost Blackwood's career six years earlier, and Belloc had regularly given a good review to every new book. In February 1912 Elodie, Belloc's American wife, had written to Blackwood to express her fascination for 'The Destruction of Smith', which Belloc was about to publish in his paper *The Eye Witness*[23]. The love and dedication that Smith showed for Smithville in that story was mirrored in Elodie's love for their home at Kings Land near Horsham.

Blackwood expressed a hope that they could meet some time and eventually a date was fixed on 6 June. Blackwood was also enchanted with Kings Land and with the Belloc children – Eleanor (aged thirteen), Elizabeth (eleven), Hilary (ten) and Peter (seven). The eldest, Louis, was away at the time. 'I really must write a story to haunt their mill,' he wrote to Elodie in thanks. 'I still see in my mind your enchanting house and meadows with the long swing of the Downs wrapping it about, and have the feeling those Downs really circle it completely round and guard it.'[24] It's a pity that Blackwood did not write this story, as by the time he began to write children's stories on a regular basis Belloc's children had all grown up and Louis had been lost in action during the war.

Never at a loss for inspiration, though, the idea of the Downs guarding the Belloc house may have inspired the short story, 'Ancient Lights'[25]. This is set just a mile or two north of the Belloc home at Southwater. It tells of a surveyor's clerk who goes to look at a wood that is to be cut down to improve the view from a house. But the wood knows, and when the clerk enters the wood, the trees close in on him.

During July Blackwood spent a couple of weeks back in Switzerland at Maloja in the Engadine. It's possible that Blackwood had tried to arrange a brief holiday with his sister but it did not work out. His regrets over this resulted in the story 'Let Not the Sun – '[26], where a brother and sister argue over a venue for a holiday and the brother dies before the sister can make amends.

That autumn he returned to Sussex with his cousin. With their son's education complete in Switzerland, the Hobart-Hampdens had returned to England and settled on a farm in Sussex. It was a large farm, of 400 acres, and in need of repair. Blackwood remarked that it was leaky, windy and rather isolated. When he wasn't writing or going for long walks across the Downs, Blackwood was picking apples and blackberries and shooting rabbits, and no doubt helping out generally on the farm. 'Sussex feels to me the biggest county of all – two-thirds of England at least, & one tastes the sea on certain days, & there are such big horizons, and the wind has room to play in.'[27]

Blackwood headed back to Switzerland in the middle of November 1912 and so missed the birth of his nephew, Patrick, on 5 December. Now Blackwood was a real uncle, and though Patrick would later refer to him as Uncle Algie, he remained Uncle Paul to all his young friends.

Blackwood returned to Bôle, but now that his cousins were in England, he decided not to stay. The last of his stories set at Bôle was 'La Mauvaise Riche'[28], a rather sombre ghost story. Out walking with his cousin the narrator finds that his niece, Izzie, is visiting the grave of an old lady, Mère Corbillard[29], who had recently died. Although no one else seemed to like the old miser, Izzie had a morbid attraction for her. Later that day both the narrator and the cousin suddenly see Izzie walking with the ghost of the old lady. The story may have grown from thoughts following the death of an English lady who had lived at Bôle for some years. She was getting old and forgetful and everyone thought of her as a bore, but they all missed her when she went. She was the basis for Miss Waghorn in *A Prisoner in Fairyland*.

In the New Year Blackwood scouted around for a new winter home and settled at the Hotel Kurhaus in Saanenmoser near Gstaad in the Valais Alps. This would become his home for the rest of his life, excluding the War years, and his ashes were scattered over the hills around the town. His love for the place is evident in one of the earliest pieces he wrote about it.

> Saanenmoser, like its admirable mountain hotel, is unique. Railways help it on all sides – to bring one home again. Apart from a dozen

smaller 'runs' of enticing beauty that start from the very door, there
are two and three day trips in other directions, all easily accessible;
and the great Wildhorn beckons just beyond the ridge – the Wildhorn,
whose head towers 10,000ft. into the sunshine, whose climbing
means a lightning descent of 6,000ft., and a night in a hut halfway
up into the bargain.[30]

That mountain hut comes alive in 'H.S.H.'[31] Delane, a climber who
has rather wasted his life, takes refuge in a hut whilst having deliberately
set himself a rigorous week's climbing in a remote part of Switzerland.
In a strangely Hoffmannesque episode the climber is visited by another
whom, it transpires, is the Devil in human form seen, like Delane, as a
wanderer and a wastrel. The Devil had focused on Delane's weakness
in the hope of claiming his soul and using him as a stepping stone to
reclaim his kingdom. Delane, having previously been reflecting on his
wasted life, now draws strength from the love he has for the World to
combat the Devil and cast him out.

V

No sooner had Blackwood arrived at Saanenmoser than he received
an intriguing telegram.

> Your psychic help urgently needed at 49 Edgware Road. Come
> immediately if you can. Isobel Dunn.[32]

The telegram had been sent by Macmillan's, who had received a
formal letter from Mrs Dunn. Blackwood had been receiving such
requests ever since the publication of *John Silence* at the end of 1908.
Alas most of these are lost, but a few survive. A couple are worth
covering here.

The letter explained the problem.

> My knowledge of the laws of vibration, which you write about in
> 'The Human Chord', is absurdly limited but I know enough to know
> that the whole trouble with my sister (whom I want you to come
> and see) is connected with these things. She doesn't know how to
> control certain notes which are in her. Thank God, I *think* her worst
> stage is over. She is now her normal self again, only I am in such
> agonies lest it shall return. She almost lost her life, though *not* her

reason, as people round her thought. They insist on thinking of 'spirit control', which it isn't. It is hardly necessary to say that I am not writing just to effect an introduction to an interesting man if that were the case it could be managed through my cousin whom I believe you have met. Neither are we – either of us – hysterical women. Indeed, we even have a sense of humour. Once more – if you are in England – for God's sake come, and come quickly.

Blackwood did not return to England until April by which time the moment may well have passed. It's typical of many letters for help that Blackwood received. He seldom wrote about these, though probably used some incidents as bases for later stories. There may be some comparison between the above request and the following episode, one of the few incidents that Blackwood did record. Infuriatingly it appears only in a draft note, perhaps for an article he was planning, and remains incomplete. Here is a real cliff-hanger indeed.

Blackwood notes that a woman had written to him for help. He was just going abroad, but when he returned she wrote to him again. He decided to go and see her, though having mislaid the earlier letter had no recollection of the problem, but hoped the lady would remind him. Her home was in the country, where she lived with her sister. They had lunch and then the lady dismissed her sister before telling Blackwood her story. Since her childhood she had been aware of a figure of a priest. It had started simply as a pair of feet, then the legs began to appear and finally the whole figure. Her sister never saw it. The priest appeared to the girl regularly, telling her it was her destiny to help unhappy people. One evening when the woman was alone the priest appeared again saying that there was a special case where only she could help. Into the room walked a gorilla, whose eyes held an expression of pitiful appeal. Although she was frightened she knew she had to help. She prayed for the stricken soul, but nothing happened. The gorilla remained in the house, though the sister never saw it. Apparently – and this is the part I'm sure Blackwood found hard to believe – the gorilla would accompany the woman on the back of her bicycle to mass. 'He always hid himself at the back of the church,' she told Blackwood, 'and never came up to take the sacrament with me'.

Blackwood's credulity must have been stretched though he says he continued to listen 'with sympathy and some degree of understanding'. Apparently over time the woman came to understand the gorilla and one day, as she stood close to it, she kissed the creature. 'A kiss, if you like, of yearning sympathy and understanding,' Blackwood explained. At that moment the gorilla was transformed into a young man, whom she saw for just an instant, and then he was gone, and she saw neither man nor ape again.

You'd think that might be the end of the story, but in this draft note Blackwood then wrote: 'This, however, is nothing to what this woman told me next.'[33]

And there his note ends. There is no record of what the woman told him next, or who she was, or where she lived. But this tells us that from time to time Blackwood would pursue requests from the public.

Such incidents may have prompted Blackwood to think more about his own life and where he was going. Here he was, now forty-four, enjoying life, but with no clear direction. Having finished *A Prisoner in Fairyland* he was less certain of his next book. There was still *Julius LeVallon* to refine and complete the second volume, but for the moment that seems to have passed from his thoughts. It's possible that a sequence of sketches that he worked on now, under the title 'Who Was She?'[34], which began to explore the ethereal nature of a being with the spirit of the air, were thoughts on the sequel to *Julius LeVallon*, but they later formed part of a separate book, *The Promise of Air*. After an early start on this it was dropped for a few years. He also turned his thoughts to his third 'Uncle' book, *The Extra Day*. Several short episodes, most of which were later worked into the novel, began to appear in *The Morning Post*. The earliest, 'Jimbo's Longest Day'[35], did not make it into the book, even though it fits admirably, but others, starting with 'The Story Hour'[36], eventually appeared as individual chapters. At this stage Blackwood was still experimenting and the book had not yet taken its final form.

After a winter in Switzerland, Blackwood moved on to Helwan for February and March 1913. Taking the steamer back to Marseilles he stopped briefly at St Raphael in France, near where his sister Ceci now lived, before returning to Bôle. He then spent some days at Champéry and Geneva before having to return to London at the end of April to resolve a problem that had arisen.

Blackwood had been approached by John Murray about a proposed collection of stories. This led to the volume *Ten Minute Stories*, which gave Blackwood more trouble than it was worth. Blackwood agreed to Murray publishing a volume of his journalism stories, that is those which appeared in *The Westminster Gazette*, *The Morning Post* and similar. He regarded these as slight, but many of them had not been published in book form and Murray felt there was an audience for them. Without thinking, Blackwood gave Murray his folder of stories and left it to him to make the selection. It was only when Blackwood was sent the proofs in April that he discovered with horror that they had used several very early stories that Blackwood regarded as 'trash'. Unfortunately the surviving records do not show which stories these were. Murray's files only identify that they were six stories for which they acquired reprint rights from the Northern Newspaper Syndicate. This suggests they may have been very early stories written by Blackwood soon after his return from America for provincial newspapers that remain untraced.

Blackwood requested that they be dropped from the collection and he promised to select better stories as replacements. Unfortunately Murray had already set the book in type and the cost of revising the volume was placed at £40 (today about £2,400). To resolve the matter Blackwood asked if Macmillan's would send Murray the sum involved and deduct it from future royalties. Murray's, to help limit the problem, decided to issue the book in a six-shilling edition with a higher royalty rate, rather than the cheap 3/6d edition with a lower royalty rate. The book took ten years to sell out its 2,000 copy print run, though an additional impression for an American edition helped costs[37].

All of this delayed publication of *Ten Minute Stories* and caused Blackwood much stress. It was further aggravated when, at the end of the year, he received details from Macmillan on royalties arising on *Pan's Garden*. This had been published on the half-profits scheme, and the sale of 3,000 copies had yielded Blackwood a royalty of only £16. Under the former arrangement of a 15 per cent royalty Blackwood would have expected £135. 'If a sale of some 3,000 copies only results in £16 profit there can only be disappointment for all concerned,' he wrote to Macmillan[38]. The half-profits system was evidently not profitable for Blackwood, and along with the *Ten Minute Stories* fiasco, made it a frustrating year.

Nevertheless, there were the high points. *A Prisoner in Fairyland* was published on 27 May, along with generally agreeable reviews and good feedback from the public. By July he was staying with the Knoops at Wadhurst, before moving on to Graham Robertson's at Sandhills in late August and September. Some of this time he was working on three long stories which would later be collected in *Incredible Adventures*, and which represent the last outburst of his golden period.

The three stories are 'The Damned', 'The Regeneration of Lord Ernie' and 'A Descent Into Egypt'. It's fairly certain that the last story was not finished until spring 1914, in Egypt, and the Lord Ernie story was not completed until his winter season in Switzerland, but it is convenient to consider all three here, as he was certainly working on them at this time. 'The Damned' may well have been started at the Knoops' at Wadhurst, since the house in the story is clearly South Park. Compare the following comments by Blackwood and Stephen Graham:

> I thought, too, of the roomy country mansion her late husband had altered to suit his particular needs, and of my visit to it a few years ago when its barren spaciousness suggested a wing of Kensington Museum fitted up temporarily as a place to eat and sleep in.[39]

And Graham's description:

> It proved to be an immense structure, a castellated aggregation of brickwork. Blackwood has described it as like a wing of a Kensington Museum temporarily fitted up for residence.[40]

Also the widow in the story, Mrs Franklyn, is called Mabel, Maya's real first name. The house is called The Towers, and Blackwood has more disparaging comments to make, noting that it looked outwardly wealthy and pretentious but was inwardly barren and austere.

Although in this story Blackwood had already disposed of Baron Knoop in the shape of the late Samuel Franklyn, a wealthy banker, his description of him is worth considering.

> Yet, in spite of this true sympathy with suffering and his desire to help, he was narrow as a telegraph wire and unbending as a church pillar; he was intensely selfish; intolerant as an officer of the Inquisition, his bourgeois soul constructed a revolting scheme of heaven that was reproduced in miniature in all he did and planned.[41]

Franklyn has his revenge, however, for the house is so saturated with his suffocatingly strong, evangelical, selfish persona, and all those with a like mind who went before him, that it continues to be intolerant of and eject any who do not conform.

When Blackwood wrote this story the Baron was still alive and he and Maya lived at South Park for five more years until his death. Yet in the story Blackwood is surprisingly accurate in his projection that Mabel will marry again and that the house will be sold to a society (in fact it became a private school). The story unites both Blackwood's and Maya's experiences of living in a house which is to all intents a prison – Blackwood's childhood restrained by the strong religious beliefs of his parents; Maya restrained by an overprotective, puritanical despot.

'The Regeneration of Lord Ernie' serves as an escape from 'The Damned', since it is about the rejuvenation of an individual who has lost the zest of life. Hendricks, a teacher who was once in Holy Orders, is charged with taking Lord Ernie ('Bindy' he calls him) round the world in the hope of shaking some vitality and spirit into him. When pregnant, Ernie's mother had suffered frostbite and deprivation in the Canadian wild, and the child was born devoid of the natural spark of life. On the last leg of their journey Hendricks brings the young man to Villaret, near Bôle in the Jura, where he had spent time in his youth with the pastor, Leysin, learning French. Then Hendricks had been in love with Leysin's daughter. He also remembered from those days stories of the wild, pagan locals who lived in huts high in the mountains. He recalls one of his fellow students, Marston, who had ventured into these mountains and returned broken and suicidal.

Hendricks is astonished to find that a new vitality has entered Ernie since they arrived. He is drawn towards the wild men of the mountains and becomes a focus for their evocation of the elemental powers of wind and fire. Ernie becomes dangerously alive, sucked into the pagan rites and is saved only by prayer and the power of the water elemental, when rain deluges the ceremony. Reborn, he succeeds to the title and goes on to become a leading world figure.

'A Descent Into Egypt' has been called by at least one critic 'perhaps Blackwood's finest single work'.[42] It translates 'The Man Whom the Trees Loved' to Egypt by reversing the motif of 'The Regeneration of Lord Ernie'. In other words the sheer cumulative intensity of the past of Egypt becomes a strong spiritual force which can absorb an individual. This is what happens to archeologist George Isley. 'Egypt was a dream-world that made the heart live backwards,' the narrator tells us.[43] And into that dream-world goes the soul of George Isley leaving an empty shell. The final paragraph of the story in which the

13

The Starlight Express (1913–15)

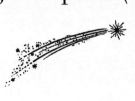

I

Now and again readers approached Blackwood, keen to adapt his books for the stage. Louis Parker had tried to create something soon after *John Silence* appeared in 1908 but found Blackwood's work too ethereal for the theatre. In June 1911 Bertram Holcroft wrote and told Blackwood that he had written incidental music to a play adapted by his sister from Blackwood's *Jimbo*. Holcroft hoped that Blackwood had no objection to it being performed for a charity, perhaps the Children's League of Pity.

Another who saw the theatrical potential in his work was aspiring playwright Violet Pearn (1880–1947). She lived in Guildford, Surrey, at St Michael's Cottage, which she shared with Gertrude Pratt, aunt of the actress Muriel Pratt. Neither Violet nor Gertrude were well acquainted with housework, and as they also kept several large dogs their house and garden was always in disarray. So was Violet. A friend from those days remembered that she was a large lady with thick heavy red hair always coming down with pins dropping everywhere – a veritable model for the Lady of the Haystack. Blackwood gave her the pet name Gingerbread. She also needed glasses but refused to wear them so went everywhere with her eyes and faced screwed up. She was, though, extremely good-hearted. She loved children almost as much as dogs and was frequently entertaining local children, writing them plays for Christmas.[1]

The exact date that Pearn contacted Blackwood is not known. Since *A Prisoner in Fairyland* was not published until 27 May 1913, her request to adapt it was unlikely to have been much before late June at the earliest, but she worked on it quickly and had a synopsis ready by August. At the outset Blackwood left Pearn alone to work on the play, not regarding it as anything he needed to get involved with, but by September he was taking a greater interest, even though he acknowledged that he had no dramatic sense. 'I am no playwright; I possess none of the necessary talents,' he later wrote[2].

Blackwood began to visit Pearn regularly. Guildford was not too far from Robertson's house at Witley – just three stations on the train. Lavender Jones was then just a young child whose family home backed on to Pearn's, and she recalled being invited round to St Michael's Cottage to meet Blackwood.

> I remember him as very tall and dark. We were told to call him 'Uncle Paul'. Blackwood joked with us and called us names – my brother Cuthbert was called Cuthbert-in-the-coal-hole I remember. I forget mine. There was a lot of talk about a play and we were given tea and a signed copy of 'Jimbo', a small book which I thought very dull.[3]

In adapting the novel Violet Pearn concentrated on the events in Switzerland and ignored the Henry Rogers' prologue and the epilogue with the Countess. She structured it into four acts for her outline, but as the play took shape this was reduced to three acts. The first introduced the Campden family and the arrival of Cousin Henry. The second was the heart of the play, set in the pine forest with the Starlight Express itself and the spirits of the children collecting the stardust to unwumble their father. The final act shows the outcome and how wonderfully unwumbled Mr Campden has become.

At this stage the adaptation was strictly a play, with no plans for music. Blackwood recalled that this emerged as an 'afterthought'[4], though Pearn had clearly intended that there be songs. The introduction of a character to link the scenes, the Organ-Grinder, demanded that. By October Blackwood was openly discussing music when he remarked that with 'the right music and the right cast this little Play, I believe, may prove to have a vitality which will mark a genuine departure in its "fairy" genre.'[5]

Muriel Pratt (1890–1945) was Pearn's key to the theatrical world. Muriel had, since 1910, performed with Annie Horniman's[6] repertory company at the Gaiety Theatre, Manchester, but by 1913 was establishing her own company at the Theatre Royal, Bristol. This company performed Pearn's first play, *Wild Birds*, in May 1914. Also at the Gaiety Theatre had been Basil Dean (1888–1978). By 1913 he had become assistant stage-director to Sir Herbert Beerbohm Tree at His Majesty's Theatre, London, and it is likely that Muriel Pratt alerted Dean to the *Starlight Express* script. Dean was an obvious target. For the Christmas seasons of 1912 and 1913 he had produced the children's fairy play *Fifinella* by Barry Jackson (1879–1961) in Birmingham and then Manchester, and had hopes of bringing it to His Majesty's Theatre, which had recently had a success with Graham Robertson's *Pinkie and the Fairies*.

The adaptation was finished by early October 1913. Blackwood wrote to Basil Dean on the 9th saying that it was being typed and that he hoped they could provide a first reading the following week, courtesy of Muriel Pratt, to Dean and Frederick Harrison, manager of the Haymarket Theatre.

Blackwood had high hopes for the play. He thought it was 'a chance to light up old London' and that it 'may start the world buzzing in a way a Manager might little dream of'.[7] Blackwood felt the play captured the public mood, all the more so with the darkening events in Europe.

Plans were sufficiently advanced by the end of November for Blackwood to tell Macmillan's that the play had been accepted for production next autumn by 'a London theatre'.[8] In this same letter Blackwood states that he has written the play, not referring to Pearn, suggesting that he had assumed a much larger role than he had originally envisaged. Dean brought in the enthusiastic young Algernon Greig as manager and financial backer, and also asked his friend Clive Carey (1883–1968) to compose the music. Carey was a gifted composer, actor and singer. He had appeared in *Fifinella* as the Man in the Moon and his performance had been one of the highlights of the production. Dean no doubt hoped that Carey could bring a sparkle to this play not only through his music but also with his wonderful voice in the part of the Organ-Grinder.

Blackwood left for Switzerland at the end of November, arriving in Saanenmoser on 3 December for a month's skiing before the season took off. He left production in the hands of Dean and Greig. George Harris, who had designed the sets for *Fifinella* and other of Dean's productions was brought in. Carey began on the music in March 1914. Meanwhile, after Christmas, Blackwood moved on to Helwan.

II

He completed several stories in Egypt. In 'A Desert Episode'[9] we are reintroduced to Paul Rivers, though this is a shadow of the man who was once Uncle Paul. It's easier to presume it is a different character, except that Blackwood probably chose the name specifically. It allows him to show a progression in a man once wild and adventurous but who now, suffering from tuberculosis, has come to Egypt to die. To Blackwood there is no death in Egypt, only eternity. Rivers becomes attracted to a woman at the hotel and the two succumb to the wave of eternity. Their bodies pass away but their souls merge with the endlessness of the desert. It was a theme Blackwood would rework in *The Wave*. Although this story seems admirably suited to the relationship between Blackwood and Maya, Blackwood may have been thinking of Hilaire and Elodie Belloc. Elodie's health had been poor for some while but it entered a severe decline in December 1913 and she died on 2 February, probably of cancer. Blackwood had not seen them for over a year, but he would have sympathized with Hilaire's distress, which was intense, and would have experienced his own loss, for Elodie was a delightful woman.

The story includes reference to an 'international dancer' who came to dine at the hotel. Elsewhere Blackwood remarks that he once saw Isadora Duncan dance in Egypt, and this may be the occasion, except that Duncan was not in Egypt at this time.[10] Perhaps watching Duncan inspired another story. 'The Wings of Horus'[11] is both a beautiful love story and an awesome story of power and belief. Binovitch is in love with Vera as is the psychiatrist Plitzinger. Binovitch believes that flight is possible if one can control the powers of the air. Urged on he calls upon the god Horus and leaps from a table. He falls to the floor but not after those present believe that, perhaps for just a second, he hovered. Binovitch feels betrayed, however, and curses Horus. Thereafter some sense that as he passes he is accompanied by the sound of wings. A few days later there is a costume ball and Binovitch arrives dressed as a hawk in a costume of bewildering reality. Vera is dressed as a dove. Plitzinger comes disguised as a Pierrot. Both Plitzinger and Binovitch vie for Vera's attention until Binovitch, calling upon the powers of the air, escapes with Vera. The others follow in pursuit and are just in time to save Vera following Binovitch over a cliff. But there were those who fancied they had seen enormous wings bear Binovitch away, for when his body is found at the bottom of the cliff, there is not a mark upon him. Fifteen years later Blackwood adapted this story into a ballet with Kinsey Peile, and it was going to be produced by Anton Dolin had finances been available. It is art's loss as this is one of Blackwood's most visually appealing stories.

Even Blackwood's lesser Egyptian stories are of interest. 'By Water'[12] arose from a sentence that kept running through his mind when he woke one morning: 'You will drown but you will not know you drown.' The idea of drowning in the desert struck him as an intriguing story challenge.

'An Egyptian Hornet'[13] is nothing more than an incident, but is an interesting study in phobia. A curate goes for his morning bath only to find a hornet obstructing his bath. He manages to avoid it, both on the way in and the way out, but is chagrined to find with what ease a grumpy individual, whom the curate dislikes, disposes of the insect. This episode almost certainly happened to Blackwood as described. He had a morbid fear of spiders and confessed he was ashamed of this fear and hated it when it was revealed to others.

Blackwood returned from Egypt via the Austrian Tyrol, stopping at Meran[14]. Two other stories from this period are worth a passing mention. 'A Bit of Wood'[15] is a short reflective piece on the workings of fate. A man musing over life kicks a piece of wood into a stream. It is carried away in the current and some miles away gets trapped in and blocks a mill wheel. A worker climbs down to clear the wheel, is caught and drowned. 'The Falling Glass'[16], which on the surface seems little more than a mood piece about mountaineers sensing the coming of a violent storm, in hindsight stands as a powerful allegory for the gathering storm of the Great War.

Five weeks after the story was published the assassination of the Austro-Hungarian archduke Franz Ferdinand in Serbia unravelled the cat's cradle of treaties that started the First World War. Britain entered the war on 4 August. With it Blackwood's hopes for the production of *The Starlight Express* were dashed. Funding was not forthcoming and there were too many other uncertainties. American interest was also curtailed, the American Play Company returning the script as 'not practical'. By September Basil Dean had enlisted in the army. He returned the script to Blackwood in the first week of October. A few days later we find Blackwood writing to Annie Horniman in Manchester asking whether she was interested in a Fairy Play for Christmas.[17] Blackwood explained that the music was mostly written and that the production was not expensive. Evidently Horniman was not interested. Dean's option on the play expired in February 1915 and, for the moment, that was that.

III

At the outbreak of the War Blackwood volunteered his services as an interpreter. He was summoned to Whitehall for an interview and a *viva voce*, which he passed, being scored 'good', but he heard no more.

While he waited Blackwood put the final touches to the collection *Incredible Adventures*. The book was published on 6 November 1914, once again dedicated 'To M. S.-K.', though this time with no message. Reviews were generally favourable. There seemed to be something for everyone. *The Bookman*, which remarked that 'Here is a book which fulfils its title', singled out 'A Descent into Egypt' as the best story because of its 'sheer beauty of craftsmanship – the magic of words'. The *Morning Post* reckoned that 'The Damned' represented 'the climax of its author's achievement'. *The Observer* decided that 'all the tales are works of supreme artistry'. However, the *Times Literary Supplement*, whilst recognizing the craftsmanship in the stories and their sensitivity, also noted how verbose Blackwood had become – 'He refines, suggests, ponders at too great length and with too much caution'. This self-indulgence and prolixity reached their extremes in *The Wave* and *The Promise of Air*.

Frustrated at the lack of action in England, Blackwood took himself back to Switzerland, to Saanenmoser and Montreux. He had hoped he might become involved in propaganda work, but there was no organization in hand and it struck Blackwood as utterly ineffective. He observed the changes already taking place. Germans were still holidaying in Switzerland as they had for years, but were being ostracized and there was a growing hatred of them among the 'allies'. Blackwood conjectured how the Germans would be perceived after the war, and how long it would take for relations to get back to normal.[18]

With no war work, Blackwood settled down to his next Uncle book, *The Extra Day*. Once again we enter the world of three children, Judy, Tim and Maria, who live in an old country house, and are visited by their otherworldly Uncle Felix. Unlike the previous two books, which were told from the adult's viewpoint, and explored the change in individual's outlook heading towards a definite conclusion, this book is seen from the children's perspective and has no firm conclusion, merely the culmination of a series of adventures. It also lacks the originality of the first two, because Blackwood is simply reworking themes. He takes the concept of 'the Crack' from *Uncle Paul* and turns that into an 'Extra Day' – a day lost in time where eternity exists. And, because he was working on *The Starlight Express*, he introduced many of the images from that, such as the Policeman, the Gardener and the Tramp, as concepts of things that mean either order or mystery. Indeed the Tramp is the secret of the book, the key to the Extra Day.

The book allows Blackwood to explore the wonder and mystery of time, asking questions as mysterious today as they were then, especially to children. Where does time come from, where does it go, why is it slow some times and fast other times, and why are some days longer than others? By exploring these ideas through children's eyes but with a mystical perspective, he was able to conjure up images of wonder and awe without becoming overly philosophical. The book is thus an easier read and more fun than *A Prisoner in Fairyland*, but it lacks the personal impact of *The Education of Uncle Paul*. Most significantly whereas the first two are definitely adult books, this one begins as a children's book, but ends as an adult's.

Blackwood admitted as much when he submitted it to Macmillan's in May.

> Whilst it deals with children in the vein of *Uncle Paul* and *Prisoner in Fairyland* it is perhaps, more than anything, a book *for* children. My idea has been to describe the sense of Wonder which, beginning with Fancy, leads on to bigger wonder which is Spiritual; and, incidentally, to show the wonder of common things.[19]

The individual parts of the book are actually better than the whole. For instance the chapter entitled 'Judy's Particular Adventure' had already appeared as a separate story called 'The Daisy World'[20]. Rather like the 'Vision of the Winds' in *Uncle Paul*, in this adventure Felix and Judy, while dozing in the garden and thinking about daisies, find themselves shrinking and becoming daisies and experiencing the world from the daisy's perspective. Blackwood was creating visions and experiences rather like computer virtual reality today. This was his delight to children. He could make them enjoy the world about them and think about it in a different way to normal, rather like *Alice in*

Wonderland. At times he plays Carrollian games with words and phrases, such as the distinction between 'Now', 'Then' and the strange adult phrase, 'Now then'.

Blackwood had read portions of the book aloud to children and he took note of their unconscious criticism. Blackwood now moved in a large circle of friends and relatives many of whom had young children, and he probably tested the individual chapters on any willing audience. These would have included his cousin's children (the originals of Jimbo, Monkey and Toby) and the children of Clara and Frederick Huth Jackson, the young Anne and Clara. Clara Huth Jackson (1870–1944), known to everyone as Tiny, was a long-time friend of Blackwood's. She was the wife of the Director of the Bank of England. They had a home at La Maison du Diable in Aix les Bains, near Grenoble in France, within easy reach of Geneva. Blackwood remembered being nearly run down by young Clara on her new bicycle.

Through fun and fancy Blackwood instilled awe and wonder in the children and this enabled him to take them beyond the everyday into worlds mystical and spiritual. In the climax of the book, 'Maria's Particular Adventure', which is almost half the book's length, they enter the Extra Day lost to time. They follow the Tramp to his world at the End of Time where they each experience their own understanding of life and get a chance to lift the veil off the world for just a moment and perceive the realities beyond.

Although the book is inspirational, full of wonderful images and creative prose, it is something of an anti-climax, because the book does not reveal the children's inner discoveries. You enjoy their wonder but it is difficult to be part of it. The first half of the book works because Blackwood describes the wonders they see. But the second half is a spiritual revelation and can only work for those attuned to Blackwood's wavelength.

When the book was published on 5 October 1915, reviewers were in a dilemma. They could appreciate Blackwood's wonderful prose and imagery but were not sure where the book was going and hoped each individual reader would find their own reward. The reviewer in *Country Life*, probably Stephen Graham, accurately summarized Blackwood's outlook on life:

> For Blackwood is a child and sees others in their ever-young aspect. He sees our angels. Those, however, who know him well, know that he is still after something new, and that not even here has he said the word he wishes to say.[21]

Just like the children in the book, Blackwood remained a seeker, ever after new perceptions, new outlooks, new interpretations of the world. Although he wrote no further 'Uncle' novels, he did revisit the world of the 'Extra Day' one more time, and rather more successfully, twenty years later in his final novel, *The Fruit Stoners*.

IV

Despairing of getting any propaganda work in Switzerland, Blackwood returned to England in March 1915 and settled into a new room built for him at the home of his brother and sister-in-law at Gillingham Street. He called it 'the house that Master Pat built'[22]. He had other books in hand, but did not tell Macmillan's about them as he was uncertain about their timeliness, regarding them as 'after-the-war' books, and far in advance of anything he had previously attempted. He does not name the books, though they were almost certainly *The Promise of Air* and *The Wave*. Both of these could be called 'after-the-war' books, if by that he meant they were books that would stimulate and rebuild people after disaster. Like everyone else, though, Blackwood did not expect the war to last as long as it did, or to be so disastrous. His one true 'after-the-war' book was yet to be written, *The Garden of Survival*, and it was a book so personal that at first he had no intention of seeking publication.

So, for the moment, Blackwood sought other outlets and other opportunities. He was frequently found at social gatherings where hosts delighted in his storytelling. At the start of June 1915 he stayed with Sir Richard Pennefather at Little Waltham Hall in Chelmsford, Essex. Sir Richard and his wife Sina were renowned hosts who held regular gatherings for the great and the famous, including the Rajah and Ranee of Sarawak. Blackwood's social status had risen remarkably since his vagrant days twenty years before, though it was this background that made him an attraction at these gatherings. He had such a fund of original and unusual stories to tell.

Blackwood occasionally attended the Quest Society meetings organized by G.R.S. Mead, though as it was becoming more of a spiritualist organization, Blackwood was losing interest. He was a charter member of the Fellowship of the Rosy Cross, inaugurated by A.E. Waite on 9 July 1915, but there is no evidence that he attended any meeting[23]. Blackwood was more interested in meeting interesting people than he was in any formal study. He kept in contact with several people who were in these esoteric orders such as Lady Frances Warwick, Mrs Alberta Montgomery, Edith and William Sawyer, William T. Horton, Margaret Lumley Brown and, of course, Waite himself,[24] but he had moved on from the need to be a regular member of a society.

Also Blackwood's work was starting to gain critical attention. His books had always garnered long and intelligent reviews, but the first full-length appreciation of his work was by the American author Grace Isabel Colbron (1869–1948) in *The Bookman* for February 1915. Although Macmillan had secured American editions of all of their volumes, the early Nash editions had not seen American printings, apart from *John Silence. The Empty House, The Listener* and *The Lost Valley* had only just appeared in America and this sudden concentration of Blackwood had caused critics to pay attention. 'Algernon Blackwood stands in a class by himself,' Colbron wrote adding, with remarkable insight, 'Blackwood has given us lyrics of childhood that will last. Children themselves may not understand them until they grow up, and then only if they are the sort of children that never grow up.'[25] Her assessment of his work was astute, noting as well that Blackwood was among that group of writers who was 'more read than talked about'. Moreover she hoped, in some ways, it would stay that way. Colbron felt she had discovered an author who was very personal to her, and to many others, and she did not want that special relationship tainted by overcommercialism.

At this same time Maude ffoulkes was completing her autobiography *My Own Past*. She had left Eveleigh Nash under acrimonious circumstances and Nash was concerned that her autobiography would say things about him he would rather left unsaid. He took the ridiculous step of taking out a court order to stop publication of the book. The court case that followed only served to publicize ffoulkes's book all the more. In fact she said nothing about Nash, but she had devoted a whole chapter to Blackwood. The book, published in October 1915, also included a wonderful sketch by Stephen Reid depicting a scene from 'Ancient Sorceries'.

The American scholar and folklorist Dorothy Scarborough (1877–1935) was undertaking her research at this time at Columbia University which would culminate in the first significant survey of weird and occult fiction in *The Supernatural in Modern English Fiction*, completed in April 1917. She gave Blackwood's work considerable attention, concluding that 'Blackwood is doing more significant form in psychic fiction than anyone else, his prose showing poetic beauty as well as eerie power.'[26]

The value of Blackwood's work was being appreciated and he was emerging from the rank and file into a celebrity of unique vision.

Once *The Extra Day* was completed Blackwood produced a number of short, ephemeral stories and articles, most of them war-inspired, and many of them propagandistic, or at least endeavouring to raise morale. Curiously his first war-related item almost welcomed the war. 'The Miracle'[27], published just two months into the war, welcomed the 'loss of self' and coming together of the British Empire into a harmonious crowd or group soul. Blackwood believed strongly in the concept of a group soul and a cosmic consciousness out of which all spirits were born and to which all things returned. He would later attempt a novel on the theme. The article was typical of Blackwood. Where others saw doom-and-gloom he saw beauty. And he hoped that after the war this sense of brotherhood would continue into a universal brotherhood.

'The Miracle' contained both a profound spiritual message and a Christian one, and the piece was reprinted in both the evangelical magazine, *The Watchword* (December 1914) and the mystical *The Quest* (January 1915). It would have worked well as a sermon. It's the first clear item by Blackwood to show his fourth and strongest 'torch', or ambition, of being a holy man. His desire to spread 'beauty' through the world, which had manifested itself in *The Education of Uncle Paul* and *A Prisoner in Fairyland* was perhaps at its best during adversity. Blackwood returned to this idea of a universal or hive mind, with all Britons united in their thinking of good thoughts and victory, rather than hate and destruction, in 'Think Victory'[28], one of a series of positive-minded essays he wrote for *The Standard*. There is also something quaint and absurdly old-fashioned, in 'The Higher Command', where Blackwood believes that the British sense of fair play is the key to victory, and almost elevates this to a form of religious understanding.

His first war-inspired story was the highly propagandistic 'The God'[29]. The narrator is an author, like Blackwood, completing his latest novel, which recreated the Greek gods. The author feeling redundant, has reconciled with himself that 'artists are necessary folk in a time like this', when he is interrupted by his secretary, Robinson. Robinson had become dreamy and listless but he suddenly seems to grow from his chair, unfurl his metaphorical wings and become like the ancient

Greek gods when he reveals he wants to enlist. The story is too saccharine today, almost jingoistic, but was just the kind of material the papers wanted to publish to encourage enlistment.

It was at this same time that his friend, Wilfrid Wilson, joined the British Red Cross as a driver in France[30] and his sister Ceci also joined as a nurse. Blackwood eventually joined the Red Cross himself, but not for another two years. He did, though, explore the possibility of being involved with the Field Ambulance Service run by Dr Hector Munro. Once again this seemed to take time and Blackwood was left to his own devices. He retained that Victorian boyhood zeal for action and righting wrongs and wanted to feel he was contributing to the war effort. His frustration at not being able to do anything was reflected in 'The Paper Man'[31] where a man, too old to serve, feels he is useless and crumbles like brittle paper.

There were two inspirational stories that Blackwood produced at this time. 'The Soldier's Visitor'[32] may be likened to Arthur Machen's 'The Bowmen', written a year earlier. In Machen's story soldiers at a crucial moment in the Battle of Mons have a vision of St George and a host of Henry V's medieval bowmen which inspires them into action. It gave rise to the legend of the Angels of Mons, which has endured to this day. In Blackwood's story an injured soldier is convalescing. He is visited by a young woman, who thanks him and blesses him and he only realizes later that this was the spirit of Britannia. 'Cain's Atonement'[33] was later selected by editor H. Cotton Minchin as one of the best short stories of the war.[34] There are two cousins, rivals more than friends, whose paths frequently cross. Smith becomes resentful because the cards always seem stacked against him, whereas Jones always benefits. In the war they are in the same unit. Advancing from the trenches, Jones is unaware that a grenade thrown from the German trenches is about to strike him. Smith is able to intervene, catch the grenade and throw it back, though he is wounded in the process. While in hospital he has a vision of a past life, millenia ago, when he and Jones hunted together. This proto-Jones is attacked by a wild beast and the proto-Smith hesitates rather than saving him. So it is that, in this life, Smith has suffered for that past deed but redeemed himself with this act of bravery.

By August 1915 Blackwood was back with Maya Knoop. Maya and her niece, Margarita, were helping refugee children. They were staying at Cowley House, in Chertsey, Surrey where, as Blackwood described it, the Baroness 'has filled the house with waifs and strays of various ages who needed a holiday'.[35] In particular there were three Polish boys, Eugene, Vladimir and Adam, whom Maya 'adopted' and looked after for many years.

Blackwood was supposed to be teaching them English though had more fun teaching them to swim and generally enjoy themselves. 'A tiny river flows through the garden,' Blackwood told Belloc, hoping that Belloc's children might join them. 'I'm trying to dam the river and make it deeper, and want help badly. But the mud is awful.'[36] They also had a punt and canoe and Blackwood was trying to recreate his journey down the Danube for the children. The Belloc children did join them for a few days. Belloc had found it difficult looking after them following Elodie's death. No matter how much he tried he realized he was no longer close to them. Yet Blackwood, even though he had no children of his own, so naturally brought children into his world, that all enjoyed themselves like one big family.

On 10 October Blackwood was saddened to learn of the death of his old mentor Alfred H. Louis. For his last few years Louis had lived at Hampstead in North London, but his mind had deteriorated and he lived increasingly in a world of his own making. At the end of September he was admitted to the St Marylebone Infirmary where he died ten days later and was buried at the Plashet Jewish Cemetery in Manor Park.

Two weeks later the Scottish publisher, Blackie & Son asked Blackwood if he would contribute the opening story to the next volume of *Blackie's Christmas Annual*. 'We have greatly enjoyed reading *The Extra Day*, and the story shows a really intimate knowledge of childhood.'[37] When Blackwood forwarded the letter to his agent, A.P. Watt, he showed interest even though he was very busy. 'I think this "children's" field may prove a lucrative one. So far I have not tapped it. Writing *about* children is not the same as writing *for* them, but I will have a good try, and if successful, it might lead eventually to a collection in volume form.'[38] Blackwood did not have the time to pursue the idea then, though he wrote 'Camping Out' for Blackie. It's a nonfantasy about children camping out on the evening of the longest day. But the idea would stay with him and develop in the 1920s.

V

At the same time that Blackwood heard from Blackie & Son, there was a sudden revival of interest in *The Starlight Express*. Muriel Pratt had not forgotten the play. She had perhaps hoped to stage it in her own repertory company in Bristol, but any plans there were shortlived as her company was disbanded in May 1915. By October, however, Muriel was rehearsing at the Kingsway Theatre in London in John Hasting Turner's play *Iris Intervenes*. The proprietor and manager of the theatre was Lena Ashwell (1872–1957). During most of 1915 Ashwell had been heavily involved in organizing concerts for the troops, for which she was awarded the OBE in 1917. Pratt brought the play to Ashwell's attention and something in its message of beauty and wonder must have appealed to her in these dark days. She agreed to stage it that Christmas.

Suddenly it was panic stations. There were less than two months in which to get the sets ready, for everyone to rehearse, to make the costumes and, above all, secure the music. It remains unknown why no one thought to contact Clive Carey and find out what had become of his music. He had continued composing through 1914 until the project collapsed and had completed several pieces of which three still survive.[39] Possibly Blackwood did not realize Carey had completed any items. When Lena Ashwell asked Blackwood for suggestions on music, Blackwood asked his friend at the Savile Club, Robin Legge, then the music critic for the *Daily Telegraph*, and Legge suggested Sir Edward Elgar. Legge tried to telephone Elgar on 9 November, but Elgar was away so both Legge and Ashwell wrote to him.

In those days a letter posted early in the morning would be delivered later that day within London (there were evening deliveries and collections). Elgar returned, read both letters and was sufficiently interested to telephone Lena Ashwell the same night. Ashwell visited Elgar the next day at his home at Severn House, Hampstead and showed him the script and the songs. Elgar spent the rest of the week thinking it over and when Ashwell visited him on Saturday he agreed to provide the score. Because time was short he believed he could do it by adapting some of the music from his *Wand of Youth* suite which had been based on a similar theme of happiness spread by children.

Blackwood met the Elgars on the following Monday (15th) and they found each other's company 'very pleasant'. Lady Elgar recorded in her diary that Blackwood dipped into his fund of stories and experiences, telling them about entering Azote in the Derby. Elgar described him as 'an unusual man and sympathetic to me'.[40] Blackwood became a regular visitor to the Elgars over the next few weeks, and it's possible that some of their 'out-of-the-world talks', as Lady Elgar noted, were added inspiration for Sir Edward. Certainly the two had much in common from music (both being violinists) to mutual acquaintances (both knew the Speyer family, for instance) to shared philosophies and ideologies (both had a fascination in the relationship between adults, childhood and the realities of life).

Blackwood was delighted. Needless to say Clive Carey was not. Carey had enlisted in the army and did not hear about the play's production until its dress rehearsal. Violet Pearn tried to smooth matters over but there was no doubt that Carey felt ill-treated. His friend Edward Dent, later commented that 'Malicious gossip had it that the author, Algernon Blackwood, was going about saying that the play was being produced by God! In that case Clive was well out of it.'[41]

It was a hectic six weeks. Changes were constantly being made to the play, partly to save costs. Blackwood was disappointed when some of his favourite characters, such as the Tramp, were lost or merged with others. These changes affected the content of the songs, which had originally been based on poems in *A Prisoner in Fairyland*. Blackwood had to write a new one, 'My Old Tunes', specially for the play, and others were adapted. The linking role of the Organ-Grinder grew until it became key to the whole production. Also Elgar's original idea that he could simply adapt his *Wand of Youth* music did not work so easily. He used some, and also drew upon some waltz music he had composed long ago but never used, but otherwise the music for the songs and most incidental music was entirely new, perhaps just borrowing a selected musical motif.[42]

Although such pressure can often bring the best out of people, it can also lead to confusion and frustration, and as the deadline for the play's opening drew near tempers began to fray. The actor O.B. Clarence (1870–1955) recorded some of this in his autobiography:

> During rehearsals there were constant bickerings and difficulties which were very regrettable and unpleasant. [. . .] There were disagreements about the symbolism of the décor, which was all rather highbrow and obscured the beauty of the story. There were even dissensions among the orchestra, which was conducted by Julian[43] Harrison. There was so much allure in the conception of this fantasy that one felt that it only wanted harmony among the interpreters to secure success.[44]

It is ironic that a play about love and goodwill should be beset by so much ill-will. In fact in early December Lena Ashwell banned

Blackwood from the theatre for a week as his presence was disruptive. This was partly because he kept playing hide-and-seek with the children, but also because he was annoyed about the stage sets and costumes. The set designer was Henry Wilson, president of the Arts and Crafts Society, and he chose to depict the sprites as Greek gods. 'It is a false and ghastly idea,' Blackwood wrote to Elgar. 'There is nothing pagan in our little Childhood Play.'[45]

Although this was changed, Wilson's sets and costumes continued to frustrate Blackwood. By the day of the dress rehearsal (24 December) Blackwood's frustrations boiled over and he sent a catalogue of complaints to Lena Ashwell and wrote also to Elgar.

> This murder of my simple little Play I can stand, for the fate of my books has accustomed me to it; but this suburban, Arts & Crafts pretentious rubbish stitched on to your music is really too painful for me to bear. If you feel inclined to help me with advice (privately and quite between ourselves) I shall be grateful. But, after a horrid night of thinking it over, I can see no course but to veto it all and face postponement, change of artist, etc. etc. – or to insist upon what compromise is possible at this late hour. We can talk on Monday if you like. I am ready to do anything. If I have to be firm and nasty, I can be so.[46]

Elgar had not been to the dress rehearsal because he was still in mourning over the death of his nephew, William Elgar, who had died on 21 December and was buried in Worcester on the 23rd. By the time Blackwood met Elgar on 27 December, just two days before the opening night, his anger had cooled and he had become reconciled to the fate of the play. The play went ahead as planned on Wednesday 29 December. Elgar did not attend. Apparently this was because Lady Elgar had been slightly injured when she was struck by a taxi-cab, though she recorded in her diary that Elgar had refused to conduct 'as the mise en scène was so repulsive'.

Although the first night went well, with rapturous applause, the critics were not so enthusiastic. The focus of their attack was not the production, or the music, or the sets or the lighting – these were all very acceptable – but the play itself:

> Were it not for the explanations thoughtfully given on the programme, it would be next to impossible to decide what 'The

Starlight Express', produced yesterday afternoon at the Kingsway Theatre, is all about. Everybody loves a fantasy, but it should not be so subtle as to elude the understanding.

That was *The Standard. The Times* was no better.

Everybody, says Cousin Henry, is thin somewhere. Where *The Starlight Express* is thin is in the story. Any tenuity there is, is bound to be felt in the theatre, as the remarkable acute Aristotle knew when he said story was the chief element of drama. And Mr Blackwood's story is thin because it is an attempt to give embodiment and visible action, a local habitation and a name to airy nothing.

And so it went on. 'Unfortunately the authors require an audience for their play gifted with an imagination at least equal to their own,' said *The Era.* '*The Starlight Express* does not stimulate the imagination; if it did the lengthy explanation given on the programme would be unnecessary.' Most cruel of all was *The Bystander*, which produced a series of cartoon sketches showing everyone getting all the more confused until the third act when 'father discovers the plot and explains'. O.B. Clarence, who played the father, also felt confused. Although he called the play 'strange and rather beautiful' and thought the music 'enchanting', the story itself was 'all rather vague and mystical and required a master hand. Granville Barker might have treated it successfully.'

Needless to say Stephen Graham, writing in *Country Life*, was more sympathetic. 'All true children of whatever age would love it. And as for old folk, it makes tears stream down their cheeks.'

Thankfully we do have a child's recollection of the play, albeit a teenager's. This was E. Wulstan Atkins, the son of Ivor Atkins, organist and master of the choristers at Worcester Cathedral, and a long-time friend of the Elgars. After his initial disappointment that Elgar was not himself conducting, Atkins recorded:

My disappointment soon disappeared, however, when Elgar's fascinating overture began and when the Organ-Grinder, Charles Mott, appeared on the apron of the stage to sing his first song, 'O Children, open your arms to me.' Soon I was completely absorbed in the play, eagerly following the dream-like sprites, the Lamplighter, the Sweep, the Dustman, the Woman-in-the-Haystack, the Starlight Express itself, and the Stardust Cavern in the Mountains.[47]

Young Atkins may not have been a typical child seeing *The Starlight Express*, but it clearly appealed to him, and it doubtless captured the imagination of many.

The star of the production was undoubtedly Charles Mott (*c*. 1875–1918) as the Organ-Grinder. His rich, baritone voice and beautiful interpretation of the songs was highlighted in every review[48]. The children Ronald Hammond and Elise Hall, who played Jimbo and Monkey, also endeared themselves to everyone, as did Clytie Hine, who had the other main singing role as The Laugher. Perhaps the best known name to appear in the production was Lynn Fontanne (1887–1983), who played one of the Pleiades. Surprisingly Muriel Pratt did not have a part.

The production had been set to run for six weeks, but falling attendances, not helped by Zeppelin raids, black-outs and poor reviews, caused Lena Ashwell to close it early, after forty performances, on 29 January 1916. Over time the production would be viewed as a failure, but that is not entirely true. Even those who frowned on the subject matter, such as the reviewer in *The Standard*, felt compelled to report that 'the production was received throughout with the warmest applause,' and noted that the acting was of a high quality. Even on the last night, Lady Elgar noted that there was a 'large audience & much enthusiasm. Lovely play & music enchanting killed by a bad setting.' There were plans for a while to revive it the following December, but these came to nought. Soon afterwards Lena Ashwell relinquished the management of the Kingsway.

Perhaps no one should have expected too much of the production. Considering that it had been produced at such short notice in such trying war-time conditions, its public reception must be regarded as a success. Clearly its weakness was in trying to adapt something as ephemeral as Blackwood's metaphysical message into a short children's play. It lacked the simplicity and immediate rapport of either *Peter Pan* or *Pinkie and the Fairies* and relied heavily on the sympathetic imagination of the audience. Even Blackwood admitted, when writing to Frederick Macmillan, that it was very far from what he had hoped it might be.[49]

Lady Elgar recorded that both her husband and Blackwood 'felt the ceasing of the *Starlight* very much'. For the rest of his life Blackwood tried in vain to secure a new production of the play. Though he would have other plays produced, both on the stage and on radio, some with critical acclaim, this first failure bit deep, and he never really recovered from it.

Many years later, when Blackwood approached J.B. Priestley over an adaptation, Priestley advised that the book was not suitable for the stage.

> My own feeling is that, apart from some minor blemishes, the faults in the dramatized version are inherent in the original story, which is very much elaborately descriptive narrative and not drama. In short, your novel does not really lend itself to dramatization.[50]

Priestley went on to say that he thought the ideal medium was the animated film, and that perhaps a copy of the book should be sent to Walt Disney. Blackwood and Pearn had perhaps been too early with their message and the right medium had not yet come along.

Yet the production had sparked other consequences. Aside from the frayed tempers, good friendships were secured, not least Blackwood and Elgar's. Blackwood, known always as 'Starlight' to Elgar, became a regular guest at the Elgars' over the next few years. It also introduced Maya Knoop to Lady Elgar's circle of friends. Moreover, it introduced Maya to her future husband, the industrialist Ralph Philipson (1861–1928). Philipson's first wife had recently died, and he had financed the production of the play because he felt its message was one that would have appealed to his wife. He also thought London would benefit from the play more than if he contributed to a variety of indiscriminate funds. It's possible Maya knew of Philipson earlier, because he was a noted patron of the arts, but they may not have met before this play. At that time, of course, Maya was still married, but perhaps a little stardust was sprinkled that day.

It also led to Blackwood meeting Henry Ainley (1879–1945), perhaps the most famous actor of his day. Elgar had known Ainley for some while and had only recently been involved with him over a recording of the poem *Carillon* to Elgar's music. Blackwood soon became close friends with Ainley and his wife Elaine.

This was not the end of *The Starlight Express*. Elgar had agreed to record the music and the songs for The Gramophone Company ('His Master's Voice') at their studio in Hayes, Middlesex. There were some revisions needed to the songs to allow them to stand alone, free from the play. Blackwood and Elgar worked quickly over the score just prior to the recording on 18 February 1916. Advance pressings of the records were sent to Elgar and arrived on 13 March, the same day that Blackwood arrived to stay for a fortnight. The official launch was given at a luncheon at the Savoy Hotel on 6 April, at which music critics were invited.

Elgar was pleased with the recordings and *The Starlight Express* was the main cause of Elgar subsequently embracing the concept of the gramophone and ensuring quality recordings of much of his music. Composing the music for the play also seemed to unlock channels deep within Elgar and allowed him to complete *The Spirit of England*, which had troubled him for some while.

Elgar was delighted to hear from an army officer serving on the Front who had acquired a copy of the record. This soldier had not previously liked the gramophone, but this record changed everything. 'It is the only means of bringing back to us the days that are gone, and helping one through the Ivory Gate that leads to fairy land or Heaven, whatever one likes to call it.'[51]

That would have meant much to Blackwood.

14

Blackwood at War (1916–18)

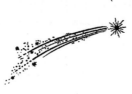

I

Despite the problems caused by *The Starlight Express* Blackwood continued to write. He gave the final polish to *Julius LeVallon* and, according to his promise, sent it to Maude ffoulkes at Cassell's on 3 January 1916. Cassell's was one of London's biggest and oldest publishers. Its editor-in-chief, Newman Flower, had a heavy workload – he was in charge of the magazine division as well as books – so would not have responded to every author himself, leaving that to his editors. But he was clearly taken by Blackwood's book.

> I hope you will not think it fulsome on my part to write and say that I think *Julius LeVallon* one of the biggest novels that ever came into this office. I read it absolutely at a sitting and it kept me up half a night. But it was a story I could not leave. It is very seldom that one comes upon a novel like that nowadays. We are proud to have it and you may leave it to me to see that Cassell's put it out well for you.[1]

The book was published in mid May to encouraging reviews and a highly receptive readership. It also led to at least two interesting cases that Blackwood investigated. One of these did not see its final denouement for another fifteen years, so I'll return to the case of 'Maria Smith' later. But the other episode happened about a year later.

Blackwood was contacted by Australian Army Staff Officer John Prentice, who was serving in Europe. He had read *Julius LeVallon* and was startled when he recognized one of the scenes Blackwood described.

There is an episode in *Julius Le Vallon* where LeVallon triggers Mason's memory and brings back a recollection of a distant life in what he calls the Temple days. Captured prisoners are forced along a narrow ledge inside a Temple Dome. Fifty feet below them spears are planted in the ground, point upwards. Eventually the prisoners have to fall and are impaled to death. Prentice not only remembered that this was how he died, but remembered the whole civilization and location, exactly as Blackwood described them. Blackwood met Prentice at Bordighera, on the Italian/French border. Blackwood believed that his story had reminded Prentice of some imaginative dream he had once had, but Prentice insisted that imagination is memory, and that he had once lived the life described by Blackwood.[2]

Julius Le Vallon went back for a second printing within a month. The finished book gives no hint of a sequel and it is perhaps unfortunate that Blackwood had not completed the second half. Not only would it have capitalised on the success of the first volume, but it may have been a more intense book. *The Bright Messenger*, when it finally appeared, is a very different volume, by a different Blackwood.

Instead Blackwood had been spending the last few months completing a long, diffuse novel, *The Wave*, subtitled 'An Egyptian Aftermath'. He had started the book as early as February 1915. The idea had literally flooded over him, but he had to break off for other work and the inspiration flagged. He was fascinated by the image of the wave, because it was prescribing a circle, the perfect form, and yet never completes it. Blackwood outlined his thinking to Macmillan's.

> I have tried to develop an interesting variant of the usual reincarnation theory, viz. that the soul's advance takes the spiral form so common everywhere in Nature. At any given point, that is, the soul finds itself exactly over a point passed earlier. Seen however from a higher point of view the earlier situation is understood and its lesson mastered.[3]

The book opens with considerable atmosphere. Throughout his life Tom Kelverdon has been haunted by a vision of a wave. As a child he had no idea what it meant though his father, a doctor, had perhaps a hint of suspicion. The doctor has a drawer full of Egyptian mementoes including some incense, the smell of which connects with Tom's vision. The doctor knows the story involving the incense (though Tom doesn't). Nearly 5,000 years ago, in ancient Egypt, the wife of a Theban prince had fallen in love with her Syrian slave. The slave was expelled but returned. He was tortured and killed and with his death his lover threw herself into the Nile. Both bodies were cast into the sea but recovered and buried in the Valley of the Kings where the prince himself was later buried. As an adult Tom falls in love with a childhood friend, Lettice Aylmer, but she has married another, a Polish prince, and is now Madame Jaretzka. Predictably the events of their previous incarnations are relived, with the added complication of Tom's cousin Tony, who also vies for Lettice's affections.

The story is set mostly in Switzerland and Egypt, and the parallels with the triangle of Blackwood, Maya and Baron Knoop are too obvious to repeat. Indeed the book reflects various incidents that occurred between Blackwood and Maya masked by the veneer of fiction. Even the episode of caring for the refugee children in Chertsey appears briefly. The novel provides further insight into Blackwood's relationship with Maya. In *A Prisoner in Fairyland* he had described the Countess as 'mothering the world'.[4] Now, in *The Wave*, he describes Lettice as follows: 'There were two persons in her. It may have been absurd to divide the woman and the mother as he did; probably it was false psychology as well; where love is, mother and woman blend divinely into one.'[5] Earlier in *The Wave*, where Tom describes his undisguised Blackwoodian upbringing, he says:

> He was in England when his mother died; and while his other experiences were ripples only, her going had the Wave in it. The enormous mother-tie came also out of the 'sea'; its dislocation was a shock of fundamental kind, and he felt it in the foundations of his life.[6]

Throughout Blackwood's life we have seen him seeking surrogate parents. First Alfred H. Louis and then W. Graham Robertson became father figures, and were even addressed as such. In New York, Mrs Kent had mothered him, and on his return to England he had sought that relationship with other women, especially his elder half-sister Lady Kintore. But it was Maya who filled that role better than any other. Blackwood worshipped her as a woman. As a married woman she may have been forbidden fruit, but that did not stop her being mother to Blackwood's world.

The Wave is the closest Blackwood came to writing a nonfantastic romantic novel. The only fantastic element is the vision of a past incarnation and the proposition of the soul's spiral advance. Read as a romance the story is competent, poetic, and at times touching. For once *The Times* reviewer appreciated it, almost certainly because it was less psychic than Blackwood's past books.

> The characters are well enough imagined, and the implied analysis of love and womanhood is sufficiently just to have made a good tale by themselves. With the characteristic Blackwood mystery to help, the book is rich in excitement and experience.[7]

The Morning Post reviewer, however, was more critical.

> *The Wave* is an extremely clever and interesting experiment, clearly absorbing the author, who conducts it with a mastery of the resources for making such. But for complete satisfaction in this genre the reader requires something more simple and spontaneous, and perhaps something less professionally carried through.[8]

The reviewer had quite rightly identified that the book fell between two markets. These are the readers of supernatural fiction and lovers of the romantic novel, especially with a touch of the mysterious. *The Wave* has scarcely any supernatural element to satisfy the first market, and was too verbose for the second, which required a simpler, more direct story. Blackwood had become carried away, 'absorbed' the reviewer perceptively notes, in his fanciful love affair, to the point where he overstates his message. We have to view the prolixity of *The Wave*, much as we do that in *A Prisoner in Fairyland*, in that both capture Blackwood's love affair with Maya. Alas *The Wave* is unleavened by the charming vision of *Prisoner*.

II

Throughout 1916 Blackwood expected to be called away to work with the Field Ambulance Service but, as he informed his literary agent in early August, there was endless delay. He took the opportunity to finalize his next collection, *Day and Night Stories*. This time it was sent to Cassell's rather than Macmillan, as the latter concentrated on his novels. Although Macmillan had stood by him through his recent books, with a mixture of good and poor sales, Blackwood felt he owed a loyalty to Maude ffoulkes, his first editor. In October 1916 there was a strange episode involving ffoulkes that is worth recounting here.

Ffoulkes lived in an apartment at 69 Curzon Street, part of which had once been an inn. Her rooms could only be reached by steps from the front door and the bedroom contained tiny windows looking out on to the roofs of houses with a dangerous drop. It was thus difficult for anyone to obtain access to the room. One night ffoulkes was awakened in the early hours by a young man peering at her from the foot of the bed. She challenged him and he responded that he was the Devil and had come to bargain with her over the souls of two people who had greatly wronged her.* Their hatred meant that she had control over them. Ffoulkes refused to believe he was there and eventually she drifted off to sleep, but the same thing happened the following Saturday night. This time, to prove he was real, the Devil placed his hand on her shoulder and left a dark blue-black imprint.

Ffoulkes was so unnerved by this that she sent a telegram to Blackwood who called promptly that Sunday morning. This was probably the morning of 22 October. Blackwood found it difficult to believe her, but dared not tell her that. A year or two earlier she had tried to commit suicide and he believed this was part of her attention-seeking, so he felt he had no right to destroy her story. Perhaps for that reason, though under the pretext of being too much of a gentleman, Blackwood did not ask her to show him the imprint as that would have meant her removing her dressing-gown, and Maude ffoulkes was a rather large woman. Yet later that same evening Maude ffoulkes dined with the ghost hunter Jessie Middleton and Dr William Brown-Thomson and happily showed them the mark. It remained visible for two or three days.[9]

Day and Night Stories brought together most of the short stories he had written since *Incredible Adventures* plus some earlier ones. This included 'A Victim of Higher Space', the story dropped at the last minute from *John Silence*, but which Blackwood had been persuaded to run in *The Occult Review* in 1914.

One of the few new stories in the collection was the highly paganistic 'The Touch of Pan'. In a rather risqué story for Blackwood, that feels more part of the liberated 1920s than of the war years, Blackwood tells of the naturalistic passion between a man and a woman, even

---

* Ffoulkes did not name these people but Blackwood identified them as the author Ada Leverson (1862–1933) and the barrister Frank Richardson (1870–1917). Both were noted humorists and wits. Ada Leverson had been Oscar Wilde's great friend during his adversity.

though both are betrothed to others. Consumed by a pagan desire the two cavort in the grounds of a country house and almost reach conjugal bliss except that the girl is suddenly frightened by something. For Blackwood, this story is remarkably explicit, especially at the climax where, hidden in the undergrowth we find the man 'clawing at her waist again with passionate eagerness that now betrayed exasperation'.[10] Unfortunately, such old-fashioned schoolboy phrases as 'By Jove, Hermione, but you're divine,' just at the point when the narrator seizes the girl on his lap, suggests that at least part of Blackwood still lived in the romantic Elysian fields of the *Girl's Own Paper* and had never quite scored through the goalposts of life.

There was one story from this period that Blackwood did not include in *Day and Night Stories*, probably because he believed it was a simple piece of propaganda, yet it is a poignant, powerful piece. 'Proportion'[11] was inspired by a letter received from a young officer the day before he was killed in action. The letter talked about the immensity of space and how insignificant a man's span of life is on the Earth. Blackwood converted this into one man's reason for fighting. The sheer scale and beauty of the heavens is too vast to comprehend whilst the beauty of the Earth can be seen and is worth fighting for.

Another story written about this time was 'Laughter of Courage'[12] where a man with an infectious laugh at a cinema turns out to be a war-invalid. These propaganda pieces, now few and far between, were designed to raise morale and are light-years removed from Blackwood's early horror stories.

Suddenly at the end of August 1916 there was a flurry of movement on the Field Hospital front. Blackwood was called down to Holmbury St Mary in Surrey, near Guildford. Holmbury House was the home of William Joynson-Hicks (1865–1932), who would become the British Home Secretary in 1924. He was chairman of the Belgian Field Ambulance Service, and Blackwood and others came to Holmbury for their training and to undergo a series of inoculations – typhoid, cholera, para-typhoid, all administered at once. Needless to say Blackwood went down with inoculation fever and was poorly for several weeks, during which time he stayed at Holmbury.

While recovering Blackwood was asked if he would be interested in undertaking 'secret service' work in Holland. He was given a week to make up his mind, and to report in London the moment he was fit to move.[13]

When Blackwood wrote about his work as a secret agent some years later his recollection was that he had first been approached at a luncheon party at Lady Brabourne's London apartments in Norfolk Square. It seems likely that once Blackwood returned to London, early in September 1916, he was sought out again. He was approached by a French officer, Count Dru.[14] Blackwood turned down the opportunity to be an agent in Holland because he could not speak Dutch. When he told Dru that he spoke French and German, Dru suggested that Blackwood operate in Switzerland.

Blackwood agreed to meet the man in charge, Colonel John Wallinger, late of the Indian Police, in his office in Lower Sloane Street. What Blackwood did not know was that the Secret Service operations in Switzerland were in chaos. Indeed military intelligence during the war had been something of a shambles. There had been parallel, almost rival, operations set up through France, Belgium and England run by individuals who had little experience in intelligence work. Colonel Wallinger had inherited the Swiss operations the year before from his younger brother Major Ernest Wallinger who was concentrating his efforts in Holland. Colonel Wallinger was determined to make his end of the operation work, but it was proving difficult. During the first year of the war many so-called agents had turned out to be fraudulent, simply taking the wages but providing no reliable information. Also few of the agents were well known in Switzerland and stood out as 'visitors'. Although the consuls in Switzerland were supposed to be neutral, they were unreliable, and many agents in Switzerland had either been forced to flee, or had been captured, and some killed. Christopher Andrew, writing in *Secret Service* says that 'by late August [1915] John Wallinger's Swiss operations were close to collapse'.[15]

It was at this time that Wallinger recruited the author W. Somerset Maugham (1874–1965). Maugham was fluent in French and passable in German and had already been serving in an ambulance unit. It was Maugham's task to rendezvous in Switzerland with agents, glean the information from them, pay them their wages and, where possible recruit new agents. He wrote about his role in the semi-fictional *Ashenden* (1928). Maugham soon grew tired of the operation, and resigned in February 1916, though he was persuaded to stay on a while longer. He was replaced in May 1916 by the American playwright Edward Knoblock (1874–1945), who had just been granted English citizenship. Knoblock is best remembered as the author of the play

Kismet (1911) – the basis for the better known musical[16]. Knoblock's operations did not prove any more successful than Maugham's to the point that Major Walter Kirke, the head of the military intelligence at French GHQ, St Omer, said in July 1916 that 'Wallinger's Swiss show, so far as we are concerned, is a waste of money'.[17] Wallinger had endeavoured to diversify his network by opening new operations on the Danish frontier, but with little success.

This was when Blackwood came upon the scene. By now Wallinger must have been desperate to make his Swiss operation work. Blackwood seemed ideal for the operation. Not only was he fluent in French and German but he was well known in Switzerland. He needed no cover, since he would simply be continuing his years of residence as a writer and pacifist.

Blackwood's role was just the same as Maugham's and Knoblock's. He was to recruit agents, provide them with the means of sending reports (paper and invisible ink) and make payments. The invisible ink was soaked into handkerchiefs and could be rinsed out. For this Blackwood received twenty shillings a week to cover expenses.

Blackwood did not leave for Switzerland immediately. His training kept him in England for a while, and no doubt the sheer disorganization of Wallinger's operations delayed matters. He spent some time with the Elgars at Hampstead. There is a charming anecdote told by Percy Young that Blackwood met Elgar on 8 October 1916. Elgar had a toad wrapped in his handkerchief, which he had bought off some children. Apparently Elgar named the toad Algernon and kept it in his garden.

Blackwood was still in London at the end of October[18] but probably left for Switzerland in early November, his usual time, just before the Season. This would have attracted no suspicion. Blackwood cabled ahead, so that he was expected. He had booked a room at the Hôtel de Londres in Montreux, which was owned by Madame Défago, a woman he knew from Champéry. However when he arrived he was informed that Madame Défago was dead and the hotel was under the management of a German Swiss called Steiner. Blackwood suspected Steiner of being a German agent and decided he could achieve nothing at the hotel. He decided to leave the next day, feigning lumbago and the need to visit a friend. He headed for Champéry where he laid low with an old American friend for ten days.

Before leaving for Switzerland Blackwood had been introduced to a French Swiss called Cruchon who was supposed to be a good contact.

Cruchon had a pass to visit Potsdam every month as his firm made fuses for the Germans. Cruchon claimed he was pro-Ally and could help Blackwood set up his network of agents. They arranged to meet in Montreux, but Blackwood had already left by the time Cruchon reached Switzerland. When Blackwood returned to Montreux he learned that Cruchon was a double-spy and he should avoid him at all costs.

That was fine by Blackwood. He was happier working alone. He felt he was safer left to his own instincts. These had become finely honed over the years. It is interesting that the man who had fallen victim to so many con artists and tricksters in New York, twenty years earlier, was now hardened by experience and his instinctive knowledge of people gained by years of observation. Blackwood had to make contact with individuals who travelled into Germany, and had to assess which side they were on. His ultimate test was to see how much money they requested. If it was high he immediately suspected their loyalty.

Blackwood gradually developed his own network of contacts spending weeks in various towns working his way into people's trust. He deduced he must have picked the right people because anyone pro-German would have reported him to the Embassy in Bern who would have sent the Swiss police round to check him out. There were strict rules about secret agents in Switzerland, because of their neutrality, and if discovered Blackwood could have been imprisoned for six months, fined 1,000 Swiss Francs, or even worse, depending on who betrayed him.

Blackwood established his base at the Hôtel Bonivard, Territet, just east of Montreux on the shores of Lake Geneva. He operated under the code name Baker. Through his courier, Blackwood received messages from his agents purporting to be cards or letters to their wives or mothers, but containing further messages written in invisible ink. Blackwood used to type his reports to Wallinger in the hotel toilet so that if he was suddenly raided by the police he could claim he was cleaning his typewriter whilst flushing his report (sometimes written on rice paper) down the toilet.

He hated it when news dried up, because he suspected his agent had been caught and possibly shot. And when news did dry up he then felt guilty for having nothing to send to London. During one of these dry periods Blackwood received a message from London saying that they were sending out a new agent, with whom Blackwood was to liaise. This turned out to be Alexander Keiller (1889–1955), of the marmalade firm, who had been invalided out of the Royal Naval Air Service.

Keiller was a young man and Blackwood felt he treated the whole operation too much like a game. He delighted in schoolboy tricks like secret pockets and special codes all of which Blackwood felt was obvious. He met him once in the mountains above Saanenmoser where they exchanged news and Blackwood filled him in on the current situation. Thereafter Blackwood avoided him like the plague, although he occasionally encountered his 'secretary'. She was an attractive young girl whom Blackwood realized had considerably more sense than Keiller and it was probably thanks to her that he was not caught.

It's a pity Blackwood did not get to know Keiller better, especially after the war. Keiller was fascinated in archaeology and in demonology and witchcraft. He spent many years (and considerable money) at the stone circle sites of Avebury and Stonehenge. He was also a frequent visitor to Switzerland, became an expert skier and was President of the Ski Club of Great Britain in 1931.

Blackwood kept the work up for six months but had by then long tired of it.

> It was a beastly job. I hated pretending to be someone else; telephoning 'meet me on Monday at noon,' which actually meant 'on Tuesday at 6.00'; changing my tram at intervals to make sure I was not being followed, and a dozen other schoolboy tricks.[19]

Blackwood told Belloc that 'I resigned, for reasons I would rather not put in writing. The W[ar] O[ffice] thanked me, saying I had showed "special ability".'[20] His reasons were probably a combination of things. A growing dislike of the work, an increasing distrust of his fellow humans and a feeling of disorganization about him, all must have pained Blackwood. There was also a possibility that the Germans had become suspicious of Blackwood and were watching him closely. One fellow worker, a Briton, unknown to Blackwood, had already worked out what Blackwood was doing. If he could, others might also. Above all there was the feeling that he was sending some men to their deaths. Someone as sensitive as Blackwood could suffer this level of guilt and tension for only so long.

III

In the end it was important that he came home as his brother was seriously ill. Blackwood was back in England by the beginning of June, when he was staying with Maya Knoop. He soon returned to London.

His brother, Stevenson, had always had a weak constitution, but over the last year this had deteriorated with chronic tuberculosis. He died on 16 June 1917 aged only forty-nine. Blackwood had once been very close to his brother and though time and business had distanced them slightly, he was still deeply affected by the loss. Only a few months earlier his cousin Arthur Hobart-Hampden had lost his wife, Henrietta, with whom Blackwood had also been close. It was also at about this time that his old lady friend from New York, Mrs Kent, died.* What with the death of Old Louis and of his sister Beatrice, this accumulated loss caused Blackwood to write *The Garden of Survival*.

> My idea in writing it was to offer an alternative to the 'return to the dead' in the current craze for séances which I find so distressing, and my theme is that the dead do not return but that those who lived Beauty in their lives, co-operate with the spirit of Beauty afterwards and for ever.[21]

The book is not really a novel. It's more of a confession or an extended prayer. Blackwood calls it 'a transcript from actual life'.[22] The nameless narrator is addressing a nameless third person throughout, identified only as 'my other half', a twin brother, though he could as easily be addressing 'you' the reader. It tells of his marriage that ended abruptly after a month when his wife, Marion, was killed in an accident. The narrator becomes concerned that he was probably not worthy of her and by way of escape he goes abroad for many years. When he returns home he finds that memories of Marion and other lost ones flood back through the spiritual beauty he experiences in his childhood garden.

Blackwood continues the message he began in 'The Prayer' and *The Centaur*, that good thoughts delivered in life and continued through the Almighty Consciousness after death enhance the beauty in the world and keep cherished memories alive. It may seem naïve these days, but Blackwood wrote the story beautifully and it struck a chord with a public who had lost so many loved ones in the war.

---

* Unbeknown to Blackwood she left him a legacy of $5,000, today equal to about $55,000 (or £36,000). Her nephew contested the will and it was a few years before Blackwood received his windfall. He promptly invested it in South African securities, which became a reliable source of income for the rest of his life.

Blackwood had not written the story for publication, but he told Macmillan that so many people had asked if it could be published. Blackwood regarded the book as too personal and considered issuing it pseudonymously, but Macmillan convinced him otherwise. Though not as intimate as parts of *The Wave*, *The Garden of Survival* was clearly written as a catharsis to help Blackwood deal with his own inner turmoil.

A.E. Waite, reviewing it for *The Bookman*, called it 'a remarkable psychological study', but also noted that 'a little patience is demanded', not because of the subject matter but because the concentrated self-focus 'repels rather than attracts'.[23] Waite was close enough to Blackwood to know, maybe first hand, the angst in Blackwood's soul, whereas most readers would simply associate themselves with the message. Blackwood was evidently continuing to carry considerable personal guilt from his youth that took years to purge. His books, and his desire to spread 'beauty', were his way of dealing with this, though it was only through such personal items as *The Garden of Survival* and his autobiography five years later, that his own catharsis was achieved.

The Garden of Survival was one of three books by Blackwood all published within a month in April–May 1918, and all credit to Macmillan for doing so.

Blackwood had been working on *The Promise of Air* since 1913. He had completed the book during his secret service work in Switzerland. Blackwood wanted to explore the consequences of humanity relying upon its instinctive or subsconscious inner being rather than on the rational mind, just as birds and animals do. It is the story of Joseph Wimble who, at the start of the book is as feckless and enervated as Lord Ernie in 'The Regeneration of Lord Ernie' – the two stories are probably offsprings of the same creative thought. Wimble is, like the young Blackwood, 'careless of consequence, indifferent to results'. His passion is the air. He dreams of flying, both spiritually and physically. He wants to escape the Earth and be as free as the birds. He marries a like-minded woman but after the birth of their daughter the mother loses this desire. The child, however, Joan, is filled with it, and the story follows her transcendence. Not until the end of the book does Wimble discover that the spirit of flight has returned to his wife.

The novel is really too long for the theme Blackwood is exploring. He had depicted flight beautifully in 'The Wings of Horus', and portrayed the instinctive elemental spirit in 'A Touch of Pan'. *The*

Promise of Air is an inconsequential novel that starts and ends delightfully but, like its subject matter, flutters every which way in between.

The book is among the first of the 'New Age' books, because Blackwood explores the dawn of the Aquarian Age. 'The Aquarian Age is pre-eminently a spiritual age,' a lecturer tells us, 'and its meaning may now be apprehended by multitudes of people, 'ungry for truth, who will now come – are already coming – into an advanced spiritual consciousness. Our air-bodies is being quickened.'[24]

With the ending of the war Blackwood hoped people would grasp the opportunity for a spiritual advance into peace and beauty. We should no longer be bound to the Earth and all things material. We should look to the air and all things spiritual. The book is thus a sermon, albeit a long one, where Blackwood looked towards a new world order built upon his desire for beauty and harmony.

The third book was a new play, *Karma*, written with Violet Pearn. He had probably discussed the idea with her when they worked upon *A Starlight Express*, and almost certainly the majority of the play would have been by Pearn, even if it is based on Blackwood's outline. To some extent it's a reworking of *The Wave*, though with new characters and settings. Its subtitle, 'A Re-incarnation Play' tells it all. It's a romance that follows four incarnations of two souls, showing their lives in Egypt in 2000BC, Greece in 325BC, Italy in the late 1400s and the present day. Throughout these lives a woman's selfish love has thwarted her husband from fulfilling his true purpose in life. It reverses the relationship between Maya and Baron Knoop, showing how the Baron's own possessive love had restricted Maya's chance to fulfil herself. Taken with *The Promise of Air*, we can see Blackwood's hope that Maya might escape her cage and fly.

Karma is easy to read, simply because you skate across the dialogue with none of Blackwood's often intense philosophy. But, devoid of Blackwood's beliefs and poetic language, the book becomes superficial. Yet Blackwood felt very possessive about it even though it was never performed. When he submitted it to Macmillan's, despite having two other books scheduled, he urged them to publish it as soon as possible. Not only did he believe that this was the first play to deal with the subject of reincarnation but he also believed that his ideas had been commandeered by others, and he was keen to ensure that his book was the first in the market.[25]

It is not clear which rival work Blackwood had in mind. Books about reincarnation were common during the last years of the war, encouraged by the hope among survivors that their lost loved ones still existed somewhere and might live again. Blackwood could hardly claim originality in this area. There are, for example, many similarities between *Karma* and various books by Marie Corelli, especially *Ziska* (1897), in which a modern-day countess is discovered to be the reincarnation of a dancing girl from Ancient Egypt murdered by King Araxes who has been reincarnated as the current artist Gervase. Likewise many of the books by H. Rider Haggard explored this theme. The idea had been given added impetus during the war with the publication of the non-fiction study *Raymond* by Sir Oliver Lodge in 1916. Lodge's son was killed during the war but Lodge and his wife purportedly established contact with their son through a medium. The interest raised by *Raymond* encouraged several books on the theme, fiction and non-fiction. Plays came in due course but I know of no other that endeavoured to compete with *Karma*.

IV

Following his brother's funeral Blackwood gave further thought to what he wanted to do. Did he wish to return to Switzerland as an agent, or were there other services that would benefit better from his abilities? He told Belloc that he spent six months at home meeting the 'big-wigs'.

> I have been to see so many people and been on so many waiting lists in vain that I despaired – and took my present job. The people were awfully nice and 'swept their hats about', as you say in one story, but nothing ever happened.[26]

Blackwood's interviews had been with the Department of Information, which had been set up in February 1917 under author and journalist John Buchan, who now had the rank of lieutenant colonel. Blackwood's meetings and interviews dragged on between August 1917 and February 1918. By the end of this period Blackwood had signed up to work as a searcher with the Red Cross at which point Buchan suddenly offered Blackwood a job in the Foreign Office. It was too late and Blackwood declined.

What is uncertain is whether Blackwood returned to Switzerland to undertake more secret service work *before* he joined the Red Cross.

Since he was pursuing work with the Department of Information it seems, on the surface, unlikely. However, in his unpublished note on his days with Intelligence, he says, 'I had been a Secret Agent for a couple of years, and having been too closely watched for some time, was on the point of leaving for Red Cross work in Rouen, when chance brought me up against Mrs J.' It seems surprising that, even writing this twenty or thirty years later, Blackwood's memory would telescope together his return home in June 1917 and joining the Red Cross in February 1918.

In the light of later events it's probable that, achieving nothing with the Department of Information and with his Red Cross work still unconfirmed, Blackwood returned to Switzerland in late November or December 1917 for just a couple of months. However, little else happened during this period until his last day. About to return to England Blackwood met an old lady, a Victorian grande-dame, at the Hôtel Byron, Villeneuve, south of Territet. He doesn't identify her, other than as 'Mrs J.', but does say that she was an English lady from the Yorkshire gentry whose father had worked with Charles Darwin, who had married a German and had spent most of her life in Frankfurt where, as a society hostess, she knew everybody of importance in Germany. When war was declared her loyalties were torn but, as Blackwood noted, 'her blood told'. She came to Switzerland to remain neutral. When she and Blackwood met, they 'clicked'. Blackwood's charm with older women never failed him. She told him that she received uncensored letters from her children and others in the diplomatic bag, and Blackwood realized that he had a major source of news but there was not the time to cultivate it. It would have to wait.

Blackwood was officially appointed as a searcher in the Red Cross on 15 February 1918, and he left for France on the 19th. It was on the 18th that the Department of Information suddenly woke up and Buchan offered Blackwood a job with the Foreign Office. Too late. Blackwood headed off to the British Red Cross Wounded and Missing Enquiry Department at Rouen (usually referred to as W&M).

The Rouen branch had opened in January 1915 on the site of a convalescent camp where there were some 6,000 patients in twelve hospitals. Initially there were just three searchers but this increased to twelve over the next three years with a thirteenth attached to an additional camp at Buchy, fifteen miles away.

The job of the searcher was to obtain information and evidence about missing men from the wounded and convalescent soldiers. The soldier may know that so-and-so had been captured or killed, and the searcher had to identify who, where, when and how. Inevitably the soldiers they were interviewing were in a state of shock and severely wounded themselves. The searcher had to win their confidence and gain accurate data, rather than rely on hearsay or third-hand information. As these enquiries formed the basis of reports back home to relatives they had to be as accurate as possible.

Since 1915 nearly 170,000 individual enquiries had been undertaken, and that figure almost doubled during 1918. It was intensive work. Every morning each searcher would check his own list of missing men against names found by searchers at other camps. Then his list was augmented by new names that came in each day. He would follow-up enquiries arriving in the post hoping for information on individuals. All this time doctors were attending to new casualties, so it was not until the afternoon that the searcher could enter the hospital to undertake his questioning.

The work required patience, sensitivity, imagination, clarity of thought, intuition and lateral thinking – all of which Blackwood had in abundance. But Blackwood also found it draining and monotonous. He recognized its value, but felt it 'hardly helps to get on with the war'.[27] He believed he could do something more positive.

Blackwood was at Rouen when the flu epidemic of 1918–19 broke out. This had started in the United States in March but rapidly spread around the globe and peaked during October–November 1918. Early cases reached Rouen in April and placed a heavy demand upon medical staff adding to the pressure on the searcher.

With a view to gaining wider recognition for the work Blackwood wrote an article called 'The Work of a Red Cross Searcher', which A.P. Watt tried to sell to major markets in Britain and America. It was bought by the prestigious *Ladies Home Journal* in Philadelphia for $150[28]. However the *Journal* was unable to schedule it before the armistice was signed in November. They still paid the money, but the article had ceased to be news and it ended up in the pages of the American *Red Cross Magazine*[29].

With ten days' leave due Blackwood returned to London on 21 June 1918. His lodgings were at the home of Lita Crawfurd in Bickenhall Mansions. She was the widow of the British diplomat and author Oswald Crawfurd and the sister of Lady Brabourne, both being daughters of the Imperial Chancellor of Vienna, Hermann von Flesch

Brunningen. Blackwood had been introduced to her by Maya Knoop. Little did Blackwood realize then that he would remain at these lodgings for the next fifteen years.

He anticipated it would be a hectic ten days upon his return. He had planned to meet Hilaire Belloc in London. Belloc was trying to find Blackwood more rewarding work with the (now renamed) Ministry of Information. Blackwood was also committed to visiting his widowed sister-in-law, Kate, and his young nephew Patrick. Blackwood was probably also shaken by the news that a few weeks earlier, on 9 May, Baron Knoop had died, aged seventy-two. He had had a fall the previous year and was confined to a wheelchair. His health, never as bad as he usually made out, nevertheless rapidly deteriorated. Maya was now a widow, and a rich one.

But uppermost on his mind was the possibility that he might return to Switzerland and regain contact with 'Mrs J.' He wrote to Colonel Wallinger at the War Office, saying that they had a rapport and he was the only one likely to gain information from her. Wallinger agreed that Blackwood should revisit 'Mrs J', and suggested that he went undercover as a reporter for the London *Times*. Blackwood was sent to the editor, Geoffrey Dawson, for a letter of accreditation. It was agreed that Blackwood would report back with articles describing internment camps in Switzerland. There was an agreement between the Allies and Germany to exchange officers and soldiers who were unable to fight due to their wounds and these exchange camps were in Switzerland.[30]

Blackwood was ready to go to Switzerland after his ten days' leave, at the end of June, but he was delayed. Lady Elgar records that he visited them at Brinkwells, near Fittleworth in Sussex, in the middle of July. The Elgars had bought Brinkwells in 1917 and had moved there on 2 May 1918 as their main home. Elgar was composing a sonata and a piano *Quintet*, both of which Lady Elgar believed were inspired by a copse of trees at Fittleworth. Elgar believed there was a legend about these trees having once been Spanish monks who were struck by lightning when practising black magic. Later research could not trace this legend, and it may be that Blackwood created it himself or embellished it from a simpler tale. Elgar had taken Blackwood to see the trees on 18 July.[31]

Atkins remembered Elgar's memories of Blackwood at Brinkwells. He called him an ideal guest, a fine walker and talker, a keen athlete and, perhaps most surprising of all, a 'rare expert at pole-jumping'.

He told how he had cut a long pole for him, and how he had demonstrated his art by leaping on to the top of a tall barred gate, jumping over a hedge, and by long horizontal jumps.[32]

No doubt it was a skill Blackwood acquired from his years of punting and rowing down rivers, and shows his strength and agility.

Blackwood must have reported back for work soon after 18 July as his note places him back at the frontier at Bellegarde, south of Paris, in late July 1918. He was recognized by someone at the railway station who addressed him by his code name, Baker. By the time Blackwood had turned to see who this was, the man had gone. It was an unnerving way to start his latest operation.

The next day he caught the train to Geneva and from there to Montreux. 'Mrs J.' was staying at the Palace Hotel, Caux, in the foot-hills beyond Montreux, where Blackwood dined with her every night. Although she was accompanied by her German maid, who would have reported immediately any leakage of information to the Swiss authorities, she was skilled at weaving words into the general discussion in such a way that her maid could not follow it. One example Blackwood quoted went, 'I never really liked Browning, as a man I mean, and his Kiel poem, where the big battle ships are now lying open to air attack was one of his very worst, I always thought.'

Blackwood dutifully passed this information back to London. He believed his coup was a revelation about the Kaiser's purported homosexuality, which he pursued further once he was back in London through interviews with John Buchan and Sir Reginald Hall. Hall (1870–1943), then a rear-admiral, was rather like a character from a John Buchan novel, as he delighted in employing agents and counter-agents and setting up false messages to deceive the Germans. News about the Kaiser's homosexuality was not exciting enough for him and he dismissed it out of hand. The war, in any case, was almost won. Blackwood returned home probably in October and with the armistice signed on 11 November, his days as a secret agent were over.

V

Several stories arose out of Blackwood's war experiences. Though some were not written until a few years later it is appropriate to consider them all here.

'Onanonanon'[33] is a reconstruction of a nightmare. It's quite probable that Blackwood caught influenza during the 1918–19 epidemic and became delirious. In this story the constant barking of a dog reminds him of similar sounds he heard when he was a child, though it was difficult to distinguish between his own dog Carlo and that of the dog that keeps barking, which he calls Onanonanon. In his delirium Carlo comes to him but mutates into the monster Onanonanon. At the same time the narrator (who like Blackwood had served as a secret agent) has to face his alter-ego, Baker, the part of him that is the undercover agent, whom he hates. The story reveals how difficult Blackwood had found it to live with his own conscience when serving as an agent.

This same torment of a split personality haunts 'Alexander Alexander'[34]. A young girl's uncle has the same first and last names and insists they are used correctly. The patronymic *Alexander* was a stern authoritarian guardian, the more friendly avuncular Alexander is difficult to find. The girl regards them as two individuals and, when the man dies in an accident, she has a ghostly vision of both personalities confronting each other.

Dreams, nightmares, visions feature in two other stories at this time. In 'Wireless Confusion'[35] a man learns that his brother is missing, probably dead, in Turkey. He begins to experience strange optical illusions – objects nearby suddenly appear as if he's looking down the wrong end of a telescope, or distant objects come close. He later learns his brother has survived and perhaps there had been telepathic contact via psychometry, because the brother had borrowed the narrator's binoculars. In 'The World-Dream of McCallister'[36] a man has a dream that he forgets except for one line, which tells him that everything is all right after all. This one line keeps recurring to him as he goes through a series of crises and helps restore his faith that perhaps, after the war, things will sort themselves out.

'"Vengeance is Mine"' is Blackwood's most overt war story. It is set at Rouen in March 1918 and its narrator is a Red Cross worker and former cleric. Typically, Blackwood is overwhelmed by the ancient past of Rouen, from the days of Joan of Arc, and the centuries of conflict that have centred on the town. It gives the locale a sombre air, one of accumulated hate. The narrator also wonders why the weather so often seems to favour the Germans, as if the gods – the old gods – are on their side. He is attracted to a young girl but as a man of the cloth he does not pursue her. However, one night when he takes a

stroll towards the woods he meets her again. This time passion rules –
not the passion of sex but of vengeance. Her soul calls out to him. It is
time the tide of the war was turned. The old gods must be won over
and that demands a sacrifice – a German prisoner of war. The cleric is
swept along by the tide of revenge but at the last minute breaks free
and stops the murder of the German. His act receives supernatural
beneficence.

During the story Blackwood muses on the innate desire for mankind
to fight and wonders whether this is passed on through the spirit,
perhaps by reincarnation, with a constant desire for revenge. He
reworked the idea in 'First Hate'[37], one of his now rare latter-day
Canadian stories. It features again the giant Scandinavian hunter
Ericssen, from 'The Sea Fit', which was his friend Wilfrid Wilson[38].
Ericssen suggests that just as there is love at first sight, so there is hate
at first sight, and that hate is the strongest. Ericssen recounts an experience he had in Canada which demonstrated how hate is the basic
survival instinct of humans passed down since primitive times.

All these ideas come together in 'The Valley of the Beasts', also based
on a discussion with Wilfrid Wilson but drawing upon a native
American Indian legend. Based in the Snow River area of Canada it
tells of a hunter, called Grimwood, who violates the valley where all
animals live in harmony and faces the wrath of the protector deity.

Blackwood never fully reconciled himself to the war that would end
all wars. The war changed him and the old Blackwood, the Starlight
Man, the man who hoped to make the world aware of beauty, had
found his vision despoiled. It was an older, wiser, more mature and,
alas, less visionary Blackwood who rose from the ashes.

15

All the World's a Stage (1919–23)

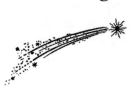

When Blackwood returned to Switzerland in November 1918 he had much to think about. The war had exhausted him. The stress of the Red Cross and Intelligence work had drained his energies, which needed refortifying in the only way Blackwood knew. Strenuous climbing and invigorating skiing did much to restore his physical self. Communion with nature would renovate his spiritual energy. His mental anguish was harder to repair.

There is some feel of this anguish in a letter he wrote to his friend Ella Maillart a few years later, when he reflected upon hitting fifty in March 1919.

> Can you fill your life adequately with adventure only? Worthily, too? – so that at 50 you can say 'my life was worth living.' Adventure – that is, mere physical adventure – as a rule is lived for self alone. With the failing of physical energy (which comes quickly after 30) it satisfies less and less. There rises a resentment in the ageing body, a bitterness in the mind.[1]

Blackwood had poured so much of himself into his recent books, and the personal losses he had sought to palliate with *The Garden of Survival* were still fresh.

Much of this sadness and loss tumbles out in the almost unbearably poignant 'The Little Beggar'[2], Blackwood's first published story after the war. It tells of a middle-aged man 'with a slight stoop' and blue eyes 'with light and courage, and a faint hint of melancholy – or was it resignation?'. He is heading to his club when he sights a ten-year-old-boy struggling with a bag. He helps the boy, though is surprised when he takes the bag to find that it weighs nothing. The boy is friendly and the man finds himself wondering who he is. He remembers other children with whom he had played: 'substitute children', he called them. When the boy asks if the man knows what is in the bag he becomes apprehensive and turns to ice when the boy tells him, 'my future'. As they reach the station the boy runs ahead to find his mother and as he thanks the man he calls him 'father'. When the man next looks the boy has gone, and his memory goes back all those years to the girl who had agreed to marry him but who had died.

Wherever Blackwood was, children were not far away. For Blackwood the reprimand that 'children must be seen and not heard' never applied. He treated them as people, as individuals and encouraged them to open their minds, use their imagination and delight in the world. The 1920s would see Blackwood explore even further the world of children. But it would always be his 'substitute children', never his own.

Did he now, in this soul-searching, reflective post-war period regret that he had not married and settled down with a family? Several stories written within a year or two of the end of the war suggest that he did. 'The Little Beggar' is the most blatant, but there are others. In 'The World-Dream of McCallister' he talks about an affair with a married woman. 'The Other Woman'[3] features an artist who yearns for a wife and children – 'their lovely ghosts walked through his canvases'. The artist has lived with years of a vision of the 'Other Woman', as he calls her, he has even tried to paint her, but without success. She is always just out of reach. He reconciles himself to the fact that the artist's soul is 'notoriously passionate and fickle', and that it could not live with one woman. He adds: 'The painter passed through many love affairs; they had no result; they interfered with his work; they dimmed his sweetest vision as they passed.'[4] It is only as he dies that the Other Woman – Death – embraces him. 'The Call'[5] is another story of un-requited love. Deane was once in love with Mary, but she was lost at sea. Years later, at a house-party, where the hostess hopes to do some match-making between Deane and another girl, Deane fancies he hears his lost love calling. Early one morning the narrator believes he sees Deane and Mary walking away across the garden, and then finds Deane has died in his sleep.

Blackwood faces the inevitable in 'The Lane that Ran East and West'. The story is an allegory of life, but written from the woman's viewpoint, a woman waiting forever for her dreams to come true.

> She saw herself, a fading figure, more than half-way now towards the sunset end, within sight even of the shadowed emptiness that lay beyond the sun's dipping edge. She had lingered over-long, expecting a dream to confirm a dream; she had been oblivious of the truth that the lane went rushing just the same. It was now too late. The speed increased. She had waited, waited for nothing. The seller of dreams was a myth.[6]

These stories, written in the cold aftermath of war, reveal a melancholic, reflective, undecided Blackwood trying to get back on terms with a world that had almost died on him. The 'old-world beauty', as he thought of it, had been sullied and spoiled by the war. Hearts were saddened, lives destroyed. It was going to be a long, long, uphill struggle.

And where was Maya in all this? The woman who had been Blackwood's spiritual Helen of Troy, who had launched a thousand visions? 'Elusive beyond capture,' reflects the artist in 'The Other Woman', and so Maya had been. The Baron had died a year ago. Maya was now free to marry . . . but there was a catch. The Baron had left Maya a considerable income in his will[7], but only so long as she remained a widow. If she remarried the annuity ceased.

Stephen Graham speculated that the Baron may have included this clause specifically to stop Maya marrying Blackwood[8], but that is unlikely. He left bequests to many widows and spinsters, but all only so long as they remained unmarried. Nevertheless, it meant that if Maya married Blackwood she would lose her wealth, and Blackwood had no appreciable income. Graham believed that Maya was in love with Blackwood – 'more than with any other man in her life'. He believes she would even have married him for love, but Blackwood did not ask her. 'Marriage has never attracted me,' he told his friend George Wrong.[9]

Today, of course, few would bother about marrying in these circumstances, but in those days society frowned on unmarried couples who lived together. However, Blackwood would not have wanted the restriction of marriage. He was too much of a free bird. All the time the Baron was alive he could still enjoy the company of Maya without any obligation. Suddenly he was now faced with an obligation. The terms of the will were almost a convenience.

Maya, however, needed the company of men. She was a sociable creature who delighted in having people about her, and who glowed in the reflected aura of men inspired by her own spirit. She still accompanied Blackwood to parties and functions, but suddenly there was a slight distance between them. After *The Promise of Air*, he never dedicated another book to her. The spirit had flown.

Apparently other men courted Maya – 'shabby suitors' Graham called them – but soon she became close friends with the rich industralist and patron of the arts, Ralph Philipson. Philipson was even wealthier than the Baron, and by marrying him, she simply lost one fortune and gained another. They were married on 9 June 1922. Blackwood was also a good friend of Philipson. They both had a fascination in antiquities – Philipson was something of a Sanskrit scholar – and in the realities of life. Philipson knew all about Blackwood and Maya, but also knew that Maya always brought out the best in Blackwood and vice versa, and that this new *ménage à trois* was more satisfying and creative than the old one with the Baron. Once Maya and Philipson married, life returned to some normality, but until then Blackwood and Maya went through a peculiar estrangement. Graham noted that their relationship 'languished but was not broken' and that Blackwood became irritable.

It was this irritated love-lorn Blackwood who produced the stories discussed above, but it was a limited depression from which he would soon recover once the Roaring Twenties took off. It's possible that 'Chinese Magic'[10] was written to overcome this loss of Maya. A psychologist, Dr Owen Francis, is not the marrying kind. 'A man in love was a man enjoying a delusion,' he declares, although one day he sees a woman who might change all that. He also meets an old friend, Edward Farque, fresh back from ten years in the Orient. Farque has discovered a Chinese drug that purports to bring seven years of happiness, but thereafter the taker has to face the consequences. Farque introduces Francis to his 'Chinese' wife of seven years. Francis recognizes her as the woman he had seen earlier and realizes that Farque has been living a life of delusion. Is it coincidental that Blackwood's years of happiness with Maya spread over seven years, 1911 to 1918?

It may be that this period of despondency hindered his completion of a novel, 'The Group-Soul'. This manuscript, which runs to just over 120 pages plus a mass of notes, is difficult to date. It has a similar mood to *The Wave* and could easily have been started soon after the war. It is the story of Richard Gale-Jones, a pleasant though predictable man. Content in himself, Gale-Jones nevertheless has a feeling of incompleteness. Over the years he has come to believe that each individual is really part of a group soul with the overall spirit in harmony. In his case, however, one of the beings that constitutes this group soul is not in harmony. The story line shifts from England to Egypt and once again there is the feeling that Blackwood is trying to understand his relationship with Maya and other individuals and how harmony can be re-established. Evidently he could not resolve this plot-line as the story just ends. Maybe the story ceased to serve any therapeutic benefit. He set it aside and never regained the urge to complete it. Yet the fact that he kept the typescript for the rest of his life shows that perhaps he still had hopes for harmony.

II

Blackwood always had a wide, continually growing circle of friends, and a few more were added during and soon after the war. In the Red Cross he met Daisy Lewis (1873–1967) – usually called Nell or Dindy. She was the wife of Frederick Lewis (1870–1944), a shipping magnate who was created a baronet in February 1918[11]. Blackwood became a regular visitor to their homes in Hatfield, Hertfordshire and Lausanne in Switzerland, and remained in regular contact with the family, especially their daughter Frieda, for the rest of his life. Blackwood became such a regular visitor to family homes over the next twenty-five years that he called himself a 'Professional Guest'. He hoped that he repaid his host's hospitality through his fund of stories, his worldly wisdom and his frequent help around the estate. More often than not he also became the resident childminder.

He also became a real Uncle Paul to Nixie and others when his sister, Cecilia, married his cousin, Arthur Hobart-Hampden, on 18 March 1920. The family spent their time between their home in England (initially in Sussex but later in Bournemouth) and Ceci's home near Menton in the south of France. Blackwood would visit them when he could.

While in Switzerland, almost certainly in 1920–21, Blackwood met the remarkable young lady Ella Maillart (1903–97), who would go on to become a renowned world traveller. Ella was only seventeen. She was at Saanenmoser perfecting her skiing and there had been an evening of song and dance in the *Baerengraben*. They were on their way back to their respective rooms when their paths crossed. Quite what made them talk to each other, Ella could not remember when I asked her years ago, but she did recall that he said she had 'tiger's eyes'. She reminded Blackwood of this in a letter in 1943, and he replied: 'Yes, I vividly recall the Tiger's Eyes that winter's night when the bise made the stars sparkle like eyes in the sky and the way to the chalet Haldi lay open.'[12] Blackwood had such a way with women.

When she learned he was an author she called on him shortly afterwards to borrow his typewriter. He steadily became her mentor. 'You are the first grown-up who gave me confidence in myself,' she reminded him in that letter.[13] She was another free spirit, almost a youthful Maya whom Blackwood could nurture. He frequently gave her help and advice and in particular the confidence to trust herself and her abilities. No doubt some of Blackwood's spirit guided the ever-zealous Maillart on the road to the 1924 Olympic Games where she represented Switzerland in sailing (single-handed category). She was the only female participant and came ninth.

There were also the Elgars. Blackwood was a regular guest at Brinkwells during 1918 and 1919, and was grief-stricken when Lady Elgar died in April 1920. 'It all makes me ache so for you – and the impossibility of helping or comforting is terrible,'[14] he wrote to Elgar. Following Lady Elgar's death, Elgar withdrew more into himself and developed a new, smaller circle of friends. He moved back to Worcestershire, and Blackwood saw less of him. They had talked of working on a new theatre piece together but now nothing came of that. It was so sad. Blackwood had proved a tonic for Elgar, and would have continued to be so throughout the 1920s had the opportunity remained.

The most important friendship Blackwood made at this time was with the actor Henry Ainley and his family.[15] Ainley was perhaps the greatest Shakespearean actor of his day – he was King George V's favourite thespian. Though regarded as tall by most (he was six foot) Blackwood still towered over him, and Blackwood's thinness compared to Ainley's fuller figure gave Ainley a look of compactness. He was graceful, handsome, with a wonderful head of hair that only 'leonine' describes. But his trademark was his voice, powerful, resonant, vivacious. Ainley was always larger than life. He lived life to the full, but was prone to mood swings, something upon which Blackwood, who was ten years his senior, provided a calming effect.

In 1902 Ainley had married the American actress Suzanne Sheldon (1875–1924). He was twenty-three, she was twenty-seven. She was the sister of the wife of Anthony Hope (1863–1933), best known as the author of *The Prisoner of Zenda* (1894). Ainley played Prince Rudolf in the stage adaptation of that novel in 1911 and also in the first silent film version in 1914. The marriage ended in 1909 when Ainley began an affair with the American socialite, Baroness von Hutten (1874–1957). The two moved in together and a son, Richard, was born in December 1910.

With the outbreak of war, the Baroness sought refuge in Switzerland and later returned to America. The affair was over. Ainley met another American divorcée, Elaine Fearon. Born Elaine Titus, she had married when she was only seventeen and divorced soon after, but she had a young daughter, Biddy. Henry and Elaine Ainley would have two children of their own, Henry Jr., usually called Sam, and Patricia, usually called Patsy. All the Ainley children, but especially Sam and Patsy, would feature heavily in Blackwood's life. Patsy was born in March 1919, two weeks after Blackwood's fiftieth birthday. There were times when Blackwood would be more of a father to her than Ainley. Patsy adored him – 'He was magical,' she told me. She always called him 'Uncle Paul', Blackwood called her his 'Best Beloved Poppet'. The relationship between them was close, perhaps the closest Blackwood ever came to a father–daughter relationship.

When Ainley starred in the film version of *The Prisoner of Zenda*, much of it was filmed at Knole, Sevenoaks and Ightham Mote in Kent. Ainley loved the area and after the war, with his growing family, he bought a large house – Chart Lodge – near Ightham – a farm in its own right. The house was so big that Blackwood came to share it with them. He rented a room above the garage where he stayed for most of the summer. When he headed for Switzerland in the winter the Ainleys sometimes came with him. Suddenly Blackwood had not simply 'substitute children', but an entire surrogate family. They all confided in him. He was Uncle Paul to them all – their mentor, friend, companion, playmate, even gardener.

At nearby Stonepitts Farm lived Lady Rhondda (1883–1957), one of the survivors of the *Lusitania* disaster. In 1920 she founded the political paper *Time and Tide*, to which Blackwood became a frequent contributor. A short car ride away at Fairlawne was the home of Thelma and Peter Cazalet, which Blackwood visited regularly, usually to play tennis[16]. He was even drafted into the local village cricket eleven.

Just over the downs at Dunstall Priory was the noted author and playwright, Lord Dunsany. Blackwood and Dunsany were very distantly related, via the playwright Richard Brinsley Sheridan. Dunsany was a great traveller, like Blackwood, and they had plenty of stories to tell each other. Patsy Ainley recalled one winter when Blackwood and Dunsany went tobogganing down the hillside near Dunstall Priory on silver tea trays.

Suddenly Blackwood's world came alive again. The melancholia of 1919 passed, and a new era began. By 1920 he was working on two plays, several short stories and had at last returned to the sequel to *Julius LeVallon*, *The Bright Messenger*.

III

Blackwood threw himself into the world of the theatre. He became acquainted with the actor and playwright Bertram Forsyth (1882–1927). Forsyth had been with the Benson Company and acted alongside Ainley in several Shakespearean productions. He had written and produced a popular children's Christmas play, *The Shepherdess Without a Heart*, first performed in 1913. It was a simple play wherein love brings various household goods to life, an idea that would have appealed to Blackwood.

Although Blackwood was still working with Violet Pearn – she was adapting *The Education of Uncle Paul* for the stage as *Through the Crack* – their relationship was a little strained. Blackwood wanted to work with someone more attuned to the theatrical world and his own philosophy on life and Forsyth was a good choice. The man was, unfortunately, prone to fits of depression.

The two set to work on a new play, *The Crossing*. The storyline was almost entirely Blackwood's. Antony Grimshaw is writing a book called *Living Beauty*. Grimshaw has lost his son in the war and wants to bring a message of hope and beauty to others who suffered loss. His wife, Margaret, has not come to terms with the loss and it has eroded her faith. She has distanced herself from her husband and become like her brother, Richard: a hard-headed northerner intent only on making money. Grimshaw's daughter, Nixie, is more in tune with her father's thoughts. They make a pact that whoever dies first will visit the other 'on the wind'. Grimshaw is killed in a road accident and only Nixie is aware of his spirit when it returns to their house. There is an epilogue which provides a key to Blackwood's philosophy. A month later the brother, Richard, returns to the household with a message from a spiritualist, but this message is irrelevant to the widow. She knows her husband's spirit is all around her because of the peacefulness and harmony in the house. This was the message of *The Garden of Survival*.

The play was staged at the Comedy Theatre on 29 September 1920, with Herbert Marshall as Grimshaw and Irene Rooke as his wife. It ran for thirteen performances – typical of the many short runs in those days. The newspapers were mixed in their reviews. *The Times*, as usual, was hostile. 'It is without unity of impression, proportion, cumulative interest – without, in short, any of the indispensable elements of a work of dramatic art.'[17] *The Stage* agreed, adding that the play 'leaves us not only unconvinced, but cold, and a little wearied by Antony Grimshaw's steady flow of carefully-chosen words'.[18] However, *The Graphic* commented on the masterly production and noted that the audience was 'spellbound'[19]. Even *The Times* had to admit that 'This curious farrago was followed at the curtain-fall with thunders of applause. The authors were enthusiastically called'.

Interestingly, when the play was considered by the Lord Chamberlain for a licence, there was some consideration about how the dead-alive should be portrayed on the stage, but the verdict was that it was 'beautifully expressed'.[20] Much of this was down to the admirable production by Donald Calthrop (1888–1940) who was daring in his use of long periods of silence to heighten the atmosphere and in his effective use of lighting. The critic for *The Era* commented on the sincerity of all the performers.

Blackwood and Forsyth worked on a second play, *White Magic*. This one betrays much less of the Blackwood trademark. A married couple have long yearned for a child, but are not blessed. The husband turns to drink. But a local witch uses her skills and brings a child to the family. The play was never performed in Britain. At the end of June 1921 Forsyth took up the appointment as director of the Hart House Theatre in Toronto. He took the play with him and staged it as part of a triple bill as his directorial début, along with *A Night at the Inn* by Lord Dunsany and *Pantaloon* by J.M. Barrie. Reports suggest that the audience were less sure how to interpret *White Magic*, as it lacked the depth of its companion plays. Nevertheless, the overall production was well received and ran for fifteen nights from 21 November 1921.[21]

Neither play has been performed again since. Unfortunately Forsyth, in one of his fits of depression, gassed himself in New York in September 1927, and nothing further became of the plays.

Even as Blackwood and Forsyth took their curtain calls at the first production of *The Crossing* in 1920, plans were already well advanced with *Through the Crack*. The Everyman Theatre, Hampstead, had opened for the first time on 15 September 1920, under the directorship of Norman MacDermott (1890–1977) with Edith Craig (1869–1947) as resident producer. Craig was the daughter of the famous actress Ellen Terry, and it's very probable that Blackwood had met Craig when he interviewed Ellen Terry for the *New York Sun* twenty-seven years before. MacDermott wanted something different from the usual London pantomimes for his Christmas children's matinées, and he settled on *Through the Crack*. Evidently memories of *The Starlight Express* had not cast shadows over Blackwood and Pearn's work. In fact the production of the play proceeded without any of the faults of *Starlight*. This was no doubt helped by Edith Craig's masterful hand, but also because more time was allowed for the production and there were no clashes of artistic temperament. It was a more friendly, co-operative environment. Music was composed by a member of the company, Laurence Hanray (1874–1947), and Harold Scott, who played the Tramp, wrote an extra song for himself.

Although *Through the Crack* takes its basic premise from *The Education of Uncle Paul* it is essentially a new story, borrowing a few features and characters from *The Extra Day*. In fact *Through the Crack* brings together all the key elements of Blackwood's Uncle novels, and is the better for that.

We meet Uncle Paul who comes under the spell of his sister's children, Nixie, Jonah and Toby, and with their childhood spirit is able to pass through the crack to the land where all lost things are found. Other characters make it through the crack as well, and there they find old, lost toys and old friends, long departed. This includes Misty-Love, the elder sister of Nixie, who had died some years before. The children hope that Misty-Love can find her way back through the crack, but the audience is left wondering until the very last moment whether she makes it or not. There are echoes in Misty-Love of the fairy Tinker-Bell in *Peter Pan* where the children in the audience have to believe in her to bring her back to life.

It's a beautiful play, sentimental without being maudlin, and not so shrouded in mysticality as *Starlight*. Children were totally absorbed by the play. One reviewer noted how the children near him hated the intermission before the last Act because they wanted to know if Misty-Love would come back. It had a strong cast of capable and experienced repertory artists. Best known at the time was Nicholas Hannen (1881–1972), who played Uncle Paul. He married actress Athene Seyler and later was awarded an OBE for his stage work. Lesser known then, but destined to become well known on stage, screen and television, was Felix Aylmer (1889–1979) (later knighted), who played the Policeman. Nixie was played by Renée Mayer, who had recently played the part of Pinkie in *Pinkie and the Fairies*. Misty-Love marked the first stage appearance of Gilly Flower, who will long be remembered for her role as Miss Tibbs, one of the two old ladies in John Cleese's *Fawlty Towers*.

For once the critics were united in their praise of the play. 'One of the most agreeable things of its kind that London has seen for a long time,' wrote one[22]. Norman MacDermott was also satisfied. 'The production was a complete success, playing to full houses, and was asked for in the following year.'[23] Unlike *The Starlight Express*, or any of Blackwood's other plays, *Through the Crack* was revived several times. Edith Craig staged a new production at the Apollo Theatre in December 1922[24]. Clare Greet repeated her role as the Cook, and Margaret Carter as Aunt Emily. Otherwise it was an entirely new cast and included Muriel Pratt as the Mother, at last being able to take part in one of Blackwood and Pearn's plays. There was a third production by Edith Craig as the opener for the first season of a new theatre, the St Christopher School Theatre at Letchworth Garden City in January 1925.[25] This marked the first professional theatrical work for Laurence Olivier. He was second assistant stage manager and general understudy, which he classified as starting 'at the very bottom'. He also added that the name of the play 'has never failed to bring a smile to the lips of the average profane grown-up'.[26]

The popularity of *Through the Crack* meant that it was the only stage play of Blackwood's that was ever published, since *Karma* was never performed. Samuel French issued an edition in 1925. It contained a brief introduction by Sybil Thorndike (1882–1976) where she called it 'a wonderful example of a true child's play'.

IV

The year 1920 had proved a remarkably productive one for Blackwood. In addition to the success of *The Crossing* and *Through the Crack*, he completed several new stories and at last finished *The Bright Messenger*. He gave it its final polish in Saanenmoser, where he retreated for the winter after the last night of *Through the Crack*.

Most of the new stories, which Watt's admirably agented around several high-paying American markets, were for a new collection, *The Wolves of God and Other Fey Stories*. This volume is shown as a collaboration with his friend Wilfrid Wilson, though when the stories appeared earlier in magazines they were credited to Blackwood alone. In fact the stories were all by Blackwood. Some of them owed their origins to ideas that came up in discussion with Wilson. Others owed something to their shared experiences over the years. Wilson has always remained a shadowy figure despite much research to bring him into focus. A tall, hearty, bluff man with a great bellow of a laugh, he weaved in and out of Blackwood's life right from the earliest times through to his last days. He was one of those stout rocks to which Blackwood could anchor now and again to rest and recuperate.

The Wolves of God is one of the hardest volumes of Blackwood's work to find, and it contains some very good stories. A few, like 'The Man Who Found Out' and 'The Empty Sleeve' date back to before the war, but most were new ones written in that heady vibrancy that came with Blackwood's rediscovery of life after the post-War melancholy.

The stories that owe most to Wilson are what may be called explorer's tales and include 'First Hate' and 'The Valley of the Beasts' discussed elsewhere. 'Running Wolf'[27] takes us way back to Blackwood's final days in America. It's set in the same territory as 'The Wendigo', north of Mattawa. A hunter, called Hyde, finds himself being followed by a wolf. It offers no threat. Curious, Hyde follows the wolf and it leads him to the skeleton of a long dead Indian. Later Hyde's friend, Morton, recounts the legend of an Indian who had killed a wolf and was banned from his tribe to wander forever, until his bones were found by a member of another race. In 'The Wolves of God', Jim Peace returns to the Orkneys from Canada having murdered a man. He is pursued by the spirits of the wolves of God who exact their revenge. 'The Tarn of Sacrifice'[28] is set in the Lake District and owes much to Wilson's Cumbrian background. It was written after the war because the main protagonist, John Holt, had fought in the war and in a strange way had enjoyed it. On a long hiking tour through the Cumbrian mountains he follows the remains of a long disused Roman road and imagines himself part of the Legion. He finds himself sucked into a re-enactment of an incident between the Romans and the native Britons.

Most of the other stories are romances spiced by the supernatural or macabre. They include 'The Call', 'Chinese Magic' and 'The Lane that Ran East and West', which are discussed elsewhere. 'Egyptian Sorcery' is one of the last Maya-inspired stories. Sanfield's astral body travels to Egypt to save the life of a woman he once loved. 'The Decoy'[29] is a doppelganger story set in the Kentish Weald, near the Knoops' home at Wadhurst. In 'Confession', O'Reilly, still recuperating from shell-shock, becomes confused and dislocated from time in a thick London fog. He encounters a young lady, also lost, and follows her back to her house where he discovers she's been murdered. He flees from the house and is saved by a doctor. The story has a clever surprise ending, which Blackwood evidently liked as he often retold the tale, and it was one of the first he used on radio.

The Wolves of God was published in April 1921[30]. Although it did not receive rapturous reviews, the critics were generally in favour, commenting on the cleverness and ingenuity of the authors. There would be two more substantial collections of new stories from Blackwood, but *Wolves* is his last significant volume. The stories lack the power of his great works, but they are competent, professional pieces that show the mature mastery of a true storyteller, able to look back over a lifetime of experience and uncover the magic and mystery in every aspect of life.

The Bright Messenger was not just the long-awaited finale to *Julius LeVallon*, but the last piece in Blackwood's grand design. The original novel had been forged in a period of white-heat creativity in early 1911. Ten years later it was a different Blackwood who continued it. This book is the culmination of Blackwood's crusade to make people aware of beauty in the world and to turn their hearts away from the commercialised, plundering world of civilization.

We are introduced to Edward Fillery, illegitimate son of a mining engineer and a wild Caucasian girl, and sympathetic to the spirits of nature. Experienced through his travels and studies across the globe, Fillery has opened a Spiritual Clinique, or a home for 'hopeless cases', as he calls it. A colleague, Paul Devonham, refers the odd case to him. He is passed the papers of John Mason, who has now died. It is twenty years on from the experiences related in *Julius LeVallon*. Mason has done his best to raise and care for the strange offspring of Julius and his wife. This child, although called Julian LeVallon, has an alien alter-ego, a spirit self which Mason calls N.H. (for Non-Human). Fillery's task is to look after LeVallon/N.H.

Blackwood re-uses concepts employed in earlier stories. *The Bright Messenger* becomes an extended study of possession and dual personality. LeVallon is 'quiescent, normal, very charming into the bargain, more like a good child or trained animal or happy peasant'; whilst N.H. is 'otherwise'. Both manifestations betray a child of Nature, where instinct rules over rationality, as Blackwood had explored in *The Promise of Air* and 'A Touch of Pan'. Blackwood repackaged these ideas in the context of the Eastern concept of *Devas*. Fillery explains.

> There rushed through him the Eastern conception of another system of life, another evolution, deathless, divine, important, the Order of the *Devas*, a series of Nature Beings entirely apart from human categories. They included many degrees, from fairies to planetary spirits, the gods, so called; and their duties, work and purposes were concerned with carrying out the Laws of Nature. . . A noble, useful, selfless work, God's messengers. . .[31]

Fillery believes that if he could unite LeVallon with his N.H. side, then Nature and Beauty would return to the hearts of men. LeVallon is an advance messenger of the gods, a kind of nature Messiah, whose very existence could turn mankind's thoughts back to the spiritual life. Devonham, on the other hand, believes that N.H. should be exorcised, like a demon, and LeVallon restored.

Most of the time it is the character of LeVallon who presents himself to the world. N.H. seldom reveals himself even though that is the real being. Once in a while Fillery breaks through and makes contact with N.H. and there is a revealing chapter (Chapter 9), where the viewpoint shifts to N.H. and he gives an account of himself. We know from *Julius LeVallon* that the elemental power now occupying LeVallon's body had been released during an illicit experiment aeons ago. That power is N.H. It feels isolated, cut off from its companions. It recalls that it has observed the human race for countless ages, but always from 'outside'. Now that it has awoken inside a human it realizes the limits of the human faculties. Yet one human trait seems to have made contact with N.H., since it becomes interested in 'the Comely One'. This is Nayan Khilkoff, a beautiful free-spirited young lady, and daughter of a Russian artist.

The power of love strengthens LeVallon's human side whilst with the coming of spring, and the return of the power of the Earth, N.H. becomes strong enough to return to his companions who are calling to him. N.H. tells Fillery that humans are not yet ready for the next stage of spiritual evolution. Fillery wishes that N.H. would still work with him and makes one last plea.

> 'Using beauty – the artists – the creative powers of the Race. . . we shall create together a new body, a new vehicle, through which your powers can express themselves. The intellect cannot serve you... it is the creative imagination of those who know beauty that you seek. You are inarticulate in this wretched body. We shall make a new one –'[32]

But it is too late. N.H. departs leaving the shell, the 'disenchanted dust' of LeVallon. Fillery realizes he has seen a glimpse of the future, a new evolution, an angelic evolution, when the god of nature would restore beauty and harmony to the world. 'That's Pan's work,' a priest says to Fillery at the end. 'Pan and all his splendid hierarchy. Always at work, though invisibly, with music, colour, beauty!'[33]

There are moments in *The Bright Messenger* when we see the Blackwood of *The Centaur* and *Julius LeVallon*. He is, after all, working with a major concept, that of restoring true spiritual beings upon the Earth as was God's original purpose. When he pushes aside the veils into the otherworldly the magic starts to work.

Unfortunately, Blackwood was finding it harder to regain that magic. It was a different Blackwood to the one who wrote *Julius LeVallon* a decade before. Blackwood had poured his creative energies into a dozen books or so in the intervening years and he had been drained by the war and his own personal losses. He now lived in a different world. Not the world of the mighty hunter, as he had seemed as he strutted across the mountains of the Caucasus and the deserts of Egypt. Now he was a celebrity, a creature of society. To the novel's loss, Blackwood places LeVallon against that society and in those moments the novel's spark dims and the energies diffuse.

Nevertheless, it should rank alongside *The Centaur* for its scope and wonder. Both books consider the mighty alternate cosmic powers of the Universe. Both books reveal, just for an instant, a blissful paradise of beauty and harmony, but one that is beyond the reach of normal man. Only ones who commune with the powers of nature, who have the sensitivity to comprehend and are not shackled by materialism and self-importance – only they may have a glimpse of what might be, just like Moses saw the Promised Land but could not enter.

The Bright Messenger is a courageous book – intelligent, unique, original. Alas, it is not a great book. Its power glows only in the context of Blackwood's ideological sequence – *Julius LeVallon, The Centaur, The Promise of Air, The Bright Messenger* – demonstrating the potential for mankind's spiritual evolution to an Edenic state.

Once he had completed *The Bright Messenger* Blackwood had nothing else to tell the world. Two other stories almost certainly started around this time, 'The Group Soul' and a short story, 'The People of the Ridge', were left discarded and unfinished. 'The People of the Ridge' is reminiscent of 'The Temptation of the Clay'. A writer signs a contract against his better judgment because it promises big money. He feels that he has sold his soul. He retires to a remote village to write but finds that the spirit of the village turns against him until he renounces the contract and regains his soul. The first draft ends in a mass of notes and alternate endings. It appears that Blackwood got bogged down in his own imagination. The stories were set aside and never resumed. Blackwood had said all he wanted to say.

V

Blackwood spent January to April 1921 in Switzerland at Saanenmoser, mostly on his own but with frequent visitors, especially the Ainleys who joined him in March at the end of Henry's run in *Peter Pan*. He returned home just in time to attend a wedding. His sister-in-law, Stevie's widow Kate, married James Eadie on 15 April. Eadie (1881–1963) was a surgeon, and became Patrick's stepfather. Although this did not relieve Blackwood of his role as Patrick's uncle – he continued to take a keen interest and care in the boy's upbringing – it did at least relieve him of certain paternal obligations that had restrained him since his brother's death. Blackwood continued to be a regular guest at the Eadie's home in Bentinck Mansions.

After the wedding Blackwood stayed in London for a while. He and Wilson celebrated the publication of *The Wolves of God* at the end of April. Wilson had recently become engaged to Agnes Henderson. It was a case of money marrying money. Wilson was already a man of considerable private means. Like Wilson, Agnes was related to a banking family and the landed gentry. She had her own personal butler and was driven everywhere in a Rolls-Royce. They were married on 5 July 1921, and it's likely that Blackwood's idea to share the credit of *The Wolves of God* with Wilson was his wedding present.

By the summer Blackwood was back in his room at the Ainleys. The Birmingham poet/playwright John Drinkwater (1882–1937) paid a visit. He had recently finished the latest in his series of historical dramas, this one based on the life of Oliver Cromwell. Drinkwater had known Henry Ainley for many years and was a frequent guest at his home, sometimes accompanied by his brother-in-law, Hugh Walpole (1884–1941). Walpole and Blackwood had much in common – both were dedicated walkers with a devotion to the countryside. Walpole had also been in the Red Cross during the war, though based in Russia, and Blackwood had met him at the Ministry of Information on his visits to see John Buchan. Walpole settled in the Lake District after he bought Brackenburn in 1923, overlooking Lake Derwentwater, and Blackwood was an occasional guest.

Both Drinkwater and Walpole were friends of the American author Sinclair Lewis (1885–1951). Lewis had rented a house for two months (August and September) in the village of Bearsted, just outside Maidstone in Kent. Here he worked on *Babbitt*. He invited Drinkwater down from Hampstead, and the playwright turned up with a carload including Ainley and Blackwood. Ainley invited Lewis back to Chart Lodge and took him on a tour of the farms and countryside – Lewis was fascinated by the hop-picking.

It's little surprise that, surrounded by these literary and theatrical greats, Blackwood was stimulated and inspired. When Bertram Forsyth left for Canada, in June, Blackwood looked for a new writing partner. For fun he and Elaine Ainley wrote a short sketch, a curtain-raiser, called *The Halfway House*. The title refers to a remote inn in Yorkshire where 'charmer' Richard Paine lures Sybil Mansfield one evening. Sybil's husband, Arthur, who has discreetly followed them, takes over the inn for the evening to save his wife. It was produced for a short run at the Victoria Palace in London, starting on 5 December. Henry Ainley played Arthur Mansfield and Elaine played his wife.

As his main writing partner, though, Blackwood settled on Frederick Kinsey Peile (1862–1934). Peile was a noted actor as well as a playwright. He had toured with George Alexander's company just before Ainley had joined. He began writing plays as early as 1896, and his reputation grew in 1903 when he adapted Rudyard Kipling's 'The Man Who Was' as a very successful stage play. By the time Blackwood and Peile entered into partnership (they had a formal agreement drawn up) Peile was nearly sixty, a tall, authoritative figure with a wealth of theatrical experience.

During the autumn of 1921 Peile and Blackwood were hard at work on various projects. The first completed was *The Decoy*, followed by *Max Hensig*. According to Blackwood they also began a three-act farce and a ballet. There are no details of the farce, and the idea may have been dropped. The ballet was based on 'The Wings of Horus' which Peile remembers in his own autobiography.[34] Considering Peile and Blackwood's connections and this sudden burst of industry, it is surprising that so little came from it, and most of their output has sunk with barely a trace. Blackwood recalled that *The Decoy* was placed with José Levy of the Little Theatre, to be followed by *Max Hensig*, and though both were ideally suited to Levy's Grand Guignol seasons, there is no record that either were produced.

Max Hensig was produced eight years later at the Gate Theatre Studio in the Strand, London by Peter Godfrey, when he put on a series of Grand Guignol plays.[35] That production was not well received, one critic dismissing it as 'a commonplace shocker with a "snap" curtain which is merely incredible'. Another critic called the ending 'a facile theatrical trick'.[36] The fate of *The Decoy* is unknown. There was a later adaptation by Margaret Dolman for the Questor Theatre in West London in 1944[37], which Blackwood was happy to approve, but he had no hand in the script or the production.

The saddest loss of all is the ballet, 'The Wings of Horus'. This was to be produced and choreographed by Anton Dolin (1904–83), who was then a principal dancer in the Diaghilev Ballet, with sets and costumes designed by Percy Anderson (1852–1928). Anderson was perhaps the leading stage designer of his day and was renowned for his exotic work on *Chu Chin Chow* and *The Mikado*. Kinsey Peile believed that the designs he made for 'The Wings of Horus' were his best. Peile says that 'circumstances prevented its being produced before poor Percy Anderson died'. Apparently Anderson was very ill when he undertook the work and was awaiting a serious operation, which he put off until he finished the designs and costumes. The last words Peile heard Anderson say were, 'If the ballet is ever produced, Fred, rest assured that I shall be present in spirit. I feel quite certain of that – think of me then. I hope we may have a great success.' Anderson died on 30 October 1928.

The work with Peile cut down Blackwood's other writing pursuits. He began an occasional series of articles for Lady Rhondda's *Time and Tide*, starting with 'Changing 'Ats'[38], a short amusing sketch upon how people's personalities change with their clothes. The only new story at this time was 'Nephelé'[39]. Its focus on dancing shows that Blackwood's mind had been following the terpsichorean theme all year. An archaeologist finds the remains of a Roman dancing girl, Nephelé, including her dancing sandals and a jewel. When a friend's sister tries on these items, she is possessed by the girl's spirit and begins to dance.

In November 1922 Blackwood was contacted by the British pianist and composer Alec Rowley (1892–1958). Rowley was interested in Blackwood's stage productions and Blackwood suggested they meet. Rowley was keen to compose music for *Through the Crack*, and Blackwood suggested that he contact 'Miss Pratt' (presumably Muriel, not Gertrude) in order to discuss the music in case of a revival another year.

However, Blackwood's real desire was for a *new* play.

> I suggest your friend, Aidan Clarke, should contrive a play for grown-up children, using the material, if he likes, from the 3 books (*Prisoner, Uncle Paul, Extra Day*). All the material is there – characters, songs, business. More could be added. Miss Pearn has no exclusive rights – nor has anyone – in the material of these 3 books, which contain all my children stuff. The *Prisoner* alone has sufficient material, and the *Starlight Express* play does not prevent its being used a second time in a new version. [40]

Rowley pursued this initially. He may even have composed some provisional music, but nothing further came of it. Clearly Blackwood's works were an inspiration to artists who hoped to widen the scope of his message through other artistic interpretations, only to find that the true mystical heart of Blackwood's beliefs did not easily lend itself to adaptation.

The day after the final performance of the Apollo production of *Through the Crack* Blackwood went abroad, but only for a few weeks. There was a deadline looming, and Blackwood needed to be word perfect. Thirty years after Blackwood had first trod the boards in New York with J.H. Gilmour's company, he was to return to the stage in the role of Colonel Pemberton in John Drinkwater's *Oliver Cromwell*. Henry Ainley had brought together his own company to tour the provinces before opening in London. The play was first performed at the Brighton Theatre Royal on 19 February 1923. Ainley played Cromwell in a role that was universally praised and which demanded curtain calls every night. Cromwell's ageing mother, whose part allows for an emotional climax in the final scene, was played by Irene Rooke (1878–1958), who had previously appeared in Blackwood's *The Crossing*. It was later regarded as her finest performance. Also in the company were such well known stars of the day as Harcourt Williams, Hayden Coffin, Milton Rosmer (Irene Rooke's husband) and Mary O'Farrell.

Blackwood's role was not arduous. Colonel Pemberton appears in only one scene, on the day of the battle of Naseby, where Blackwood acted alongside Douglas Jefferies as General Fairfax and Milton Rosmer as Henry Ireton. He had about a dozen lines. Blackwood had to perform dressed in a partial suit of armour – breastplate and helmet – which may have made moving around the stage difficult and there is, of course, far more to acting than just delivering lines. Nevertheless, at least one critic commented that Blackwood was 'excellent'.

The played toured the provinces, including Birmingham, Oxford and Nottingham, before coming to His Majesty's Theatre in London on 29 May where it ran for nine weeks. Blackwood was first mooted to appear in the London production, but in the end he did not and the role was taken over by J. Fisher White (1865–1945).

Blackwood's presence on stage must have been striking, just as it was years later on television. The Irish theatrical impresario, Micheál MacLiammóir, who met Blackwood soon afterwards, described him as follows.

> No one who had pierced through those careless rambling books of his to the splendours of the mind beneath could be disappointed by that extraordinary personality, and when he towered up from his chair to greet me, lean and bald and bronzed, a fabulous, blue-eyed hawk, my doubts fled for ever. . . . The afternoon wore away,

crowded with enchantment; we parted at some street corner near the park, and as I watched the tall figure a phrase I had forgotten came to me about men who walked like trees at night.[41]

The tour gave rise to the story 'Malahide and Forden'. While they were at Nottingham, Harcourt Williams (who becomes Forden) wanted to check out the church and other antiquities at the nearby village of Barton-in-Fabis. Ainley (Malahide) and Blackwood (the narrator) join him. In the story they become lost and trapped in a repeating cycle of time.

The fascination with time and space had always intrigued Blackwood and it now came into sharper focus as Blackwood moved into the multi-dimensional worlds of Gurdjieff, Ouspensky and J.W. Dunne.

16

Elsewhere and Otherwise (1923–27)

I

On 4 February 1922 Blackwood wrote to one of his devoted readers, who had sent him some books to autograph. The books had arrived two months earlier, missing Blackwood as he set off to Switzerland for his usual winter skiing. In typical tantalizing fashion, when he returned the autographed books and apologized for the delay, Blackwood said, 'Your letter of December 18/21 has only just reached me, as I have been travelling beyond bounds where letters could safely follow me.'[1]

What a delightful way of saying 'I've been abroad'. But why explain something so prosaic when you can be so much more mysterious. In the twenty years between the wars Blackwood travelled all over Europe, but it's not always easy to track him from one place to the next. Switzerland remained his base during the ski season, but he also spent time in Italy, France, Germany, Austria, Hungary and, of course, Egypt. He was like a migrating bird, who returned during the summer to nest in the Ainley garret and flit out from time to time to visit friends, before migrating back to winter haunts.

In the summer of 1922 Blackwood was in Venice. It was soon after the marriage of Ralph and Maya Philipson in London on 9 June. He was contacted by Lady Rothermere (1875–1937) and asked out to lunch. Blackwood must have been intrigued. He knew Lady Rothermere slightly, more by reputation than personally. She was the estranged wife of Lord Rothermere the newspaper tycoon, publisher of the *Daily Mirror* and *Sunday Pictorial*, and younger brother of Lord Northcliffe. Despite her wealth, her beauty and her connections she was rather a sad individual. She had lost two of her sons in the war and though she put on a brave face and strove to be the bubbly society hostess, deep down she was looking for an explanation for the way life had treated her.

At lunch Lady Rothermere entreated Blackwood instantly. 'There are two people in Paris just now you ought to know – Ouspensky and Gurdjieff.'[2]

Blackwood already knew of Pyötr Demianovitch Ouspensky (1878–1947), though apparently not of Georgei Ivanovich Gurdjieff (1866?–1949). Blackwood had encountered Ouspensky's name the previous year when American publisher Claude Bragdon sent Blackwood a copy of his translation of Ouspensky's *Tertium Organum*. Published in Russia (St Petersburg) in 1912, this book, which Ouspensky regarded as his 'weakness', challenged the whole philosophical basis of scientific thinking, especially concerning our perception of space and time. Ouspensky drew upon the thinking of the English author, Charles H. Hinton (1853–1907), whose pioneering work *Scientific Romances* (1886) had inspired H.G. Wells, and whose *A New Era of Thought* (1888) and *The Fourth Dimension* (1904) were among Blackwood's favourite reading. Hinton had postulated the idea of a fourth dimension in space, the next stage on from a cube, which he called a tesseract. He even argued that under certain conditions you could see a ghost of this fourth dimension by constructing a series of specially coloured cubes. These Hinton cubes were especially popular in Theosophical circles and Blackwood would have been familiar with them from his earliest studies.

Ouspensky took that thinking further, like Wells and Einstein, stating that the fourth dimension was time, and recognizing that our own perceptions were limited, trapped, by our current thinking. In order to become aware of the fourth and other dimensions we had to liberate ourselves from our existing way of thinking and expand our consciousness. That was what the title *Tertium Organum* meant. Usually translated as 'The Third *Canon* of Thought'[3], Ouspensky argued it should have been 'The Third *Weapon* of Thought', meaning he was providing a means whereby you could fight current philosophical limitations and broaden our understanding. Like Gurdjieff, Ouspensky wanted to set aside the rules and rebuild with an open mind. Both were keen to bring a scientific rationale to mysticism, provided both strains of thought allowed for liberated not closed thinking.

Blackwood liked that. It was what he had done. After he had shed his mind of his evangelical background he returned to basics, rediscovering the world from natural sources and beliefs. Through his own studies, Blackwood had reached much the same view as Ouspensky. Ouspensky was proposing the same mental and spiritual evolution that Blackwood had been exploring in *The Centaur*, *The Promise of Air* and especially *The Bright Messenger*. Blackwood was thus keen to meet the man, but knew of no way to contact him.

Blackwood had presumably not known that Ouspensky had been in London in 1913 and met A.R. Orage (1873–1934), the editor of the socialist magazine *New Age*, and G.R.S. Mead, of the Quest Society, both well known to Blackwood. Ouspensky even travelled from there to Egypt on his way out to Ceylon and the Far East. Their paths so very nearly crossed.

Blackwood could almost have rubbed shoulders with Gurdjieff, as well. As Lady Rothermere told him more about this Armenian mystic, so Blackwood's interest grew. Gurdjieff had been born in the town of Alexandropol[4] in Armenia, though he spent most of his later youth in Kars. Though his mother was Armenian, his father was Greek. He was raised in that turbulent area of the Caucasus that would capture Blackwood's spirit in 1910. Like Blackwood Gurdjieff had a wanderlust, and was a seeker after truth – he was involved in the development of an esoteric organization called the Seekers of Truth as early as 1894. He purportedly travelled throughout Russia, the Middle East and Central Asia, as well as Egypt and Ethiopia. He is even supposed to have travelled into Tibet as a political agent, and was there at the same time as Blackwood's later friend, Vincent Nesfield. Whereas Blackwood had suffered the privations of New York, Gurdjieff's existence had been even more perilous. He was shot and injured on several occasions and involved in several accidents. He later believed that individuals needed to experience near-death and appreciate their own mortality before they could take their studies seriously.

Gurdjieff settled in Tashkent in what was Turkestan (now Uzbekistan) in 1905 and by 1908 had emerged as an idiosyncratic and unpredictable teacher – a 'Professor-Instructor of Supernatural Sciences'. That was where he was when Blackwood was in the Caucasus. If he heard of him then by reputation, Blackwood didn't say. By 1912 Gurdjieff was in Moscow, having established a psychospiritual school. This was when he first heard of Ouspensky and the two eventually met in 1915.

Ouspensky and Gurdjieff were very different characters. Ouspensky was the intellectual of the two. He had reached his conclusions through academic study, which he then tested by experience. Gurdjieff was the opposite. He had learned directly through experience, instinct, intuition, and then sought to apply his understanding through experimentation and study. Ouspensky could be aloof, superior, vain, with a tendency to didacticism and autolatry. Gurdjieff remained mysterious, obscure, obtuse, unpredictable. They even looked different. Ouspensky looked a serious scholar, stern-faced, impenetrable, lacking humour. Gurdjieff enjoyed looking unusual. By the 1920s he had a completely bald, domed head (on which he frequently wore an astrakhan hat) and he had shed his tailored suit in favour of a more traditional Greek outfit. He was shorter, portlier, with a lugubrious face, but with eyes that captured and haunted. Everyone talks about how his eyes would capture you, read you, control you.

Ouspensky later felt that upon their first meeting Gurdjieff had lifted him in his hand, weighed him, and placed him back. Blackwood's view of the two is typical of many. He found Ouspensky intriguing but ultimately lightweight. 'I owe him much,' Blackwood wrote. 'At the same time, it is to Gurdjieff that I owe most.'

The war uprooted Gurdjieff and Ouspensky but by 1919 Gurdjieff had settled in Tbilisi (Tiflis) and established his Institute for the Harmonious Development of Man. The following year he settled in Constantinople where he again met Ouspensky.

This is where Lady Rothermere entered the picture. She had read *Tertium Organum* in May 1921 and, like Blackwood, was keen to meet the author. Unlike Blackwood, Lady Rothermere had the money to achieve her aim. She cabled the American publisher, Claude Bragdon, asking to meet him and the author. Bragdon had also just received a letter from Ouspensky. He was delighted to learn of the translation (and of the royalties arising) and asked for help to travel to England or the United States. Bragdon told Lady Rothermere of this and she promptly sent a telegram to Ouspensky in Constantinople, expressing her desire to meet him, and sending him £100.

Ouspensky reached London in August 1921. A circle of followers soon gathered around him, most prominently Orage and Mead, and he lectured to the Quest Society. Once again Blackwood missed him.

Blackwood later wrote that he was looking for an opening to meet Ouspensky, and yet here was the man lecturing virtually on his doorstep. Ouspensky began a series of regular meetings in November 1921, first at Lady Rothermere's own studio in St John's Wood but soon after at the Theosophical Hall in Warwick Gardens. Gurdjieff made it to London in February 1922. There had been problems over his visa, and he was not allowed to stay, but he did deliver a speech at Warwick Gardens on 13 February and again on 15 March. At the second of these meetings he challenged Ouspensky's right to act as his apostle, seeking to spread his word.

Gurdjieff argued that Ouspensky could not have the necessary depth or breadth of understanding of Gurdjieff's beliefs to teach it independently. On his part, Ouspensky had been harbouring doubts about Gurdjieff's person (but not his teaching) since they had left Russia in 1917. This led to a decisive fracture in their relationship from here on. Ouspensky never forgave Gurdjieff this admonition in front of his own colleagues.

Blackwood missed all this. He was in Switzerland, as usual, not returning to England until late March 1922, when he again stayed with the Ainleys and visited Vita Sackville-West. He may not have known about the meetings, though Maya Knoop and Ralph Philipson attended them. For this one brief period Blackwood was so absorbed in his other work and temporarily distanced from Maya, that he missed an opportunity.

They say that opportunity does not knock twice, but for Blackwood it did, via Lady Rothermere. She gave Blackwood Gurdjieff's address in Paris. Because Gurdjieff could not obtain a work permit for England he was forced to return to Germany, and then settled in Paris on 14 July 1922. His friends helped him find a flat, and soon after there was a meeting about finances. Both Lady Rothermere and the Philipsons were present, and both matched each other's donations to support Gurdjieff's work.

Blackwood tells us that after his meeting with Lady Rothermere he cut short his holiday and left the next day for Paris. Why was it that urgent? Did he suddenly realize he had missed out on something that Maya had discovered?

According to Blackwood, when he met Gurdjieff in his Paris flat he found it difficult to communicate with him. He says that Gurdjieff's French and English were poor as was Blackwood's Turkish and Russian.

But was Gurdjieff's French or English that bad? He was a very capable linguist and had a basic but passable knowledge of French and probably of German. Perhaps Gurdjieff was using the opportunity to assess Blackwood, as he had Ouspensky. It was arranged they would meet again that afternoon at the Dalcroze Institute, which Gurdjieff's followers had hired for the summer. There Blackwood met Orage. If Blackwood's memory is correct, then it was only now that he learned of Ouspensky's lectures at Warwick Gardens. Blackwood states in his *Prediction* article that Ouspensky had just started his lectures as a precursive sieve to assess who was suitable to pass on to Gurdjieff's school at Fontainebleau, but that was not established until October 1922.

Blackwood does not record further memories of Gurdjieff at that time, though he had some intense discussion with Orage and others of the circle. Gurdjieff's beliefs would have been second nature to Blackwood, and he would have been keen to know the man more.

Blackwood returned to England and began to attend Ouspensky's lectures. But he found that the 'evenings' bored him.

> Much wisdom, I am sure, was sprayed over us, many valuable hints offered, practical as well as theoretical, but the net result when I made my way home was negligible. To get a straight intelligible answer to a straight question was almost impossible. I listened attentively, but I never heard an intelligible – yes, an intelligent – question receive a satisfactory reply. The questioner was made to feel that his or her question was rather silly.[5]

Blackwood was already far and away ahead of this group, and Ouspensky's superficiality was only too apparent. No matter that Blackwood had delighted in his book and his ideas, the man himself was disappointing. Blackwood talked it over with Orage and then agreed with Ouspensky that he was already sufficiently prepared for Fontainebleau. According to Blackwood he then 'went off at once . . .': another impulse.

We have to consider this time sequence. Little is recorded in Blackwood's letters at the time, and his own personal recollections are all from over twenty-five years later. Time has a remarkable ability for telescoping events together. Also we have to allow for authorial licence. It's much more dramatic to imagine Blackwood racing across Europe in search of the latest guru.

Just how many Ouspensky 'evenings' Blackwood attended is not recorded. If he was bored and found them intellectually insulting he probably did not last more than two or three. This could mean that Blackwood returned to Gurdjieff at the earliest opportunity within weeks of the opening of the Prieuré at Fontainebleau in October 1922, but that is unlikely. Although the Prieuré was open for pupils – with about fifty in attendance – there is no record that Blackwood was among them. Most of Gurdjieff's energies (and those of his disciples) were given over to refurbishing the Prieuré and building a special study room. The official opening was on 12 January 1923, a date made all the more public by the death of one of Gurdjieff's followers, the author Katherine Mansfield on 9th January, aged only thirty-four, and her funeral on the day the Prieuré opened. Orage had sent her there because it was known she was dying, and it was hoped that time spent with Gurdjieff would soften her final days.

During the autumn and winter of 1922 Blackwood was with the Ainleys in Kent. He was back in London by the last week of November, when he was involved in the new production of *Through the Crack* and thereafter in the rehearsals for *Oliver Cromwell*. The next opportunity was when he went abroad on 14 January 1923. The reporter E.C. Bowyer produced a series of articles for the *Daily News* between 15 and 19 February, some of which ran front-page coverage alongside the opening of Tutankhamun's tomb. Bowyer included Blackwood and J.D. Beresford among those who were 'deeply interested'.

Blackwood could not stay there long as he needed to be back for final rehearsals for *Oliver Cromwell* in early February. He was committed to the play for the next three months and the earliest he could return to Fontainebleau would have been June or July 1923.

All this suggests that Blackwood learned of Gurdjieff in late July 1922 and visited him briefly soon after. He began to attend Ouspensky's lectures during the autumn of 1922 but rapidly grew bored. He paid a fleeting visit to the Prieuré in mid/late January 1923, sufficient to capture his interest, and then returned for a more prolonged stay that summer.

Blackwood tells us that he 'stayed at the Fontainebleau establishment on several occasions, with repeated visits'. I also know from a letter he wrote to a devotee in November 1949 that his final visit was after 'G's dreadful accident'.[6] Gurdjieff's accident was on 8 July 1924. He was a reckless self-taught driver and he crashed his car into a tree at 90 kph. Miraculously he survived, but on 26 August he announced the closure of the school. Although he dismissed his pupils, a core remained. Blackwood may have been one of these, but more likely he had planned to visit the Prieuré at this time and following the accident returned (perhaps in September) in order to see what was happening.

So Blackwood's main involvement with Gurdjieff is concentrated into the short space of a year. Soon after his first involvement that summer, Blackwood wrote to his old Toronto friend, George Wrong. Without mentioning Gurdjieff he nevertheless states clearly his current outlook:

> I think, honestly, the deepest interest in my life is to find any knowledge, in book or practice, that may widen the field of consciousness and waken powers which, I feel convinced, lie dormant in our greater self – the subconscious so called. I still believe we have latent powers which could bring us nearer, if only a little nearer, to Reality. This is the insatiable quest in my blood and compared with it other things, money least of all, do not count.[7]

It is worth comparing this letter to one written seven months later (before Gurdjieff's accident) when Blackwood was renewing his acquaintance with Edward Carpenter.

> You rightly say, now. that I am wandering over the globe 'seeking rest', though 'finding none' is not quite my case. The slowness of progress & its difficulty, both racial & my own, I do, however, find disheartening. I have long since reached a stage where I feel that there can be little progress until the subconscious powers become developed & accessible. Without these we can become better, but not greater, I feel. In my search for someone who may point a practical way in this direction, I have been interested lately in the man at Fontainebleau of whom, & of whose Institute, you may have heard.[8]

The tone of the letter shows that Gurdjieff's teachers were providing a glimmer of hope to Blackwood in accessing his latent subconscious powers.

We can understand why this might be. There was much in Gurdjieff's approach that attuned with Blackwood's outlook, even more than Ouspensky's. Ouspensky's ideas and concepts appealed to Blackwood, but Ouspensky had no way to develop this. Stephen Graham noted how Blackwood 'cared little for Ouspensky, who shut down Wonder behind doors of common sense'.[9]

However, Blackwood felt instantly that Gurdjieff was right.

> The preliminary training in Yoga convinced me it was genuine and
> helpful for any serious student. The methods of changing one's *type*
> of consciousness, rather than merely extending what one already
> possesses, seemed to me true and practical, for it was both severe
> and painful.[10]

There were many ways that Gurdjieff achieved this. He relied heavily
on music and dance, and we have seen how important this was to
Blackwood's work and outlook. Gurdjieff composed a considerable
amount of music with the help of his acolyte, the classically trained
Russian musician Thomas de Hartmann (1886–1956). His emphasis
on emphatic rhythms and harmonics gave his music an hypnotic and
evocative mood. Gurdjieff played the guitar adequately and in later
years often played the harmonium.

His Sacred Dances or Movements were central to his entire approach.
These were not formal dances in the accepted sense, but a series of
exercises, rituals or tableaux. Some may be frenzied 'dervish' style
dances, others more languid and pensive. Gurdjieff desired that his
pupils dance to certain patterns that fitted in with his philosophy and
for which he had designed an 'enneagram' – a nine-pointed star within
a circle. This design was a visual representation of Gurdjieff's basic
concepts. The dances were mathematically precise and concentration
on this movement, rhythm and pattern provided a means of moving
beyond the intellect through a more balanced, multi-centred sensory
awareness. Gurdjieff believed that dance was a form of communication,
and this was exactly Blackwood's philosophy where he believed that
the whole rhythm of life was inherent in nature.

Gurdjieff believed there were three paths to immortality, epitomised
by the fakir, the monk and the yogi. The fakir is the crudest of the three
in that he submits himself to all manner of pain and humiliation for
minimal reward, and with no emotional or intellectual outlet. The monk
is more sophisticated, in that he has considerable faith and commitment
but also suffers physical and intellectual deprivation. The yogi is the
smartest of the three as he is the most focused and knows how to get
what he wants, but has no emotional or physical expression. However
there is a fourth path, sometimes called the sly way. The sly man has a
special secret, though he may not know how he acquired it. It may be
instinctive, but it gives him a short cut, a route no one else knows whereby

to achieve his goal without physical, intellectual or emotional starvation. This was everyone's ultimate goal, though most would have to be satisfied with harmonizing all the paths and looking for those sudden flashes when the fourth way might open.

In helping people achieve this development Gurdjieff was constantly challenging them, pushing them out of their normal lifestyle. Thus someone who was an accountant he would set looking after chickens. Titled ladies found they had to grub up tree roots with nothing but spoons. Orage found himself digging the foundations for a Turkish bath and wondering what he had let himself in for. The point was that people had to find new ways within themselves to tackle problems for which they were not prepared.

Sometimes this might force them through the equivalent of an emotional or spiritual death and rebirth. This is what Gurdjieff wanted to achieve. By voluntary suffering and strenuous effort you may penetrate through to your individual essence and release that in its raw state. Blackwood spent time cutting down trees till he was utterly exhausted. He did not do this just at Fontainebleau. He kept it up on the Ainley estate and on other large estates where he stayed. I have heard memories of many people who remember watching Blackwood head off for the woods with an axe to cut down tree after tree until he entered an almost mesmeric state.

Perhaps the most unusual part of Gurdjieff's teaching was his celebration of the idiot. At mealtimes there would be a toast to the idiot, with liberal shots of vodka or armagnac, where Gurdjieff categorized individuals by one of the twenty-one levels of 'idiocy'. This began with an 'ordinary idiot' up through 'super', 'arch', 'hopeless', 'compassionate', and so on. Orage was classified as a 'squirming' idiot. Blackwood's grouping is not recorded. This may seem unnecessarily demeaning, but Gurdjieff maintained that we are all idiots, of one form or another. Understanding that allows us to set ourselves goals and a direction of attainment. Even before meeting Gurdjieff Blackwood had used just the same analogy in 'A Touch of Pan', where he considered the distinction between an idiot and a lunatic.

> An idiot, Heber understood, was a person in whom intelligence had been arrested – instinct acted but not reason. A lunatic, on the other hand, was someone whose reason has gone awry – the mechanism of the brain was injured. The lunatic was out of relation with his environment; the idiot had merely been delayed *en route*.[11]

This was exactly Gurdjieff's point. We are all arrested in the idiot stage and need to know what type of idiot we are and what is holding us back in order to move forward.

As we can see there was so much in Gurdjieff's approach and techniques that fitted in with Blackwood's outlook on life. It is impossible here to go into the detail of Gurdjieff's ideas and teachings, but there is no doubt that they considerably influenced Blackwood's lifestyle in the last quarter of his life. They gave him a framework in which he could seek his spiritual goal. He may not ever attain it, but he had a way of getting there, something that Theosophy and Hermeticism had never satisfied. They had opened doors, and widened awareness, but had not provided a map. During the rest of the 1920s and 1930s Blackwood felt more content, fulfilled, at ease with himself. It allowed him to help others more. He was now becoming the mentor that Old Louis had been to him thirty years before. He was at last edging towards that fourth and most difficult 'torch' or ambition he had set himself as a young man – that of a 'holy man'. Gurdjieff gave back to Blackwood the belief in himself that he had before the war and which he had temporarily lost at the end of the war. This didn't set him off on a new wave of creative writing – he did not need to. Blackwood was now reaching a spiritual fulfilment that had hitherto eluded him.

But even this had its limitations. As we have seen Blackwood did not continue to visit Fontainebleau much after Gurdjieff's accident. Although Gurdjieff reopened the school, and though Blackwood continued to associate with people who remained close to both Gurdjieff and Ouspensky, Blackwood did not feel he needed the continual attendance to move forward.

It was unfortunate that what was special about Gurdjieff – his unpredictability, his desire to break rules, his determination to turn everything on its head, his need to challenge – meant that Gurdjieff trod a dangerous path between genius and madness. His methods could easily degenerate into circus and farce unless everyone were dedicated and positive about their goals. Sinclair Lewis, who was staying near Fontainebleau, visited it in August 1923, probably when Blackwood was there, and told his father that the house, as decked out for dancing and ceremonies, looked like a cross between a cabaret and a harem.

Blackwood's correspondent, A. Webster Stinton, who studied under Gurdjieff for several years but later grew disillusioned, apparently echoed Blackwood's view when he wrote:

On the whole, the strongest impression that remains with me is of a rather tired, very benevolent Father Christmas, who enjoyed the company of his guests and who, I am sure, got a good deal of private amusement out of their excessive earnestness and impressionability.[12]

Blackwood's views of the man were possibly even more extreme. In 1950 the author Anne Fremantle, daughter of Blackwood's friend Clara Huth Jackson, whose husband Christopher Fremantle was a leading official in Ouspensky's latter-day organization, sent Blackwood a copy of Gurdjieff's *Beelzebub's Tales to His Grandson*, which had been published posthumously in 1950. Blackwood thanked Anne for the book adding:

The G. book I heard read aloud at Fontainebleau when I was last there, or parts of it at any rate, and I judged it sheer megalomania that got me nowhere. And as I wade through its verbose pages now I find my first impression confirmed. The word paranoia even occurs to me. Yet it is certainly a magnum opus on the largest scale, an achievement indeed, that gives me nothing more than eye-strain! I cannot imagine it being really helpful to any seeker.

Blackwood's frustration with some of Gurdjieff's practices can be seen in the story 'A Continuous Performance'[13]. It refers to the 'Great Man' (almost certainly Gurdjieff) reading from his own 'Works' to the ladies in the blue drawing-room. The narrator (O'Malley again, Blackwood's alter-ego) is bored with the reading and ventures out into the garden where he watches the far greater wonders of nature functioning continuously and yet unappreciated.

But having demolished Gurdjieff's famous work, Blackwood added:

I am almost too busy to do all I still want to do. But for what PDO taught me, and therefore G. too, I should never find the energy I still have.[14]

II

At a time when Blackwood's written output looked as though it had slowed down, he was busier than he had been for years. When not travelling, or studying at Fontainebleau, or working with Kinsey Peile or Bertram Forsyth or others, he was writing the occasional new story, new essays and literary criticism, and working on his autobiography, *Episodes Before Thirty*. This had been commissioned by Cassell's in

1922, and he delivered it in March 1923[15]. He was still working on it at the start of the *Oliver Cromwell* tour – he even refers to it in the book.

The book was extremely well received, perhaps even more so in the United States, where it was published the following January. The book concentrates on Blackwood's New York years, and proved to be Blackwood's best selling book in America[16]. In Britain devotees of his fiction who knew little about the man himself, were amazed to learn of the hardship and travail he had in his youth. *The Times*, in its typical blinkered way, was sceptical about how much was fact and fiction. But those more in sympathy with Blackwood's outlook were in wonder at just what experiences Blackwood had. Edmund Candler, writing in *Time and Tide*, said:

> This, the latest of his twenty odd volumes, easily transcends in its appeal the best of his imaginative work. The glamour he has thrown over us may have injured perspective, but in the flush of the adventures we have shared with him we feel that he has given us one of the most poignant human documents we have ever read.[17]

Blackwood had indeed been open, revealing much about himself and his deepest thoughts during those dark days. It's possible he may not have written the book had he not felt relaxed and at home staying with the Ainleys. When responding to his half-sister, Lady Kintore, on her comments about the book, he said:

> I feel 24 rather than 54. I hope you will find a house soon and, if in Kent, perhaps it will be near my 'home' with the Ainleys. That woman [Elaine Ainley] has been a real brick to me – I can't think why – and without 'complications' of any sort or kind, which is such a mercy.[18]

The Ainleys had been a tonic to Blackwood and brought him back out of the slough of despond he had fallen into after the war. *Episodes* was also therapeutic. At last Blackwood faced publicly his relationship with his father, his feelings about his father's death and what a failure he had felt for many years. 'I have tried to given an honest picture of what I was then – in distant 1891,' he told George Wrong, 'but much of it was impossible to recapture. In the end I had to make selections. Even now it is too long, though I cut out 30,000 words.'[19]

Blackwood regarded *Episodes* as the end.

I feel that I have written my last book. Twenty-one books is enough! But, apart from that, I have said all that was in me – and how it used to boil up and boil over in me – and from now on shall earn my living by articles, journalism, etc. Canada is a long way off. It is the older lands I feel drawn to. I have been asked to lecture in America, and could make some money by it, only I cannot face it. Money does not mean enough to me to pay that price![20]

As if to finally hammer the nail in the coffin of his former life, a few months before Blackwood's autobiography was published, Maya Philipson published her fictional autobiography, *Pauline* (published as by Baroness de Knoop). It is dedicated to R.H.P., her new husband, Ralph Philipson. The book is transparently autobiographical, tracing the exploits of the young Pauline who leaves home at the age of seventeen with nothing but her violin and heads off for Cassel, near Hanover, to find her distant relative Princess George of Hessen-Nassau. She undergoes various romantic adventures until she marries an elderly count. He is fiercely protective of her, taking her first to Egypt and then settling in England. Eventually he dies and she rediscovers her freedom and marries a new paramour, Reginald.

One looks keenly to see how Blackwood features in the book, but he doesn't. Obviously not by name, but not even by character. The whole relationship is sidestepped. Perhaps she saw it as unwise to dedicate a book to a new husband and include within it a relationship so long-standing. There are references to her New Thought Alliance and to Gurdjieff and Ouspensky. She refers to being involved in a community that included all kinds of arts and crafts plus 'rhythmic dancing'.[21] The whole feeling in reading the book is that Maya Knoop had recrafted her life and that Blackwood no longer featured. Barbara Lindsay recalls Maya telling her that Blackwood helped with the writing of *Pauline*, which might also explain his absence, otherwise there is a distinct feeling that the relationship with him had been rubbed out of existence.

In fact Blackwood continued to visit Maya and Ralph Philipson regularly throughout the 1920s until Philipson's sudden and tragic death from food poisoning in 1928. The Philipsons's main home was in Portland Place, London, but upon their marriage, Philipson bought a large house at Sandgate, near Hythe in Kent. Called Encombe, it became their summer home. He allowed Maya *carte blanche* in converting it and she employed one of the leading architects of the day, Basil Ionides, to rebuild and restyle the original brick house into a white Italianate villa. He added a colonnaded loggia along the south front and a large archway for the drive approach on the north side. The main bathroom included a feature where the window slid into the wall. The rest of the Philipson family was aghast at Maya's extravagance, but the house became one of the architectural dreams of Kent. It was officially 'opened' in December 1924, with major coverage in *Country Life* and *The Architectural Review*.

Maude ffoulkes recalls the days at Encombe.

> Sometimes I went to Encombe, which Maya Philipson had made unique. Glamour and enchantment were inseparable from it and its owners – Ralph Philipson, most understanding of men, and Maya – at times the woman of the world, at others the Blessed Damozel – welcomed the unusual in brains and attainment, and never influenced by contras in pounds, shillings and pence. The person, *as a person*, alone mattered.[22]

Encombe was the centre of literary attraction. Visitors included H.G. Wells, Ford Madox Ford, Noël Coward, Rosamund Bland (the daughter of Edith Nesbit), Lady Rothermere, Mary Borden, Syrie Wellcome, Sir Denison Ross and Stephen Graham. Ouspensky himself came down on at least one occasion. Blackwood was often the centre of attraction, telling stories out in the loggia, usually in the evening, so that he could end his story as darkness fell. There were many musical evenings. Occasionally Blackwood would play his violin, accompanying Maya on the piano. They were blissful days at Encombe, but all too short. When Ralph Philipson died, on 1 December 1928, Maya closed it down. She continued to return for a few weeks every summer until 1935, but seldom held such large gatherings. She had her husband's study demolished. She then sold the entire house with all its fittings and never returned. Tragically the house was severely damaged in a landslip in the 1950s and thereafter fell into ruin. It was vandalized, became the home of vagrants and eventually burned down in 1978.

III

Another individual whom Blackwood knew at this time was the author, engineer and latter-day philosopher J.W. Dunne (1875–1949). Dunne became famous in 1927 with the publication of his book *An Experiment*

With Time, which he had put off publishing for years for fear of being regarded a crank. During the war Dunne, who had designed one of Britain's first military aircraft, the Dunne D.8, had become aware that events he remembered in dreams were coming true. From 1917 on he methodically recorded his dreams and discovered that about half of them related to events in the past but the other half were precognitive. He formed this into his theory of the serial universe, which he equated to a piano keyboard. When we are awake, or in conscious mode, we can only play one note at a time – the note for that day, and each day we progress along this enormous keyboard, moving always to the right – one day into the future. But in our dreams our subconscious has free range up and down this keyboard.

This idea appealed to Blackwood[23]. He knew of Dunne's experiments before the book appeared, as Dunne had read him extracts. In an incomplete, undated note, Blackwood says that long before the book appeared he was staying at Montreux as the house-guest of author Alice Perrin (1867–1934). The Perrins had settled in Switzerland in 1925, hardly 'long before', but we are relying on Blackwood's memory. He learned that Dunne was staying at Bouveret, just across Lake Geneva, and arranged to visit him. Frustratingly, Blackwood's note ends with the words 'Dunne welcomed us. . . ', and reveals no more. Whatever the circumstances, from 1922 on Blackwood's studies with Ouspensky and Gurdjieff and his association with Dunne led to several stories involving time and higher space.

In 'The Pikestaffe Case', two individuals, experimenting with higher mathematics, create a path to the fourth dimension and travel beyond. Blackwood's description of a fourth-dimensional movement, as witnessed through a mirror that serves as a portal, is ingenious and effective. This was soon followed by 'The Man Who Was Milligan'[24] where an old Chinese painting acts as a portal and conveys Milligan from his lodgings in London to China.

'Playing Catch' is more mystical. The narrator, grieving over the loss of his wife, Mabel (which was Maya's real name), has a fourth-dimensional vision of gigantic beings playing catch with the Moon. This and later visions of infinity lead him to believe that we are all part of a fourth-dimensional game where our extra-dimensional body is pitched to and fro and is sometimes dropped.

In 'Full Circle'[25], Jordan, from the age of thirty-six, periodically sees another individual whom he realizes, as he gets older, is an alternate younger version of himself. He sees images of himself as he might have been. The two aspects unite at death. 'The Land of Green Ginger'[26] is similar. A man sees a purported antique Chinese mirror, which reflects images of what might have been. Alarmed by one image the man finds himself rushing towards the mirror and the two images merge. Thereafter the man feels renewed and reinvigorated. These stories suggest that Blackwood, reflecting over different aspects of his own life – the traveller, the mystic, the author, and his 'torches' – may at last have felt that they were merging into one and that his life at last had unity.

'The Land of Green Ginger' was also the first story Blackwood wrote for the BBC. It was completed at Encombe at the end of October 1927, inspired in part by a magnificent mirror Maya had acquired for one of the bedrooms. Blackwood had been asked the previous winter if he would be interested in reading one of his own stories on the radio, but Blackwood was about to depart for Switzerland. The BBC could not tie him down over the next twelve months and gave up, but did at least secure a story for the *Radio Times*. The next opportunity to broadcast did not arise for another seven years.

'The Man Who Lived Backwards'[27] was Blackwood's most Dunne-inspired story. In later life Professor Zeitt regrets his marriage and wishes he had married another. He has a mystical experience whereby he is able to communicate with his own younger self and attempts to change his life. In a way he does. His present wife leaves him and he marries the girl he had always loved.

Although written some years later 'Elsewhere and Otherwise' belongs to this sequence of stories. It is Blackwood's longest and most detailed exploration of higher space, though it is more a series of episodes than a straight story. Told in retrospect it begins at the start of the Great War where the narrator, aged twenty-five, is aware how young his cousin Mantravers is looking. Though sixty-five, Mantravers looks closer to forty. Somehow Mantravers, like Dorian Gray, has escaped time. Mantravers disappears during the war, and some felt he had gone into hiding, but the circumstances of his reappearance and his ultimate fate, show that Mantravers had found a way of moving through time and higher space.

The strangest of all these stories, and the hardest to explain, is 'Adventures of Miss de Fontenay', published in *Shocks*. The narrator is a reader for a publishing house who has been sent a book which, the reader decides, is possibly a series of true accounts. The name on the manuscript is Janet de Fontenay, but when the reader asks the author to visit him he finds it is a man, John Smith-Jones. He discovers that Smith-Jones, though he looks only thirty says he is forty-five. Since childhood he has had a series of experiences which his book tries to explain. The narrator cannot comprehend Smith-Jones, and thereafter the story simply relates some of these episodes, without conclusion. Blackwoods seems to be trying to describe an individual who is really two beings – his own normal self and some ultra-being, perhaps some elemental-driven force, which exists within its own time frame (another Julian LeVallon). Smith-Jones shifts between these two existences scarcely without realizing, as anything may trigger it.

Although Blackwood had proclaimed *Episodes Before Thirty* as his final book, Ouspensky, Gurdjieff and Dunne revitalised his creativity. Many of these stories were issued as *Tongues of Fire*, published on 23 November 1924. Though it was his last new story collection for eleven years, even Blackwood would have been astonished to think there would be *seventeen* other books published between them. New worlds and new opportunities were opening to Blackwood.

One was the ability to recycle his stories. New volumes appeared collecting together a retrospective of his short stories. Collins published *Ancient Sorceries and Other Tales* in March 1927 and Herbert Jenkins (who published *Tongues of Fire*) issued *The Dance of Death and Other Tales* in October 1927. Neither volume is especially representative, but at least they provided cheaper editions of his stories to a wider audience. More significant was the bumper volume, *Strange Stories*, published by William Heinemann in October 1929. This reprinted twenty-six of Blackwood's best stories and was nearly a quarter-of-a-million words long. Blackwood made the selection himself and though he was limited in what he could select from the original Eveleigh Nash volumes (because all of these were being reissued in 1929–30) his selection is reasonably representative. While he was compiling this volume, publisher George Harrap contacted him for a volume in their *Short Stories of To-Day and Yesterday* series. This was a smaller selection, made by their general editor F.H. Pritchard, but did not overlap with *Strange Stories*, and contained much good material.

Blackwood also came into the world of Cynthia Asquith (1887–1960). She was tall and demure, with an elfin smile and an infectious sense of humour. Daughter of the Earl of Wemyss, wife of the poet

Herbert Asquith (son of the 1st Earl of Oxford and Asquith) and secretary to the playwright Sir J. M. Barrie, Lady Cynthia Asquith had all the right society connections. She also knew most of the major literary men of the day. She began compiling collections of stories for both children and adult readers, and called upon the literary establishment to contribute. She delighted in ghost stories and in 1926 compiled *The Ghost Book*, published by Hutchinson's that December. It had a first-class line-up including stories by May Sinclair, D.H. Lawrence, Arthur Machen, Desmond MacCarthy, Oliver Onions and L.P. Hartley.

Blackwood contributed 'Chemical', the first genuine ghost story he had written in over ten years. It is reminiscent of 'The Listener', though is more sinister. It is a story narrated by Moleson about something that happened to him before the war. He had rented lodgings opposite the British Museum but took an instant dislike to a fellow lodger who had once had the room Moleson is now in. Yet he also felt strangely attracted to him. That is the 'chemical' of the title – the chemistry that like bodies attract. Moleson witnesses the re-enactment of a murder that had happened twenty years before, the notorious case of the Warley Parricide. Blackwood's writing had taken on a new sophistication since he had last dabbled with something as mundane as a ghost story, and here we find him creating an ingenious identity puzzle as he allows the characters to make assumptions about who is who. The story proves to be far more than a simple ghost story.

He became a regular contributor to Cynthia Asquith's anthologies. And not just her ghost-story ones. She also compiled children's annuals. At long last Blackwood had turned to a market he should have explored years earlier.

17

Fairylands (1927–34)

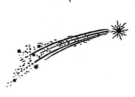

I

Despite the intensity of his workload, Blackwood was settled and happy, domiciled with the Ainleys during the 1920s. At the outset it was they who had saved him from his postwar melancholy, but he soon became the rock around which they anchored. This was especially true for the children. By 1924, Henry Jr (who was always known as Sam or Sambo) was six and Patsy five. Blackwood spent many hours with them. They had their own nanny, but Blackwood was their extra-special friend. They knew not to interrupt him during the morning when he worked (and most mornings he was up with the sun), but often in the afternoons he would play with them in their nursery or take them out into the surrounding fields for walks. They would explore woods, ford streams, build hideaways. He was like some great mystical American Indian leading them on an adventure. And they revelled in his mystery. He could sense things and would tell them when it was going to rain, just by smelling the air. He identified all the birds and flowers and animals and insects. He was just a constant joy, the ultimate Uncle Paul.

This was their salvation. There was considerable pressure on their father, especially when he became exhausted through his performance in the demanding play *Hassan*. He was often away, and when home there were frequent outbursts of temper and raging arguments between him and Elaine. By 1927 Ainley's health was suffering and he was drinking heavily. He ended up in a nursing home and then a convalescent home in the Isle of Wight. He did not return to the stage for two years.

Blackwood was usually there to keep the children sheltered. 'I'm sure he stopped me going mad,' Patsy remarked[1]. Of course Blackwood told them stories. His adventures in New York and Canada, canoeing down the Danube, climbing in the Caucasus. And when all else failed he created new stories. One day, in 1924, Blackwood began a story about a six-year-old boy called Sambo and his younger sister Topsy. Sambo comes across a lizard that has lost its tail. He's amazed to find the lizard can talk. He calls it Snitch because of the noise it makes when it sneezes. The two become friends and Snitch shows Sambo and Topsy how to reduce in size and grow large again. When tiny they have adventures in the garden at night, guided by glow-worms. They get chased by their cat, climb up on to the cow's horns, and learn the 'Garden-Writing' of sounds, smells and signs.

Blackwood had started the story for fun, but it went so well that he wrote it down. A.P. Watt sent it to *The Merry-Go-Round*, a children's magazine published in Oxford by Basil Blackwell. It had been running since November 1923 and was originally edited by the poet and playwright, Rose Fyleman (1877–1957), who has become immortalized by the opening of her poem, 'Fairies'[2] – 'There are fairies at the bottom of our garden!' Fyleman had known Blackwood for several years. It was Blackwood who suggested to her that she should write a poem about a girl who was told to blow out a candle but blew so hard that she blew out the moon. When that poem, 'Temper', was bought by *Punch* in 1920, Fyleman wanted to co-credit it to Blackwood, but Blackwood's response was that ideas were not merchandise to buy and sell. There may be other works by various authors that Blackwood contributed to without credit.

It was Fyleman who bought 'Sambo and Snitch' for the magazine, but by the time it began serialization in the April 1926 issue, poet and artist Hugh Chesterman (1884–1941) had taken over as editor. It ran through to the May 1927 issue, after which Blackwell issued it as a hardcover book including the illustrations by Audrey Teago that had featured in the magazine.

Blackwood was invited to a lunch with the staff of *Merry-Go-Round* on 18 November 1926. Chesterman encouraged further contributions from Blackwood and he submitted several poems – or rather children's doggerel, starting with 'Engine' (about a train, but not another Starlight Express)[3]. None of these was significant, simply pieces of fun, although one of them, 'If I Were You', was set to music by Cyril Winn[4].

Cynthia Asquith was also an occasional contributor to *Merry-Go-Round* and she had recently started editing children's annuals to which Blackwood became a regular contributor. His first was 'Toby's Birthday Presents' in *The Treasure Ship*, published in December 1926. Toby wants a cat, a tortoise and 'a nowl' for his birthday but his Uncle isn't interested because none of these animals is useful. Toby sets out to show how useful they are. 'The Water Performance' in *Sails of Gold* (published October 1927) is especially interesting. Not only does it retell Blackwood's own childhood adventure, at Shortlands, where he and his sister visited the pond at night in their garden, but Blackwood tried to develop it into a full children's novel, with the working title *Rose and Ditt*. 'When Nick Dressed Up' in *The Treasure Cave* (published September 1928) is just a piece of fun where Nick, punished for being naughty, finds an old pantomime bear outfit and escapes dressed in the skin.

Blackwood became friends with Basil Blackwell, the publisher of *Merry-Go-Round*. He published many children's books, including the popular *Joy Street* annual, which had started in 1923. Blackwood became a contributor to this, starting with 'Mr Cupboard, or the Furniture's Holiday' in *Number Five Joy Street* (September 1927). During a game of hide-and-seek young Jackie befriends a large old cupboard and joins in the furniture's adventures during the annual spring clean.

Always resourceful, Basil Blackwell published selected stories from the *Joy Street* series as separate small books. Blackwood's stories were all (bar one) reissued in this format starting with *Mr Cupboard* in September 1928. They are among Blackwood's hardest books to find.

The only story that wasn't reprinted as a separate book was 'The Chocolate Cigarettes' in *Number Six Joy Street* (September 1928). Blackwood was a regular cigarette smoker, though never a heavy one. He always had one after a meal, and usually smoked at social gatherings. In this story Mr Tumps, who hates children, cats and his name, forgets young Tommy's birthday, but Tommy surprises him by giving Mr Tumps a present – a cigarette case with three chocolate cigarettes. Tommy tells him they are magic cigarettes that grant a wish that will work only so long as you're eating the chocolate. Mr Tumps thinks it's all childish poppycock so each wish is made before he realizes it. By the end of the third wish he has come to like children, cats and his name.

These early stories are all fun. Blackwood occasionally imparts some of his worldly wisdom but generally they are straight stories written as he would have told them to children. Just occasionally Blackwood used the stories to convey a message. 'Mr Bunciman at the Zoo', for instance, in Asquith's *The Children's Cargo* (1930), is an anti-hunting story. All the animals at a zoo bring Mr Bunciman, a big-game hunter, to trial. Blackwood had not always been against hunting – it was part of his upbringing, but in his later years he began to question it. Bunciman is probably based on Lord Dunsany.

One other story that began life in the Ainley nursery rapidly outgrew its origins. This was *Dudley & Gilderoy*. Dudley is an African Grey parrot and Gilderoy is a ginger cat. They live together in a nursery in a big country house in Kent. Dudley is old and wise, and often grumpy. Gilderoy is young and keen to learn. The two pets escape from the nursery and head off to London for adventures. The story grew in depth and meaning until it took on philosophical proportions. Dudley has some Great Work that he is seeking to achieve, though he doesn't know what it is. He is always spouting aphorisms or curses (sometimes in French or Latin, such as '*A bas les Boches!*' or '*Parva sed goddam apta*') and using his wisdom to get them out of scrapes, whilst Gilderoy uses his instincts.

After the first few chapters the story ceases to be a children's book, other than superficially. Blackwood, perhaps without realizing it, was drawn back into the world of adult novels, which he believed he had finished with *The Bright Messenger*. He had found a vehicle whereby he could comment upon the human world via other eyes, and be mercilessly scathing if he chose. We learn Blackwood's views about the nature of the animal kingdom, the shallow superiority of the human world, the wonderful world of the cat and the marvels of the egg, plus thoughts about destiny and the meaning of life. Like some Gurdjieffian guru, Blackwood detaches himself from society and observes life from outside. *Dudley & Gilderoy* is Blackwood's philosophy upon human life as he saw it during the 1920s.

Sometimes Dudley's homespun philosophy, whilst fun, detracts from the story – Blackwood's usual problem of overburdening a story with his ever-active fascination for life. But other times it brings a sophistication to the tale, especially at the climax where Dudley, always hitherto of indeterminate sex, suddenly discovers 'his' purpose in life.

When Blackwood brings the book to a conclusion you realize that Gilderoy is also Blackwood. He is the rebel, the unknown factor, the unpredictable 'otherwise', as he describes the cat, the free-spirited alterego compared to Blackwood the philosopher. When Dudley/Blackwood completes his life's work, Gilderoy/Blackwood is released back into the world. Blackwood's final paragraph about Gilderoy encapsulates that moment of magic.

> Without another look, he left the room, he left the house, he became what he had been before the Great Friendship entered his life – a stray, alien, independent cat that walked by himself across the universe.[5]

When Blackwood submitted the story to A.P. Watt in March 1928, their reader felt that the story was a 'masterpiece' and couldn't lay it down. Blackwood had subtitled it 'a Nonsense', his idea of a children's story which was also fun for adults. When it was published, *The Times* reviewer was as caustic as usual, saying that the book was not a nonsense, but 'a good deal too sensible'. The book does fall between two stools. It does not really work as a children's novel, other than in summary, and the adult parts don't work as a novel, but as a series of sketches and parodies, best understood if you know Blackwood's world. *The Times* reviewer was understandable if blinkered when he wrote that 'the children who read it will no doubt ignore what does not suit them and very much enjoy the rest, and their elders had better follow their example'.[6]

The character of Dudley is beautifully realized in the book and it is clear that it is based on a parrot known to Blackwood. The book's dedication is twofold: 'To Mrs Muir Mackenzie owner of Dudley & Louis N. Parker.' There is also a copy personally inscribed 'To Felicity, the owner of Dudley and the inspiration of this book of Nonsense from Pan, 1929'. Felicity was Lady Constance Felicity Muir Mackenzie (1884–1975). Though she lived to be ninety-one and died comparatively recently, no one in her family had any recollections of Blackwood or any relevant family papers. I do not know how they met but she certainly brought Dudley to Encombe and they may have met via Maya. He told Vera Wainwright that:

> Dudley belongs to a friend of mine and I have known the ruffian many years and built up the story out of all the fanciful stuff his owner used to invent about him.[7]

He further elaborated in a preface he wrote for an adaptation of *Dudley & Gilderoy* several years later:

> Dudley is still alive, growing prouder every year of his immense age. No one knows exactly how old he is, and he's not telling anybody, either; though he gladly talks about anything else – very loud and very fast – he won't even whisper when I ask him his age; he just looks the other way and pretends he isn't listening.[8]

There were three other African grey parrots whom Blackwood knew. There was the one in the Ainley nursery that was the real starting point of the story. There was one owned by Blackwood's friend Dr Vincent Nesfield that was still alive in the 1980s[9]. But most important of all, and the reason for the second part of the book's dedication, was Koko, owned by Louis N. Parker. Koko is the real Dudley and Parker reveals all about him in his autobiography, *Several of My Lives*. Koko hated being in a cage and would squawk 'Let me out' in such a tone that he soon regained his freedom. He would learn whole sentences and whistle entire tunes, including 'Rule Britannia' and 'God Save the King'. He had a repertoire in at least four languages and '*A bas les boches!*' and 'Any 'ope doctor?' were two regular phrases. Alas poor Koko died in 1916 when he was left in the garden all night. Blackwood knew Koko well and it's a shame he is not also mentioned in the dedication. Soon after the book's publication the news people tried to film a short sequence with Blackwood and Dudley, but the parrot refused to talk.

As for Gilderoy, Blackwood told Vera Wainwright that the cat was 'an invention of my own', but in his later preface he says that he was a stray that turned up at Blackwood's apartment one night and stayed for a while until he wandered away.

It had taken Watt's some while to sell the book, simply because it did not seem to have an obvious market – beyond cat lovers. Although Blackwood had finished it in March 1928 it was not sold until December, to Ernest Benn, and was published the following September. Blackwood had suggested that the book lent itself to sketches, perhaps in the margins. Benn commissioned an artist to produce several line drawings but the final results are little more than scribbles, investing no character in either animal. Blackwood did not like the artwork and requested that it be dropped from the American edition, due to be published by Dutton's the following month. John Macrae, President of E.P. Dutton, agreed and was only too happy to comply.

In fact Blackwood was not happy with how Benn handled the book at all. Three years later, when Benn's enquired about a second book, Blackwood wrote to his agent:

> I found the firm poor in advertizing, slipshod in execution, stupidly unimaginative in general treatment of my *Dudley & Gilderoy*. It was quite clear to me that Mr Keogh (or was it Keans?) who had charge of that particular book was not 'up to his job'. Much more might have been made of that book in my humble judgment.[10]

And yet this became one of Blackwood's more profitable books, remaining in print for over twenty years and selling regularly every year.

Encouraged by the reception to the book Blackwood was approached by *The Sketch*, one of the leading slick society papers of the day, to contribute further stories. Blackwood produced a series of six short episodes under the collective title 'The Graceless Pair'[11]. These are delightfully humorous stories. In 'The Saving of Colonelsirarthur', Dudley creates a diversion to allow his owner to sneak in after a late night out. In 'French and Italian' Dudley succeeds in ridding the household of the annoying piano teacher, Signor Ravelli, whilst in 'Burglars' Dudley and Gilderoy's nightly escapades lead the Lady of the household to think they are being burgled. One of the stories, 'Anyopedoctor? Abaslesboches! etc.', tells of Dudley's early days in Louis Parker's house (here just called the Playwright).

These six stories, totalling around 17,000 words, were too short to publish as a book in their own right, though a specialist press might have done so.[12] As a consequence they have never been reprinted and Blackwood's humorous side, with almost Wodehousian wit, has not been as widely recognized. Blackwood wrote one other story, 'The Parrot and the – Cat', which retold how the two animals came together. It appeared in *Number Eight Joy Street* in August 1930 and was reprinted in bookform the following September. Although 'The Graceless Pair' was written for an older age group, it would have been a fitting companion piece.

So entranced was Blackwood with his children's stories that he wrote one specifically for an adult readership. 'The Adventure of Tornado Smith' appeared in the Christmas 1929 issue of *Country Life*. It's about a city stockbroker who wakes up one morning full of the joys of spring. On his way to work his alter-ego, Tornado Smith, takes over and Smith finds himself following directions to Fairyland and encountering a dragon, until he pops out of his dream and returns to the mundane world.

For Blackwood, though, the 1920s had been anything but a mundane world. He had revelled in the Roaring Twenties as much as anyone who was part of high society.

II

His association with Henry Ainley's circle of friends, and the publication of his autobiography, had made Blackwood something of a celebrity. His face frequently featured in the society and popular papers of the day. He was photographed by Howard Coster and his portrait was sketched by Walter Tittle. He was called upon for his views especially in the world of the unusual. When *T.P.'s-Cassell's Weekly* brought together a symposium of authors for their 'favourite spooks'[13], Blackwood was among them. When the *Daily Mail* ran a series of articles on reincarnation[14], Blackwood was consulted alongside such heavyweights as Sir Oliver Lodge and Sir Arthur Conan Doyle. And, needless to say, when Lord Carnarvon died soon after the discovery of Tutankhamun's tomb in 1923, the *Daily Express* called upon Blackwood for his thoughts[15].

Despite his frequent desire to escape humanity and civilization, Blackwood enjoyed the celebrity status. It brought with it a pleasurable and rewarding living (though not necessarily a lucrative one) but, more to the point, it opened doors for Blackwood to meet even more interesting people. As a consequence his travels in the 1920s were on an entirely different level to those of the previous decades. Although he still sought the solace of the Swiss Alps he seldom ventured anywhere remote and certainly undertook no risky adventures. Compared to his life of thirty years before, it was like living in a fairyland.

In July 1924, for instance, he attended the revived Bayreuth Festival. Hugh Walpole had taken the great tenor, Lauritz Melchior (1890–1973) under his wing and had promoted him at Covent Garden in May 1924, where Blackwood heard him. Melchior had auditioned for Siegfried Wagner and was commissioned to perform at Bayreuth that summer. Walpole, Blackwood and others set off at the end of July. They returned home in August. It was sometime around now that Blackwood visited Fontainebleau for the last time. He was back in time for the grand opening of the Philipsons's new house at Encombe, but a few weeks later had returned to Switzerland, at the Bahnhof Hotel, Gstaad.

Blackwood continued to spend his winters at Gstaad and his summers with the Ainleys at Chart Lodge and the Philipsons at Encombe. He visited the ancestral home of the Dufferins at Clandeboye in Northern Ireland in May 1925 and spent part of the summer of 1925 climbing in the Alps with Freddie Dufferin.

It was on this climbing holiday that Blackwood at last solved a mystery that had plagued him for years and which, unbeknown to him had been a trick played on him by a young friend. He revealed all to Vera Wainwright:

> One day before the War I got an anonymous telegram, "I see what you're at!" which made me uneasy, for who among us has an unstained conscience. Some dozen years later a snow blizzard made skiing impossible and I took a party into the forest and made a great fire round which we told stories. Then, remembering that odd telegram, I told about it. Up jumped a small figure by the fire and said, "I sent you that wire!" Little Elizabeth Belloc.[16]

By 1926, Blackwood was back in Hungary for the first time in many years. Blackwood had become friends with Sir Colville Barclay (1869–1929), then the consul-general in Hungary, and he attended an embassy ball in Budapest. This was the earliest memory that Sir Colville's wife, Sarita, had of Blackwood, though they may have met earlier. When I spoke to her sixty years after this meeting, she still had a clear recollection. Blackwood was more interested in the night sky and the view from the balcony than he was in the official function, and she vividly remembered his roguish smile, his charming manner and his hypnotic eyes. Lady Sarita Barclay became Blackwood's latest devotee and remained so for many years. Sir Colville Barclay died, aged only fifty-nine, in 1929, leaving Sarita with three children, Colville, Cecil and Robert. Two years later Lady Barclay married Sir Robert Vansittart (1881–1957), then a senior civil servant in the Foreign Office. They established a new home at Denham, in Buckinghamshire which, along with their London apartment in Park Street, became regular ports-of-call for Blackwood.

Through his friendship with Compton Mackenzie at the Savile Club, Blackwood was introduced to Capri. He was fascinated with the whole area around Naples, Ischia, Pompeii and Herculaneum and became a regular visitor over the years to Capri, particularly from 1927 onwards. His great friend was the Swedish physician and author Axel Munthe (1857–1949), whose villa on Capri Munthe immortalized in *The Story of San Michele* (1929). Munthe now lived at Torre di Materita in Upper Capri, where Blackwood was a regular guest. Blackwood also befriended the English entertainer Gracie Fields (1898–1979) who had a villa on the other side of Capri, and he often spent several weeks each year alternating between the two.

While at Capri, in the spring of 1927, Blackwood developed a toothache that led to one of those odd episodes he liked to relate. He was recommended a Russian dentist in Naples, but he was not inspired. The dentist was dirty, a chain-smoker, in a small garret which had seen better days. Nevertheless Blackwood persevered. The dentist spent half-an-hour fiddling inside Blackwood's mouth but never once touched the affected tooth or did any drilling or filing. Blackwood had no idea what he was doing, but the pain went. The dentist asked Blackwood to call back the next day when the same routine followed. Then he was told to come back a third day. This would have continued *ad infinitum* if Blackwood had not already booked to go on a train to Florence. He had to stop the treatment but was curious to know what the dentist had done. The dentist told Blackwood he had killed the nerve, but when Blackwood visited an American dentist in Florence he was told the dentist had done nothing at all, and the nerve in that tooth had been dead for years. The pain had been a small abscess, which had healed itself. Blackwood was left utterly puzzled over what the dentist had spent all his time doing – and for no payment.

There was another meeting on Capri that finally resolved a strange matter that Blackwood had first encountered soon after *Julius LeVallon* was published in 1916. A woman, whom he called Maria Smith, had contacted him because she believed her son was the reincarnation of the American statesman at the time of the War of Independence, Alexander Hamilton (1757–1804). The way Maria described this to Blackwood was as follows.

About fifteen years earlier, around 1901, when she was eighteen, Maria had a vision of a man sitting near her. This man said, 'I need you, and I shall wait for you,' and vanished. The man's face remained fixed in Maria's mind. Over the next few years two incidents occurred which made her convinced she had some kind of guardian angel. First, she was involved in a bazaar in Paris but was called away by a telegram to report to a certain address. There was no such address and no one was expecting her, but while she was away a dreadful fire killed 126 people at this bazaar, mostly women. Maria believed the summons had saved her. A few years later, when Maria was married, she and her husband were at St Malo in France about to travel on a new liner, the *Titanic*. Maria had a sudden irrational panic about her pet dogs and she insisted on returning home. Once again Maria believed she was saved. After her child was born, she saw a portrait of Alexander Hamilton in a magazine and realized that this was the face of the man she had seen all those years earlier. She became convinced that his spirit had sought her out, wanting to be reborn to her, and had protected her until the child was conceived. Furthermore, the young boy had remarkable memories of the War of Independence and other incidents from that period even when he was too young to have learned them.

Blackwood found her convincing. He could do nothing to prove or disprove her story. Then, around 1928, he was travelling with a man from Saanenmoser to Naples and on to Capri. They exchanged stories, and Blackwood related the story of Maria Smith and her child. He was then staggered and embarrassed to discover that he was talking to Maria's husband. He apologized, feeling he had invaded the man's privacy, but the man was happy to talk. It transpired that he and Maria were now separated. The marriage had not worked. But he could explain all these strange episodes, except the first vision of the man, as he had not known Maria then. The fire at the bazaar, which was a well known historical event known as the Bazaar de la Charité, happened in May 1897, when Maria was only fourteen. She had never been there but had read about it at the time and been horrified. Over time she began to imagine what it must have been like and gradually imagination took over from reality. The same applied to the *Titanic*. They had never been booked on the *Titanic*, though they had gone to see it at Cherbourg. With the disaster Maria began to imagine that she could so easily have been on board. As for the child – the father could not recall a single instance when the boy had memories of Alexander Hamilton's time. Rather the opposite. The child, whom Blackwood later met, and was then in his early twenties, was a scientist experimenting with radio. The father recalled that on one occasion his wife had visited a gypsy fortune-teller and, in the discussion, reference had come to Maria being descended from Alexander Hamilton. All these factors had been sucked into the melting pot of Maria's excessive imagination and fabricated the whole story. Blackwood was delighted to have a solution to something that he regarded as a text-book case of delusion.

By the end of the 1920s Blackwood's world was changing. The death of Ralph Philipson on 1 December 1928 brought an end to the halcyon days at Encombe. His passing did not bring Maya and Blackwood together again. Those golden days were history. Ralph's death drained Maya's spirit sorely, and she retreated into their apartment at Portland Place. Blackwood continued to visit her, but that precious spark of vitality had gone. She was now more a creature of his past than his future.

With Henry Ainley's breakdown, Elaine had left him and moved to Highgate Village in 1927. She later married again, this time Henry Clews, Jr. They lived at the Château La Napoule near Cannes in the south of France. Blackwood occasionally visited them there, as it was conveniently close to other friends and relatives. En route between his regular resorts in Switzerland and Cannes were the Jacksons at Aix-les-Bains. His close friend Mary Borden lived just beyond Cannes at Mouans-Sartoux. His sister, Cecilia, lived in the hills behind Cannes at Menton. She was now estranged from her husband, Arthur Hobart-Hampden. Alas, Cecilia died on 18 March 1929, on her ninth wedding anniversary. She was sixty-six. Within a month of her death her husband married for a third time.

Blackwood was probably with his sister at her death, or soon after. He had left Gstaad on 24 February and was in Cannes at the start of April. She had died just four days after Blackwood's sixtieth birthday, a potent milestone for considering his own mortality. Blackwood had now lost two sisters and his brother. There were just he and Ada left. She lived in the village of Itchen Abbas, near Winchester, which became an occasional refuge for Blackwood.

With the split in the Ainley household in 1927, young Patsy was sent to a school at Bexhill in Sussex, run by two sisters, Marjorie and Jessie Baird. Blackwood would visit the school occasionally to see Patsy, and he became friendly with the sisters, especially Jessie, who adored him. Through Jessie, Blackwood came to know her sister, Grace, and Grace's husband, Dr Vincent Nesfield (1878–1972). Nesfield had been born in the Holy City of Benares, in Bengal, India, where his grandfather had been a missionary. Soon after he had qualified as a doctor, Nesfield joined the expedition of Francis Younghusband in Tibet in 1901, where he could well have met Gurdjieff. Nesfield remained in India, in the Indian Medical Service, until 1919, when his grandfather died, and decided to come to England. He practised as a doctor in London and, in 1930, he set up a nursing home called Ellenden near Sandhurst in Kent.

Blackwood and Nesfield first met in either 1927 or 1928. By 1929 the Nesfield family had joined Blackwood on his winter trip to Saanenmoser, and over the next twenty years remained close friends. They shared many common interests in Eastern religions, Theosophy, psychology and pathology, as well as the occult. Blackwood and Nesfield would occasionally attend séances where both were disruptive. On one occasion Nesfield snatched the so-called ectoplasm issuing from the medium's mouth to discover it was butter muslin. Both believed that about 99 per cent of mediums were phony.

The few surviving medical notes about Blackwood from this period and into the early 1930s, tell us that Blackwood stood six foot two inches tall (he had shrunk an inch since his thirties), weighed 86kg (189lbs) and his blood pressure at rest was 130 over 78. After six hours' skiing it was 115 over 68. He was immensely fit, even in his early sixties, and took regular exercise every day. He was still into his Gurdjieff regime of excessive exercise, such as cutting down trees, in order to reach his spiritual essence. One eccentricity is that he would never bathe in hot water as he believed this dried out the skin's natural oils. He washed in cold water and rubbed his body in olive oil, to keep it supple. If olive oil was not available, he used vinegar, which meant he must always have been accompanied by a slightly acrid aroma. Generally Blackwood's eyesight was good, but as he aged he grew long-sighted and needed strong reading glasses.

Both Blackwood and Nesfield vowed they would live to be 100. Nesfield got closer than Blackwood, living until he was ninety-three. Nesfield was interested in the experiments being conducted by Sergei Voronoff (1866–1951) into rejuvenation. Since the early 1920s Voronoff had treated hundreds of elderly patients by grafting tissue from monkey testes to human's. Later this process was discredited and greater credence was given to the discovery of the male hormone, testosterone, in 1929. Experiments were undertaken where testosterone was drawn from the testicles of monkeys and injected into the male scrotum. This was believed to increase the sex drive and contribute towards longevity. Both Nesfield and Blackwood undertook this treatment upon themselves. It does not seem to have caused either of them any harm, but it is difficult to say whether it contributed towards Blackwood's longer life. Although he lived far longer than his parents or his elder siblings, his younger sister Ada lived to be 103, without any additional aids. I believe Blackwood owed far more to his healthy lifestyle than to any monkey-gland experiments.

Reminders of mortality were still haunting Blackwood, however. On 3 March 1930 his half-sister's husband, Lord Kintore, died at the age of seventy-seven. His half-sister, Sydney, would follow two years later (21 September 1932) when she was eighty. His second cousin, Freddie Blackwood, Lord Dufferin, was killed in an aeroplane accident in July 1930.

Maybe this was why Blackwood's short fiction took on a rather morbid aspect for a while, with an unhealthy emphasis on suicide. In 'The Survivors'[17], two people meet up after an accident only to realize that they are both dead. In 'The Colonel's Ring'[18], Hendrik returns home after ten wasted years in America and visits his Uncle. The old man seems despondent and Hendrik has a vision of the man's suicide. In 'A Threefold Cord . . .'[19], Malcolm meets a woman and discovers, almost too late, that she is the ghost of a suicide and is trying to lure him to his death. Only 'Revenge'[20] is slightly more positive. An embezzler murders his nephew in the Alps but then becomes lost and is rescued by his nephew's ghost.

Blackwood also began to doubt his beliefs. He had written a couple of pieces about reincarnation for newspapers and these must have channelled his thinking, for he then wrote a more extensive piece, 'On Reincarnation' for *The Aryan Path*[21]. Whilst he acknowledged that, after a long life, 'I have yet to find a solution that solves its problems better than the explanation of reincarnation,' he also admitted that 'Personally, I know no proof that reincarnation is true. My youthful acceptance has disappeared. Doubts have crept in since that happy ardent period.' The reason for his doubts was not so much the lack of proof, but a wider understanding of the philosophical issues involved. There were questions of what constituted an 'individual' and upon what basis each reincarnation would happen, and whether it happened to all souls or only selected ones. Blind faith had been replaced by a tenuous hope kept afloat by scientific reasoning and philosophical logic. At least Blackwood was reassured that he was not alone in his dilemma. He received a letter from Sir Arthur Conan Doyle admitting that the piece echoed his views entirely.

There was one other unusual piece to appear at this time. This was 'The Fire Body'[22], which Blackwood called 'one of the episodes in the "Alexander Hamilton" series'. Blackwood had started to dabble with a series of reminiscences for a possible book of occult adventures. It was the first hint of a sequel to *Episodes Before Thirty*. This piece, which reads as much like fiction than fact, recounts a meeting with a woman who could see Blackwood's elemental spirit – his 'fire body'.

Thankfully Blackwood's life was not so depressing as those few stories might suggest. The death of Lord Kintore meant that his favourite niece, Lady Stonehaven – or Ettie – returned from Australia with her husband, where he had been governor-general. They lived at Ury, near Stonehaven in Scotland and Blackwood visited them there at whatever opportunity he could.

In the summer of 1931 he was visited, for the first time, by the remarkable Cornelia Lunt (1843–1934). She had discovered Blackwood through his autobiography and had written to him in 1927. Miss Lunt, who lived in Chicago, had been a sweetheart of Alfred H. Louis in Evanston, Illinois in the 1860s. They had parted soon after but for all the years since she had held his memory close. Suddenly here was a book that brought those memories flooding back. Blackwood had dedicated the book to Louis and told much about him. Cornelia Lunt, known as the 'first lady' of Evanston, wrote to Blackwood wanting to have more memories of Louis. She had kept all Louis's love letters to her and she sent them to Blackwood. They struck up a correspondence. She had much to tell. After all she had been a debutante in American society before the Civil War. She and her father, Orrington Lunt (who had helped found the township of Evanston) had been guests of Abraham Lincoln in the White House. In 1864 she was escorted through the camp of the Army of the Potomac.

In the summer of 1931, aged eighty-seven, she came all the way to England to see Blackwood and talk about his days with Louis. Blackwood adored her. 'She had the most wonderful understanding of anyone I ever knew,' he wrote later to Miss Lunt's secretary and companion of her later years, Rachel McFerran. 'I think she understood everything in the human heart.'[23] It seems Cornelia Lunt adored Blackwood, too. Blackwood told his stepsister, 'Now this old lady, thinking of her past love, which went ugly for some reason, has transferred this unsatisfied emotion, it seems, to me. She calls me Figlio and I call her Madre.'[24]

She returned for a period over each of the next three years, and Blackwood became her guest at the Connaught Hotel in London. She was a remarkably fit lady for her age and Blackwood escorted her to many venues in London as well as to certain society events. The two of them even found themselves part of the Cliveden Set when they became guests at one of Nancy Astor's famous weekend parties at the Astor home at Cliveden in Buckinghamshire[25]. Cornelia Lunt was so well known in the United States that Lady Astor, herself American, would have felt honoured to meet her.

These American memories were timely because an opportunity presented itself for Blackwood to revisit New York for the first (and last) time in over thirty years. Frederick Lewis had been created Baron Essendon in June 1932. Blackwood was a frequent guest at their large nineteenth-century mansion, Essendon Place, at Hatfield in Hertfordshire. The Essendons' daughter, Frieda, had in February 1927 married Ian Napier, and Blackwood was godfather to their son, Malcolm, who was born in December 1927.

Lord Essendon was, among many other duties, chairman of the shipping company Furness, Withy & Co. This company had financed the construction of a new liner, *The Queen of Bermuda*, which replaced the previous liner, *Bermuda*, damaged in a fire in June 1931. *The Queen of Bermuda* was a high-class cruise ship operating between New York and Bermuda. It was 580 feet (178m) long, with a 77 foot (23m) beam, 22,500 gross tonnage and was built at a cost of $8 million. It had accommodation for 731 first-class passengers. It had spacious sports and sun decks, a large main restaurant, and a luxury swimming-pool. Every cabin had a private bathroom, something of a novelty even then.

Launched in September 1932 it underwent extensive sea and speed trials before undertaking its maiden voyage from Glasgow to Bermuda, via New York. It left Glasgow on 21 February 1933. Among its guest passengers were Lord and Lady Essendon, Frieda and Ian Napier, Lady Galway (one of Lady Essendon's colleagues in the British Red Cross) and Algernon Blackwood.

The crossing was fairly smooth. The ship docked in New York on the morning of 3 March, at berth 95 at the end of West 55th Street. It was within walking distance of some of Blackwood's old haunts, especially Central Park, and the area where Blackwood pursued and arrested his former friend Arthur Bigge. The liner remained in New

York for four days, but this was long enough for Blackwood to explore the city. Surprisingly, he left no written record of this return to New York. He told Ella Maillart of the trip but saw fit to write only 'I had a few days in New York – for the first time since 1893.'[26] (He even got the year wrong.) It was a difficult time to be in New York. The Depression was biting hard. President Roosevelt had just come to power and introduced his New Deal and one of his first acts was temporarily to close all banking operations, just at the time *The Queen of Bermuda* arrived. Even so, it would be surprising if Blackwood did not take the opportunity to show his friends many of his old haunts.

Blackwood remained with *The Queen of Bermuda* for her inaugural voyage to Hamilton, Bermuda. She left New York on 7 March. The weather was appalling. The *New York Times* reported:

> The liner battled high seas and winds of hurricane proportions. Few travelers left their staterooms. Seas broke high over the prow as the ship pitched along for thirty hours and ports were covered to prevent water from dashing into the staterooms.
>
> Experienced travelers to Bermuda said it was the stormiest trip they had ever made. The public rooms were deserted and most meals were served in staterooms. The velocity of the wind was estimated at eighty miles an hour and tales of seas of fabulous heights were exchanged this morning by hardy souls who had ventured on deck during the storm.[27]

Blackwood was probably in his element, watching the raw power of air and water.

Blackwood remained in Bermuda for several weeks, as he did not return to England until May. It was financial chaos in Bermuda at that time and the British found it difficult to access funds from home. Also many first-class passengers who had booked on the maiden voyage had to cancel their trip in order to deal with their financial affairs. On 3 April *The Queen of Bermuda* established a new speed record between New York and Bermuda of 20.33 knots. The liner remained in service for over thirty years and was one of the best remembered and most profitable of the company's ships.

III

The time for reflection that Blackwood had on the cruise allowed him to return to producing one last novel about childhood. *The Fruit Stoners* is not a children's book but, like his Uncle books, is about childhood, and also about time, growing up, and the loss of innocence. It is perhaps the profoundest of Blackwood's childhood books because not only is it written with the experience of age, it is written from the perspective of years of watching how his young friends are affected by the world about them.

This time there is not a group of children, but one, Maria. It was a name Blackwood had used before, most recently with 'Maria (of England) in the Rain', his contribution to *Number Ten Joy Street* (September 1932). In that story, where Maria has adventures in a flood, Maria is Patsy Ainley. The story starts on her twelfth birthday, and Patsy had been twelve in March 1931.

In *The Fruit Stoners*, Maria is more of an amalgam of many children Blackwood knew, but I suspect Patsy Ainley is again at the heart of it. Maria is an only child, ten years old, who has lost her mother. Her father is nearly always too busy to play with her and she is left to devise her own games. She has a vivid imagination and enjoys creating characters out of the old nursery game for girls that gives names to prune stones. In that game you place all your stones around the rim of the plate and count round them reciting the names (in Blackwood's version) – 'Tinker, Tailor, Soldier, Sailor, Gentleman, Ploughboy, Apothecary, Thief . . .' and so on. These characters are the Fruit Stoners. Depending on how many stones you have, the last one you count will be the type of man you marry.

One day Maria is given five minutes to fetch her father's slippers. She dashes off but in her search she encounters the sinister figure of the Man Who Wound the Clocks. This is a real individual who comes once a week to wind up all the clocks in the house. But now he takes on a mystical perspective. To allow Maria time to find the slippers he slows time down so that it passes at an infinitesimally slow rate. In her search Maria finds herself in a part of the house she never normally enters, rather like in the story 'The Other Wing', and here she encounters the Fruit Stoners as real live characters. They personify the different trials, necessities and demands of life.

She forgets what she is looking for, so the object of her quest becomes the Pearl of Great Price. The Fruit Stoners help her, though she feels she must also seek the help of Jack Robinson, who is faster than Time and knows where the Pearl is. Time seems to stretch on forever, even though it is also rushing past. She finds life passing her by, while she remains fixed on her goal, but she also realizes that so much else is happening. At last, she finds the slippers and manages to get back before her five minutes is up and the clock stops striking. Once back she wonders about all she has experienced and tries to work out which is real and which is false. One of the Fruit Stoners whispers to her saying that all that she has experienced could be real and one day she will awake, a second time, and discover life and the realities.

Although deeply philosophical, the book is devoid of the oversentimentality of *The Education of Uncle Paul*, and the verbosity of *A Prisoner in Fairyland*, and has a stronger narrative drive than *The Extra Day*, which makes it the most accomplished of his childhood books. It has moments of brilliant perception, with a remarkable array of images that personify our choices as we go through life. It is also a reminder of our mortality and how fast life passes us by, and what we may miss in the process. It is a book that only the elderly Blackwood could have written, and it is also one of his masterpieces. For just about every good reason this book is dedicated to Cornelia Lunt: 'To Madre from Figlio'.

Although he had not collaborated with Violet Pearn in fourteen years, they had kept in contact, and he arranged for her to see proofs of *The Fruit Stoners*. She was happy to prepare a treatment either as a stage play or as a film scenario. Pearn would continue to work on this adaptation for several months. At one point Blackwood was happy with it, but later he became highly critical. It was not until almost a year later that Blackwood seemed satisfied with her work. However, like so many theatre projects Blackwood worked on, nothing came of it, though he long remained convinced that the story would work as a film.

Rather curiously Blackwood wrote another story called 'The Fruit Stoners', this time for *Number Twelve Joy Street*, which was published in September 1934, a month before the book *The Fruit Stoners* from Grayson & Grayson. The two stories are totally different. This story, which features Imogen and her older sister Susan, concentrates on the fruit-stone game and what happens when Imogen meets each of the fruit stoners. The story is devoid of the mystical imagery and is simply a romance for adolescent girls. It shows, rather strikingly, how Blackwood could use exactly the same basic idea and develop it in two very different ways. As usual, Blackwell reissued the story as a slim hardback in April 1935, just six months after the novel. This means there are two different books by Blackwood, both with the title *The Fruit Stoners*.

Blackwood published just one more children's story, a fairly mundane circus adventure, 'How the Circus Came to Tea', for *Number 12a Joy Street* (September 1935)[28]. But by the end of 1934, the children weren't young children any more. Henry Ainley Jr was sixteen, and Patsy fifteen. Blackwood's own nephew, Patrick, was twenty-two. There would be others. Frieda Napier's eldest son, Malcolm, was just seven, and there were the children of Lord Essendon's friend Basil Sanderson. But Blackwood did not spend as much time with them as he had with the Ainley children.

The Man Who Wound the Clocks had done his job and time moved on. And so did Blackwood. In April 1934 the BBC contacted him again. This time Blackwood was not about to leave the country. Opportunity struck a second time, and Blackwood's career was about to take a new turn.

18

The Storyteller (1934–39)

I

Blackwood's sixty-fifth birthday fell on 14 March 1934. He was, as usual, in Saanenmoser. The hotel made him a large sugared cake with 'bonne fête' written on it in cream. He told Patsy Ainley that he ate it all and then felt sick, but that may just be Uncle Paul talking.

Nevertheless he was enjoying life. He told Patsy that 'I've written so many new short stories here that I am blue with the effort.'[1] These no doubt included both 'Elsewhere and Otherwise' and 'Adventures of Miss de Fontenay', the only two stories in Blackwood's last full-scale original collection, *Shocks*, not to have seen prior publication. There were other stories that Blackwood did not think appropriate for *Shocks*, and so never made it into a Blackwood collection.

One such was 'That Mrs Winslow'. On the surface it's untypical of Blackwood, but beneath it tells another story. It's about a widow who will be disinherited, apart from a small annuity, if she remarries, and the money will pass to research into Egyptian antiquities. The widow, Mrs Winslow, uses her ingenuity to defeat the will and win a new husband. Echoes of Maya and the Baron. The story was rejected by three markets before it was bought by *Pearson's Magazine* in August 1934. Even then it was two years before it was published.[2] 'The Man-Eater', a fairly mundane story of a were-tiger, also took a long while to sell. No British market took it, and Watt's American agent, David Lloyd, hawked it around four major magazines before it sold to the pulp *Thrilling Mystery* for the sum of $50. Unusually for Blackwood this is set in Malaya, which he had not visited – which suggests it's a story idea from one of his traveller friends, such as Wilfrid Wilson or Orientalist Sir Denison Ross.[3]

It was good that he had some new material, because a new market was about to open. Two months before Blackwood's sixty-fifth birthday, journalist and BBC talent-spotter, Jack C. Cannell contacted Blackwood for permission to adapt some of his stories into radio-drama format. Cannell was head of the Magic Circle's psychic-research committee and had recently had a best selling book, *The Secrets of Houdini* (1931). Blackwood gave him permission, though nothing came of it.

Soon afterwards Cannell contacted Blackwood again and asked whether he would be prepared to appear on the popular BBC radio programme, *In Town Tonight*[4]. It had a simple magazine format whereby celebrities who happened to be 'in town' popped in to talk about their current activities. Blackwood appeared live in the edition broadcast on the Saturday evening, 7 April 1934. He told a ghost story, but no record survives of which one.

Cannell had also suggested to the BBC's Director of Talks, Lionel Fielden, that Blackwood be included in a forthcoming short-story series. The series was full, but Fielden agreed to listen to Blackwood's *In Town Tonight* broadcast, and was suitably impressed. Fielden thereupon wrote to A.P. Watt requesting a story for broadcasting. Blackwood liked the idea and told Watt's that 'I owe a good deal to Mr Cannell's help and interest'.[5]

Blackwood had missed his first opportunity to broadcast back in 1926 when producer Lance Sieveking asked Blackwood for a story just as he was heading off to Switzerland. The BBC turned to another storyteller, L.H. Lambert (1883–1941), better known as A.J. Alan, who told many strange, often darkly humorous stories on the radio over the next decade.

Fortunately Blackwood grasped his second chance with gusto. He suggested that Watt submit two stories – 'The Prophecy', which he had specially adapted from 'By Water', and 'Lock Your Door'. A week later he submitted a third story, 'The Blackmailers'. Both of the new stories are macabre. 'Lock Your Door' is about a woman spending a night alone in a haunted house. Blackwood had often told the story to friends and said it never failed to thrill. 'The Blackmailers' is another ghost story but far bleaker.

Lionel Fielden was a little alarmed at the subject matter of both stories. He favoured 'The Blackmailers' but felt 'that we shall have a good many letters from listeners saying that we are corrupting the youth of England with morbid fancies and distasteful subjects'.[6] He relied on Blackwood's 'charm of manner' in how the story was delivered.

Blackwood understood Fielden's caution, but remarked: 'My own public, whatever that may mean, expect a queer sort of grim story from me and would be disappointed with an ordinary tale.'[7] Blackwood assumed that 'the young' would be in bed by the time the story was broadcast, at nine-thirty p.m. Fielden agreed and the necessary arrangements were made.

The BBC had originally offered 21 guineas for the broadcast but Blackwood and Watt's pushed for more, partly on the grounds that it was a new story but also because Blackwood would have to give up several hours to cover its rehearsal and broadcast. They eventually agreed on 25 guineas (equal to about £1,000 now) which is far greater than the BBC's equivalent terms today. Blackwood's response is interesting, bearing in mind his recent comments that he was not interested in the money so long as his works were read and appreciated. He said, 'I heartily approve getting as much as we can out of everybody! If this can be achieved without ill-feeling, so much the better, but I particularly want a "pleasant atomosphere" when I go.'[8] The broadcast fee became a sore point with Blackwood. A year later he wrote directly to the BBC Talks Executive explaining that the time spent reworking stories for broadcasting plus having to stay in London was not worth the fifteen guinea fee. He stated he would not do any broadcast for less than 20 guineas

Blackwood agreed to come in for a rehearsal earlier on the projected day of broadcast, set for 15 June. In the event Blackwood had a cold and the broadcast was rescheduled to 11 July, for 8.00 p.m. All went well and the story was broadcast in the BBC London Regional service. There is no record of the public's reaction, though when producer, J.R. Ackerley, wrote to Blackwood on 13 July, seeking a spot for another story, he remarked that they were pleased with the broadcast. For this second broadcast Ackerley said that they wanted to experiment and see the difference in quality between a story read from a script and one extemporized. Blackwood was enthused by the idea and decided to tell four short anecdotes, just as he did at house parties.

This broadcast was on 28 August at ten p.m. under the umbrella title of 'Queer Stories'. Blackwood was more intimate with his audience, chatting to them and speaking in the first person. The stories were brief and chatty but still atmospheric. 'Yogi' is about an old Holy Man who exchanges bodies with that of a dead younger man. 'Blank Cartridges' tells of friends who play a practical joke on another sleeping in a haunted room. In 'Homicidal Dream' a girl has a repetitive dream about a man strangling her and how she eludes destiny. 'Evidence in Camera' is a puzzling piece about a man who has long believed he is being followed. Two friends agree to photograph him next time he sees this apparition, but the photo is so puzzling they dare not show it to him.

This talk was immensely popular, and was reprinted in the BBC's literary magazine, *The Listener*[9]. By now one of the BBC's senior producers, Cecil Madden (1902–87) had got his claws into Blackwood. Madden was very impressed by Blackwood's first radio performance. Broadcasting late at night, Blackwood created a pregnant atmosphere and an immediate rapport with listeners. Blackwood's only fault was that he sometimes smacked his lips together and made a slight clacking sound with his teeth. Madden made a recording and played it back to Blackwood and thereafter he generally controlled it, though you can still hear it even in some of the later recordings.

Madden was the senior producer for the BBC Empire Service. Among his many programmes he hosted an informal chat show called *The Gossip Hour*, rather like *In Town Tonight*. Blackwood appeared on the edition for 1 August 1934 and, once again, told a couple of ghost stories. It went well, though Blackwood later commented 'how appallingly difficult it was to tell a ghost story immediately after bagpipes and a comedy Abyssinian prince!'[10]

Madden was planning a series of stories under the heading of *Nightmare*. This included contributions by J.B. Morton ('Beachcomber'), Noel Langley, Marjorie Bowen, Noel Streatfeild and H. de Vere Stacpoole. Madden was keen for Blackwood to launch the series. In fact he broadcast the pilot episode, 'The Empty House'[11], on 4 September 1934, and the first in the regular series, 'By Water' on 30 October. The series was such a success that Madden compiled an anthology of the stories, published as *My Grimmest Nightmare* the following autumn. He wanted to use both of Blackwood's stories, but Grayson & Grayson (who had taken over Blackwood's early titles from Eveleigh Nash) would not release 'A Haunted Island' so Madden substituted 'The Blackmailers', marking its first appearance in print.

Blackwood made seven radio broadcasts during 1934. He took to it instantly and everyone at the BBC enjoyed working with him. He was charming and professional. Blackwood also enjoyed the medium, though was concerned about how time-consuming it was. It tied him to being in London, and for that reason alone he did not want a regular slot. He was happy to broadcast when he was in London, but that meant coinciding an opportunity when he was around. Because few programmes were pre-recorded in those days, this concentrated his broadcasts into the summer and autumn.

II

A week after his broadcast of 'By Water' Blackwood was off to Capri to stay with Gracie Fields. Although he was writing his children's story 'How the Circus Came to Tea', most of his time was spent reading and generally enjoying himself. He was still very active but life had slowed down by his standards, although 1934 had suddenly raised his profile again. His radio popularity led to a number of reprints of his stories in anthologies or newspapers. Furthermore, Jonathan Cape issued a slightly abridged version of his autobiography in their Travellers' Library series, retitled *Adventures Before Thirty*. Along with the publication of *The Fruit Stoners* Blackwood's name was well before the public.

He stayed with Gracie Fields through to early December, even having the villa to himself for some time. Axel Munthe heard that he was on the island and invited him over. Munthe had lost his sight four years before, but after a difficult operation in Zurich and six weeks of suspense he was overjoyed to find it restored. Just back on the island, Munthe welcomed his old friend.

By the middle of December Blackwood was back at Saanenmoser for the ski season. He spent some of this time with the Vansittarts and their children. Lady Vansittart's eldest son, Colville Barclay, was now twenty-one and at Trinity College, Oxford. He and Blackwood had been discussing the question of what constituted a 'civilized' life, and how one should measure humanity's progress. Their discussion developed into a story idea, and during this winter Blackwood gave it further thought. He wondered if it might work better as a film and put together an outline entitled 'Gold, or the Uncharted Island'. A yachting party of socialites under Lord X is shipwrecked on a previously uncharted island where, two centuries before, ancestors of Lord X had emigrated and whose descendants live in Arcadian peace. The outline contrasts the two societies. Blackwood sent the treatment to a film agency, but nothing came of it.

The next spring Blackwood travelled to Montreux for a month before returning to Capri in April. It was there that he received news of the death of Cornelia Lunt in Chicago the previous December, and this brought on a melancholia.

> A great part of my life seems to have gone dead now without her, for she was so tremendously in my mind and thought always, and now there is just a blank. I am now 66, and though that seems a long way from 91, the end of course cannot be so very far away. [. . .] Life is not too easy for me, what with Pat and his mother and my small uncertain income, but it is a full life, anyhow, though no longer so full as it was before she left us.[12]

Blackwood returned to London in the middle of May 1935, staying initially with his sister-in-law in Duke Street, and then at the London apartment of the Vansittarts at 44 Park Street. Blackwood was never at a loss for somewhere to stay as all his friends delighted in his company. One of these friends was Guy Cooper-Willis, a solicitor in the Public Trustee's Office whom Blackwood had come to know at the Savile Club. Cooper-Willis was a charming but fastidious man, always full of ideas. The interest in radio sparked them into adapting one of Blackwood's stories. They selected 'The Man who Was Milligan' and worked on an outline which they retitled 'Chinese Magic'. It became almost a new story. In this version a Chinaman seeks revenge upon a man who kidnapped and murdered his girl. The Chinaman paints himself into a picture and bides his time until he can step out of the picture to exact his revenge. Nothing came of the play, though Blackwood broadcast an abbreviated story version on 1 September.

In August Blackwood was visiting an old family friend, Captain Edward Boylan (1894–1959) in Drogheda, Ireland. While there he was struck with an idea for an unusual story, which he called 'At a Mayfair Luncheon'.[13] Monson is called at the last minute to make up the numbers at a luncheon party. He finds himself sitting opposite an empty chair. Monson, who has been in a dreamy mood all day, is suddenly aware of a presence in the vacant chair, someone with a holy aura. This is among the best of his later stories, and it remains a mystery why he did not offer it to August Derleth ten years later when Derleth was seeking to publish a collection at Arkham House.

For the first time that autumn Blackwood took part in a regular series. *Young Ideas* was broadcast at seven-thirty p.m. each Friday evening. It was a magazine programme where guests talked about current projects. Blackwood was commissioned to tell a short five-minute story each week. He began on 4 October with 'The Train Ghost'. No record survives of this talk, but it may have been the same as 'Lock Your Door'. Next week he told 'Come With Me'. This was among his favourite anecdotes as he told it on radio and television several times, under varying titles, and everyone who knew him remembered him telling it. Two men are crossing a field. One of them hears a voice saying several times 'Come with me'. On the last occasion he realizes his companion has vanished. The third story was 'The Wig', a humorous squib about an old lady who sleeps in a haunted room occupied by a little gnome-like ghost which steals her wig. He missed a week and then broadcast his fourth story on 1 November. This was 'Lion in New York City', another anecdote he never tired of telling, about the time the lion escaped from the circus. His final spot was on 29 November when he told 'A Backwoods Adventure', about the moose-hunting trip in Canada. Blackwood took Maya Philipson along to that recording. This is the last reference to her among the surviving Blackwood papers, though it is no reason to believe it was the last time they met. In a letter to a friend on 4 January 1940 Blackwood said, 'I have rather lost sight of Mrs Philipson.' Maya spent her last days in Hans Court, London, where she died on 6 May 1945 of cancer, aged sixty-nine.

The day after that broadcast Blackwood packed his bags and headed off to Lech in Austria. Just two weeks earlier, on 17 November 1935, his old friend Mary Bevan had died, at the age of only sixty-four. Blackwood makes no reference to her passing, and may not even have known of it. Although he seems to have lost touch with the Bevans in recent years, their early association was a vital part in Blackwood's life. Edwyn Bevan spent most of the rest of his life at his home near Cannes, in the south of France.

III

After a winter's skiing in Lech, with many of his usual circle of friends, Blackwood headed to Montreux on 24 February and a week later moved down to the south of France. At the age of sixty-seven Blackwood was to venture on the last significant trip of his life. He was going to hike through Spain – in the months just before the outbreak of the Civil War.

Blackwood took the train to Barcelona and then settled in a hotel at Sitges, a few miles further south. He stayed there for a couple of weeks, finding the people delightful, the oranges 'gorgeous' and the cost of living cheap. Having arrived soon after the recent elections when the sweeping reforms of the Republicans were causing considerable unrest, Blackwood witnessed first hand much of what led up to the Civil War. He told Patsy Ainley:

> Although there's a good deal of rioting, arson and murder going on here, tourists seem safe enough, and it's chiefly churches and convents that get burnt. At any rate, I wander about with my infallible sense of direction and, if we're in a car and see trouble ahead, we just reverse and buzz back. But foreigners are watched all the same and, if you wire abroad you have to translate it into Spanish first, and if you telephone, an official who understands is by your side in the box.[14]

The weather was rather cold for Blackwood and he planned to head south, but not before he had seen a bull-fight in Barcelona. 'Though rather dreadful', he wrote, 'I want to see how it's done – once.' He was also meeting Herr Wactjen, who was translating some of his stories into German. No such book subsequently appeared and as Wactjen died in 1941 it may never have found a publisher.

Blackwood headed south, visiting Malaga and Seville (to see the Alhambra) and Algeciras before arriving at Gibraltar in early April. He stayed there for three weeks, using it as a haven to explore southern Spain, before he caught a steamer back home.

Twenty-five years earlier Blackwood would have been captured by the magic of the places he was visiting which, despite the civil unrest, still held a fascination, and these experiences would have poured out of him in stories. Now he had all but run dry. Spain yielded nothing by way of new stories or articles. Blackwood the visionary had become Blackwood the tourist.

Back in England Blackwood spent the weeks around Whitsun with the Essendons and only broadcast once that summer. This was 'King's Evidence' on 27 June 1936. It was a revised version of 'Confession', concentrating on the mystery aspect. Although the story is not so powerful as the original, it is easier to follow over the radio.

Interestingly, a film company suggested to Blackwood that it might make a good film, but again nothing came of it.

The producer, Malcolm Brereton, chose this story as an opportunity to test the comprehensibility of stories to the listener. He compiled a questionnaire, which was given, in a sealed envelope, to various members of his department. They were asked to open the envelope after they had heard the broadcast and to record their views. Whilst all agreed it was 'first-class', they also felt the second half needed to move more quickly in order to reach the climactic scene (where the narrator realizes the man who has rescued him is a murderer), because the seed for this had been sown some while earlier. Blackwood took the comments in good spirit, reflecting upon how careful one has to be in placing an emphasis at certain points of the story to help the reader along without giving the game away. Blackwood was, of course, an old hand at this, but radio was a different medium as he was not able to see the listener reaction, which he could at camps or house parties. He had to judge his emphasis carefully. What with this and his lip-smacking and teeth-clenching, Blackwood realized he had much to think about when broadcasting, while still trying to sound informal and spontaneous.

He used this experience to write an article for the *Radio Times* the following year. It was called 'You Can't Tell Ghost Stories on the Radio'[15], where he makes the point that there must be an affinity between the storyteller and his audience. A rapport, where the body language is all important, and where the recipient must listen, and not be distracted. The raconteur requires an atmosphere, which he or she can create in an intimate setting, but which is elusive on radio. It is rather ironic that Blackwood should conclude that radio is not a good medium for ghost stories, when it was the very medium in which he would become better known to the whole nation than at any other time in his life.

It was a hectic round of visits that summer and autumn. He was whisked away in August for an unexpected 'glacier tour' of Obergurgl and Innsbruck. On his return he visited friends in Cornwall, and on the way back visited his sister, Ada, at Itchen Abbas. From there he visited one of his devoted correspondents, Vera Wainwright (1893–1967), who lived at Cerne Abbas in Dorset. She was a poet, painter and sculptress who kept in touch with many of the creative artists of the day, including Walter de la Mare, E.H. Visiak, Henry Savage and

Victor Neuberg. She maintained a correspondence with Blackwood for nearly twenty years, right up until his death.

Back in London he had a letter from Gracie Fields hoping he would visit her at St John's Wood, but a few days later he was with friends at Malvern. He managed to return from there to attend an astronomy lecture by Sir James Jeans at Margate, and from Margate he returned to London on the afternoon of 2 November 1936 for a landmark event – the first television broadcast in Britain.

After the opening ceremonies and a song-and-dance act in the afternoon, the first formal television programme went out at nine-twenty-three p.m. that Monday evening. It was called *Picture Page* and was produced by Cecil Madden. Blackwood recounted the details of the historic event to Patsy Ainley.

> We all went out to Alexandra Palace in a private BBC bus, each of us performing for 3 minutes. The light being quite different to cinema lighting, our make-up was something fierce and my bright blue lips and eyelids made me horrifying or fascinating according to taste. The others did their bit in the big studio but, as they wanted close-ups of my face while telling my stories, I was put in a smaller studio, pitch dark, with two experts who moved huge machines about to light up the different sides of my face, just as in a photographic studio, except that the rays these machines emitted were invisible, and the air remained black as night. I could not rely on my notes and when the man pinched my elbow as a sign to start I was in such a dither I nearly 'dried up'. The knowledge that I was being watched on a screen by experts in the Board Room upstairs made me nervous. I emerged at the end into the lighted corridor dripping with perspiration – to be met with the unexpected verdict that I had been 'marvellous'.[16]

Blackwood told a couple of short anecdotal stories (alas the record does not say which). He was delighted to find that the next day *The Times* singled him out as 'excellent', and Cecil Madden wrote to thank him more formally saying that 'All the reports say that your stories came over exceptionally well, as I knew they would!'[17] Madden also apologized for the state of the journey home, even though Blackwood had quite enjoyed it, rolling around in the bus with the Pearly King and Queen of Blackfriars – a cockney costermonger tradition that goes back centuries. They swapped stories and sang cockney songs and had a rare old time.

IV

The emergence of Blackwood the Storyteller further raised his profile among publishers. In October 1938 Martin Secker published *The Tales of Algernon Blackwood*, an omnibus volume of his best work. This was the biggest collection published during his lifetime. The stories were chosen by Blackwood's long-time correspondent Mrs Lamont, and this time came entirely from the early Eveleigh Nash volumes and thus did not clash with *Strange Stories*. The volume is still the best selection of Blackwood's early material and includes all the stories from *John Silence*.

Despite the desire to have Blackwood broadcasting more regularly he made only two further radio broadcasts between the end of 1936 and the start of the Second World War. Part of the problem was that Blackwood was out of the country for over half of each year, and when he was in England he travelled extensively. But another problem was that the BBC preferred new stories, and Blackwood had few such stories of the right length. He adapted 'Running Wolf' as 'The Curse of the Wolf', broadcast on 12 September 1937, but was not on radio again until the eve of the war.

Blackwood had in fact completed five new stories during this pre-war period, but only two of them were of broadcastable length, and Watt's chose to offer those to the magazines.

The first was 'By Proxy', which he completed at Lech, in the Austrian Alps in February 1937, and which was later adapted for radio. It's a macabre story about a thug who tricks a young boy into killing his own mother. Soon after Blackwood headed to Cannes to see his nephew, Patrick[18]. Blackwood and Patrick became regular companions over the next few years and Patrick adored his uncle. Patrick had been well educated and was something of a multi-lingualist. During the mid-thirties he turned to medical studies, in the footsteps of his stepfather. He had been engaged to another medical student who sadly died of cancer. Patrick understandably lost interest in his studies. Like his uncle, Patrick was more artistic and had an ambition to run an art gallery, but it was some while before he achieved his goal. In the meantime he held a variety of jobs, including working in the Chase Manhattan bank and for the East India Company. Patrick enjoyed the good life and was always fun to be with.

While at Cannes Blackwood met Wilfrid Wilson who suggested ideas for several stories. The first completed was 'The Reformation of St

Jules'. It's a skit on the fashion for advertizing by sky-writing. A man invents a way of projecting writing on to the sky accompanied by a loud voice, but the superstitious locals in a small French village believe it's divine intervention and amend their ways. From Cannes they moved on to Monte Carlo and, while there, Wilson, who enjoyed playing the tables, came up with another story idea, which became 'The Magic Mirror' – the mirror reveals the winning numbers at roulette but there is a price to pay.

Watt had trouble selling the first two of these stories. They were rejected by the four main fiction magazines of the day, but eventually sold to the popular women's society magazine, *The Bystander*.[19] Their payment rate was not very high – ten guineas per story – but Blackwood agreed. Consequently Watt also pitched 'The Magic Mirror' at *The Bystander*. Watt's American agent, David Lloyd, had been unable to sell 'By Proxy' or 'St Jules' but he did place 'The Magic Mirror' with *Weird Tales*[20], where editor Farnsworth Wright offered thirty-seven dollars (then about the equivalent of nine guineas). The story had previously been rejected by the more lucrative markets, such as *The Saturday Evening Post*, and Lloyd commented that the story 'has not a wide magazine market in this country'.

Weird Tales had been the primary market for such material since 1923. When he learned of the sale to *Weird Tales*, Blackwood remarked: 'I think we might keep our eye on this *Weird Tales* magazine. "The Blackmailers" might surely have suited it, having never been broadcast out there. In any case, though its fees are small, it may come in useful for odds and ends of similar kind in future.'[21] Yet Watt submitted nothing further to *Weird Tales*.

Blackwood stayed rather longer in Switzerland than he had planned. This was partly because he was enjoying himself, meeting up with many friends, old and new, but also because he had been commandeered by the English colony in Geneva to help out with a special dinner to celebrate the coronation of George VI on 12 May. It was not Blackwood's scene. 'We shall sit down some 250 strong, all bored,' he wrote to Patsy.

Blackwood's letters from this period are full of people who visited him, far too many to mention and all too few of them remembered today. His constant companion was an elderly gentleman, well into his seventies by then, and known to everyone as Old Bell[22]. His friendship with Blackwood went back a very long way, and it is believed they met during Blackwood's Intelligence days. Everyone loved Bell. Like Blackwood he was always cheerful and a great raconteur. Just to confuse matters Blackwood was also close friends with the retired British diplomat, Sir Henry Hesketh Bell (1864–1952). He had retired to Cannes in 1924, but continued to travel in the Far East as well as the West Indies where he had served as a governor. He was fascinated in voodoo and wrote several books on the subject.

Another regular companion was Elaine Clewes. By the mid 1930s she had separated from her third husband and later reassumed the name of Elaine Ainley. She was frequently with Blackwood in Saanenomoser, usually with her eldest daughter, Biddy. Once in a while Patsy and Henry, Jr would join them. It was much rarer for Henry Ainley himself to come out, though he did in 1937, seeking refuge with Blackwood in order to reacquaint himself with his role in *Hassan*, which he was performing again both on the stage and on radio.

Blackwood occasionally visited Ella Maillart at her home in Chandolin, though he saw her less in the 1930s as her travels took her to Turkistan and China and beyond. The Essendons had a home in the Avenue Eglantine in Lausanne, where Blackwood would visit, just as he would Alice Perrin at Tour de Peilz at Vaud, until her death in 1934. Lord and Lady Vansittart would also join Blackwood at Saanenmoser, along with their children, and sometimes with Lord Vansittart's private secretary, Clifford Norton. Norton and his wife had been ardent followers of Ouspensky.

Blackwood returned to London immediately after the Coronation dinner. Wilson had given Blackwood access to his London apartment for the summer in Lennox Gardens, and he settled down to a programme of writing. This time, though, rather than fiction or radio talks it was a series of reminiscences. The recent reprinting of *Adventures Before Thirty* had revived requests from people for the sequel, but Blackwood always deferred. In fact he had no good reason to write *Episodes After Thirty*. Much of what he had experienced since 1899 had already been expressed in his stories. Many of these events were still too close to him, emotionally, and many of the people still alive. New York had been sufficiently distant, and many of the people had died or could be safely disguised, but that was less easy for his more recent years.

Instead he reached a compromise. Rather than a new autobiography, he would write a series of articles, anecdotes and reminiscences that looked at various unusual experiences, and explored any conclusions drawn. He had been dabbling with these for some years, at least since 'The Fire Body' in 1931. By the summer of 1937 he had completed at least four, most of them interlinked by the subject of time and reincarnation. 'Coincidences' discussed the case of the Australian who had memories of a past life from *Julius LeVallon*. 'Alexander Hamilton' was the case of Maria Smith. 'The Russian Dentist' was the odd dentist in Naples who did nothing to Blackwood's tooth. The fourth, 'The Giant in Khaki', is more amusing than strange. Blackwood had followed up a letter from a woman in distress. But he had lost the letter and though he knew the apartment block he wasn't sure of the flat number. Nevertheless a woman responded to the doorbell. While she made tea he noticed a picture of an army officer nearby. This, it transpired, was the woman's husband who was so jealous that he had turned almost homicidal and was currently in an institution. He would be let out now and again, and indeed the lady had only just escorted him back to the nearby 'home'. Needless to say Blackwood was unnerved. Every sound he heard was this lunatic about to return and murder him. It was all he could do to remain calm for an hour or so before he could make his escape.

Blackwood submitted 'Alexander Hamilton' and 'The Russian Dentist' to Christopher Salmon at the BBC as possible broadcasts but they came to nothing. Over a year later Patsy Ainley asked him why he had not broadcast and his response was that he couldn't find a suitable story.[23]

Blackwood was also struggling to complete stories he had started but had somehow lost the way. One was 'Rose and Ditt', a novel developed from his children's story 'The Water Performance'. Once again it's a story about childhood which can be read at many levels. It's also his most existential novel. It tells of two children, Peter and Rose (based on Henry Ainley, Jr and Patsy), who believe that at night they and everyone else has another existence. Even the House. Everything that they know and see is but the tip of the iceberg. Beyond is a greater existence of which they are only aware under certain circumstances. They name these extra-beings by reversing their names, so that the night-time Peter is Retep and the night-time Rose is Esor. Peter teaches Rose special yoga techniques which allow her to widen her perception and she becomes aware of her other self. In this heightened state Rose sees something special in her father's friend Mr

Ditt, whom she calls 'the Glamour Man'. Ditt is able to take her further into this extra-world.

Blackwood created some highly imaginative scenes but was unable to bring the novel to a conclusion, though there are copious notes exploring final scenes. He almost completed it, yet must have lost interest or energy. One draft is dated 'Encombe, 1936' and again 'Bishopsteignton, 1940'. The original short story was published in 1927, suggesting that Blackwood experimented with this novel for perhaps thirteen years or more. Eventually it joined the pile with 'The Group-Soul' and 'The People of the Ridge' of stories not for this world. He mentioned them when writing to Vera Wainwright in December 1938:

> I myself at the moment am beautifully bogged over an idea that came rushing in one day with a force that it seemed easy at first. Once the inspiration flags I drop it and turn to something else, so that I now have a thick dossier of two half-finished books and numerous shorter things. Once the real inspiration fades nothing, least of all hard work and cooking up, can replace it.[24]

The 'numerous shorter things' probably included the following. There is a strange piece called 'The Introduction', which is missing a page and may not be complete where it ends. It is set in Paris and may have been inspired by Blackwood's Gurdjieff days. The female narrator has an experience in a cemetery when she discovers she is bound to the spirits of the dead by invisible 'psychic' threads. 'The Bugle' is labelled a 'Wilson tale', meaning the idea came from Wilfreid Wilson. A man inherits a bugle that sounds a warning when danger is imminent. 'Wishful Thinking', possibly planned as a radio talk, is only 1,700 words long. It's an echo of 'Keeping His Promise'. A colonel's nephew insists on repaying a debt even after his death.

None of these was published. The idea that 'rushed at him' was probably one of the two remaining stories he did finish before the War. He refers to them in a letter to Patsy Ainley in January 1939, when he was in Montreux. He says simply, 'I've finished two new stories – one an awful thing called "The Doll".' The other is almost certainly 'The Trod'. 'The Doll' is a chilling story of revenge. A doll is left as a present at the house of Colonel Masters. Though asked to dispose of it the housemaid gives it to the colonel's daughter, Monica. The doll is there to right an ancient wrong and comes alive. The scene where the malignant doll climbs over the counterpane of the bed to wreak its revenge is an especially strong moment. 'The Trod' is more like the Blackwood of old, though never quite achieving that same visionary power. It is set on the remote Yorkshire Moors near a track called the trod. This is avoided, especially at the time of the equinox, because it is the road that the fairies and little people use. Norman is in love with Diana, the daughter of his host. On the night of the equinox Diana's spirit self, Dis, is attracted to the trod which comes alive with creatures and he only just rescues her in time.

These two stories were the best Blackwood had written since 'At a Mayfair Luncheon', but there is little evidence that Watt's did anything with them, or even that Blackwood sent them to his agent. The potential of *Weird Tales* seems forgotten. It was a difficult time. Many of the British fiction magazines had folded, or soon would do with the onset of war.

Blackwood had watched this darkness fall with the Nazi take-over of Austria on 13 March 1938. 'I must renounce Austria,' he told Vera Wainwright, 'as I detest the Nazi system too much to be happy in its atmosphere. I was out there in March during the Anschluss fuss and shall never forget it.'[25] A few months later he wrote to Patsy Ainley saying, 'I expect the worse; I believe we must fight NOW or accept a Nazi domination of all Europe.'[26] However, like many Britons, the more proceedings dragged on with apparent entente between Britain and Germany, the more Blackwood felt the likelihood of war was receding. In April 1939 he went so far as to tell Vera Wainwright that he thought war was 'most improbable'.

Blackwood needed to watch his own health. He was not getting any younger. The previous June (1938) he had a fall in the snow and landed awkwardly on his spine. Back at the hotel he was having some soup when a sudden weakness came over him. He broke out into a sweat but was too weak to do anything but scribble down his name and the address of Old Bell. The weakness passed after twenty minutes and he felt fine again but he consulted the doctor the next day who told him it was delayed concussion from the fall.

Blackwood stayed in Switzerland as long as he could during 1939. He travelled to Nice in May and finally returned to England in early July. Little did he think then it was the last he would see of Switzerland for six years.

19

The Ghost Man (1939–48)

I

When war was declared, on 3 September 1939, Blackwood volunteered again for Intelligence work. He was told he was too old but that there may be some work in Censoring. While he waited for confirmation of this – and none came – he turned to his friend Mary Borden to help equip and despatch the Field Hospital service for France.

In the end Blackwood was rather relieved that he was not involved in Intelligence work. He wrote to a friend saying: 'This is my first winter in England for 30 years, and I don't like it awfully, while yet life is so amazingly interesting these days that I wouldn't be abroad for anything.'[1] On the eve of war Blackwood had been involved in a variety of projects. The American editor, Marion Cothren, had sought permission to adapt *Dudley & Gilderoy* into a children's book. She met him in London at the start of August and he was delighted with the result. In his usual charming manner Blackwood praised her work but felt awkward about asking where he fitted into the picture financially. When Watt's approached her about it she was surprised, believing that Blackwood's original permission was sufficient. What began as a pleasant relationship steadily devolved into something acrimonious and it took over a year to resolve. The book was eventually published by E.P. Dutton in March 1941 as *The Adventures of Dudley and Gilderoy*. Ernest Benn were not interested in publishing the abridged edition in Britain, so it was sold to Faber & Faber who published it in October.

Blackwood's gentlemanly approach to deals shows that he found it hard to act as a businessman. That's why he needed A.P. Watt. At the same time as the Cothren case, Blackwood was also in dispute with the BBC over their broadcasting of music and songs from *The Starlight Express* without further payment. The BBC had not realized that the permission they had been granted by Elgar's music publisher, Elkin & Co., had covered the music only. No further thought was given to this until Blackwood heard a broadcast of the music on the BBC Home Service on 26 November 1939 and he queried the position with Watt's. Watt's had not acted on Blackwood's behalf for *The Starlight Express*. The arrangement with Lena Ashwell had been managed by Hughes, Massie, but that agreement had long since lapsed. Once again A.P. Watt had to resolve the situation, which they did amicably.

For the time being Blackwood was tied to London. He had moved in with his nephew, Patrick, at 3 Lawn Road in Hampstead, North London. When war broke out Patrick was not called up immediately, though he subsequently joined the RAF where he became a corporal.

Because he was in London Blackwood was more easily accessible for radio broadcasts and he threw himself into the medium. There was a series called *At the Black Dog* on the BBC Empire Service. It was an informal chat show set in a fictional public house. It was another format where Blackwood could turn up and tell a story. He appeared twice in the series (on 16 August 1939 and 3 May 1940). On the second occasion he regaled his audience with some of his experiences in Canada.

He also returned to the BBC Home Service. Blackwood had been adapting several of his stories to fit into convenient ten- or fifteen-minute slots. He broadcast 'Two of a Kind' (adapted from 'The Survivors') on 17 December 1939, and this worked well. He was scheduled again to broadcast on Christmas Eve but, early in December, Christopher Salmon found he had control over a half-hour slot at lunchtime on Christmas Day. He hoped Blackwood could read *three* of his stories in that slot. 'This trio will make wonderful listening, I believe, and I think you will have half the world at your feet.'[2]

Blackwood chose 'Transition', 'The Laughter of Courage' and 'A Boy and His Bag' (adapted from 'The Little Beggar'). He was nervous, not because of the size of his audience, but because of what he called 'the Terror of the Clock'. Blackwood did not like reading from a script. He knew these stories inside-out anyway. He submitted a script simply as a formality (a requirement, in any case, for censorship), but when he came to tell the story he told it by heart. He knew he could not improvise over radio during the war, but he still liked to experiment with inflection and pauses to create the atmosphere. With one story he knew he could bring this in on time to within a few seconds, but three stories aggravated the problem. He feared that his eye would be so fixed on the clock that he might rush the story and not sound natural. He need not have feared.

> My own Terror of the Clock was killed on Xmas Day for good. I had allowed myself one minute margin – ample – when I was started 1 1/2 minutes late and begged in addition to cut out another 2 minutes if possible. I managed it somehow during reading, ending precisely on the Pip-Pip. The clock no longer haunts me after that![3]

Blackwood continued to submit story ideas to Christopher Salmon but there were not enough appropriate ones to allow him to broadcast regularly. Blackwood's favourite among his stories, such as 'The Willows', were too long to broadcast, and many of the shorter pieces were too abstract. Nevertheless, he broadcast five times during 1940, two of these being repeat broadcasts. His new stories included 'By Proxy' (29 February), 'The Voice' (adapted from 'The Reformation of St Jules') on 17 April and 'The Destruction of Smith', a particularly difficult subject to convey on radio but which Blackwood achieved in a masterly way. The first two stories were read in the morning and afternoon, but the third story, broadcast on 6 September, went out at eleven p.m. on the Friday night. Rather than attempt to return to Hampstead that late at night the BBC arranged that Blackwood sleep over. It was an eventful night as there were air raids and a bomb landed nearby at the Langham Hotel, just opposite Broadcasting House.

When not broadcasting Blackwood undertook firewatching from Hampstead, which is on high ground and thus allowed a clear view over the capital.

On 13 October 1940 disaster struck. The newspapers later reported it as the 'Worst Night Raid of the War'. Germany's air force had increased its *Blitzkrieg* over London, returning for raid after raid every night. On 13 October London had its worst raid yet, with high explosive and incendiary bombs raining down on the city and suburbs. Blackwood's home received a direct hit. Fortunately Blackwood and Patrick were in the air-raid shelter in the garden. Nevertheless, they were extremely lucky to survive as Blackwood revealed.

> You'll be amused to know that sausages literally saved me & a
> nephew, for we were cooking them in our A[nderson] Shelter for
> supper when a bomb removed the house next but one. The Shelter
> merely rose and sank again with earth-vibration. When dust settled
> we crawled out to examine our building – all windows gone but no
> structural damage – when my nephew remembered the burning
> sausages and we ran back in the brilliant moonlight. Five minutes
> later our house caught it and again the Shelter just rose and sank,
> heavily smothered but intact. So we were saved by sausages.[4]

Their house was destroyed and with it went what remained of
Blackwood's personal papers and memorabilia. His radio scripts survived because he was working on them in the shelter, whilst Patsy and
his sister, Ada, had his books and a few other old files. But his scrapbook, with photographs and papers going back to the 1890s, was
destroyed.

Blackwood was invited by his old friend, Louis N. Parker, to retreat
to the safety of the West Country. Parker lived at Bishopsteignton, in
Devon, and there were lodgings available just along the road.
Unfortunately it removed Blackwood from immediate access to the
BBC. He came up specially on Christmas Eve, 1940, as Christopher
Salmon was keen for Blackwood to read a story at Christmas.
Originally they spoke about a new story, but Blackwood said that his
'muse' was unable to rise to the occasion. 'I don't feel anything in me
these days as good as the, alas, unsuitable tales we have already re-
hearsed together, and the conditions here, without boring details, are
not favourable either to new ideas or composition.'[5]

Eventually it was decided that Blackwood read 'King's Evidence'
again. It was an opportunity to experiment with the story that Malcolm
Brereton had analysed. It was touch and go, though. Blackwood no
longer had a copy of the script, which he needed to refer to. The BBC
suggested mailing one, but Blackwood feared it would be delayed in
the post and cross with him coming up to London, so he had to refresh
his memory of the story within hours of his live broadcast at six forty-
five p.m. Even so the broadcast was a success, and this version of the
story was published in the BBC's magazine *London Calling* on 9
January and was selected for *Best Broadcast Stories* in 1944.

While in Devon Blackwood gave thought to his reminiscences, urged
on by correspondence from his American publisher John MacCrae at

E.P. Dutton. He told Vera Wainwright in March 1941 that 'I spend part of my time making a few notes of various queer adventures that might be used someday in *Episodes After Thirty*. I say "might" only.' He clearly remained unsure about the value of producing these reminiscences. Although undated and incomplete, the drafts of chapters headed 'Maude ffoulkes', 'Letters from Strangers' and 'Three Old Ladies' probably all date from this period.

With the help of Louis Parker, Blackwood gave thought to how he might adapt his stories as radio plays. Blackwood had always maintained that he had no gift for scripts but under Parker's guiding hand, he gave it a go. Between them they worked on 'The Willows', 'The Wolves of God', 'The Decoy', 'That Mrs Winslowe', 'Tongues of Fire' and 'Old Clothes', sometimes abandoning them after a first draft. Blackwood made three different attempts at 'The Wolves of God', but noted across the last version, 'A suggested dramatic treatment never finished because it was beyond me.'

He persevered. Together with Parker he completed, in February 1941, a fifteen-minute adaptation of 'Shocks'. This was not a supernatural story but a spoof, about a solicitor who plays a practical joke on a client about a significant legacy. The original story was one of the few that Blackwood had sold to the prestigious *Strand Magazine* back in 1930. It was accepted by the Director of Features and Drama, Val Gielgud (1900–81), elder brother of the actor John Gielgud, and was broadcast on 16 July 1941.

Blackwood made another special trip to London in June 1941 to broadcast again the story 'By Water', but he was soon back in Devon. Blackwood now had the drama bit between his teeth. 'I shall always be glad to let your department see any new radio play,' Blackwood wrote in response to Gielgud's request for more. 'Many of my short stories should provide material. I am now at work on one of these with Louis Parker, whose playwright experience is valuable.' He further added. 'It is a comedy – bright and cheery, I hope. . . I have rather specialized in creepy or spooky stories, but I feel these are not easy to get across, as a couple I sent in didn't suit. So I won't waste time on these.'[6] The new play was 'That Mrs Winslowe'. Blackwood finished the final version of it himself at Socknersh Manor. He had discovered on his trip to London that Frieda Mason's boys, Malcolm and Andrew, had gone to Canada to stay with relatives, where it was safer, so that there was room at Socknersh. Frieda Napier and her first husband had divorced in 1940 and she married longtime friend, Cecil Mason. He owned Socknersh Manor in Sussex, near Burwash, which became a regular place of refuge for Blackwood. He moved there during the first week in July 1941 and despatched the play to Gielgud on the 22nd. Alas this one did not fit the bill.

Now that Blackwood was back within striking distance of London, albeit still in the deep countryside of the Sussex/Kent border, it was hoped he might read more of his stories. Christopher Salmon enticed him back to read 'The Chinese Picture' on 18 August. Unfortunately this led to something of a disagreement. First Salmon told Blackwood he had to read it in eighteen-and-a-half minutes, but when Blackwood did a read through at Socknersh he discovered it took him twenty-three minutes. His original broadcast of the story in 1935 had been just under twenty-one minutes, so he had clearly slowed a little over the years, but the prospect of reducing it to less than nineteen minutes frustrated him. 'Drastic cuts and alterations can do this, though the tale will suffer,' he told Salmon, but his annoyance was evident when he added, 'You can rely absolutely on my being within time. By now you ought to know that if I say that, I mean it.'[7]

As if that was not annoying enough Blackwood then discovered that because the BBC already owned the broadcast rights to the story they proposed to pay him a fee of only five guineas[8]. Yet not only did Blackwood have to edit his script for the new timing, but this fee had to include the cost of both his rail fare and an overnight stay at a hotel. This remained a sore point with Blackwood.

But that was not all. Salmon had suggested that someone else read the story, and this made Blackwood see red.

> No story of mine has ever been read by someone else, and I should greatly dislike this to happen; this particular story, moreover, needs the author's personal interpretation to help it get across. In view of this I am returning the contract – with my most reluctant signature.[9]

Blackwood remained convivial in his dealings with Salmon and his successor, Hilton Brown, but it still irked beneath the surface. Brown asked Blackwood to come in and rehearse his next story, 'Violence', which Blackwood needed to trim from twenty minutes to fifteen. Blackwood declined. He disliked rehearsing anyway, especially on the same day, because it removed the spontaneity from the performance, but he disliked it all the more when this time commitment was supposed to be covered by the smaller fee. 'I've done a lot of "hard labour" with this tale, more than any other two tales combined, and – well, I think I've done enough to earn my little fee,' he told Brown.[10] Without Watt's to act for him, and after the hassle of the Marion Cothren and Elkin affairs, Blackwood was at last stamping his authority. Blackwood's point struck home. He seldom rehearsed another radio talk.

Nevertheless, all went quiet for a while. Blackwood did not broadcast another story for almost a year. When Edward Sackville-West asked Blackwood if he would take part in a programme of short readings in April or May 1942 Blackwood politely declined. It was not worth the effort.

Instead he concentrated on adapting his stories as plays and was delighted in October 1941 when Gielgud accepted *Told in a Mountain Cabin*. This was the first play Blackwood had written entirely on his own. It was loosely based on 'Revenge' and ran for thirty minutes. A climber finds himself lost in the Alps but a woman's voice guides him to safety and shelter in a cabin. There he learns the story of Saint Julie, a girl who had been killed fifty years before.

The play was not broadcast until 13 April 1942. It was produced by Lance Sieveking, who had tried to lure Blackwood to radio fifteen years earlier. Sieveking was a renowned pioneer radio producer, noted especially for his development of sound effects and atmosphere. Blackwood himself commented on the effectiveness of the sound of wind and running water.

Blackwood followed this with a play called *The Astronomer*, but that was rejected and is now lost.

It might have encouraged Blackwood if he had known that the American film producer Val Lewton (1904–1951) was giving serious thought to filming 'Ancient Sorceries'. Lewton had been appointed head of a unit at RKO studios to make low-budget horror films and one of the titles he was allocated as having public appeal was *Cat People*. Casting around for a plot to fit that title he latched on to 'Ancient Sorceries' and even got so far as to enquire about the availability of film rights. In the end it did not proceed as Lewton commissioned an original script from his screenwriter DeWitt Bodeen. The film, released in 1943, is justifiably one of the classics of horror cinema. The film critic and historian Kim Newman has commented that Bodeen may have used 'Ancient Sorceries' in the background to the film, making *Cat People* something of a sequel to Blackwood's story. The history of the heroine, Irena, and of her cursed people, could easily have come from 'Ancient Sorceries' and the character of the New York psychiatrist, Dr Judd (who reappears in another Lewton film, *The Seventh Victim*) has much in common with John Silence.

Like many of the English at the start of the war, Blackwood was optimistic that it would soon be over, but as the war dragged on, and especially during the Blitz, morale was severely damaged. Nevertheless, even in March 1942, we find Blackwood telling Vera Wainwright, albeit rather tongue-in-cheek, that an astrologer had told him the war would end in June.

Blackwood remained at Socknersh Manor for fourteen months. The grounds were to his liking and frequently he would take his axe and fell a few trees, continuing the practice of exhaustion and elation that he had started with Gurdjieff. There was plenty of space for walks – sometimes he would cross the fields to Kipling's old house at Bateman's, where he knew the tenant, Clement Woodbine Parish. Dr Nesfield's Nursing Home was also only a short car ride away.

However, in August 1942 Malcolm and Andrew Napier came back from Canada and Blackwood returned to London. He rented rooms at 3 North Drive in Highgate, near to where the Ainleys lived. There is a wonderful memory of Blackwood at this time from the children of Basil Sanderson (1894–1971), a partner of Lord Essendon in the Furness, Withy company. His children Alan, Murray and Pauline often stayed at the home of Elaine Ainley during the war, and met Blackwood there. Murray Sanderson remembers Blackwood teaching him tricks with pennies, which he would make move along his fingers. He also recalls Blackwood making a cracking sound with his nose. Pauline had a strong memory of Blackwood.

> The fact that I remember him so clearly is due to two things. First his considerable presence – he was quite unlike anybody else I came in contact with: tall, almost gaunt, permanently suntanned as though he'd stepped out of the African bush. Secondly, he was prepared to talk to the young, which few adults then did, and without condescension. I remember sitting wide-eyed and tongue-tied drinking in, as I thought, great draughts of Life.[11]

Even in his seventies, Blackwood sustained that rapport with children that he had displayed for at least forty years.

Blackwood tried two further stories with the BBC. A topical one, 'Black Market', was rejected and has not survived. The other was an adaptation of 'The Magic Mirror' as a twenty-minute story. Hilton Brown liked this and it was broadcast late on the evening of 13 December.

Over the next year Blackwood stopped submitting stories and proposals to the BBC. Blackwood was missing a number of his friends. Patrick was serving with the RAF in Assam. Ella Maillart was also in India, whilst Patsy Ainley was in the British Red Cross in Syria and the Middle East. He was able to keep in touch by sporadic correspondence, but Blackwood missed the direct contact. He was also losing other old friends. Edwyn Bevan died on 18 October 1943, Clara Huth Jackson on 12 January 1944 and Lord Essendon on 24 June 1944. With this dwindling circle of contacts Blackwood kept in touch as much as he could. In addition to the Ainleys at Highgate, there were the Nesfields at Sandhurst in Kent, the Vansittarts at Denham in Buckinghamshire, and the Masons at Socknersh Manor. He also kept in regular touch with Mary Borden, and visited Guy Cooper-Willis and Wilfrid Wilson in Sussex whenever he could.

On 3 March 1943 Blackwood attended the eightieth birthday celebration given for Arthur Machen at the Hungaria Restaurant in the Haymarket. Many of those present had contributed to a collection for the author, though Blackwood confessed he had been unable to. It was the first opportunity Blackwood had to meet Machen for many years, and there were plenty of other associates there – Max Beerbohm, Compton Mackenzie, John Masefield, A.E.W. Mason, George Bernard Shaw, Arthur Quiller-Couch, W.W. Jacobs and H.G. Wells. The somewhat younger Frank Baker (1908–82), who had helped with the organization, recalled seeing 'the wrinkled mummified visage of old Algernon Blackwood'.[12] Blackwood could probably have benefited from just such a collection. His own bank account survives from the mid 1940s showing that it seldom rose above £800 during the year, the equivalent today of about £17,000, and that was mostly because of dividend pay-outs from shares shrewdly invested years before. Andrew Napier recalled the following from the 1940s. Blackwood had stayed for a weekend houseparty and as he was leaving on the Monday morning, Blackwood made a great show of fumbling through pockets until he found ten shillings to give as a gratuity to the butler. Apparently the butler took one look at it and gave it back to Blackwood saying, 'I think this would help you more than it would me, sir'.

It may have been the anxiety about his finances that brought on a case of eczema. Apparently Dr Nesfield cured this by extracting some of Blackwood's blood and then immediately re-injecting it. 'It appears that blood thus injected immediately coagulates and in doing so automatically produces the toxin needed,' Blackwood explained.[13]

In September 1944 his place at Highgate became unsafe when a bomb blast caused ceiling damage which might have collapsed at any moment. Thereafter he slept in a basement room at a friend's empty house nearby but then the windows there were blown out by another blast and were boarded up.

Despite all this Blackwood continued to work on plays and stories for the BBC and managed to hit an active streak in 1944. This was probably encouraged by some hope over *The Starlight Express*. The actress Muriel Pratt was now working in the Features and Drama department. In May 1944 Blackwood sent her a copy of the script in the hope it might work for children's programmes. However, they rejected it instantly, the head of children's programmes calling the play 'complete lunacy'. Muriel Pratt decided that she would try to adapt the play for radio. Blackwood's view was that the original version 'should be scrapped as wholly useless'. Pratt undertook considerable revision, especially the ending, but unfortunately died in January 1945 before she could finalize it. Violet Pearn acquired the revision, had it typed up and then submitted it to the head of radio drama, Val Gielgud. She had already sent him the original version of the play early in 1939 but he had never commented upon it returning that to Pearn in January 1945. She sent him Pratt's version a few weeks later. She thought it was a great improvement and Blackwood was also impressed, but Gielgud again rejected it as unworkable.

Blackwood approached J.B. Priestley for his advice. Priestley, in his usual blunt Yorkshire manner, told Blackwood that the original novel did not lend itself to stage adaptation but might work as an animated film. Blackwood would not let it rest. He sent a synopsis of the play along with a copy of *A Prisoner in Fairyland* to Mary Hayley Bell, the wife of actor John Mills, whom Blackwood knew via the Vansittarts (both lived at Denham). She thought it was 'too good for a picture. It is not commercial enough unless people were prepared to make it in a child's fantasy picture, which would be wonderful. What a pity, because it is so beautiful.'[14]

In the meantime he at last had some success with his own material. In the summer of 1944 he sold the BBC a fifteen-minute play, *Running*

Wolf, based on his story of that name and a new story, 'The Castlebridge Cat'. Both were broadcast in October. 'The Castlebridge Cat' is a macabre little tale, not unlike Poe's 'The Black Cat'. A travelling salesman returns to a town where six months earlier he had murdered a blackmailer, but he is betrayed by the victim's cat. It was broadcast in *The Wednesday Story* series at 10.15 in the evening of 25 October. It was the only broadcast that story had, and it has never been published.

Blackwood was invited to the rehearsal and recording of 'Running Wolf' on 12 October 1944. Producer Leslie Stokes reworked Blackwood's script a little to avoid too many scene changes but otherwise the play was as per Blackwood's script. At last Blackwood was feeling comfortable with composing radio plays. He sold two more in quick succession. In 'It's About Time', a physicist, engaged on secret war work into two-dimensional time, is contacted by a man whose life he had saved forty years ago and who has travelled out of time to save the Professor. The second play was 'In a Glass Darkly', adapted from 'The Magic Mirror'. This led to a major problem when it went out live on 23 July 1945. It was a twenty-minute play but, on the day, producer, Hugh Stewart, tried to squeeze it into a fifteen-minute slot with disastrous results. 'It ruined the play,' Blackwood complained to Leslie Stokes, then head of drama, 'and has done me a lot of harm which I'm still having to live down'.[15] Blackwood sought reassurance that if the play were repeated it would be restored to its proper length. Although no reassurance was given, thankfully when the play was reproduced, in January 1949, it ran the full twenty minutes.

The winter of 1944/45 was intensely cold and it was difficult to get adequate heating in Blackwood's flat because of the coal shortage and resultant low gas pressure. He took to riding up and down in the Underground between Archway and Waterloo where he said it was as warm as toast. He also had to sleep at night clutching hot water bottles, although the rubber on one of these had almost perished, causing him and the sheets to be covered in an alarming red stain. Worse was yet to come:

> Recently I woke up feeling something pricking against my bare back, something hard. Thought it was some insect biting me but didn't dare lift the pressure lest I got a bad nip. A frog? A stagbeetle? Finally I HAD to leap out of bed and, onto the floor dropped my – dentures! Bitten by my own teeth![16]

Increasingly his letters became optimistic. Victory seemed but weeks away and snowdrops and crocuses were out in the London parks. When VE day came on 8 May 1945, Blackwood doubtless joined in the celebrations in London like everyone else, though he doesn't record them. Soon after, he attended the wedding of Lady Ava Baird, the daughter of his niece Ettie Stonehaven. The reception was held at Claridge's on 21 June 1945. Wartime restrictions, which were still in force, meant they had been unable to acquire any champagne and it was cider all round.

Nevertheless, Blackwood had good grounds to celebrate. His most famous days were around the corner.

II

At the end of June, Blackwood moved into new rooms at 15 Sheffield Terrace. This was the first settled home Blackwood had had in London since he had left Moore Street in Chelsea thirty-six years earlier. It wasn't the most central of locations, but it was close to Kensington Gardens and Hyde Park, through which he could stroll on his way to Broadcasting House.

It was a sad day when Henry Ainley died on 31 October. He had had a stroke in his sleep in July and had been left severely incapacitated. Speech was difficult. Blackwood visited him as often as he could but was very saddened to see his old friend's plight. In particular Blackwood missed Ainley's hearty laugh. There was a memorial service at St Martin's-in-the-Fields in London on 13 November 1945 at which Laurence Olivier and Sir Lewis Casson read the lessons. It was yet another chapter closing in Blackwood's life.

Blackwood was looking forward to seeing his nephew for the first time in nearly four years. He was due home on leave in the autumn. It came as something of a surprise when Patrick announced his impending marriage to divorcée Ellen Hammond, whom he had met in the air force. They were married at Poole registry office on 19 November 1945, with Blackwood as one of the witnesses. Fortunately, Patrick and Ellen returned to London, settling in a flat in Belgrave Square.

In November 1944 Blackwood had received a letter from the American author August Derleth (1909–71), who ran his own small publishing business called Arkham House. He enquired whether Blackwood had any unpublished stories. Blackwood asked Watt's to send Derleth both 'The Doll' and 'The Trod', adding:

Since the war I have had no time for writing; possibly, too, there has been so much horror in life that my imagination turned away from adding to it. At any rate, inspiration, even if time had allowed, did not prompt that way.[17]

Derleth asked whether there might be further material not collected in book form. Unaccountably, Blackwood responded that there was not, even though there were several stories, not in his collections, that would have fitted the bill, especially 'The Man-Eater' and 'At a Mayfair Luncheon'. Derleth ran with the original two stories. It took him time to finance his publishing operation, so it was not until March 1946 that he was able to issue a 3,000-copy edition of *The Doll and One Other*. Although only a slim volume, Blackwood was very pleased with it.

The book itself delights me – print, margins, general set up and all, and I am particularly pleased with Robert Clyne's jacket, with its restraint and fine taste especially; it strikes just the right note.[18]

He was also grateful of Derleth's generosity in sending him extra copies of the book and in the payment for and copy of the anthology *Who Knocks?*, in which was reprinted Blackwood's 'Running Wolf'. He told Derleth that he felt 'you treat your authors very handsomely'.

Derleth was the champion of many writers of weird fiction, most especially H.P. Lovecraft, whose works he had rescued from the magazines and published in hardcover collections and anthologies. Derleth was keen to know Blackwood's reaction to Lovecraft and to other writers. Blackwood was widely read in supernatural fiction and he remarked to Derleth that authors like A.E. Coppard, H. Russell Wakefield, Henry S. Whitehead, May Sinclair and Mary Wilkins Freeman never fail to please. But he was less convinced about Lovecraft.

Sheer horror, without this sense of wonder – wonder about the universe, I mean, 'cosmic wonder', to use a dreadful phrase – never quite stirs me. I have asked myself why Lovecraft often fails in my case, since he writes so well and all the raw stuff of true horror is at his command. Is it that he often overdoes the piling up of material horror without relating it to bigger issues – cosmic, spiritual, literally 'unearthly'? Something in me turns instinctively from decay, the grave, a glut of too material detail. 'The Turn of the Screw', I feel, points the right way.[19]

Lovecraft, who had died in 1937, believed that Blackwood was among the greatest writers of supernatural fiction and that 'The Willows' was one of the two best short supernatural stories ever written. Lovecraft's shift to more cosmic horror in the early 1930s owed much to Blackwood's work. One of Lovecraft's most popular stories, 'The Colour out of Space', contains elements redolent of 'The Willows'.

By this time Blackwood's radio profile was growing rapidly. Geoffrey Dearmer, the head of children's programmes, had adapted Blackwood's 'Mr Bunciman at the Zoo' for *Children's Hour* in July 1945, starring Norman Shelley, who was a considerable presence in children's radio because of his roles in *Winnie the Pooh* and *Toytown*. The BBC's schools programmes had run a two-part adaptation of *Dudley and Gilderoy* in September 1945 and just before Christmas there was a broadcast of Blackwood's own play 'Chinese Magic' in the series *Mystery and Imagination*. Blackwood was puzzled by the broadcast of 'Confession' in the same series on 17 January 1946. Blackwood had submitted his own dramatization of this story in April 1945 under the title 'Soldier in the Fog'. It had been accepted and paid for, but he had heard no more until the broadcast when he discovered the play had been attributed to Robert G. Newton. In fact the BBC had commissioned Newton to adapt Blackwood's original story without realizing they had already accepted Blackwood's play!

In addition to his plays, Blackwood was in demand for his stories and talks and was a popular guest on chat shows and magazine programmes. He was invited on to *At the Bowler Hat* (a successor to *At the Black Dog*) on 16 October 1945 when he chatted away about his days as a reporter in New York and told a humorous ghost story. He was involved in a Christmas special called *Five Men*, where five travellers were invited to tell of their adventures. Blackwood's story, which came at the end, was 'The Curate and the Stockbroker' which was a blend of experience and fiction.

Blackwood was to give another talk in February 1946 but had a bad cold and lost his voice. But after that his radio appearances steadily increased. In the rest of 1946 he made five further broadcasts, in 1947 three (though because of repeats this amounted to six), plus a new play, *The Secret Society*[20]. In 1948 these appearances increased to fifteen. They included a short series of five- or six-minute 'strange stories' which he broadcast late each night during a week in mid May, and included his popular anecdotes 'Texas Farm Disappearance', 'The

Holy Man', 'Pistol Against a Ghost', 'Japanese Literary Cocktail' and 'The Curate and the Stockbroker'. He was a guest on various literary programmes such as *Books and Authors* (where he talked on the subject of 'gooseflesh' and what made him shiver) and *New Books and Old* (where he spoke about one of his favourite books, *Confessions of an Opium-Eater* by Thomas de Quincey and reviewed Lewis Spence's new book, *The Fairy Tradition in Britain*). He was also involved in a panel game called *Stump the Story-Tellers* where guests are given a box containing four objects and they have four minutes in which to improvise a story featuring all four objects.

Throughout all of this Blackwood had tried to return to his old routine. On 31 October 1946 he flew out to Geneva from Northolt airport. Previously he had always taken the boat and train. This is the first time he had flown, and may be why he made his will just before he left. He moved on to Montreux, then Saanenmoser for the New Year, skiing for the first time since 1939. He noticed that much had changed. So much had become standardized – the outfits, the skiing – 'a true herd performance' he called it. 'The people are dull and colourless and the old cheery Baerengraben bar at the Sports is empty at night.'[21] He felt the life and gaiety had gone. Also, although he could still ski, a knee problem hampered his manoeuvres and knocked his confidence. Now approaching seventy-eight he realized he could not do all he once could. 'Old age is grim,' he told Patsy. Still, he generally enjoyed himself – 'Anything's better than freezing England,' – but when money ran out he returned, on 3 March 1947.

It was now he began his programme of writing for radio. Blackwood was determined to convert his favourite story, 'The Willows', into a play. He sent a draft to producer Felix Felton in October 1947 who liked it, and agreed to collaborate with Blackwood on a final version. He thought it might work as a double-bill with 'Chinese Magic' on the new BBC radio station, the Third Programme. However, soon afterwards Felton left the BBC and the play was shelved.

Probably the hardest radio broadcast Blackwood ever did involved, ironically, children. On 9 November 1948 he was invited to the studios in Swansea to record a discussion programme *Speak for Yourselves*. Each week in this series a guest met twelve young people who asked him questions about his life. The children were acutely perceptive and asked Blackwood uncomfortable questions about why he had left home and whether he had acted responsibly. He was asked point-blank what had he 'put into life', a question he found hard to answer on the spur of the moment. The lack of an answer caused the children to think that Blackwood had been selfish and had wasted his life. He found it difficult to explain to them his concept of beauty and wonder in Nature and to make them understand that he preferred to live life without any possessions. Blackwood admitted that if he had his life over again he would still do all that he had done. After the broadcast he was exhausted. Douglas Allen, who chaired the discussion, said that it had prompted a fascinating discussion and was excellent radio.

During 1947 Blackwood finished what would be his last published weird story, 'Roman Remains', which he sent to August Derleth. The chief character is a young airman, on sick leave from India, while the character's elder brother is a 'retired surgeon', suggestive of Patrick and his stepfather, James Eadie. Set in a remote valley on the Welsh border it tells of the vision of a satyr and its influence upon a young lady. It contains some of the atmosphere of Blackwood's old stories and is fair as a swan song. Derleth had originally enquired after anything he might publish in his little magazine *The Arkham Sampler*, but realizing that Blackwood's story should have a wider readership he passed it on to *Weird Tales*, where it appeared in the March 1948 issue.

It was in September 1947 that Blackwood was contacted by producer Robert Barr. Television broadcasting had resumed after the war and Cecil Madden was back in charge of programming. Madden thought that something special was needed for Hallowe'en and he asked Barr to contact Blackwood and see if he would tell a story on television. Barr and Blackwood met at Broadcasting House and Barr knew instantly that here was a man destined for television. 'What a wonderful face,' Barr told me. 'Lined like a walnut. And the eyes of a storyteller, eyes that held you while the story was woven.'[22]

Blackwood suggested telling his favourite anecdote of the Curate and the Stockbroker. Barr thought this would work well and was struck by an idea. At the end of Blackwood's story the stockbroker disappears. Suppose they could perform a camera trick and make Blackwood disappear? Today that trick is simplicity itself, but in 1947 it required much planning. Barr acquired two identical chairs so that at the end of Blackwood's broadcast they could 'dissolve' from one chair to the other, giving the impression that he had vanished, even though his voice could still be heard saying: 'How simple. How wonderful.'

The broadcast was superb. Blackwood was in complete control. He needed no script. He knew the story from a thousand tellings. He greeted his viewers at the start, sitting back comfortably in his chair, reading a book. He laid the book aside, took off his glasses and began his tale. As the story proceeded so he slowly, almost imperceptibly, leaned forward, moving that weatherbeaten, lined, feature-full face nearer the camera. Viewers found themselves also leaning forward[23]. Then, at the climax and before their very eyes, Blackwood faded away. The result was electric. Even staff at the BBC wondered what had happened. The switchboard was jammed with callers saying they had seen Mr Blackwood disappear.

It was one of the most memorable moments in early television. Everyone thought it was excellent. In fact the only person who was not satisfied was Blackwood himself. He thought his performance was poor. It lacked the spontaneity he preferred, because they had had to do several rehearsals to get the camera positions correct. By the time they got to the performance Blackwood had lost that edge. The television hierarchy were keen for Blackwood to do a regular series. Blackwood was less sure. He agreed to do one more on 24 January – 'The Magic Mirror'. This time there were no camera tricks – he just told the story straight. Once again the reception was excellent and Robert Barr was very satisfied. But not Blackwood. The rehearsals stifled his technique. 'Under television conditions my natural story-telling instinct just doesn't work. The result is unsatisfactory for your audience; it is also bad for me.'[24]

He asked Barr to cancel his contract – the most lucrative he had ever had. He was to be paid fifteen guineas for writing each story and a further fifteen guineas for reading it. They had planned to do six stories, making a total payment of £189 (equal today to around £3,500).

Blackwood's reaction called for a drastic response. The head of BBC Television, Cecil McGivern, contacted Blackwood in Switzerland, where he had escaped for a month, and pleaded with Blackwood to return. He agreed to comply with any of Blackwood's demands. It transpired that another problem was Blackwood's dressing-room, where he was made up before the broadcast. It was small, dark and dismal, and in no way inspired him in his storytelling mood. Blackwood saw no reason for make up. When they first encountered him he was so bronzed by the sun that the make-up girls were convinced he had rubbed something on and tried to scrape it off. Blackwood admonished them saying it had taken him eighty years to acquire a visage like that and there was nothing they could do with it in ten minutes. McGivern agreed that Blackwood need do no rehearsal, provided he arrived in time for a lighting and sound test, and a quick dusting by the make-up people so that his bald pate did not reflect the studio lights.

Whether it was the spring air in Switzerland or whether he was talked into it by his friends – who now included the actress Jill Balcon and her father, the film director Michael Balcon – Blackwood agreed. The next talk, 'The Chinese Picture', went out on 6 March 1948 followed by 'Lock Your Door' on 27 March. Thereafter they followed roughly every six to eight weeks. Blackwood was not the only author to broadcast in the *Saturday Night Story* slot, but he was the featured star. Others included his two friends Compton Mackenzie and Lord Dunsany.

Robert Barr, and his successor Stephen McCormack (who took over producing the series in May 1949), used to meet Blackwood at the Savile Club about a week before the broadcast to discuss story ideas. Blackwood was invariably ensconced in one of the smaller side rooms with one or two of his friends, usually Compton Mackenzie or the broadcaster Gilbert Harding, both of whom were also great raconteurs. Sometimes these meetings would go on far longer than planned because the three men would keep swapping stories and Barr or McCormack could not get a word in. When they did settle on a story the producer would try to tie Blackwood down to a closing line, so that they knew when to fade the camera. Blackwood, though, never told a story the same way twice. Although he gave them a final line, come the day, he'd invariably end the story differently, leaving the producer befuddled. But they could never get angry with him. Both Barr and McCormack agreed what an absolutely charming person Blackwood was. Never affected or self-opinionated. Always caring and courteous. Always a gentleman.

Only once did Robert Barr panic. It had become Blackwood's habit to get the Underground to Wood Green and walk the mile-and-a-half up the hill to the studio. One night, with an impenetrable pea-souper fog, he was late. Robert Barr stood on the steps of Alexandra Palace waiting anxiously.

With only minutes before the broadcast, Blackwood's tall figure loomed out of the fog. Barr rushed upstairs to the studio, but Blackwood urged him to be calm. 'Don't worry, old boy,' he said. 'Coming up the hill I have been rehearsing the story by myself, with the fog as the audience.' He went on the air moments later and was word perfect. If ever there was a person suited to storytelling on television it was Algernon Blackwood. He was the consummate storyteller. And everyone knew it. Critics were united in their praise. Blackwood's postbag overflowed. There were plans to reissue several of his books and produce an omnibus volume of his best stories[25].

In December 1948 Blackwood was astonished to receive notification from the Prime Minister's Office that he was going to be awarded the CBE – Commander of the British Empire – medal in the New Year's Honours list. Blackwood was delighted to accept and was proud of the medal, though he noted in his diary: 'Odd to be a Commander of an Empire which the bestowers of the honour have destroyed!' The medal ceremony was held at Buckingham Palace on 1 March. Blackwood had to hire a top hat and tails. It was all rather expensive and to save money Blackwood used an old top hat with no top.

Then on 1 April 1949, Blackwood was awarded the Television Society Medal, then television's equivalent of the Oscar, as the outstanding television personality of 1948. In his presentation speech at the TV Society's luncheon at the Waldorf Hotel, Sir Robert Renwick said that Blackwood's performance was 'unique, for he cannot rely on scenery or stage settings, effects or supporting cast. He must hold our interest by the sheer exercise of his own personality and ability.' Blackwood merely rose, accepted his award from Lady Fleming, presented her with a bouquet of flowers and sat down again. For once in his life Blackwood was speechless.

20

A Very Wonderful Adventure (1949–51)

Although broadcasting dominated Blackwood's final years, and it is how many people remember him, it was not all that he was doing. Indeed the fame of his radio and television work opened other doors, so that in his final years he was busier than he had been for a long while. He was asked to be president of various organizations – most of which he declined, although he did become president of the Writer's Guild for a year in 1949. He also joined the Ghost Club and attended their dinners. His books were being reissued, stories were reprinted in magazines and anthologies, and he was in demand for interviews or talks.

Although never wealthy, these activities brought in more money than usual. His London bank account, which had averaged around £700 or so in 1946, had increased to around £2,000 by 1949 (now about £37,000). He also had a Swiss bank account. He still did not want any possessions and hated it if anyone gave him a present. One of his television contacts remembered a day when Blackwood was presented with a clock, and he did not know what to do with it. Cecil Madden believed that by the end of his life Blackwood had fine-tuned his possessions down to a change of clothes, his hold all, his pyjamas and his typewriter. With no fear of losing anything, plus some financial comfort, and being a celebrity, Blackwood's final years were happy ones.

Generally he was in good physical shape for someone approaching eighty, though his body was winding down. The stress of all his recent engagements had given him high blood pressure and brought back his eczema, and he was also suffering from prostate trouble. He recorded in June 1948 an odd experience – perhaps all the worse for having been out celebrating and drinking the night before – when he woke during the night in a friend's flat but was convinced he was in his London flat. Of course, nothing matched and for at least ten minutes he was in total confusion. He wondered afterwards whether he had suffered temporary amnesia or perhaps a delusion. Although he regarded the incident as trivial, he did wonder if it was the start of a 'decay of the mind' as he called it.

But it did not stop his regular circuit of visiting friends, plus his radio and television broadcasts. He returned to the Alps for a month from the end of January 1949, though noticed how much his body was slowing down. It depressed him slightly, but did not stop him. While in Montreux he met a young student, Peter Penzoldt (1925– 69), who was researching for his Ph.D. thesis at the University of Geneva on 'The Supernatural in Fiction'. Penzoldt had written to Blackwood the previous November and struck up an interesting correspondence. Blackwood admired the young student, speaking of his 'deep intelligence'. Penzoldt was the first to produce a perceptive analytical insight into Blackwood's fiction. Blackwood's work had been subject to several assessments but few critical analyses. Apart from the references in Dorothy Scarborough's *The Supernatural in Modern English Fiction* (1917), the only scholar to consider Blackwood in any detail had been Stuart Gilbert. In 'Algernon Blackwood: Novelist and Mystic'[1], Gilbert had considered the evolution of the literature of the 'supernormal' and showed how Blackwood was pre-eminent in its development. But he concentrated his analysis on *The Centaur* and *The Human Chord*. Writing at the end of Blackwood's career Penzoldt was able to consider his entire output in the context of the key authors and themes of weird fiction. He devoted a full chapter to Blackwood's works. Penzoldt's analysis was perceptive. Whereas too many critics pigeon-holed him as a 'mystic' or 'ghost-story writer'[2], Penzoldt states clearly that Blackwood does not fit into the mould of the typical horror or ghost story writer, *à la* Edgar Allan Poe or M.R. James. 'The main part of his work shows that in every respect he refused to tread the beaten path. It is wholly impossible to place him in any school.'[3] He adds: 'Blackwood is probably, both as a personality and as a writer, the most impressive figure among contemporary writers of supernatural short stories.'

Blackwood had an opportunity to check the draft of Penzoldt's chapter, and he also recommended the final thesis to his publisher Peter Nevill. Thus it was thanks to Blackwood that the book was published in England in 1952, too late for Blackwood to see it. Penzoldt dedicated the book 'with deep admiration and gratitude to Algernon Blackwood, the greatest of them all'.

Apart from his radio and television work, 1949 featured three or four significant projects.

The first and perhaps the strangest was that Blackwood made a series of films. Envious at the success of Blackwood's *Saturday Night Story* series, and believing that films could do better, Twentieth Century-Fox charged the film director Anthony Gilkison, of their short-film company Rayant Pictures, to make a film with Blackwood suitable for a 1,000-seater cinema. Gilkison contacted Blackwood and they discussed it over lunch at the Savile Club on 28 April. The original suggestion was to do perhaps four films – it was later extended to six – each of about fifteen to twenty minutes. Blackwood was to forward some suggested stories and they hoped to start filming in about three weeks. He was assured that it should not take up more than two days of his time, in total.

Perhaps the passage of time stifled their enthusiasm but over two months passed before Rayant agreed that they would film one story, 'Confession', as a pilot, and if that went well, would film the series. Filming began at Wembley Studios on 14 July after some delay while Rayant resolved several technical problems. Gilkison explained:

> To keep the Blackwood films moving I had to employ no less than four cameras at a time – something quite unheard-of except for the chariot race in *Ben-Hur* or similar epics. It caused electrical and synchronization problems as well. I think we were still photographing sound then and sending it off to be developed![4]

On the first day they filmed only three minutes of usable film. They had to keep stopping for blown fuses, reloading film or loss of synchron-ization. Blackwood was not used to the idea of several cameras and wanted to stroll around talking, so they had to stop him wandering off camera. This stop-start restriction severely limited his spontaneity and he found himself becoming confused and having to start over again.

When they looked at the rushes the next day Gilkison thought they were 'not too bad', but Blackwood thought them mechanical and colourless. The second day's shooting was not much better and it left Blackwood weary and feeling stupid. They eventually wrapped it up on the third day. It was decided the film might suit a Christmas audience, and it was trialled around a few cinemas at the end of November. Blackwood saw it at the Granada cinema, Greenford, on 3 December, and regarded it as 'mediocre – but no flop'. The manager reported that the audience was 'spell-bound', and the trade paper, *The Cinema* called it 'first rate', saying it was 'an imaginative and unusual offering, well out of the rut'. Twentieth Century-Fox were satisfied and gave their approval to the remaining films. Blackwood, who had been exhausted after making just one, had to face the prospect of another five.

It was the first week in January before they agreed on which stories to use. By then Blackwood was heading off to Switzerland. They scheduled shooting upon his return and began on Monday, 20 February. They had planned to shoot one story a day and finish within that week. This time they used three cameras and extended the single shots from three minutes to five or six. This helped Blackwood's rhythm but still left him uneasy. Stephen McCormack met Blackwood on the Wednesday evening to talk about the next television film and found him nervous and unsure. The films weren't finished that week, and Blackwood had to gear himself up for a TV *Saturday Night Story* that weekend.

The films were eventually finished on 6 March. Blackwood was not happy with the results. The five stories filmed were 'The Reformation of St Jules', 'The Rendezvous' (based on 'Keeping His Promise', 'The Dress Rehearsal', 'Lock Your Door' and 'Two of a Kind' (based on 'The Survivors'). Only two of these have survived, 'St Jules' and 'Lock Your Door'. They show a nervous, uncertain Blackwood who occasionally gets into his stride but is clearly fazed by a need to reshoot or stop filming, when he becomes hesitant and repetitive. Blackwood had not learned from a script but simply told the story straight as he would at a party. He treated the cameramen as his audience. The films are clearly not Blackwood at his best, but the reviews all found favour with the strength of Blackwood's personality as a storyteller, even if the stories themselves may have been weak. They were released roughly one a month between May and September 1950.

II

During 1949 Blackwood was involved in a psychic research project. On 15 June 1948 the BBC had broadcast a programme about spiritualism. Harold Vigurs of the Marylebone Spiritualist Association spoke in favour of the subject whilst Eric Dingwall gave the scientific view and Canon Marcus Knight the church's view. Following that meeting a panel was set up under the chairmanship of Lord Amwell, and sponsored by *The People* newspaper, to investigate mediums. Vigurs selected the mediums. Also on the panel were Sir John Anderson, Dr Laurence Bendit, Mrs Charlotte Haldane (wife of the philosopher J.B.S. Haldane), the author L.A.G. Strong (a close friend of Blackwood's), the Reverend Dr Leslie Weatherhead and Canon Marcus Knight. There was also an unnamed Harley Street surgeon. The panel could co-opt other experts into the investigation if they wished and Blackwood was one of these. The only séance where Blackwood is mentioned in the final report was that held by Annie Brittain on 5 October 1949. Blackwood appears briefly in the write-up of the séance where the medium appears to have contacted his aunt Lucy and her husband Charles, though it is not convincing.

The Reverend Dr Marcus Knight later recalled that Blackwood did not attend many séances but usually joined in the overall assessment. He had the impression that Blackwood was not over-enthusiastic. Blackwood's diary comments support that. He was at a séance given by Mrs Powell at 42 Russell Square on 15 October, which he noted as 'Drivel! *Und wie!* [And How!]', and at one given by Vigurs himself on 25 October at the same address, which he calls 'usual rubbish'. He added 'Declined to go on council'. Clearly even a scientific investigation such as this did nothing to change Blackwood's life-long antipathy towards spiritualism. He commented to his nephew: '*The People* investigation is childish. Well out of it. Fuss they all make of me v. amusing. Almost think I was Conan Doyle. Fills odd moments anyhow.'[5] The Panel's full report was eventually published as *Into the Unknown* in September 1950, after a series of extracts had been run in *The People*.

In the meantime Blackwood continued to hold out hopes for *The Starlight Express*. In January 1948 A.P. Watt had advised Blackwood that CBS were considering making a television film out of 'Ancient Sorceries'. This dragged on and eventually came to nothing, but while the option was open Blackwood heard from dramatist Basil Ashmore who also wanted to adapt the same story. Blackwood arranged to meet Ashmore, in March or April 1948. During their discussion Blackwood learned that Ashmore called himself a 'play doctor'. He had a skill for revising plays that had not worked or were incomplete. Blackwood told Ashmore to forget the script for 'Ancient Sorceries' and to consider what could be done to salvage *The Starlight Express*. Ashmore agreed. Unfortunately, Ashmore was in the habit of overcommitting himself. He was already working on a new libretto to Mozart's *Il Seraglio* for Glyndebourne and had at least three other plays in the works plus a new production of Bizet's *Carmen* with the Carl Rosa Opera Company. Months passed and Blackwood heard nothing. Growing frustrated he checked with Ashmore only to find he had been taken ill. In the end Ashmore was not able to progress *Starlight* any further. It was a shame. He would have been ideal for it, not only because of his skill at new adaptations but also because he was fascinated in folklore and fairy tales. When I spoke to Ashmore in 1985 he was still sorry he had not been able to complete the project as he knew how anxious Blackwood was to get the play back into production.

Ashmore returned the papers to Blackwood but recommended television playwright Nancy Bush, who might be able to help. Blackwood contacted her in November 1950, and she got to work very quickly. She had an outline ready by December and a draft script completed by February 1951, with which Blackwood was delighted. The idea was to discuss it with the BBC but once again nothing came of it. This was Blackwood's last opportunity to give *Starlight Express* a new lease of life. His continued faith in the project for over thirty years shows that even to his final days he so wanted to have a successful stage play conveying his message of beauty and universal harmony.[6]

It was during 1950 that Blackwood completed his last published story. Late in 1949 Cynthia Asquith asked Blackwood for a new children's story and he completed 'Eliza among the Chimney Sweeps'. To Blackwood sweeps, like tramps, are outsiders who explore worlds beyond our own and belong to their own secret society, which Eliza wants to join. I suspect Eliza is Elizabeth Belloc as she always wanted to be something different. Although she was now in her late forties, Blackwood was probably remembering back to some episode in her young life. Kingsland, where she grew up, had many fire places and had a regular visit from the sweep. The story appeared in *The Children's Ship* published in November 1950, along with a photograph of Blackwood as a very young child, with long hair and wearing a dress. Over seventy-five years spanned the photograph and the story.

III

So we arrive at 25 September 1949, when Blackwood walked to Broadcasting House to give his talk 'On Being Eighty'. His conclusion to that talk says much about his attitude to life.

> So what about those seductive Torches that flickered out or went on burning today? So wonderful and inspiring while they blazed. Am I still lighting new ones? Of course I am. Am I despondent about the burnt-out ones? Not a bit. I would like to go on living till 100 and beyond it. Life is far too short. The machine can wear out – though we seem on the way to halt that nonsense – but the spirit . . . never.[7]

Blackwood never stopped enjoying life. Never tired of the fascination of meeting people and learning new things. He never ran out of ideas for radio talks even after he had stopped broadcasting new stories. Several of these talks revealed what he most liked doing as he grew older. He would sit in a local café or public bar, perhaps with a sandwich and a glass of beer, and see whose eye he could catch. On one occasion he started talking to his window cleaner about the days of the week and how they might be perceived pictorially or in colours. This led to his radio talk, 'Is Monday Black and the Rest of the Week Uphill?'[8]

In another radio talk – in fact his last – 'The Human Touch', broadcast on 12 September 1950, he talks about meeting people in a pub and responding to their questions about his television broadcasts. He said that the secret was to be natural. On one broadcast he went to light a cigarette and the lighter did not work. He only just resisted in time the temptation to lean right at the camera and ask the viewer for a light – that shows how natural and relaxed he was. The difference between his radio and television was concentration. On the radio he had a script handy in case he ever dried up and also a clock he could check for time. On television he had no script, it was all memorized, and the camera would catch his eye wandering to the clock. The producer, Stephen McCormack, had a large clock face put right by the side of the camera with the exact time slot (fifteen or twenty minutes) marked so he could see it without taking his eyes off the camera. One night he overran because he had been thrown by the previous programme overrunning and being told he had to cut ninety seconds. After the broadcast McCormack asked why he hadn't kept his eye on the clock. 'What clock?' Blackwood responded – so deep was his concentration.

Blackwood continued his television talks even after he had stopped radio broadcasts. But he was becoming frail. When the BBC asked him to repeat his Halloween story at the end of October 1950, he found it hard to be spontaneous. His memory troubled him and he frequently hesitated or repeated himself. As a consequence they pre-recorded the programme, a rarity in those days.

Unfortunately, soon after that he had a fall, almost certainly occasioned by a burst blood vessel due to high blood pressure – it may even have been a minor stroke. He spent much of December at the Nesfields's nursing home in Kent[9] and was well enough to travel to Switzerland in January for a couple of months skiing. His balance, though, was seriously impaired and he found it difficult to do much walking let alone ski-ing. The fact that he could do *any*, though, says something about his willpower. While he was in Switzerland the *London Mystery Magazine* published his radio talk 'Spiders and Such' (which had been broadcast on 10 June 1950) as 'Along Came a Spider'[10]. It was his last new piece of work to appear in print, and told of his fear of spiders.

The convalescence worked to some degree. He was keen to do more television but, as he told Robert Barr in May 1951:

> I can't trust myself yet quite, for it was a stroke I had and memory is affected. There was 'delayed action', which made my mind go haywire for a time. (I don't want to advertize this, of course.) I'm now improving rapidly and hope soon to be quite normal.[11]

Blackwood was especially cheered in September to receive a letter from an aspiring young writer, Ron Hall (1929–85) who was so enthusiastic about Blackwood's works, that Blackwood regarded the letter as 'the most encouraging one I have ever received'.[12] Hall had discovered Blackwood via the writings of Henry Miller (1891–1980), best known for *Tropic of Cancer* (1934) and *Tropic of Capricorn* (1939). Hall had been in correspondence with Miller, and was also preparing for publication in Britain Miller's *The Books in My Life*, where Miller singles out Blackwood's *The Bright Messenger* as 'the most extraordinary novel on psychoanalysis, one which dwarfs the subject'.[13]

Later that same month, on 29 September, Blackwood was delighted to accept the invitation to be a Fellow of the Royal Society of Literature, which he regarded as a singular honour. He even paid his first year's subscription, further evidence that he had every intention of fighting back to good health.

In August Blackwood told Robert Barr that he felt up to doing a new television broadcast, especially as Barr had suggested they could pre-record it. They hoped to do another Hallowe'en programme and Blackwood suggested a talk on what had first made him interested in ghosts. Barr was determined that everything could be done to make this recording as convenient to Blackwood as possible. In his instructions to the film unit he emphasized this point, adding, 'He is an old man and a very valuable television personality'. It was recorded on 6 October and broadcast on the 13th, though had to be severely edited as some footage was lost. It is the only recording of Blackwood's television broadcasts that survives. Despite his frailty Blackwood's voice comes over strongly and there is no suggestion of poor memory or incapacity. There are slight hesitations, but his personality overrides everything else and you are soon hooked by his story. It shows that if he could have this effect at eighty-two, after a stroke, just how magical and gripping he had been at the height of his powers.

Blackwood managed to get around London for a short while. On 9 October he met Gerald Gough, the librarian of the Society of the Inner Light. This had been one of the many off-shoot societies of the Golden Dawn which proliferated after the First World War. Blackwood had never joined. It was most famous for Dion Fortune (1890–1946). Fortune, whose real name was Violet Firth, regarded Blackwood as the pre-eminent writer of occult fiction. Gough found the meeting rather depressing as he saw Blackwood as a man who had been constantly seeking but had never found what he really desired. Apparently Blackwood told Gough that he had lost his faith, a comment that troubled Gough for many years and had an interesting aftermath.

A few days later Blackwood had another stroke. He believed that he had overstretched himself and had had a relapse. When, at the end of October, Robert Barr enquired whether he was ready for another television broadcast, Blackwood could only write in a shaky hand to say that he was confined to bed and in danger of falling. Two weeks later, when Blackwood wrote to Ella Maillart, he said that he was no longer safe to be left alone and needed a nurse day and night to look after him. He was too frail to write his letter to her and needed someone else to type it, and he could not even sign it. But he told her, 'I shall soon recover again; meanwhile I send you my warm love and encouragement'.[14]

Patsy Ainley visited him as regularly as she could, trying to stop him smoking in bed for fear of causing a fire. The landlady at his lodgings in Sheffield Terrace also saw him as often as possible, checking on his every need. Though frail Blackwood remained cheerful, if frustrated at his incapacity.

On the morning of Monday, 10 December 1951, Patsy Ainley called again to see how Uncle Paul was doing. She found the landlady in great distress saying that he did not look at all well. It did not take Patsy long to realize that Blackwood had died. The death certificate gave the primary cause of death as cerebral thrombosis with arteriosclerosis as contributory.

Blackwood was cremated at Golders Green crematorium and, a few weeks later, his nephew took his ashes to Saanenmoser and scattered them over the mountains that he had loved for over forty years. Blackwood had embarked on his next 'very wonderful aventure'.

IV

For a while many people found it difficult to believe that Blackwood had died. They were so used to him coming and going, one moment being there, another moment off on a journey, that they just expected him to turn up again some day, even after they had seen all the obituary notices.

Most obituarists, few of whom knew him personally, churned out the usual platitudes, not always accurate, but occasionally perceptive. *The Times* at least recognized that Blackwood brought to weird fiction 'uncommon gifts'. The *Manchester Guardian* noted that he was 'a traveller by ways unknown to tourists'. The *Daily Express* homed in on his television storytelling talents: 'Few people equalled him. None surpassed him.'

But the best encomiums came from those who knew him personally. There is real heartfelt passion in Michael Hall's tribute in the *London Mystery Magazine*. Hall had only come to know Blackwood in his last few years but he regarded him as a 'great and kind friend' saying: 'Above all he belonged to that vanishing race of true gentlemen,' and that 'I don't remember hearing him speak evil of anybody'. Hall concluded by saying: 'Algernon Blackwood never lost interest in the world and humanity; perhaps "timeless" might describe him, but he would have dismissed this notion as pompous. Please join me then, dear reader, in believing that Algernon Blackwood was beloved by the gods and died young.'[15]

Another close friend, L.A.G. Strong, wrote a wonderful personal memoir for *Light*, in which he regarded him as 'ageless' and echoed Hall's views. 'I cannot imagine him ever hurting the feelings of the most sensitive, vulnerable person. Courteous, kindly, claiming no special consideration, refusing to be old, but miles removed from the artificial jauntiness of so many who try to stay young: Algernon Blackwood asked little of life, and much was granted to him – including the affection of men and women everywhere. That was the one tie which even he could not escape.'[16]

The BBC searched to find another storyteller. According to actor Preston Lockwood, who was on the short list, they held auditions at Alexandra Palace early in 1952. Other candidates included H.E. Bates, Gerald Kersh and Hugh Massingham. Lockwood told a short story that he had written. In later years Lockwood looked rather like Blackwood but in 1952 he was only just forty and had a long way to go to acquire the Blackwood wrinkles. Nevertheless Lockwood was selected as the best performer and did one broadcast, but thereafter the idea was dropped. There could only be one Algernon Blackwood.

Blackwood had left his personal effects to be shared equally between his sister-in-law, Kate, and her son Patrick, though any income from his writings was granted solely to Kate to pass to Patrick on her death. Kate retired to Kenya where she died in 1974, aged eighty-five. Ada continued to live at Itchen Abbas, near Winchester, but in her final days moved into a nursing home in Winchester where she died in April 1974 aged 103. Patrick did not long survive his mother or aunt. Since his uncle's death he had moved into the hotel trade. He died in November 1975 aged only sixty-three. He was Blackwood's last surviving close relative.

Blackwood's work remained popular. Several books stayed in print, especially the omnibus volume *Tales of the Uncanny and Supernatural*. Unfortunately, because so few of his radio broadcasts (and even less of his television ones) had been recorded, there were few opportunities to hear him on the radio. However, ten years after his death, when most people still recalled his radio and television stories, Independent Television began a series of plays adapted from his stories called *Tales of Mystery*. The plays were introduced each week by the Scottish actor John Laurie, who took the part of Blackwood himself: thus it captured the atmosphere of his earlier broadcasts without attempting to reproduce his story-telling skills. The first programme, 'The Terror of the Twins' was broadcast on 24 March 1961 and the series ran to eight programmes ending with 'The Decoy' on 17 May. It was highly successful and two more series followed during the summer of 1962 and winter of 1963. Twenty-nine stories were adapted (out of a possible 221) and kept Blackwood's name alive into the 1960s. It prompted reprints of more of his books, including *The Empty House* (1964) and *John Silence* (1969), plus a collection *Selected Tales* (1964) and a new omnibus *Tales of the Mysterious and Macabre* (1967). Penguin Books issued a paperback edition of *Selected Tales* as *The Insanity of Jones* (1966) and a new collection, *Ancient Sorceries* (1968) so that a fair selection of his stories remained accessible.

The series even prompted reporter David Griffiths to try and contact Blackwood via a medium. He was unsuccessful because the mediums said they'd rather not know whom he was trying to contact and, indeed, the one medium to whom he didn't give Blackwood's name, seemed to come closest. Blackwood would have been heartily amused at the idea of someone trying to contact him after his death. He had been disparaging of spiritualism for so long, one could imagine that even if it were possible, Blackwood would avoid contact. His own belief was that individual souls did not exist after death but merged back into a group or cosmic soul from which all new spirits were reborn. Thus new spirits may take with them memories or traits of one or more previous spirits. It is entirely unlikely, therefore, in Blackwood's belief, that his complete soul could be recontacted, though elements of it may already have been reborn.

Nevertheless, in 1962 Gerald Gough, who had been one of the last people to meet Blackwood, hoped to make contact with Blackwood at a sitting held by Ivy Northage. Also present were Kathleen Raine, Rosamond Lehmann and Paul Beard. Gough wanted to explore that feeling he had from Blackwood that he had lost his faith. The medium, through her guide 'Chan' explained that this meant he had found his spiritual freedom. 'Chan' also described the spiritual planes in terms extremely close to Blackwood:

> The colours in the spiritual planes are quite indescribable; and the
> music and harmony that come from the world of nature is all part
> of the colour and harmony, like an orchestration: sound producing
> colour, colour producing sound.[17]

The discussion about Blackwood does accurately reflect much of his lifestyle and although there is no 'message' from Blackwood, Chan did conclude by saying:

> Know that it is not something which just exists in your thought, he really is there with you when you think of him. And I appreciate very much those brief years, he says, and the very long intervals, apparently, between your meetings. He appreciates this very much in recollection.

Was this the last word from Blackwood?

Memories of Blackwood faded during the 1970s. Books went out of print and his work and reputation slipped into history. When Andrew Lloyd-Webber's *Starlight Express* began its long run in 1984 there was no mention of Blackwood's name. The musical is, of course, not based on Blackwood's play, but on Watty Piper's wonderful children's book *The Little Engine That Could* (1945). The title was borrowed from Blackwood's play, though all the references at the time were to Elgar's music. The fact that the phrase itself was Blackwood's had long been forgotten.

Now critical and public recognition is returning to Blackwood. There have been several studies of his works in such excellent books as Jack Sullivan's *Elegant Nightmares* (1978) and S.T. Joshi's *The Weird Tale* (1990). There have been several student theses on his works, including a full-length doctorate study by Professor Jean-Louis Grillou. And there are plans to reprint all of his short fiction and novels for a new generation.

Blackwood's message is even more important today than it was a hundred years ago. He firmly believed that by an expansion of consciousness you could sense a wider world, and that brought into focus a greater understanding of life and nature. His ideas and stories thus fit straight down the middle of the ecological and New Age beliefs of this generation. And he went beyond that. He believed that through our greater understanding of nature we could tap into the Earth Soul or Consciousness and through that we could generate harmony throughout the world. One man alone could not do it, and Blackwood did not try and recruit an army of others to help him. He simply hoped that by expressing these views in some of the most remarkable and thought-provoking wonder stories ever written he might increase our awareness of our own potential and set us on the road to the New Age.

He could still do it.

He had seen the Face of Nature, heard her Call, tasted her joy and peace; and the rest of the tired world might do the same. It only waited to be shown the way.

The Centaur, pp. 289–90.

Notes and References

CHAPTER 1: THE WEIGHT OF AGES

1. *Episodes Before Thirty*, p. 44. Hereinafter the book is simply referred to as *Episodes*.
2. 'Minor Memories', BBC Third Programme, 8 September 1949 [BBC Written Archives].
3. *A Prisoner in Fairyland*, p. 21.
4. *Ibid.*, p. 40.
5. The meetings moved to Mildmay Park, in Islington, in 1864.
6. Speech given at the Mildmay Conference on 29 June 1883 and quoted in *Some Records of the Life of Stevenson Arthur Blackwood K.C.B.* (London: Hodder & Stoughton, 1898), p. 318, hereinafter called *Life*.
7. *Episodes*, p. 23.
8. *Incredible Adventures*, 1914.
9. *Episodes*, p. 33.
10. 'Christmas in England', *The Methodist Magazine*, December 1890.
11. 'The Water Performance', *Sails of Gold*, edited by Cynthia Asquith (London: Jarrolds, 1927).
12. *Life*, p. 370.
13. *The Education of Uncle Paul*, p. 344.
14. *Episodes*, pp. 32–33.
15. *Ibid.*, p. 34.
16. Letter, Sir Arthur Blackwood to Lucy Wright, 22 May 1888, reprinted in *Life*, p. 450.
17. *Episodes*, p. 35.

CHAPTER 2: SPIRITS AWAKEN

1. *John Silence*, pp. 245–6.

2   'The Little People', BBC Third Programme, 25 December 1948 [BBC Written Archives].
3   BBC Television, 13 October 1951. Unpublished.
4   This story is also told in *Episodes*, p. 30.
5   'How I Became Interested in Ghosts', *op. cit.*
6   *Episodes*, p. 28.
7   All quotes come from Bhagwan Shree Patanjali, *Aphorisms of Yoga* (London, 1938).
8   'On Being Eighty', BBC Home Service, 1948 [BBC Written Archives].
9   Letter, John Macrae to Blackwood, 17 May 1935 [Blackwood estate].
10 Letter, Percy Radcliffe to Blackwood, 21 August 1947 [Blackwood estate].
11 'In the Jura – Neuchatel', Canadian *Methodist Magazine*, June 1891, p. 554.
12 This and following quotations come from an unpublished diary kept by Sir Arthur Blackwood entitled C.P.R. Tour 1887 [Blackwood estate].
13 Letter, Blackwood to his sisters, 31 August 1887 [Blackwood estate].
14 Letter, Blackwood to Vera Wainwright, 29 May 1936 [British Library].
15 Letter, Blackwood to his sisters, 31 August 1887 [Blackwood estate].

CHAPTER 3: GHOSTS AND SCHOLARS

1   In *The Empty House*, 1906.
2   For full details about Gurney's death and the probable reasons why see *The Strange Case of Edmund Gurney* by Trevor H. Hall (London: Duckworth, 1964, revised 1980).
3   'The Midnight Hour', *The Queen*, 24 November 1948.
4   Letter, Blackwood to unknown, 21 May 1943 [New York Public Library].
5   'The Midnight Hour', *op. cit.* p. 64.
6   *Episodes*, p. 14.
7   *Episodes*, p. 53.

CHAPTER 4: NORTHERN LIGHTS

1   *Episodes*, p. 14.
2   Undated note reprinted in *Life* (p. 454).
3   Quotes are from Blackwood's article 'Over the Splügen', *Canadian Methodist Magazine*, June 1893.
4   'The Song of the Sea', *The Week*, 7 August 1891; 'Lines to a Dreamer', *The Week*, 9 October 1891.
5   *Episodes*, p. 54.
6   See 'Algernon Blackwood's Brief "Episode" in the T.S.' by Ted Davy, *The Canadian Theosophist*, September/October 1991. Smythe settled in Toronto on 10 September 1889 and soon began issuing propaganda.
7   *Episodes*, pp. 55–57.

8   Mrs MacPherson contributed the woman's page. The paper ran from 5 December 1890–2 October 1891. She returned to New York soon after and there published a book on tapestry painting.

9   This story had also been heard by Ambroise Bierce, who incorporated it in 'Mysterious Disappearances' in *Can Such Things Be?* (New York: Cassell, 1893). Blackwood was unaware of Bierce's account though was accused of plagiarising it for his radio talk.

10 This and subsequent quotes are from Franz Hartman *Magic, White and Black* New York: Theosophical Society, seventh edition, 1904. It was first published in 1884.

11 'Thoughts on Nature', *Lucifer*, December 1890, p. 315.

12 Letter, Judge to Blackwood, 6 February 1891 [Theosophical Society archives].

13 Letter, Judge to Blackwood, 29 December 1891 [Theosophical Society archives].

14 Letter, Blackwood to Wrong, 12 November 1923 [University of Toronto Library].

15 *Episodes*, p. 27.

16 'From a Theosophist's Diary', *Lucifer*, January 1892.

17 His brother, Edward Klaas Pauw (1871–1899) was at Balliol College, Oxford but failed to graduate.

18 Colombo, *Blackwood's Books* (Toronto: Hounslow Press, 1981), p. 104.

19 Letter, Blackwood to Lady Kintore, 4 August 1892 [private].

20 *Episodes*, p. 79.

CHAPTER 5: THE DEPTH OF HELL

1   *Episodes*, pp. 83–4.

2   *Harper's Young People*, 11 October 1892.

3   *Episodes*, p. 85.

4   Blackwood refers to him as 'elderly' though he was only in his late forties, in fact younger than Blackwood was at the time he wrote his recollection of the incident.

5   'Looking Back at Christmas', *The Leader Magazine*, 25 December 1948.

6   'Max Hensig', *The Listener*, p. 57.

7   See 'A Lion Loose in a Stable', *The Sun*, 27 October 1893, p. 3 and 28 October 1893, p. 4. Blackwood rewrote the account for *The Boy's Own Paper* (2 June 1906) when he states the event happened on a 'gloomy winter's morning'.

8   See 'My Strangest Christmas', *Radio Times*, 24 December 1948, p. 10.

9   'A Case of Eavesdropping', *The Empty House*, p. 63.

10 Blackwood only refers to this man as an 'Exchange Place banker'. Although several individuals would fit this description, Belmont (1853–1924) is the most likely because he had also been swindled by Bigge.

11 The complaint sheet states that the theft of $32 took place on 1 November 1892, whereas according to Blackwood's chronology in *Episodes* it was

at the end of November (pp. 147–148). The complaint sheet is more likely to be correct, yet it prolongs the period during which Blackwood knew of Bigge's actions and still forgave him. Blackwood said that he forgave Bigge three times. He refers to another occasion when he received money from his father and placed this in a drawer and that was also taken by Bigge. Possibly Blackwood confused the two events one of which was on 1 November.

12 Unaccountably Blackwood gives the date as 18 December 1892 (*Episodes*, p. 191) though he also calls it 'the Tuesday before Christmas', which was the 20th. The newspaper reports all clearly state that Bigge was arrested on Tuesday 27 December. Blackwood remembered the wrong Tuesday.

13 Letter, Blackwood to Lady Kintore, Christmas 1923 [private].

14 *Episodes*, p. 111.

15 *Episodes*, p. 116.

16 *Episodes*, p. 152.

16 In *Episodes* (p. 23) Blackwood refers to some sporting friends of the revivalist Dwight Moody. He calls them 'manly fellows, good cricketers like the Studd brothers or Stanley Smith and Montague Beauchamp, men who had rowed in their University boats, and who were far removed from anything effeminate.' The reference to 'effeminate' is *a propos* of nothing and suggests that in his teens, Blackwood abhorred the idea of effeminacy.

18 Letter, Blackwood to Ella Maillart, undated but probably 1923 [Maillart archives].

19 *The Education of Uncle Paul*, pp. 74–75.

CHAPTER 6: DREAMS AND ILLUSIONS

1 *The Sun*, 25 December 1892.

2 'Ancient Sorceries', *John Silence*, pp. 77–8; my thanks to Jean-Louis Grillou for highlighting this. Though Blackwood decried snobbery he was sometimes inadvertently guilty of it himself.

3 'The Messenger', *Pan's Garden*, p. 170; my thanks to Alan Bundy for highlighting this.

4 *Episodes*, p. 182.

5 *Episodes*, p. 178.

6 *Episodes*, p. 181.

7 *The Centaur*, p. 47.

8 In *Episodes* (p. 231) Blackwood states that he took his holiday around the middle of October and heard the news of his father's death on his return, two weeks later, the end of October. But his father died on 2 October, giving plenty of time for Blackwood to be notified before he went away. His father was buried on 9 October.

9 *McBride's Magazine*, November 1915.

10 *Episodes*, p. 259.

11 The full caption says: 'I say, Jane, what is the difference between a bill-

board and a board-bill?' Answer, 'Well, you can't jump the bill-board.'
Bill-board was a common phrase for posters and board-bill means the bill
for lodgings, i.e. bed-and-board.

12 According to *Episodes* Blackwood met Hamilton soon after the Bigge
affair, i.e. early 1893. But he also says Hamilton was about twenty-one,
which would make it early 1895. I'm inclined to place it later in 1893.
Hamilton left Cheltenham College in December 1891 and, like Blackwood,
spent a year in Germany and France. He first visited New York in late
January 1893 on tour.

13 Compare *Episodes*, p. 15, 'From that day to this I have never set eyes on
him again,' with p. 255, 'Kay was in my life again'.

14 *Episodes*, p. 241.

15 *Episodes*, p. 266.

16 Alexander Woollcott, 'In Memoriam: Cornelia Lunt', *The Atlantic
Monthly*, April 1939, p. 468.

17 Blackwood and others came to believe that Eliot had based Daniel Deronda
himself on Louis. In fact Deronda was purportedly based on Edmund
Gurney, whom we have already encountered in Blackwood's youth.

18 Maude ffoulkes, *My Own Past* (London: Cassell, 1915), p. 193.

19 *The Listener*, 1907.

20 Although Blackwood recalls his interview was with Mitchel he also reports
that Mullins was doing a feature on the 'new fire marshal'. Mitchel's
successor, Hollister, had been appointed at the end of June 1895 but could
not take up his appointment until Mitchel resigned. Mitchel went on 16
July 1895. The fire coming right in the middle of this upheaval probably
worked in Blackwood's favour as Mitchel was unable to exercise his
authority. Blackwood remembers him as being 'not quite sure of himself'
(*Episodes*, p. 286).

CHAPTER 7: THE ROAD TO RECOVERY

1 *Episodes*, p. 288.

2 *Episodes*, p. 291.

3 Abbott eventually ran his lectures in *The Outlook* the following year.
They were collected together in book form at the end of 1897.

4 Giving him an income equivalent then to about £8 a week, which is today
equal to £28,000 a year.

5 *Longman's Magazine*, January 1901.

6 This could be the home of Emily Stowe on Stowe Island. In *Emily Stowe*
(1978), Janet Ray says, 'They built small summer cottages around the
main house and soon turned the island into a perfect spot to rest and
relax and enjoy the quiet beauty'. Blackwood may also have visited the
island in 1891, when he first met the Stowes.

7 *Macmillan's Magazine*, May 1900.

8 In *The Empty House*.

9   See *Episodes*, p. 304.
10 Blackwood wrote about the expedition in "Mid the Haunts of the Moose' (*Blackwood's Magazine*, July 1900). He said the trip happened 'last year in October'. That could not be October 1899 as Blackwood was back in England by then.
11 I include 'Running Wolf' in this total even though it was not written for another twenty years.
12 Adeline Loomis (1868–1944).
13 *Boy's Own Paper*, 31 December 1904.
14 Florence, the sister of Reggie Moreton, used to tell her son of the days when she and her brother sat round campfires in Canada with Reggie's friends telling stories.
15 First published in *The Eye-Witness*, 29 February 1912.
16 'The Destruction of Smith', *Pan's Garden*, p. 412.
17 'The Wendigo', *The Lost Valley*, p. 97.
18 *The Education of Uncle Paul*, p. 2.

CHAPTER 8: MAGICAL MOMENTS

1   Published in editions for 14 April 1900 and 18 August 1900 respectively.
2   *Episodes*, p. 223.
3   Private diary of Hilda Keith for 1900, unpublished.
4   *The Listener*, p. 11.
5   *Boy's Own Paper*, 23 August 1902.
6   Wilson was born at Ashurst House, Headley in Surrey on 2 October 1875, son of James Christopher Wilson. His name is spelt as Wilfrid on all official documents even though it appears as Wilfred on the book *The Wolves of God* and in several other reference books.
7   Sir Edward Inglefield was a leading Freemason and Provincial Grand Master for Buckinghamshire.
8   *Macmillan's Magazine*, September and October 1901.
9   *Westminster Gazette*, 30 April 1910.
10 E.F. Bleiler, *The Guide to Supernatural Fiction* (Kent, Ohio: Kent State University Press, 1983), p. 52.
11 Jack Sullivan, *Elegant Nightmares* (Athens, Ohio: Ohio University Press, 1978), p. 113.
12 Blackwood, 'The Little People', BBC Third Programme, 25 December 1948 [BBC Written Archives].
13 Vincent Starrett, *Born in a Bookshop* (University of Oklahoma Press, 1965), pp.248–49.
14 'With Intent to Steal', *The Empty House*, p.138.
15 The author E.F. Benson was also at the British School at that time.
16 'Smith: an Episode in a Lodging-House', *The Empty House*, p.198.
17 Chic and Sandra Tabatha Cicero, *Self-Initiation into the Golden Dawn Tradition* (1995).

18 John Symonds & Kenneth Grant, *The Confessions of Aleister Crowley*, (London: Cape, 1969), p. 180ff.
19 Their real names were Editha and Frank Jackson.
20 In 1947 Blackwood told a BBC producer, who had invited him to give a talk on the Golden Dawn, that 'I remained in it for a short period only'.
21 Arthur Machen, *Things Near and Far* (London: Martin Secker, 1923), p.130.
22 *Time and Tide*, 16 March 1923, p. 293.

CHAPTER 9: THE ROAD TO FREEDOM

1 Louis lived his last years at Hampstead and died on 19 October 1915 aged eighty-seven.
2 In *Episodes* (p. 223) Blackwood says that by 1906 he had written 'a couple of dozen' stories. Allowing for his boys' stories and light romances the total number of known stories by Blackwood, including those in *The Empty House* and *The Listener* totals 25.
3 He told it on several occasions. It will be found in 'Oddities', *The Listener*, 9 September 1948, p. 383, and in 'Adventures in Thought-Transference', *Prediction*, December 1949, pp. 7–9.
4 This account was in an unpublished note called 'Three Old Ladies'.
5 Blackwood may have made a second trip down the Danube in 1901. In his radio talk 'Two Holidays' (1949) after mentioning his first canoe trip he refers to 'another incident a year later when I was going down it [the Danube] from Ulm in a great double-ender barge with an 8 ft. oar to steer by'. When Blackwood wrote about the 1905 trip for *Boy's Own Paper* he refers to having been down the river only 'once before' by canoe. Blackwood did a final journey in July 1907 when he talked about previous 'trips', but did not say how many.
6 See 'A Holiday Down the Danube with Punt and Tent', *Boy's Own Paper*, 1 September 1906 and 'Summer Camps on the Danube', *Fry's Magazine*, July 1909.
7 When Blackwood wrote about his next Danube trip two years later for the *Boy's Own Paper* (9 January 1909) he states that the party was of two men and two women. He refers to two as being his cousin and his wife. That would be Arthur Hobart-Hampden and his wife Henrietta. The other lady remains a mystery.
8 Maude C. ffoulkes, *My Own Past* (London: Cassell, 1915), p. 178.
9 See Appendix 2 for a full listing.
10 [Hilaire Belloc], 'The English Ghost Story', *The Morning Post*, 3 January 1907.
11 *The Academy*, 15 December 1906, p. 612.
12 *The Bookman*, February 1907, p. 232.
13 *Selected Tales*, p. 10.

[14] Quoted in Ellic Howe, *The Magicians of the Golden Dawn* (London: Aquarian Press, 1985), p. 70.

[15] *The Academy*, 28 December 1907, p. 297.

[16] Maude ffoulkes had become a partner in Nash's publishing firm in September 1907.

[17] Maude ffoulkes's answer is not recorded and it is not certain she did have an ancestor called Silence. It isn't mentioned in either of her autobiographies, or in Violet Powell's biography of her, *A Substantial Ghost*.

[18] 'Two Holidays', BBC Home Service, 13 July 1949 [BBC Written Archives].

[19] The name Hubbard is derived from that of Blackwood's cousin Arthur Hobart-Hampden: Hobart is pronounced Hubbard. But the character of Hubbard is more akin to Blackwood.

[20] My thanks to Bengt Dahlqvist for his painstaking work in identifying this island.

[21] See the write up by Raymond Radclyffe in the *Daily Sketch*, 24 August 1910.

[22] Mary Bevan, 'Odd Memories of an Ordinary Person', Part III, p. 7, unpublished.

[23] Hatmaker was already making changes. The London branch of the Dried Milk Company was wound up in August 1907. Blackwood may have continued to work as an agent for Hatmaker's Paris branch.

CHAPTER 10: THE WORLD OF UNCLE PAUL

[1] 'A Monte Carlo Episode' (December 1898) about revenge upon a cheat at gambling, and 'The Secretary' (December 1902) written with A.M. Graeme.

[2] The Hobart-Hampden family is complicated. Also in Switzerland, a few years earlier, had been Ernest Miles Hobart-Hampden (1864–1949), Arthur's cousin. Ernest served in the British Consulate in China and Japan from 1888 to 1919 and was only occasionally in Europe. However in November 1901 he married Marie Hélène Langel, the daughter of Blackwood's old pastor, and spent much time in Bôle and Neuchâtel until they returned to Japan in 1904. Both Ernest and Hélène became writers of children's books.

[3] 'The Poetry of Ski-running', *Country Life* (27), 26 February 1910, p. 293.

[4] He recalled this in 'Some Remarkable Dreams', *The Strand Magazine*, February 1933, pp.144–5.

[5] *The Education of Uncle Paul*, p. 21.

[6] See *Synesthesia: a union of the senses* (1989) and *The Man Who Tasted Shapes* (1993) both by Richard Cytowic and *Bright Colours Falsely Seen* (1998) by Kevin T. Dann.

[7] *Episodes*, p. 123.

[8] *Education of Uncle Paul*, p. 170.

[9] See Walter Hooper (editor), *They Stand Together: the Letters of C.S. Lewis to Arthur Greeves* (London: Macmillan, 1979).

10   Blackwood was surprised when A.P. Watt sold this story to *Country Life*.
      He had been selling them articles and reviews but had not considered
      them for stories even though it was an excellent market. *Country Life*
      paid a higher word rate for fiction than for articles, up to three guineas a
      thousand words, so Blackwood received £20 for this story (the equivalent
      today of about £1,250). The story was published in two parts, 30 October
      and 6 November 1909.

11   It was published under this title in *Pall Mall Magazine*, March 1910, but
      appeared in *The Lost Valley* as 'Perspective'.

12   *Nash's Magazine*, December 1909.

13   First published in *The Lost Valley*, 1910.

14   *Westminster Gazette*, 6 November 1909.

15   The play came about as follows. A frequent guest at Robertson's home at
      Witley was his friend, the artist Arthur Melville, who came with his baby
      daughter Marion, whom Robertson called Binkie. Binkie was fascinated
      by a gate leading to a wood at the bottom of Robertson's garden. Robertson
      told Binkie that the gate led to Fairyland and could only be passed by
      people over four years old. That was fine until Binkie reached four, when
      she wanted to go through the gate. Robertson created a grand ceremony
      to admit Binkie into Fairyland. They decked the wood in fairy lanterns,
      friends dressed as elves and fairies and she was greeted by the Guardian of
      the Gate. Soon after Robertson wrote the play showing a day and a night
      as seen through a young child's imagination. H.G. Wells regarded it as the
      best of all plays for children and it may well have influenced Blackwood's
      Education of Uncle Paul.

16   Letter, Blackwood to Robertson, 13 Feb [1911] [Henry E. Huntington
      Library].

17   *The Human Chord*, p. 65.

18   It is this episode that Hilaire Belloc highlighted for special comment in his
      review of the book for *The Westminster Gazette* (29 October 1910)
      describing the episode as 'as powerful as can be'. Belloc called the book
      'unique, and should be a matter of national pride'.

19   In February 1911 Macmillan informed Blackwood of the first three months
      sales figures for *The Human Chord*. Blackwood felt that 'considering the
      nature of the book I feel they are not discouraging at all'. However a year
      later, in response to a note from Siegfried Sassoon, he said: 'Your short
      note is particularly welcome to me because my books find hardly any
      market and so a word from an understanding reader is the greatest help
      and encouragement I can have.'

20   Both Jepson and Blackwood were members of the Square Club. This was
      a literary club founded in 1908 by Conal O'Riordan and G.K. Chesterton.
      Every month various literary lights gathered for an evening meal to discuss
      current literary issues. I don't know when Blackwood became a member,
      but it could have been from the start. Other members included Edward
      Garnett, Arthur Machen, John Masefield, Walter de la Mare, J.D. Beresford
      and John Galsworthy. It is possible that Jepson and Blackwood discussed

their ideas about the power of sound and invocations without realizing both were developing them into a book.

CHAPTER 11: THE PEAKS OF INSPIRATION

1   'From My Caucasus Note-Book', *The Tramp*, January 1911, pp. 333–4.
2   See *The Centaur*, pp. 193–4.
3   Letter, Blackwood to Macmillan, 18 August 1910 [British Library].
4   'The Genesis of Ideas', *The Writer*, February 1937, p. 36.
5   *The Tramp*, December 1910.
6   *London Magazine*, January 1911.
7   Stephen Graham, *Part of the Wonderful Scene* (London: Collins, 1964). p. 70.
8   Graham, *Part of the Wonderful Scene*, p. 40.
9   *New Weekly*, 27 June 1914.
10 *Julius LeVallon*, p. 63.
11 Letter, Blackwood to Robertson, 13 February [1911] [Henry E. Huntington Library].
12 Letter, Blackwood to unknown, 29 March 1911 [private].
13 *Westminster Gazette*, 17 June 1911.
14 *The Eye-Witness*, 29 December 1911.
15 *The Eye-Witness*, 20 July 1911.
16 *Westminster Gazette*, 2 September 1911.
17 There is a significant body of novels, stories and articles considering the possibility of a German invasion of Britain prior to the outbreak of war in 1914. The best known at this time was *The Invasion of 1910* by William Le Queux which had been serialized in the *Daily Mail* during 1906 with considerable publicity and was published by Eveleigh Nash later that year. It sold more than two million copies around the world and was, I believe, Nash's best selling book. It could be argued that this helped subsidize the publication of Blackwood's first few books.
18 Letter, Blackwood to Stephen Graham, 28 February 1914 [University of Texas].
19 *Pall Mall Magazine*, May 1910.
20 *The Eye-Witness*, 22 June 1911.
21 *Country Life*, 25 June 1910.
22 *The Eye-Witness*, 19 October 1911.
23 *Country Life*, 9 December 1911.
24 Peter Underwood, *Exorcism!* (London: Robert Hale 1990), p. 138.
25 *Country Life*, 20 January 1912.
26 *Pall Mall Magazine*, December 1911.
27 *Westminster Gazette*, 20 April 1912.
28 Letter, Blackwood to Elodie Belloc, 7 March 1912 [Boston College, John L. Burns Library].
29 'The Second Generation' (*Westminster Gazette*, 6 July 1912) bears

comparison with this story. A man returns home after ten years away in primitive lands, and calls on the woman he had loved but left behind. The woman appears and there is a momentary reunion before he realizes she is a ghost and his lost-love had died several years before.

30 *Time Literary Supplement*, 16 November 1911.
31 *The Bookman*, February 1912.
32 Robb Lawson, 'Algernon Blackwood', *The Bookman*, November 1917, p. 50.
33 'The Little People & Co.', BBC Third Programme, 25 December 1948 [BBC Written Archives].
34 As an aside, Carpenter was born at 45 Brunswick Square in Brighton in a house facing the haunted house that Blackwood investigated and inspired 'The Empty House' nearly sixty years later.
35 Letter, Blackwood to Carpenter, 7 January 1912 [Sheffield Library, Carpenter Collection.]
36 *The Centaur*, p. 336.

CHAPTER 12: THE SPELL OF MAYA

1 Mrs Lamont had written to Blackwood earlier in the year praising his stories and he had visited her at Iver in Buckinghamshire, during the summer. They remained in touch for many years and she later assembled a major omnibus of his stories, *The Tales of Algernon Blackwood* (1938).
2 *Country Life*, 27 January 1912.
3 Letter, Blackwood to Lamont, 4 December 1911 [private].
4 *The Morning Post*, 26 December 1911.
5 *The Eye Witness*, 23 May 1912 as 'The Empty Room'.
6 *The Education of Uncle Paul*, pp. 242–3.
7 Letter, Blackwood to Graham, 15 November 1911 [University of Texas].
8 Stewart M. Ellis, 'The Ghost Story and its Exponents', *The Fortnightly Review*, December 1923.
9 Locally it is called Hulwan today, but Helwan remains the most common spelling. In Blackwood's day it was often spelled Helouan.
10 'The Egyptian Desert from Helouan', *Country Life*, 16 March 1912, pp. 381–2.
11 'Egypt: an Impression', *Country Life*, 8 November 1913, p. 626.
12 'Helouan in the Desert', *The Morning Post*, 30 April 1912. Despite that publication date I suspect the essay was written a month or more earlier.
13 Hereward Carrington, *The Problems of Psychical Research* (New York: W. Rickey, 1914), p. 298.
14 Letter, Blackwood to B.J. Morse, 28 September 1949 [University of Cardiff].
15 Letter, Rilke to Princess Marie, 29 March 1912, in *The Letters of Rainer*

Maria Rilke and Princess Marie von Thurn und Taxis, translated by Nora Wydenbruck (London: The Hogarth Press, 1958), p. 39.

16 See Eudo C. Mason, *Rilke, Europe, and the English-Speaking World* (Cambridge University Press, 1961), pp. 88, 224–5.

17 Letter, Princess Marie to Rilke, 14 May 1912, in *The Letters of Rainer Maria Rilke, op. cit.*, p. 44.

18 Letter, Rilke to Princess Marie, 18 May 1912, in the original German edition of *The Letters of Rainer Maria Rilke* (Insel Verlag, 1951), not included in the Wydenbruck translation. Excerpt translated especially for this book by Elsbeth Schmidt-Marty.

19 Stephen Graham, *Part of the Wonderful Scene, op. cit.* p. 67.

20 *A Prisoner in Fairyland*, pp. 473–476.

21 Stephen Graham, *ibid.* pp. 67, 70–71.

22 It was also the year that Maya joined the newly created International New Thought Alliance, which New Age message is reflected in *The Promise of Air*.

23 *The Eye-Witness*, 29 February 1912. Elodie wrote to Blackwood on 24 February.

24 Letter, Blackwood to Elodie Belloc, 8 June 1912 [John J. Burns Library, Boston College].

25 *The Eye-Witness*, 11 July 1912.

26 *The Morning Post*, 19 November 1912.

27 Letter, Blackwood to Elodie Belloc, 12 November 1912 [John J. Burns Library, Boston College].

28 *Westminster Gazette*, 30 November 1912.

29 Corbillard means 'hearse'.

30 'Before the Season', *Country Life*, 27 December 1913.

31 *The British Review*, October 1913.

32 Telegram, Dunn to Blackwood, 6 January 1913.

33 Extracts taken from an unpublished, untitled, typed note among Blackwood's papers.

34 *The New Witness*, 26 June, 17 July and 28 August 1913.

35 *The Morning Post*, 24 June 1913.

36 *The Morning Post*, 18 November 1913.

37 At six shillings, the British edition eventually brought Blackwood royalties of £90, which helped cover the loss of £40, though it was several years before this accumulated. At the original price and royalty rate Blackwood would have earned only £40, and would have had no profit at all.

38 Letter, Blackwood to Macmillan, 30 November 1913 [British Library].

39 *Incredible Adventures*, p. 132.

40 Stephen Graham, *Part of the Wonderful Scene*, p. 68.

41 *Incredible Adventures*, p. 137.

42 See S.T. Joshi, *The Weird Tale* (Austin: University of Texas Press, 1990), p. 103.

43 *Incredible Adventures*, p. 275.

CHAPTER 13: THE STARLIGHT EXPRESS

1   I am indebted to Mrs Lavender M. Jones and her daughter Mrs Rosemary Linnell for their help and memories of Violet Pearn.

2   A.E. Keeton, 'Elgar's Music for "The Starlight Express"', *Music and Letters*, January 1945.

3   Letter, Lavender Jones to Ashley, 27 December 1984.

4   Keeton, *op. cit.*

5   Letter, Blackwood to Basil Dean, 20 October 1913 [John Rylands Library, Manchester University].

6   Annie Horniman had been a key figure in the Golden Dawn. Blackwood knew her during his more active days in the Order.

7   Letters, Blackwood to Basil Dean, 9 and 20 October 1913 [John Rylands Library, Manchester University].

8   Letter, Blackwood to Macmillan, 30 November 1913 [British Library]. The theatre was probably the Haymarket. Dean had plans for the Savoy Theatre, but agreement over the lease came through too late.

9   *Country Life*, 10 January 1914.

10 In a letter that she wrote from Florence in 'Autumn 1913', Duncan stated 'I am on my way to Rome – & then perhaps to Egypt – to Karnak to rest in that Great Temple. . . .' (Francis Steegmuller, *Your Isadora*, New York: Random House, 1974, p. 338). However she never completed that journey, returning to Paris soon after.

11 *Century Magazine*, November 1914.

12 *Westminster Gazette*, 18 April 1914.

13 *New Weekly*, 27 June 1914.

14 Blackwood mentions in 'A Bit of Wood' that his cousins were visiting a sanatorium at Meran. It is probable that Mrs Hobart-Hampden had come here for a rest-cure as she had developed poor health.

15 *Morning Post*, 28 April 1914.

16 *Country Life*, 23 May 1914.

17 Letter, Blackwood to Horniman, 12 October 1914, [John Rylands Library, University of Manchester].

18 See 'After the War', *The Standard*, 7 October 1915.

19 Letter, Blackwood to Macmillan, 12 May 1915 [British Library].

20 *The Quest*, July 1914.

21 *Country Life*, 1 January 1916, p. 29.

22 Letter, Blackwood to Stephen Graham, 20 February 1915 [University of Texas].

23 Curiously Blackwood was entered into this Order on the Grade 5–6, which is Adeptus Minor, but there is no record that Blackwood was ever initiated into the Adeptus grades.

24 Blackwood had also recently written a substantial review of *The Collected Poems of A.E. Waite* for *The Bookman* (January 1915).

25 *The Bookman* [US edition], February 1915, pp. 618–621.

26 Dorothy Scarborough, *The Supernatural in Modern English Fiction* (1917), p. 285.

27   *Saturday Westminster Gazette*, 31 October 1914.
28   *The Standard*, 25 November 1915.
29   *Saturday Westminster Gazette*, 7 August 1915.
30   Wilson was formally engaged on 26 July 1915.
31   *Saturday Westminster Gazette*, 9 October 1915.
32   *Land and Water*, 9 October 1915.
33   *Land and Water*, 20 November 1915.
34   See *Great Short Stories of the War*, edited H. Cotton Minchin (London: Eyre & Spottiswoode, 1930) and in the US as *Best Short Stories of the War* (New York: Harper Brothers, 1931).
35   Letter, Blackwood to Hilaire Belloc, Sunday [15 August 1915] [Boston College].
36   *Ibid.*
37   Letter, Blackie to Blackwood, 26 October 1915 [A.P. Watt].
38   Letter, Blackwood to A.P. Watt, 28 October 1915 [New York Public Library].
39   These are his *Opus 18*, 'Oh! Children', 'The busy dustman', and 'Stars are seeding in the air'.
40   Letter, Elgar to Sidney Colvin, 20 December 1915.
41   Hugh Carey, *Duet for Two Voices* (Cambridge University Press, 1979), p. 88.
42   For a detailed study of the evolution of the music in *The Starlight Express* see 'Elgar and the Wonderful Stranger' by K.E.L. Simmons in *Elgar Studies* (Aldershot: Scolar Press, 1990) and *Edward Elgar: A Creative Life* by Jerrold Northrop Moore (Oxford University Press, 1984).
43   His name was Julius Harrison.
44   O.B. Clarence, *No Complaints* (London: Jonathan Cape, 1943), p. 145.
45   Letter, Blackwood to Elgar, undated [but early December 1915] [Novello Archives].
46   Letter, Blackwood to Elgar, 25 December 1915 [Novello Archives].
47   E. Wulstan Atkins, *The Elgar–Atkins Friendship* (Newton Abbot: David & Charles, 1984) p. 271.
48   Tragically Mott was killed at the Second Battle of the Marne on 13 May 1918.
49   Letter, Blackwood to Macmillan, 5 January 1916 [British Library].
50   Letter, Priestley to Blackwood, 26 January 1945 [Blackwood estate].
51   Letter in *Edward Elgar: A Creative Life* by Jerrold Northrop Moore (Oxford University Press, 1984), p. 695.

CHAPTER 14: BLACKWOOD AT WAR

1   Letter, Flower to Blackwood, 25 January 1915 [Blackwood estate].
2   See 'Our Former Lives', *Prediction*, May 1947.
3   Letter, Blackwood to Macmillan, 28 April 1916 [British Library].
4   *A Prisoner in Fairyland*, p. 482.

5   *The Wave*, pp. 279–280.

6   *The Wave*, p. 57.

7   *The Times*, 12 October 1916.

8   *The Morning Post*, 13 October 1916.

9   The episode was included in the uncredited *Weird Stories* (London: Illustrated Newspapers, 1927), pp. 79–81. Blackwood wrote about it in his unpublished essay 'Maude ffoulkes'.

10 *Day and Night Stories*, p. 56.

11 *Saturday Westminster Gazette*, 5 August 1916.

12 I have yet to trace the original publication date of this story. Blackwood refers to it being *re*printed in a paper in a letter dated 3 April 1917.

13 This data comes from a letter between Blackwood and Hilaire Belloc dated 29 August 1916, which helps tie down an otherwise elusive date.

14 Dru may not be this man's real name. Professor Grillou suggests that Blackwood may have created a pun. 'Dru' is French for 'thick' (as in 'thick-set'), but Blackwood may have intended it to mean 'thick' as in stupid, and that this reflects his condescension of the Intelligence Service.

15 Christopher Andrew, *Secret Service* (London: William Heinemann, 1985), p. 225.

16 In fact Knoblock may best be remembered in future years because of Sir John Gielgud's *faux pas* of describing Knoblock as the most boring man in London when he was actually dining with him.

17 Entry in Kirke's diary for 19 July 1916 (held at the Imperial War Museum). Kirke also noted that Wallinger's 'organization is useless' and he has 'not produced one report of any real value'.

18 On 26 October Blackwood wrote to Stephen Graham saying 'This is goodbye'. But two days later he was still in London having dinner with Maya Knoop and Lady Elgar. He must have left very soon afterwards.

19 From Blackwood's unpublished note, 'Three Old Ladies'.

20 Letter, Blackwood to Hilaire Belloc, 20 May 1918.

21 Letter, Blackwood to Macmillan, 21 January 1918 [British Library].

22 *The Garden of Survival*, p. 85.

23 A.E. Waite, *The Bookman*, December 1918, p. 108.

24 *The Promise of Air*, p. 215.

25 Letter, Blackwood to Macmillan, 8 April 1918 [British Library].

26 Letter, Blackwood to Belloc, 30 May 1918 [Boston College].

27 Letter, Blackwood to Belloc, 20 May 1918 [Boston College].

28 Today the equivalent of about $1,650 or £1,100.

28 Published as 'Missing', *The Red Cross Magazine*, December 1918.

30 Blackwood says that he wrote reports about the internment camps at Murren and Château d'Oex, but that none of these 'saw the light'. There were reports published about other camps in Switzerland and the work of the Red Cross but according to the *Times*' archives these were by the paper's regular correspondent Hubert Walter and his assistant A.F. Maconochie.

31 E. Wulstan Atkins, *The Elgar–Atkins Friendship* (Newton Abbot: David & Charles, 1984), pp. 294–295.

32 Atkins, *op.cit.*
33 *The English Review*, March 1921.
34 *Saturday Westminster Gazette*, 6 September 1919.
35 *The Quest*, October 1919.
36 *Vision*, September 1919.
37 *Nash's Illustrated Weekly*, 14 February 1920.
38 The story was collected in *The Wolves of God*, which consisted mostly of stories conceived jointly by Blackwood and Wilson.

CHAPTER 15: ALL THE WORLD'S A STAGE

1 Letter, Blackwood to Maillart, undated, but probably 1923 [Maillart archives]. Blackwood was asking himself the same questions that would be put to him by children in a radio broadcast 'Speak for Yourselves' nearly thirty years later. Blackwood found them just as difficult to answer then.
2 *Westminster Gazette*, 10 May 1919.
3 *Saturday Westminster Gazette*, 8 November 1919.
4 *Tongues of Fire*, p. 185.
5 *Nash's Illustrated Weekly*, 6 December 1919.
6 *The Wolves of God*, p. 275.
7 The total value of Baron Knoop's estate was £281,854, the equivalent today of about £8.5 million. Most of this, including his houses, passed to his son, but Maya received an annuity of £5,000 (equal to £150,000 today).
8 See Graham, *Part of the Wonderful Scene*, p. 253.
9 Letter, Blackwood to Wrong, 12 November 1923 [University of Toronto Library].
10 *Romance*, June 1920.
11 He was elevated to the peerage as Baron Essendon in June 1932.
12 Letter, Blackwood to Maillart, 24 January 1944 [Maillart archives, Bibliothèque Publique et Universitaire].
13 Letter, Maillart to Blackwood, 11 November 1943 [Blackwood estate].
14 Letter, Blackwood to Elgar, 23 April 1920 [Elgar archives].
15 Blackwood had met Ainley via Elgar. Their paths could have crossed before. When Blackwood knew Arthur Machen in the Golden Dawn, Machen was touring with Ainley in the Frank Benson company. Compton Mackenzie, whom Blackwood had known at the Savile Club since 1912, had also acted with Ainley.
16 Thelma Cazalet became a notable tennis player in her day, though her fame rests as one of Britain's earliest female Members of Parliament. Her brother, Peter, married Leonora, the stepdaughter of P.G. Wodehouse, who was also a frequent visitor to Fairlawne.
17 *The Times*, 30 September 1920, p. 9.
18 *The Stage*, 30 September 1920, p. 16.
19 *The Graphic*, 9 October 1920, p. 546.
20 Report by the Lord Chamberlain, 22 September 1920 [British Museum].

21   My thanks to the Theatre Department of the Metropolitan Toronto Library for finding details on this play's production.

22   Unidentified newspaper cutting among the papers of the Pearn estate.

23   Norman MacDermott, *Everymania* (London: Society for Theatre Research, 1975), p. 25.

24   23 performances, 18 December 1922 to 13 January 1923.

25   14 performances, 1 to 10 January 1925.

26   Laurence Olivier, *Confessions of an Actor* (London: Weidenfeld & Nicolson, 1982), p. 25.

27   *Century Magazine*, August 1920.

28   Sold to *Romance Magazine* for January 1921 but magazine folded before publication.

29   *Lloyd's Magazine*, December 1919 as 'The Substitute'.

30   This is the printer's publication date although the official release date was 26 May 1921.

31   *The Bright Messenger*, p. 69.

32   *The Bright Messenger*, pp. 358–9.

33   *The Bright Messenger*, p. 372.

34   Details come from Blackwood's letter to A.P. Watt, 25 November 1921 [Watt archives] and F. Kinsey Peile, *Candied Peel* (London: A. & C. Black, 1931), p. 191.

35   18 September to 5 October 1929, 17 performances.

36   Uncredited newspaper clippings in the British Museum manuscript archives.

37   It was one of fifteen plays performed as part of the Questors Twelfth Annual Drama Festival. So far as I know there was only one performance, on 4 June 1944.

38   *Time and Tide*, 16 December 1921.

39   *Pears Annual*, Christmas 1921.

40   Letter, Blackwood to Rowley, 11 January 1923 [Ellen Terry archives].

41   Micheál MacLiammóir, *All for Hecuba* (London: Methuen, 1946), p. 223.

CHAPTER 16: ELSEWHERE AND OTHERWISE

1   Letter, Blackwood to unknown, 4 February 1922 [private].

2   This and subsequent Blackwood quotes are from Blackwood, 'Passport to the Next Dimension', *Prediction*, March 1948.

3   The first two were *Organum* by Aristotle and *Novum Organum* by Francis Bacon.

4   Alexandropol has had various name changes. It was known as Leninakan until recently and is now called Kumayri in Armenia.

5   'Passport to the Next Dimension', *op. cit.*

6   I do not have Blackwood's letter but his comment is quoted in the response from the correspondent, A. Webster Stinton, 3 November 1949 [Blackwood estate].

7   Letter, Blackwood to Wrong, 12 November 1923 [University of Toronto Library].

8   Letter, Blackwood to Carpenter, 3 June 1924 [Sheffield Library].

9   Stephen Graham, *Part of the Wonderful Scene, op. cit.* p. 253.

10 'Passport to Another Dimension', *op. cit.*

11 *Day and Night Stories*, p. 22.

12 Letter, Stinton to Blackwood, 3 November 1949 [Blackwood estate].

13 In *Tongues of Fire*, 1924.

14 Letter, Blackwood to Anne Fremantle, 23 November 1950 [New York Public Library].

15 Advance excerpts from the book were serialized in *Cassell's Magazine* from July 1923, and the book was published on 20 October.

16 This is according to Dutton's files, though probably *John Silence*, which also had a pirated edition, sold more.

17 Edmund Candler, *Time and Tide*, 16 November 1923, p. 1149.

18 Letter, Blackwood to Sydney Kintore, Christmas 1923 [private].

19 Letter, Blackwood to Wrong, 12 November 1923 [University of Toronto Library].

20 Letter, Blackwood to Wrong, *op. cit.*

21 In the novel, Maya writes, 'in the cause of Brotherhood Pauline sold a lovely row of pearls and the Community set to work again prosperously.' (p. 196). Maya had done the same at the start of the Prieuré.

22 Maude ffoulkes, *All This Happened to Me* (London: Grayson & Grayson, 1937), p. 114.

23 In fact it appealed to many authors, the best known being J.B. Priestley, who used the idea in his time plays such as *Time and the Conways* (1937).

24 *Pearson's Magazine*, November 1923.

25 *The English Review*, May 1925.

26 *The Radio Times*, 23 December 1927.

27 *World Radio*, 12 December 1930.

CHAPTER 17: FAIRYLANDS

1   Private remark to the author. I am indebted to Patsy Ainley for her memories of these days.

2   'Fairies' first published in *Punch*, 23 May 1917.

3   Blackwood's poetry in *Merry-Go-Round* ran 'Engine' (November 1926), 'The Star' (December 1926), 'Questions and Answers' (March 1927), 'If I Were You' (August 1927) and 'The Haystack' (July 1928).

4   Winn was a teacher and later school inspector on musical education, and was keen to develop children singing. His music with Blackwood's lyrics appeared in the January 1929 issue.

5   *Dudley & Gilderoy*, p. 281.

6   *The Times*, 5 December 1929, p. 16.

7   Letter, Blackwood to Wainwright, 25 August 1938 [British Library].

8   'Preface' to *The Adventures of Dudley and Gilderoy*, 1941, p. 7.

9   I met the parrot in 1985 but, alas, he revealed no memories of Blackwood.

10   Letter, Blackwood to Watt, 20 January 1933 [Watt archives].

11   *The Sketch*, 23 April to 28 May, 1930.

12   Elkin Mathews & Marrot had reprinted Blackwood's short story *Full Circle* in a limited edition of 530 copies in December 1929 in their Woburn Books series.

13   See 'Famous Authors on their Favourite Spooks', *T.P.'s-Cassell's Weekly*, 8 December 1923.

14   See 'Have We Lived Before?', *Daily Mail*, 10 December 1929.

15   See 'Superstition and the Magic "Curse"', *Daily Express*, 9 April 1923.

16   Letter, Blackwood to Wainwright, 20 February 1937 [British Library].

17   *Occult Review*, December 1930.

18   *The Morning Post*, 31 December 1930.

19   *When Churchyards Yawn*, edited by Cynthia Asquith, London: Hutchinson, 1931.

20   *The Radio Times*, 19 December 1930.

21   *The Aryan Path*, March 1930. The earlier pieces were 'Have I Lived Before?', *London Weekly Despatch*, April 1927 and 'Have We Lived Before', see note 15.

22   *North American Review*, September 1931.

23   Letter, Blackwood to Rachel McFerran, Easter 1935 [private].

24   Undated note [1932] by Blackwood to Sydney Kintore [private].

25   Nancy Astor (1879–1964) was Britain's first woman Member of Parliament, elected in 1919. She had married the 2nd Viscount Astor in 1906 when they settled at Cliveden.

26   Letter, Blackwood to Maillart, 11 July [1933] [Maillart archives].

27   *The New York Times*, 10 March 1933.

28   There was one other, 'Mr Slumbubble and Mr Minkrat'. He refers to having despatched this to *Joy Street* in a letter dated only 'Jany 31' but which is almost certainly 1935, but it was not published. *Joy Street* continued until 1938 but ran no more stories by Blackwood.

CHAPTER 18: THE STORYTELLER

1   Letter, Blackwood to Patsy Ainley, 19 March 1934 [private].

2   *Pearson's Magazine*, October 1936.

3   Blackwood's 'Hands of Death' (*Bolton Evening News*, 5 December 1925) is set in Bolivia, which he also never visited.

4   *In Town Tonight* was first broadcast on 18 November 1933 and ran for nearly thirty years.

5   Letter, Blackwood to Watt, 11 June 1934 [Watt archives].

6   Letter, Fielden to Watt, 17 May 1934 [BBC Written Archives].

7   Letter, Watt to Fielden (quoting Blackwood), 28 May 1934 [Watt archives].

8   Letter, Blackwood to Watt, 11 June 1934 [Watt archives].

9 'Queer Stories', *The Listener*, 12 September 1934.
10 Letter, Blackwood to BBC, 4 August 1934. The comedy Abyssinian prince was Prince Monolulu, a well known racing tipster of the day.
11 'The Empty House' was not the same as Blackwood's early story but a retitling of 'A Haunted Island'.
12 Letter, Blackwood to Rachel McFerran, Easter 1935 [private].
13 *The Windsor Magazine*, March 1936.
14 Letter, Blackwood to Patsy Ainley, 19 March [1936] [private].
15 *Radio Times*, 11 December 1936.
16 Letter, Blackwood to Patsy Ainley, undated [November 1936] [private].
17 Letter, Madden to Blackwood, 3 November 1936 [BBC Written Archives].
18 This was the trip where Blackwood discussed the planned Mount Palomar Observatory with H.G. Wells.
19 'By Proxy', *The Bystander*, 17 November 1937; 'The Reformation of St Jules', *The Bystander*, 29 December 1937.
20 *Weird Tales*, September 1938.
21 Letter, Blackwood to Watt, 6 February 1938 [Watt archives].
22 People were so used to calling him Old Bell that most forgot his first name. His name was J.W. Bell (*c.* 1862–1948).
23 Letter, Blackwood to Ainley, 21 June 1938 [private].
24 Letter, Blackwood to Wainwright, 17 December 1938 [British Library].
25 Letter, Blackwood to Wainwright, 25 August 1938 [British Library].
26 Letter, Blackwood to Ainley, undated but almost certainly 24 October 1938 [private].

CHAPTER 19: THE GHOST MAN

1 Letter, Blackwood to Mrs Ridgeway, 4 January 1940 [Case Western Reserve University Libraries]. In fact it was his first winter in England since 1915/16.
2 Letter, BBC to Blackwood, 1 December 1939 [BBC Written Archives].
3 Letter, Blackwood to BBC, 22 February 1940 [BBC Written Archives].
4 Letter, Blackwood to BBC, 9 November 1940 [BBC Written Archives].
5 Letter, Blackwood to BBC, 11 December 1940 [BBC Written Archives].
6 Letter, Blackwood to BBC, 3 July 1941 [BBC Written Archives].
7 Letter, Blackwood to BBC, 9 August 1941 [BBC Written Archives].
8 Wartime inflation had already increased the cost of living, and five guineas is today equal to about £135.
9 Letter, Blackwood to BBC, 9 August 1941 [BBC Written Archives].
10 Letter, Blackwood to BBC, 3 October 1941 [BBC Written Archives].
11 Letter, Pauline Matarasso to Mike Ashley, 24 September 1985 [private].
12 Frank Baker, *I Follow But Myself* (London: Peter Davies, 1968), p. 240.
13 Letter, Blackwood to Wainwright, 14 March 1944 [British Library].
14 Letter, Mary Hayley Bell to Blackwood, 12 November 1945 [private].
15 Letter, Blackwood to BBC, 26 September 1945 [BBC Written Archives].

16 Letter, Blackwood to Patsy Ainley, 16 January 1945 [private].
17 Letter, Blackwood to Derleth, 10 November 1944 [State Historical Society, Wisconsin]
18 Letter, Blackwood to Derleth, 26 April 1946 [State Historical Society, Wisconsin].
19 Letter, Blackwood to Derleth, 10 June 1946 [State Historical Society, Wisconsin]. 'The Turn of the Screw' is, of course, by Henry James, and Blackwood's work has occasionally been alikened to James's.
20 *The Secret Society* was based on Blackwood's dream story of cannibalizm, 'The Price of Wiggins's Orgy', and was broadcast on 22 October 1947. This was Blackwood's last original radio play. He was discouraged because the BBC lost his original script, after they accepted it, and having no copy he had to do a second adaptation.
21 Letter, Blackwood to Patsy Ainley, 7 February [1947], [private].
22 Letter, Barr to Ashley, 6 October 1985 [private].
23 Blackwood used this to good effect when he broadcast 'Lock Your Door'. His voice gradually dropped so that everyone craned to listen and then he suddenly shouted 'Lock the Door!' and everyone jumped out of their skins.
24 Letter, Blackwood to BBC, 25 January 1948 [BBC Written Archives].
25 The omnibus volume was *Tales of the Uncanny and Supernatural* published in October 1949. Also reissued were *John Silence* (Richards Press) in August 1947, *The Empty House* (Richards Press) January 1948, and *Episodes Before Thirty* (Peter Nevill) March 1950. Benn issued a new edition of *Dudley & Gilderoy* in May 1951.

CHAPTER 20: A VERY WONDERFUL ADVENTURE

1 *Transition* #23, July 1935, pp. 89–96.
2 Since his radio broadcasts Blackwood had acquired the epithet 'the Ghost Man', which he regarded as almost derogatory, as it showed a lack of understanding of the thrust of his work.
3 Peter Penzoldt, *The Supernatural in Fiction* (London: Peter Nevill, 1952), p. 247.
4 Letter, Gilkison to Ashley, 6 September 1986 [private].
5 Letter, Blackwood to Patrick Blackwood, 8 November 1949 [Blackwood estate].
6 Eventually the BBC broadcast a new adaptation of the play by Raymond Raikes on 10 December 1965. A special children's production was made by Thérèse Kitchin in 1978.
7 'On Being Eighty', BBC Home Service, 25 September 1949 [BBC Written Archives].
8 BBC Light Programme, *Woman's Hour*, 30 May 1949 [BBC Written Archives].
9 He may also have had an operation on his prostate at this time. He was being treated for a prostate problem and Michael Hall, the editor of *London*

Mystery Magazine, related how Blackwood 'underwent a daring operation at an advanced age and insisted on having a local anaesthetic so that he could watch every detail of the surgeon's work'.

10 *London Mystery Magazine*, January/February 1951.
11 Letter, Blackwood to BBC, 23 May 1951 [BBC Written Archives].
12 Letter, Blackwood to Hall, 14 September 1951 [Blackwood estate]. It was this letter that first inspired me to research Blackwood's life, as it's here that he said that all his work was more or less autobiographical.
13 Henry Miller, *The Books in my Life* (London: Peter Owen, 1952), p. 14.
14 Letter, Blackwood to Maillart, 24 November 1951 [Maillart archives].
15 Michael Hall, *The London Mystery Magazine*, February 1952, p. 5.
16 L.A.G. Strong, *Light*, February 1952.
17 'Discovery Group: Algernon Blackwood', *Light*, Autumn 1977, p. 130.

Appendix

Blackwood's Family Trees

Through both his parents Blackwood was related to many peers of the realm and landed gentry. They influenced his upbringing and, in the years after his return from America, he maintained contacts with many of them. Although they do not all feature in this biography, many were a regular part of his life, especially the Kintores and the Dufferins.

This appendix includes three family trees, one showing his forebears and the others showing his closer family connections.

The Blackwood family originated in Scotland, at least as far back as authentic records go. Adam Blackwood (1539–1613) had been born in Scotland, but fled to France in his youth and was educated in Paris. His works in praise of Mary, Queen of Scots, then married to the French Dauphin, brought him to her attention and she appointed him Judge of the Parliament at Poitiérs. He later became a Privy Councillor to the Queen in Scotland. Adam's own descendants lived in France and the last of them died out in the nineteenth century.

It was from one of Adam's brothers that Algernon was descended. John Blackwood (1591–1663) acquired several large estates in Bangor in the early 1600s. They eventually established an estate at Ballyleidy, Upper Clandeboye[1]. His great-grandson, Robert Blackwood (1694–1774), was created the first Baronet Blackwood in 1763. His son, Sir John Blackwood (1722–1799), the 2nd Baronet, married Dorcas

---

[1] Sometimes spelled Claneboye.

Stevenson (1726–1807) in 1751, who was heir to the Hamilton estates of Clandeboye. She was created Baroness of Dufferin and Clandeboye in her own right after her husband's death.

Through her son Hans Blackwood (1758–1839) are descended all the Lords of Dufferin, including Frederick Temple Blackwood (1826–1902), the 5th Baron who became the first Marquess of Dufferin and Ava in 1888. It was he who was Algernon's most influential relative. He was Governor-General of Canada (1872–8) and Viceroy of India (1884–8). Algernon knew his sons Terence (1866–1918), Basil (1870–1917) and Frederick (1875–1930) – it was the latter he went mountain climbing with in the 1920s. Their ancestral home is at Clandeboye Castle, just outside Belfast, which Algernon visited on several occasions.

Dorcas's younger son Henry Blackwood (1770–1832) was created first Baronet Blackwood in 1814. He was one of the great naval figures during the Napoleonic Wars, rising to the rank of vice admiral in 1825. Sir Henry was married three times. Through his second wife, Eliza Waghorn, are descended the Baronets Blackwood. Algernon was less close to these cousins, though in his day he knew Francis Blackwood (1838–1924), the 4th Baronet.

Algernon was descended from Sir Henry Blackwood and his third wife, Harriet Gore, daughter of the Governor of Grenada.

On his mother's side, Algernon was descended from Sir Richard Dobbs, who was Lord Mayor of London in 1551. His grandson, John Dobbs, settled in Ulster in 1596 and married into the O'Neil family, whereby Blackwood can trace his descent back to the High-Kings of Ireland. A little closer in time was Arthur Dobbs (1689–1765), who had an interest in North America and financed expeditions to the Hudson Bay territory, trying to find the North-West passage. Cape Dobbs in the far north-west of Hudson Bay is named after him. He became Governor of North Carolina from 1754 to his death.

Arthur Dobbs's nephew was Francis Dobbs (1750–1811). He was a religious fundamentalist and produced a *Universal History* in 1787 which sought to prove the fulfilment of the Messianic prophecies. His reputation remained strong in the Dobbs family during Blackwood's mother's childhood.

Blackwood's maternal grandfather, Conway Richard Dobbs (1795–1886), was the High Sheriff of County Antrim. He caused something of a stir by marrying a second time when he was eighty. His second wife, Winifred, outlived him by over forty years and died in 1928.

Blackwood's half-sister, Sydney Montagu (1851–1932), married the future Earl of Kintore and although Blackwood was not directly related to the Kintores, their family was very close. Late in life Blackwood's sister Cecilia married Arthur Hobart-Hampden (1864–1952), who was her and Algernon's second cousin. Through him Blackwood was distantly related to the Earls of Buckinghamshire.

There are scores of other family connections, though they become increasingly complicated and tenuous. This did not stop Blackwood associating with these distant relatives. For instance, he called the author Algar Thorold (1866–1936) a 'cousin' because he was married to the niece of his mother's first husband, so in fact was not directly related at all. By a similar method Blackwood may be found related to Lord Dunsany, J. Sheridan Le Fanu and Graham Greene. It was an aristocractic network that Blackwood used to his advantage whenever necessary, but one that he could just as easily slip out of if he chose.

1. BLACKWOOD FAMILY TREE

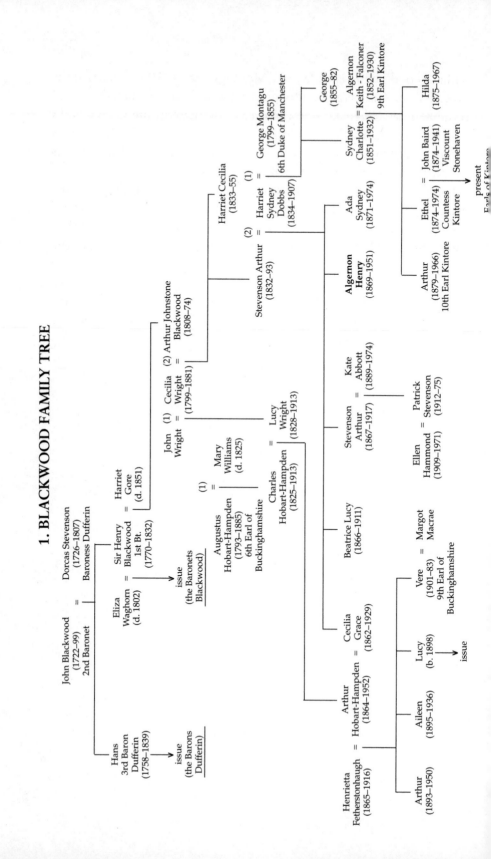

2. THE BLACKWOOD-DUFFERIN FAMILY (simplified)

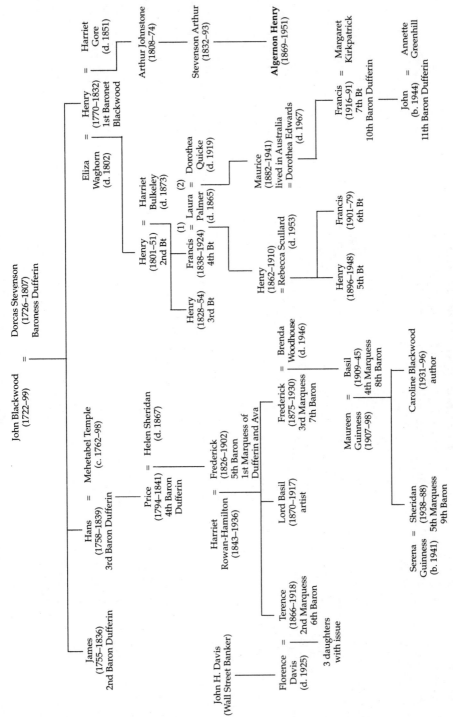

3. BLACKWOOD'S FOREBEARS

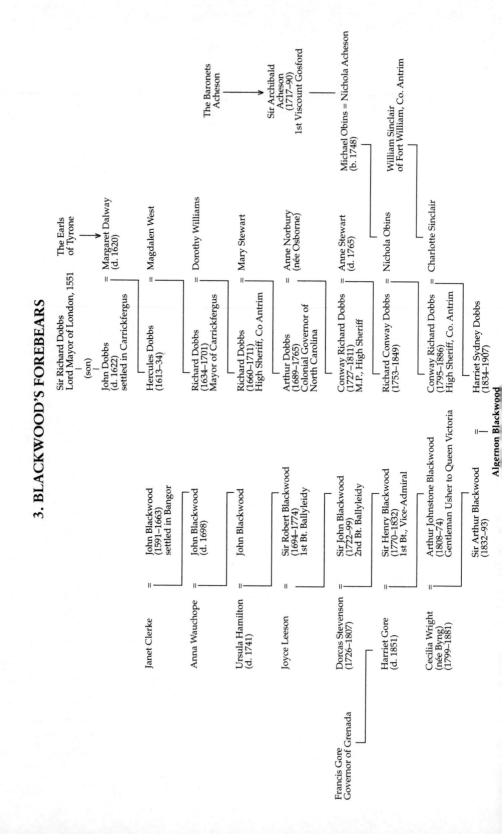

Blackwood's Books and Stories

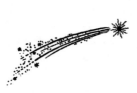

All Blackwood's published books and collected short stories are listed below This list does not include his uncollected stories, or nonfiction, or his radio talks; it includes solely the first English and first American editions. For a complete index and guide to all of Blackwood's output see *Algernon Blackwood: A Bio-Bibliography* by Mike Ashley (Westport, CT: Greenwood Press,1987).

Original Collections

The Empty House and Other Ghost Stories (London: Eveleigh Nash, 1906; New York: Donald C. Vaughan, 1915). Contains: 'The Empty House', 'A Haunted Island', 'A Case of Eavesdropping', 'Keeping His Promise', 'With Intent to Steal', 'The Wood of the Dead', 'Smith: an Episode in a Lodging House', 'A Suspicious Gift', 'The Strange Adventures of a Private Secretary in New York', 'Skeleton Lake'.

The Listener and Other Stories (London: Eveleigh Nash, 1907; New York: Vaughan & Gomme, 1914). Contains: 'The Listener', 'Max Hensig', 'The Willows', 'The Insanity of Jones', 'The Dance of Death', 'The Old Man of Visions', 'May Day Eve', 'Miss Slumbubble – and Claustrophobia', 'The Woman's Ghost Story'.

John Silence – Physician Extraordinary (London: Eveleigh Nash, 1908; New York: J.W. Luce, 1909). Contains: 'A Psychical Invasion', 'Ancient Sorceries', 'The Nemesis of Fire', 'Secret Worship', 'The Camp of the Dog'. The 1997 US edition issued as *The Complete John Silence Stories* (New York: Dover, 1997) adds the story 'A Victim of Higher Space'.

The Lost Valley and Other Stories (London: Eveleigh Nash, 1910; New York: Vaughan & Gomme, 1914). Contains: 'The Lost Valley', 'The Wendigo', 'Old Clothes', 'Perspective', 'The Terror of the Twins', 'The Man from the "Gods"', 'The Man Who Played upon the Leaf', 'The Price of Wiggins's Orgy', 'Carlton's Drive', 'The Eccentricity of Simon Parnacute'.

Pan's Garden: A Volume of Nature Stories (London: Macmillan, 1912; New York: Macmillan, 1912). Contains: 'The Man Whom the Trees Loved', 'The South Wind', 'The Sea Fit', 'The Attic', 'The Heath Fire', 'The Messenger', 'The Glamour of the Snow', 'The Return', 'Sand', 'The Transfer', 'Clairvoyance', 'The Golden Fly', 'Special Delivery', 'The Destruction of Smith', 'The Temptation of the Clay'.

Ten Minute Stories (London: John Murray, 1914; New York: Dutton, 1914). Contains: 'Accessory before the Fact', 'The Deferred Appointment', 'The Prayer', 'Strange Disappearance of a Baronet', 'The Secret', 'The Lease', 'Up and Down', 'Faith Cure on the Channel', 'The Goblin's Collection', 'Imagination', 'The Invitation', 'The Impulse', 'Her Birthday', 'Two in One', 'Ancient Lights', 'Dream Trespass', 'Let Not the Sun – ', 'Entrance and Exit', 'You *May* Telephone from Here', 'The Whisperers', 'Violence', 'The House of the Past', 'Jimbo's Longest Day', 'If the Cap Fits – ', 'News v. Nourishment', 'Wind', 'Pines', 'The Winter Alps', 'The Second Generation'.

Incredible Adventures (London: Macmillan, 1914; New York: Macmillan, 1914). Contains: 'The Regeneration of Lord Ernie', 'The Sacrifice', 'The Damned', 'A Descent into Egypt', 'Wayfarers'.

Day and Night Stories (London: Cassell, 1917; New York: Dutton, 1917). Contains: 'The Tryst', 'The Touch of Pan', 'The Wings of Horus', 'A Bit of Wood', 'Initiation', 'A Desert Episode', 'Transition', 'The Other Wing', 'The Occupant of the Room', 'Cain's Atonement', 'An Egyptian Hornet', 'By Water', 'H.S.H.', 'The Tradition', 'A Victim of Higher Space'.

The Wolves of God and Other Fey Stories (London: Cassell, 1921; New York: Dutton, 1921). Contains: 'The Wolves of God', 'Chinese Magic', 'Running Wolf', 'First Hate', 'The Tarn of Sacrifice', 'The Valley of the Beasts', 'The Call', 'Egyptian Sorcery', 'The Decoy', 'The Man Who Found Out', 'The Empty Sleeve', 'Wireless Confusion', 'Confession', 'The Lane That Ran East and West', '"Vengeance is Mine"'.

Tongues of Fire (London: Herbert Jenkins, 1924; New York: E.P. Dutton, 1925). Contains: 'Tongues of Fire', 'The Little Beggar', 'Malahide and Forden', 'Playing Catch', 'The Pikestaffe Case', 'Alexander *Alexander*', 'Lost!', 'The Olive', 'A Continuous Performance', 'The World-Dream of McCallister', 'The Other Woman', 'Picking Fir-Cones', 'The Open Window', 'Petershin and Mr Snide', 'The Man Who was Milligan', 'The Falling Glass', 'The Spell of Egypt', 'A Man of Earth', 'The Laughter of Courage', 'S.O.S.', 'Nephelé'.

Shocks (London: Grayson & Grayson, 1935; New York: Dutton, 1936). Contains: 'Elsewhere and Otherwise', 'The Stranger', 'Full Circle', 'Dr Feldman', 'A Threefold Cord', 'Chemical', 'Shocks', 'The Survivors', 'The Adventure of Tornado Smith', 'Hands of Death', 'The Land of Green Ginger', 'The Colonel's Ring', 'Revenge', 'The Man Who Lived Backwards', 'Adventures of Miss De Fontenoy'.

The Doll, and One Other (Sauk City: Arkham House, 1946). Contains: 'The Doll', 'The Trod'.

The Magic Mirror: Lost Supernatural and Mystery Stories (Wellingborough: Equation, 1989). Contains: 'A Mysterious House', 'The Kit-bag', 'The Laying of a Red-haired Ghost', 'The Message of the Clock', 'The Singular Death of Morton', 'La Mauvaise Riche', 'The Soldier's Visitor', 'The Memory of Beauty', 'Onanonanon', 'The First Flight', 'The Vision of the Winds', 'The Call of the Urwelt', 'The Summoning', 'The Blackmailers', 'The Wig', 'King's Evidence', 'Lock Your Door', 'Five Strange Stories', 'At a Mayfair Luncheon', 'The Man-eater', 'By Proxy', 'The Voice', 'The Magic Mirror', 'Roman Remains', 'Wishful Thinking'.

Reprint Collections

Ancient Sorceries and Other Tales (London: Collins, 1927). Contains: 'Ancient Sorceries', 'The Willows', 'The Return', 'Running Wolf', 'The Man Whom the Trees Loved', 'The Man who Played upon the Leaf'.

The Dance of Death and Other Tales (London: Herbert Jenkins, 1927; New York: The Dial Press, 1928). Contains: 'The Dance of Death', 'A Psychical Invasion', 'The Old Man of Visions', 'The South Wind', 'The Touch of Pan', 'The Valley of the Beasts'.

Strange Stories (London: Heinemann, 1929; New York: Arno Press, 1976). Contains: 'The Man Whom the Trees Loved', 'The Sea Fit', 'The Glamour of the Snow', 'The Tryst', 'Transition', 'The Occupant of the Room', 'The Wings of Horus', 'By Water', 'Malahide and Forden', 'Alexander *Alexander*', 'The Man Who was Milligan', 'The Little Beggar', 'The Pikestaffe Case', 'Accessory Before the Fact', 'The Deferred Appointment', 'Ancient Lights', 'You *May* Telephone from Here', 'The Goblin's Collection', 'Running Wolf', 'The Valley of the Beasts', 'The Decoy', 'Confession', 'A Descent Into Egypt', 'The Damned', 'The Willows', 'Ancient Sorceries'. An abridged US edition, omitting the last three stories, was issued as *The Best Supernatural Tales of Algernon Blackwood* (New York: Causeway Books, 1973).

Short Stories of To-Day & Yesterday (London: Harrap, 1930). Contains: 'The Regeneration of Lord Ernie', 'The Sacrifice', 'Chinese Magic', 'The Land of Green Ginger', 'The Stranger', 'First Hate', 'The Olive', 'Two in One', 'Dream Trespass', 'Cain's Atonement'.

The Willows and Other Queer Tales (London: Collins, 1932). Contains: 'The Willows', 'Ancient Sorceries', 'The Return', 'Running Wolf', 'The Man Whom the Trees Loved', 'The Man Who Played upon the Leaf', 'The Tryst', 'By Water', 'The Occupant of the Room', 'The Decoy', 'Dream Trespass'.

The Tales of Algernon Blackwood (London: Martin Secker, 1938; New York: Dutton, 1939). Contains: 'The Empty House', 'A Case of Eavesdropping', 'Strange Adventures of a Private Secretary', 'With Intent to Steal', 'Keeping his Promise', 'The Wood of the Dead', 'A Suspicious Gift', 'The Listener', 'Max Hensig', 'The Willows', 'The Insanity of Jones', 'The Dance of Death', 'May Day Eve', 'The Woman's Ghost Story', 'A Psychical Invasion',

'Ancient Sorceries', 'The Nemesis of Fire', 'Secret Worship', 'The Camp of the Dog', 'The Man from the "Gods"', 'The Wendigo'.

Selected Tales of Algernon Blackwood (Harmondsworth: Penguin Books, 1942). Contains: 'The Empty House', 'Strange Adventures of a Private Secretary', 'Keeping his Promise', 'The Woman's Ghost Story', 'Ancient Sorceries', 'The Camp of the Dog'.

Selected Short Stories of Algernon Blackwood (New York: Armed Services, 1945). Contains: 'The Willows', 'The Wendigo', 'A Psychical Invasion', 'The Woman's Ghost Story', 'Max Hensig', 'The Wood of the Dead', 'The Listener'.

Tales of the Uncanny and Supernatural (London: Peter Nevill, 1949; Secaucus: Castle Books, 1974). Contains: 'The Doll', 'Running Wolf', 'The Little Beggar', 'The Occupant of the Room', 'The Man Whom the Trees Loved', 'The Valley of the Beasts', 'The South Wind', 'The Man Who was Milligan', 'The Trod', 'The Terror of the Twins', 'The Deferred Appointment', 'Accessory Before the Fact', 'The Glamour of the Snow', 'The House of the Past', 'The Decoy', 'The Tradition', 'The Touch of Pan', 'Entrance and Exit', 'The Pikestaffe Case', 'The Empty Sleeve', 'Violence', 'The Lost Valley'.

In the Realm of Terror (New York: Pantheon Books, 1957). Contains: 'The Willows', 'The Man Whom the Trees Loved', 'The Wendigo', 'A Haunted Island', 'A Psychical Invasion', 'Smith: an Episode in a Lodging House', 'The Empty House', 'The Strange Adventures of a Private Secretary in New York'.

Selected Tales (London: John Baker, 1964). Contains: 'The Willows', 'The Woman's Ghost Story', 'Max Hensig', 'The Listener', 'The Old Man of Visions', 'May Day Eve', 'The Insanity of Jones', 'The Dance of Death', 'Miss Slumbubble', 'The Wendigo', 'The Camp of the Dog'. The US edition was issued as *Tales of Terror and the Unknown* (New York: Dutton, 1965). The UK paperback edition was issued as *The Insanity of Jones and Other Tales* (Harmondsworth: Penguin Books, 1966).

Tales of the Mysterious and Macabre (London: Hamlyn, 1967; Secaucus: Castle Books, 1974). Contains: 'Chinese Magic', 'First Hate', 'The Olive', 'The Sacrifice', 'The Damned', 'Wayfarers', 'The Sea Fit', 'The Attic', 'The Heath Fire', 'The Return', 'The Transfer', 'Clairvoyance', 'The Golden Fly', 'Special Delivery', 'The Destruction of Smith', 'The Tryst', 'The Wings of Horus', 'Initiation', 'A Desert Episode', 'Transition', 'The Other Wing', 'By Water', 'A Victim of Higher Space'.

Ancient Sorceries and Other Stories (Harmondsworth: Penguin Books, 1968). Contains: 'The Empty House', 'A Haunted Island', 'Keeping his Promise', 'A Case of Eavesdropping', 'Ancient Sorceries', 'The Nemesis of Fire'.

Best Ghost Stories of Algernon Blackwood (New York: Dover, 1973). Contains: 'The Willows', 'Secret Worship', 'Ancient Sorceries', 'The Glamour of the Snow', 'The Wendigo', 'The Other Wing', 'The Transfer', 'Ancient Lights', 'The Listener', 'The Empty House', 'Accessory before the Fact', 'Keeping his Promise', 'Max Hensig'.

The Best Supernatural Tales of Algernon Blackwood – see *Strange Stories*.
Tales of Terror and Darkness (Feltham: Hamlyn, 1977). Omnibus volume of *Tales of the Uncanny and Supernatural* and *Tales of the Mysterious and Macabre* but omitting 'By Water' and 'A Victim of Higher Space'.
Tales of the Supernatural (Woodbridge: The Boydell Press, 1983). Contains: 'The Willows', 'The Wendigo', 'The Other Wing', 'First Hate', 'The Destruction of Smith', 'The Occupant of the Room', 'The Terror of the Twins', 'The Man Who was Milligan', 'The Wings of Horus', 'The Sea Fit', 'Violence', 'The Touch of Pan'.
The Willows and Other Strange Stories (New York: Penguin Viking, 2002). Contains: Smith: an Episode in a Lodging-House', 'The Willows', 'The Insanity of Jones', 'Ancient Sorceries', 'The Wendigo', 'The Glamour of the Snow', 'The Man Whom the Trees Loved', 'Sand', 'The Man Who Found Out'.

Novels and Single Story volumes

Jimbo: a Fantasy (London: Macmillan, 1909; New York: Macmillan, 1909)
The Education of Uncle Paul (London: Macmillan, 1909; New York: Henry Holt, 1910)
The Human Chord (London: Macmillan, 1910; New York: Macmillan, 1911)
The Centaur (London: Macmillan, 1911; New York: Macmillan, 1912)
A Prisoner in Fairyland (London: Macmillan, 1913; New York: Macmillan, 1913)
The Extra Day (London: Macmillan, 1915; New York: Macmillan, 1915)
Julius LeVallon: an Episode (London: Cassell, 1916; New York: Dutton, 1916)
The Wave: an Egyptian Aftermath (London: Macmillan, 1916; New York: Dutton, 1916)
The Promise of Air (London: Macmillan, 1918; New York: Dutton, 1918)
The Garden of Survival (London: Macmillan, 1918; New York: Dutton, 1918)
The Bright Messenger (London: Cassell, 1921; New York: Dutton, 1922)
Dudley & Gilderoy: a Nonsense (London: Ernest Benn, 1929; New York: Dutton, 1929)
Full Circle (London: Elkin Mathews & Marrot, 1929) short story
The Fruit Stoners: Being the Adventures of Maria among the Fruit Stoners (London: Grayson & Grayson, 1934; New York: Dutton, 1935)
A Mysterious House (Edinburgh: The Tragara Press, 1987) short story

Plays

Karma: a Reincarnation Play (London: Macmillan, 1918; New York: Dutton, 1918)
Through the Crack (London: Samuel French, 1925)

Autobiography

Episodes Before Thirty (London: Cassell, 1923; New York: Dutton, 1924).
   Abridged as *Adventures Before Thirty* (London: Jonathan Cape, 1934)

Children's Books

Sambo and Snitch (Oxford: Basil Blackwell, 1927; New York: Appleton, 1927)
Mr Cupboard (Oxford: Basil Blackwell, 1928)
By Underground (Oxford: Basil Blackwell, 1930)
The Parrot and the – Cat (Oxford: Basil Blackwell, 1931)
The Italian Conjuror (Oxford: Basil Blackwell, 1932)
Maria (of England) in the Rain (Oxford: Basil Blackwell, 1933)
Sergeant Poppett and Policeman James (Oxford: Basil Blackwell, 1934)
The Fruit Stoners (Oxford: Basil Blackwell, 1935)
How the Circus Came to Tea (Oxford: Basil Blackwell, 1936)
The Adventures of Dudley and Gilderoy (New York: Dutton, 1941; London:
   Faber & Faber, 1941). Adapted from *Dudley & Gilderoy* by Marion B.
   Cothren

Bibliography

In addition to Blackwood's own books, articles and radio talks cited throughout the biography, I have drawn upon the following for background information or commentary. The listing covers the more significant titles only.

Biographical or Contemporary Sources

Samuel Hopkins Adams, *Alexander Woollcott, His Life and his World* (London: Hamish Hamilton, 1946)

Christopher Andrew, *Secret Service: The Making of the British Intelligence Community* (London: Heinemann, 1985)

Mike Ashley, 'Algernon Blackwood: The Ghostly Tale's Great Visionary', *Rod Serling's 'The Twilight Zone' Magazine*, May/June 1985

Lena Ashwell, *Myself a Player* (London: Michael Joseph, 1936)

E. Wulstan Atkins, *The Elgar–Atkins Friendship* (Newton Abbot: David & Charles, 1984)

Kenneth Baily, *Here's Television* (London: Vox Mundi, 1950)

Frank Baker, *I Follow but Myself* (London: Peter Davies, 1968)

J.G. Bennett, *Witness: The Story of a Search* (London: Hodder & Stoughton, 1962)

Daisy Bevan, *Odd Memories of an Ordinary Person* (unpublished typescript, 1927)

Henrietta Blackwood (editor), *Some Records of the Life of Stevenson Arthur Blackwood* (London: Hodder & Stoughton, 1898)

H.P. Blavatsky, *Isis Unveiled* (New York: J.W. Boulton, 1877)

—— , *The Secret Doctrine* (London: Theosophical Publishing, 1888)

E.F. Bleiler, 'Introduction' to *Best Ghost Stories of Algernon Blackwood* (New York: Dover Books, 1973)

Theophilus E.M. Boll, *Miss May Sinclair: Novelist* (Cranbury, N.J.: Associated University Presses, 1973)

Martin Booth, *A Magick Life: A Biography of Aleister Crowley* (London: Hodder & Stoughton, 2000)

Mary Borden, *The Forbidden Zone* (New York: Doubleday, Doran, 1930)

Charles Boswell & Lewis Thompson, *The Carlyle Harris Case* (New York: Collier Books, 1961)

R.M. Bucke, *Cosmic Consciousness* (New York: Innes & Sons, 1901. Volume consulted, New York: E.P. Dutton, 1923)

Arthur Calder-Marshall, *The Magic of My Youth* (London: Rupert Hart Davis, 1951)

Bruce F. Campbell, *Ancient Wisdom Revived: A History of the Theosophical Movement* (Berkeley: University of California Press, 1980)

J.C. Cannell, *In Town To-night* (London: Harrap, 1935)

Hugh Carey, *Duet for Two Voices: An Informal Biography of Edward J. Dent* (Cambridge University Press, 1979)

Edward Carpenter, *Civilization: Its Cause and Cure* [complete edition] (London: Allen & Unwin, 1921)

———, *Towards Democracy* [complete edition] (London: Allen & Unwin, 1905)

William Carr, *The Spot That is Called Crayford* (Crayford U.D.C., revised, 1965)

Hereward Carrington, *The Problems of Psychic Research* (New York: W. Rickey, 1914)

Thelma Cazalet-Keir, *From the Wings* (London: The Bodley Head, 1967)

Chic & Sandra Tabatha Cicero, *Self-Initiation into the Golden Dawn Tradition* (St Paul, MN: Llewellyn Publications, 1995)

Michael Davis, 'Spotlight on Story-Teller Algernon Blackwood', *Scan*, July 1949

Basil Dean, *Seven Ages, an Autobiography 1888–1927* (London: Hutchinson, 1970)

Alan Denson, *Printed Writings by George W. Russell (Æ): a Bibliography* (Evanston: Northwestern University Press, 1961)

Isadora Duncan, *Isadora: My Life* (London: Gollancz, 1928)

Richard Ellman, *Yeats: The Man and the Masks* (London: Macmillan, 1948)

Maude M.C. ffoulkes, *All This Happened to Me* (London: Grayson & Grayson, 1937)

———, *My Own Past* (London: Cassell, 1915)

———, *True Ghost Stories* (London: Hutchinson, 1936)

R.F. Foster, *W.B. Yeats, a Life: I: The Apprentice Mage* (Oxford University Press, 1997)

Anne Fremantle, *Three-Cornered Heart* (London: Collins, 1971)

R.A. Gilbert, *The Golden Dawn: Twilight of the Magicians* (Wellingborough: The Aquarian Press, 1983)

———, *Revelations of the Golden Dawn* (Slough: Quantum, 1997; US title: *The Golden Dawn Scrapbook*, York Beach, ME: Samuel Wesier, 1997)

———, *The Sorcerer and His Apprentice* (Wellingborough: The Aquarian Press, 1983)

Stephen Graham, *Part of the Wonderful Scene* (London: Collins, 1964)

Mary K. Greer, *Women of the Golden Dawn*, Rochester (VT: Park Street Press, 1995)

Mary Greer & Darcy Kuntz, *The Chronology of the Golden Dawn* (Edmonds, WA: Holmes Publishing Group, 1999)

David Griffiths, 'In Search of Algernon Blackwood', *TV Times*, 12 May 1961

G.I. Gurdjieff, *Beelzebub's Tales to His Grandson* (originally published 1950; edition consulted, New York: Penguin Arkana, 1999)

—— , *Meetings With Remarkable Men* (London: Routledge, 1963)

Trevor H. Hall, *The Strange Case of Edmund Gurney* (London: Duckworth, 1980 new edition)

Ethel Hardie, *Henry Ainley: Portrait of a Great Actor* (unpublished, seen in typescript)

George Mills Harper, *W.B. Yeats and W.T. Horton: The Record of an Occult Friendship* (Atlantic Highlands, N.J.: Humanities Press, 1980)

Harper's Magazine, *New York: a Collection from Harper's Magazine* (New York: Gallery Books, 1991)

Franz Hartman, *Magic, White and Black* (New York: Theosophical Society, 1904 edition)

Renée Haynes, *The Society for Psychical Research, 1882–1982* (London: Macdonald, 1982)

Walter Hooper (editor), *They Stand Together – The Letters of C.S. Lewis to Arthur Greeves* (London: Collins, 1979)

Ellic Howe, *The Magicians of the Golden Dawn* (Wellingborough: The Aquarian Press, 1985)

Derek Hudson, *A Study of Algernon Blackwood* [#14 in series *Essays and Studies*] (London: John Murray, 1961; incorporated in *Talks With Fuddy and Other Papers*, Fontwell: Centaur Press, 1968)

William James, *A Pluralistic Universe* (London: Longmans, Green, 1909)

—— , *The Varieties of Religious Experience* (London: Longmans, Green, 1902)

Richard Joseph, *Michael Joseph: Master of Words* (Shedfield: Ashford Publishing, 1986)

Moses King, *Handbook of New York City 1893* (Boston: Moses King, 1893)

—— , *Notable New Yorkers of 1896–1899* (New York: Moses King, 1899)

Darcy Kuntz, *The Battle of Blythe Road* (Edmonds, WA: Holmes Publishing Group, 2000)

—— , *The Golden Dawn Source Book* (Edmonds, WA: Holmes Publishing Group, 1996)

James Leigh, *Manual and Who's Who of Spiritualism and Psychic Research* (London: Francis Mott Company, 1936)

Sir Oliver Lodge, *Reason and Belief* (London: Methuen, 1910)

Sir Alfred Lyall, *The Life of the Marquis of Dufferin and Ava* (Edinburgh: Thomas Nelson, 1905)

Maud Gonne MacBride, *A Servant of the Queen* (London: Gollancz, 1938. Volume consulted, Woodbridge: Boydell Press, 1983)

Micheál MacLiammóir, *All for Hecuba* (London: Methuen, 1946)

John McTaggart, *Some Dogmas of Religion* (London:Edward Arnold, 1906)

Ella Maillart, *The Cruel Way* (London: Heinemann, 1947)

———, *Cruises and Caravans* (London: J.M. Dent, 1942)

———, *Gypsy Afloat* (London: Heinemann, 1942)

Juan Mascaró (trans), *The Bhagavad Gita* (Harmondsworth: Penguin Books, 1962)

G.R.S. Mead, *Some Mystical Adventures*, (London: John Watkins, 1910)

Raymond Monk (editor), *Elgar Studies* (Aldershot: Scolar Press, 1990)

James Moore, *Gurdjieff, a Biography* (Shaftesbury: Element Books, 1991)

Charles Morgan, *The House of Macmillan* (London: Macmillan, 1943)

G[ilbert] M[urray], *Edwyn Robert Bevan* (London: Humphrey Milford, 1944)

Lynda J. Murray, *A Zest for Life: the Story of Alexander Keiller* (Swindon: Morven Books, 1999)

Eveleigh Nash, *I Liked the Life I Led* (London: John Murray, 1941)

Vincent Nesfield, *Viscosity of the Blood and its Bearing on High Blood Pressure* (London: Cobden-Sanderson, 1937)

Louis N. Parker, *Several of My Lives* (London: Chapman & Hall, 1928)

Kinsey Peile, *Candied Peel* (London: A. & C. Black, 1931)

Whitall N. Perry, *Gurdjieff: In the Light of Tradition* (Bedfont: Perennial Books, 1978)

Frank Podmore, *The Newer Spiritualism* (London: T. Fisher Unwin, 1910)

Violet Powell, *A Substantial Ghost* (London: Heinemann, 1967)

Donald Prater, *A Ringing Glass: The Life of Rainer Maria Rilke* (Oxford University Press, 1986)

Harry Price, *Search for Truth: My Life for Psychical Research* (London: Collins, 1942)

Kathleen Raine, 'Discovery Group – Algernon Blackwood', *Light*, Autumn 1977

Janet Ray, *Emily Stowe* (Don Mills, Ontario: Fitzhenry & Whiteside, 1978)

Alan Richardson, *Dancers to the Gods: The Magical Records of Charles Seymour and Christine Hartley 1937–1939* (Wellingborough: The Aquarian Press, 1985)

———, *Priestess: The Magical Life of Dion Fortune* (Wellingborough: The Aquarian Press, 1987)

Arthur Compton Rickett, *I Look Back* (London: Herbert Jenkins, 1933)

———, *Portraits and Personalities* (London: Selwyn & Blount, 1937)

W. Graham Robertson, *Time Was* (London: Hamish Hamilton, 1931)

Berta Ruck, *A Story-teller Tells the Truth* (London: Hutchinson, 1935)

The Savile Club, *The Savile Club 1868–1923* (privately printed, 1923)

Mark Schorer, *Sinclair Lewis: An American Life* (New York: McGraw-Hill, 1961)

Kathleen Shackleton, 'Algernon Blackwood the Mystic', *John O'London's Weekly*, 3 September 1921

Eleanor Mildred Sidgwick, *Phantasms of the Living* (New York: University Books, 1962)

K.E.L. Simmons, 'A Message, an Oath, and a Bag of Stardust', *The Elgar Society Journal*, May 1982

Society for Psychical Research, *Proceedings*, volume xv (London: Kegan Paul, Trench, Trübner & Co., 1901)

Kathleen Riordan Speeth, *The Gurdjieff Work* (New York: Jeremy P. Tarcher, 1989)

Francis Steegmuller, *Your Isadora* (New York: Random House, 1974)

Alfred Sutro, *Celebrities and Simple Souls* (London: Duckworth, 1933)

R. St C. Talboys, *A Victorian School, being the story of Wellington College* (Oxford: Basil Blackwell, 1943)

Gregory Tillett, *The Elder Brother: a Biography of Charles Webster Leadbeater* (London: Routledge & Kegan Paul, 1982)

Evelyn Underhill, *Mysticism* (London: Methuen, 1910 revised 1942)

Peter Underwood, *Exorcism!* (London: Robert Hale, 1990)

—— , *No Common Task* (London: Harrap, 1983)

Lord Vansittart, *The Mist Procession* (London: Hutchinson, 1958)

Vera Wainwright, *Poems and Masks* (Thame: Mandrake Press, 1991)

James Webb, *The Harmonious Circle* (New York: Putnam's, 1980)

T. Earle Welby, 'Algernon Blackwood: Story-teller and Mystic', *John O'London's Weekly*, 7 August 1920

Theresa Whistler, *Imagination of the Heart: The Life of Walter de la Mare* (London: Duckworth, 1993)

A.N. Wilson, *Hilaire Belloc* (London: Hamish Hamilton, 1984)

Literary or Bibliographic sources

Mike Ashley, *Algernon Blackwood: A Bio-Bibliography* (Westport, CT: Greenwood Press, 1987)

—— , 'The Cosmic Connection', *Crypt of Cthulhu* (St John's Eve, 1988)

Julia Briggs, *Night Visitors* (London: Faber & Faber, 1977)

Glen Cavaliero, *The Supernatural & English Fiction* (Oxford University Press, 1995)

Grace Isabel Colbron, 'Algernon Blackwood – An Appreciation', *The Bookman* [US], February 1915

John Robert Colombo, *Blackwood's Books* (Toronto: Hounslow Press, 1981)

Louise Maunsell Field, 'The Prose Poet of the Borderlands', *New York Times Book Review*, 18 December 1921

R.F. Fleissner, 'No Ghosts Need Apply'? or, 'The Adventure of the Empty House's Empty House', *Studies in Weird Fiction*, no.6, Fall 1989

Stuart Gilbert, 'Algernon Blackwood: Novelist and Mystic', *Transition* no.23, July 1935

Jean-Louis Grillou, *Algernon Blackwood en son temps (1869–1951)* (University of Toulouse-Le Mirail, 1995. Unpublished doctoral dissertation)

S.T. Joshi, *The Weird Tale* (Austin University of Texas Press, 1990)

A.E. Keeton, 'Elgar's Music for *The Starlight Express*', *Music and Letters*, January 1945

Robb Lawson, 'Algernon Blackwood', *The Bookman* [UK], November 1917

Russell Letson, 'The Approaches to Mystery: The Fantasies of Arthur Machen and Algernon Blackwood' (doctoral thesis, Ann Arbor, MI: Xerox University Microfilms, 1975)

Dr Constance E. Long, *Collected Papers on the Psychology of Phantasy* (London: Baillière, Tindall and Cox, 1920)

H.P. Lovecraft, 'Supernatural Horror in Literature' in *Dagon and Other Macabre Tales* (Sauk City: Arkham House, 1965, revised 1986)

Peter Penzoldt, *The Supernatural in Fiction* (London: Peter Nevill, 1952)

David Punter, *The Literature of Terror* (London: Longman, 1980)

J. Russell Reaver, 'From Seed to Fruit: The Doubling of Psychic Landscapes in Algernon Blackwood's *The Centaur*', *The Romantist* nos. 4/5, 1982

Henriette Reeves, 'Algernon Blackwood: A Writer of Mysteries', *Touchstone*, volume 7, 1920

Dorothy Scarborough, *The Supernatural in Modern English Fiction* (New York: Putnam's, 1917)

A.P. Sinnett, *Esoteric Buddhism* (London: Trübner, 1883; revised extensively by eighth edition, London: Theosophical Publishing Society, 1903)

Jack Sullivan, *Elegant Nightmares: The English Ghost Story from Le Fanu to Blackwood* (Athens, OH: Ohio University Press, 1978)

S.L. Varnado, *Haunted Presence: The Numinous in Gothic Fiction* (Tuscaloosa: University of Alabama Press, 1987)

Aubrey J.C. Walters, 'Algernon Blackwood and Occult Literature', *Manchester Literary Club Papers*, volume 54, 1928

Index

Note: family relationships to Algernon Blackwood are identified with the initials AB.